Accounting for AQA A-level Part 1

the complete resource for the AQA examinations

David Cox

Published by Osborne Books Limited
Tel 01905 748071
Email books@osbornebooks.co.uk
Website www.osbornebooks.co.uk

Cover design by Windrush Group (www.windrushgroup.co.uk)

Printed by CPI Group (UK) Limited, Croydon, CR0 4YY.

British Library Cataloguing in Publication Data
A catalogue record for this book is available from the British Library

ISBN 978-1-911198-89-5

Contents

Introduction

Accounting for AQA A-level Part 1 provides the first part of a study resource for students of the Assessment and Qualifications Alliance's A-level in Accounting. Together with our other book, **Accounting for AQA A-level Part 2**, it provides comprehensive coverage for the AQA A-level examinations.

The book is divided into three sections:

- **Introduction to Financial Accounting**, which is designed as a foundation for the course and covers double-entry procedures as applied to the accounting systems of sole traders.
- **Financial Accounting**, which provides the opportunity to develop knowledge and understanding of financial accounting and introduces some of the ways in which financial accounting can provide valuable information for measuring and monitoring business performance.
- **Management Accounting**, which introduces techniques to assist with the financial decision-making, planning and control of businesses.

Accounting for AQA A-level Part 1 has been designed to be user-friendly and contains:

- clear explanations and numerous worked examples
- chapter summaries to help with revision
- a wide range of questions, appropriate for the AQA examinations
- answers to selected questions, set out in the fully worked layout that should be used

Resources for tutors – Tutor Zone

For the questions where answers are not given in this book, separate **tutor support material** provides the answers, together with a range of photocopiable layouts.

These resources are available to tutors who adopt this textbook for their students. For more information, visit www.osbornebooks.co.uk

Use of Accounting Terminology

The AQA examinations in Accounting make full use of international terminology as set out in International Financial Reporting Standards (IFRSs). The following shows the international terminology, together with the terminology used previously.

International Terminology	Terminology used previously
Financial statements	
Cash and cash equivalents (limited companies)	Cash in hand, cash at bank/bank overdraft
Financial statements	Final accounts and balance sheets
Income statement	Trading and profit and loss account
Inventory	Stock
Irrecoverable debt	Bad debt
Loss for year	Net loss
Non-current assets	Fixed assets
Non-current liabilities	Long-term liabilities
Other payables	Expenses due; income received in advance
Other receivables	Expenses prepaid; income due
Profit for year	Net profit
Revenue (within an income statement)	Sales
Statement of financial position	Balance sheet
Trade payables	Trade creditors (creditors)
Trade receivables	Trade debtors (debtors)
Accounting ratios	
Expenses in relation to revenue %	Expenses in relation to sales %
Profit to revenue %	Net profit to sales %
Rate of inventory turnover	Rate of stock turnover
Trade payable days	Creditor payment period
Trade receivable days	Debtor collection period

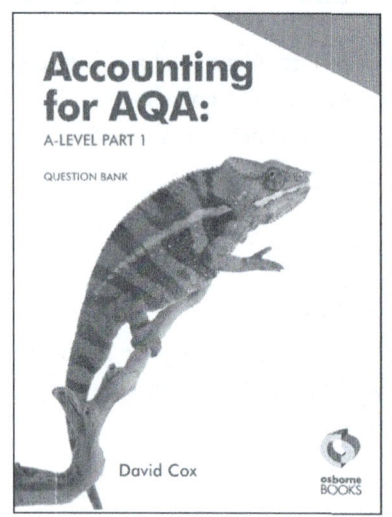

Electronic Resources for students

Online Multiple Choice Tests for each chapter

At the beginning of the questions at the end of each chapter you will see a screen that indicates that an additional 'True or False' multiple choice test is available online to test understanding of the chapter. These tests can be accessed in the Products and Resources section of www.osbornebooks.co.uk

Online Resource Documents

Also available in the Products and Resources section of www.osbornebooks.co.uk are downloadable pdf files which will help with the practice questions in this book. These include:

- ledger accounts
- invoice
- sole trader income statement and statement of financial position
- limited company income statement, statement of changes in equity and statement of financial position
- financial ratios

Introduction to Financial Accounting

This section of the book is designed as a foundation for AQA's A-level Accounting course, and covers:

- double-entry procedures, business documents
- verification of accounting records, including correction of errors
- use of the trial balance
- income statement and statement of financial position

This section focuses on the accounting systems of sole traders. A sole trader is a person in business on his or her own, not involving partners and avoiding the costs of forming a limited company. Later on, in Chapter 13, we will compare the advantages and disadvantages of the different types of business organisation – sole traders, partnerships and limited companies.

1 WHAT IS FINANCIAL ACCOUNTING?

Accounting – known as 'the language of business' – is essential to the recording and presentation of business activities in the form of accounting records and financial statements. Financial accounting involves:

- recording business transactions in financial terms
- reporting financial information to the owner of the business and other interested parties
- advising the owner – and other stakeholders – how to use the financial reports to assess the past performance of the business, and to make decisions for the future

Throughout this book we will see how the three main elements of the definition – recording, reporting and advising – are carried out. First though, in this chapter we will look at an outline of the financial accounting system.

an important note about VAT

As you will know, many of the goods and services that we buy are subject to Value Added Tax (VAT), which is a tax on sales. You should note that AQA's specifications for A-level Accounting do not include VAT. Although this will simplify your study of accounting, it does mean that some documents and layouts in this book and in examination questions will differ slightly from those you will see in day-to-day use by individuals and businesses.

The Financial Accounting System

Businesses need to record transactions in the financial accounting system for very practical purposes:

- to quantify items such as sales, expenses and profit
- to present the accounts in a meaningful way so as to measure the success of the business
- to provide information to the owner of the business and to other stakeholders (eg the bank manager, who may be providing a loan)

Business accounting records can be complex, and one of the problems that you face as a student is having difficulty in relating what you are learning to the financial accounting system of the business as a whole. In this chapter we will summarise how a typical business records and presents financial information in the form of accounts. The process follows a number of distinct stages which are illustrated in the diagram on the next page.

the financial accounting system

SOURCE DOCUMENTS

sales and purchases invoices
credit notes
cash receipts
till rolls
bank paying-in slip counterfoils
cheque counterfoils
information from bank statements

sources of accounting information

BOOKS OF PRIME ENTRY

sales journal
purchases journal
sales returns journal
purchases returns journal
general journal
cash book

gathering and summarising accounting information

DOUBLE-ENTRY BOOKKEEPING

sales ledger or **receivables ledger** – accounts of trade receivables

purchases ledger or **payables ledger** – accounts of trade payables

general ledger

- 'nominal' accounts for sales, purchases, expenses, capital, loans etc
- 'real' accounts for items, eg non-current assets, cash, bank balance

recording the dual aspect of accounting transactions in the ledger accounts

TRIAL BALANCE

a summary of the balances of all the accounts at the end of the accounting period

arithmetic checking of double-entry bookkeeping

FINANCIAL STATEMENTS

- income statement

  and

- statement of financial position

measures profit or loss for an accounting period

list of assets, liabilities and capital at the end of an accounting period

The financial accounting system can be summarised as follows:

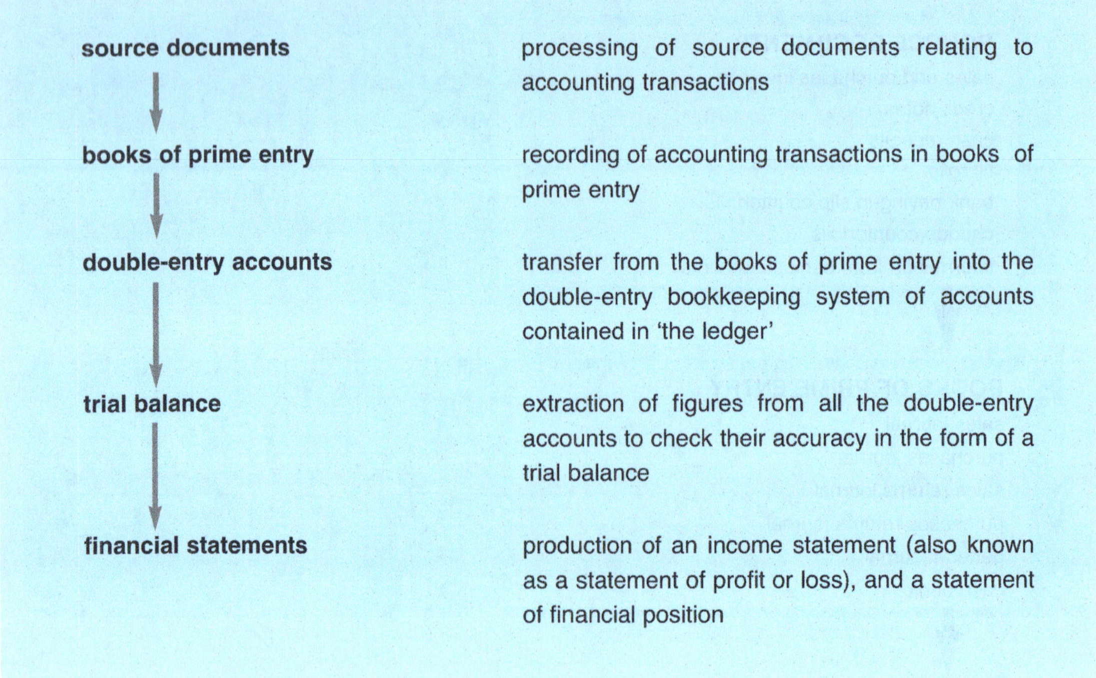

source documents
processing of source documents relating to accounting transactions
books of prime entry
recording of accounting transactions in books of prime entry
double-entry accounts
transfer from the books of prime entry into the double-entry bookkeeping system of accounts contained in 'the ledger'
trial balance
extraction of figures from all the double-entry accounts to check their accuracy in the form of a trial balance
financial statements
production of an income statement (also known as a statement of profit or loss), and a statement of financial position

Over the next few chapters we will look at these stages – the financial accounting system – in detail. If you should at any time lose sight of where your studies are taking you, refer back to this chapter, and it should help to place your work in context.

Before summarising each stage in the financial accounting system we will first examine what form accounting records can take.

Accounting Records

Accounting records are usually kept in one of two forms: handwritten records or computer records.

written accounting records

This is the traditional form of keeping 'the books', particularly for the smaller business. The main record is the ledger which, at one time, would be a large leather-bound volume, neatly ruled, in which the bookkeeper would enter each business transaction in immaculate copperplate handwriting into individual accounts. In modern times, the handwritten ledger is still used, and stationery shops sell ledgers and other accounting books, designed especially for the smaller business.

computer accounting records

Nowadays, computers are relatively cheap so that they can be afforded by most businesses. With computer accounting, business transactions are input into the computer. The major advantage of computer accounting is that it is a very accurate method of recording business transactions; the disadvantage is that it may be time-consuming to set up, particularly for the smaller business. Interestingly, the word 'ledger' has survived into the computer age but, instead of being a bound volume, it is represented by data files held on a computer.

Whether business transactions are recorded by hand, or by using a computer, the basic principles remain the same.

practical points

When maintaining financial accounts you should bear in mind that they should be kept:

- accurately
- up-to-date
- confidentially, ie not revealed to unauthorised people outside the business

Maintaining financial accounts is a discipline, and you should develop disciplined accounting skills as you study with this book. Your studies will involve you in working through many questions and practical examples. These will require you to apply logical thought to the skills you have learned. In particular, when attempting practice questions you should:

- be neat in the layout of your work
- use ink (the use of pencil shows indecision and can be altered easily)

Source Documents

Business transactions generate documents. In this section we will relate them to the type of transaction involved and also introduce other accounting terminology which is essential to your studies.

sale and purchase of goods and services – the invoice

When a business buys or sells goods or a service, it is the seller who prepares an invoice stating:

- the amount owing
- when it should be paid
- details of the goods sold or service provided

The sales invoice is then sent to the purchaser.

An invoice is illustrated on page 45.

cash sales and credit sales – trade receivables

An invoice is prepared by the seller for:

- **cash sales** – where payment is immediate, whether in cash, by cheque, by debit card, by credit card, or by bank transfer. (Note that not all cash sales will require an invoice to be prepared by the seller – shops, for instance, normally issue a **cash receipt** for the amount paid and record the sale on their **till roll**.)
- **credit sales** – where a sales invoice is issued to the purchaser, with payment to be made at a later date (often 30 days later)

A **trade receivable** is an individual or a business who owes you money when you sell on credit.

Note that, in accounting, the term 'sales' is used for the sale of goods – whether on credit or for cash – in which the business trades; for example, a shoe shop will record as its sales the money amounts of shoes sold.

cash purchases and credit purchases – trade payables

To the business buying goods:

- **cash purchases** – where goods are bought and paid for immediately, whether in cash, by cheque, by debit card, by credit card, or by bank transfer
- **credit purchases** – where a purchases invoice is received from the seller for goods bought, with payment to be made at a later date (often 30 days later)

A **trade payable** is an individual or a business to whom you owe money when you buy on credit.

Note that, in accounting, the term 'purchases' is used for goods bought – whether on credit or for cash – which are intended to be resold later.

return of goods – the credit note

If the buyer returns goods which are bought on credit (they may be faulty or incorrect) the seller will prepare a credit note (see page 47 for an example) which is sent to the buyer, reducing the amount of money owed. The credit note, like the invoice, states the money amount and the goods or services to which it relates.

banking transactions – paying-in slips, cheques, bank transfers

Businesses, like anyone else with a bank account, need to pay in money, and draw out cash and make payments. Paying-in slip counterfoils, cheque counterfoils, bank transfers and information from bank statements are used frequently as source documents for bank account transactions.

further reading

The subject of business documents is covered in detail in Chapter 4, while Chapters 7 and 8 deal with the use of information from bank statements.

Recording of Transactions – Books of Prime Entry

Many businesses issue and receive large quantities of invoices, credit notes and banking documents, and it is useful for them to list these in summary form, during the course of the working day. These summaries are known as books of prime entry. They include:

- **sales journal** – a list of credit sales made, compiled from invoices issued
- **purchases journal** – a list of credit purchases made, compiled from invoices received
- **sales returns journal** – a list of returns inwards, ie goods returned by customers, compiled from credit notes issued
- **purchases returns journal** – a list of returns outwards, ie goods returned by the business to suppliers, compiled from credit notes received
- **cash book** – the business' record of the bank account and the amount of cash held, compiled from cash receipts, till rolls, paying-in slip counterfoils, cheque counterfoils, bank transfers and information from bank statements
- **general journal** – a record of non-regular transactions, which are not recorded in any other journal

The books of prime entry are explained in detail in Chapter 6. The point you should bear in mind is that they provide the information for the double-entry bookkeeping system.

Double-entry Accounts – the Ledger

The basis of the accounting system is the double-entry bookkeeping system which is embodied in a series of records known as the **ledger**. This is divided into a number of separate accounts.

double-entry bookkeeping

Double-entry bookkeeping involves making two entries in the accounts for each transaction: for instance, if you are paying wages by cheque you will make an entry in bank account and an entry in wages account. The reasoning behind this procedure and the rules involved are explained in detail in Chapters 2 and 3. If you are operating a manual accounting system you will make the two entries by hand, if you are operating a computer accounting system you will make one entry on the keyboard, but indicate to the machine where the other entry is to be made by means of a code.

accounts

The sources for the entries you make are the books of prime entry. The ledger into which you make the entries is normally a bound book (in a non-computerised system) divided into separate accounts, eg a separate account for sales, purchases, each type of business expense, each trade receivable, each trade payable, and so on. Each account will be given a specific name, and a number for reference purposes (or input code, if you use a computer system).

division of the ledger

Because of the large number of accounts involved, the ledger has traditionally been divided into a number of sections. These same sections are used in computer accounting systems.

- **sales ledger** or **receivables ledger** – personal accounts of trade receivables, ie customers to whom the business has sold on credit
- **purchases ledger** or **payables ledger** – personal accounts of trade payables, ie suppliers to whom the business owes money
- **general ledger** – the remainder of the accounts: income and expense accounts, eg sales, purchases, wages, and accounts for assets and liabilities of the business, eg non-current assets, inventory, cash, bank, non-current liabilities, owner's capital

trial balance

Double-entry bookkeeping, because it involves making two entries for each transaction, is open to error. What if the bookkeeper writes in £45 in one account and £54 in another? The trial balance – explained in full in Chapter 5 – effectively checks the entries made over a given period and will pick up most errors. It sets out the balances of all the double-entry accounts, ie the totals of the accounts for a certain period. It is, as well as being an arithmetic check, the source of valuable information which is used to help in the preparation of the financial statements of the business.

FINANCIAL STATEMENTS

The financial statements of a business comprise the income statement and the statement of financial position.

income statement

income minus **expenses** equals **profit or loss**

The object of the income statement (also known as the statement of profit or loss) is to calculate the profit or loss due to the owner of the business after the deduction of cost of sales to give gross profit, and also after the deduction of all expenses (overheads) to give profit for the year.

The figures for these calculations – sales revenue, purchases, expenses of various kinds – are taken from the double-entry system. The layout of income statements is explained in Chapter 9.

statement of financial position

The double-entry system also contains figures for:

assets items the business owns, which can be

- non-current assets – items bought for use in the business, eg premises, vehicles, computers
- current assets – items used in the everyday running of the business, eg inventory, trade receivables (money owed by customers), cash, and money in the bank

liabilities items that the business owes, eg bank loans and overdrafts, and trade payables (money owed to suppliers)

capital money or assets introduced by the owner of the business; capital is in effect owed by the business to the owner

The statement of financial position always balances in numerical (money) terms:

assets	minus	**liabilities**	equals	**capital**
what a business owns		*what a business owes*		*how the business has been financed by the owner*

The layout of statements of financial position is explained in Chapter 9.

the accounting equation

The statement of financial position illustrates a concept important to accounting theory, known as the accounting equation. This equation is illustrated in the diagram above, namely

Assets – Liabilities = Capital

Every business transaction will change the statement of financial position and the equation, as each transaction has a dual effect on the accounts. However, the equation will always balance.

Consider the following transactions made through the business bank account:

	Transaction	**Effect on equation**
1.	Business pays a trade payable	decrease in asset (bank) decrease in liability (money owed to trade payable)
2.	Business buys a computer for use in the office	increase in asset (computer) decrease in asset (bank)
3.	The owner introduces new capital by paying a cheque into the bank	increase in asset (bank) increase in capital (money owed by the business to owner)

How is the equation affected by these particular transactions?

1. Assets and liabilities both decrease by the amount of the payment; capital remains unchanged.
2. Assets remain the same because the two transactions cancel each other out in the assets section: value is transferred from the asset of bank to the asset of computer.
3. Both sides of the equation increase by the amount of the capital introduced.

In short, the equation always balances, as will the statement of financial position of a business.

In conclusion, every transaction has a dual aspect, as two entries are involved: this is the basis of the theory of double-entry bookkeeping, which will be described in detail in Chapters 2 and 3.

Accounting Concepts

Accounting concepts are broad assumptions which underlie the preparation of all accounting reports. For the moment, we will consider two very important aspects:

- business entity
- money measurement

Business entity means that the accounts record and report on the financial transactions of a particular business: for example, the accounts of J Smith Limited – a limited company – record and report on that business only. The problem is that, when a business is run by a sole trader, the owner's personal financial transactions can be sometimes mixed in with the business' financial transactions; the two should be kept entirely separate.

Money measurement means that the accounting system uses money as the common denominator in recording and reporting all business transactions. Thus, it is not possible to record, for example, the loyalty of a firm's workforce or the quality of a product, because these cannot be reported in money terms.

Who Uses Financial Accounts?

Before answering the question of who uses the accounts, and why, it is important to draw a distinction between the processes of bookkeeping and accounting.

Bookkeeping is the basic recording of business transactions in financial terms – literally 'keeping the books of account'. This task can be carried out by anyone – the owner, or by a full-time or part-time bookkeeper. The bookkeeper's role is to record the day-to-day financial transactions, including:

- maintaining accounting records
- entering transactions in the books of prime entry (journals) and ledger accounts
- checking the accuracy of the bookkeeping

Accounting involves the financial accountant taking the financial information recorded by the bookkeeper and preparing and presenting it in the form of financial reports to the business owner or managers. Such reports include the income statement and the statement of financial position. In particular, the accountant will ensure that:

- accounting concepts (see above and Chapter 14) are applied
- the financial statements show a true and fair view of the business

Financial reports help the owner or managers – who are stakeholders in the business – to monitor the financial progress of the business, and to make decisions for the future.

information for the owner or managers

The accounting system will be able to give information about:

- purchases of goods (for resale) to date
- revenue (cash and credit sales) to date

- expenses and overheads to date
- trade receivables – both the total amount owed to the business, and also the names of individual trade receivables and the amount owed by each
- trade payables – both the total owed by the business, and the amount owed to each trade payable
- assets owned by the business
- liabilities, eg bank loans, owed by the business
- profit made by the business during a particular time period

The owner will want to know how profitable the business is, and what it may be worth.

information for outsiders

As well as the owner and managers, other stakeholders interested in the accounts of a business include:

- the providers of finance, eg the bank manager if the business wants to borrow from the bank
- suppliers, who wish to assess the likelihood of receiving payment from the business
- customers, who wish to ensure that the business has the financial strength to continue selling the goods and services that they buy
- employees and trade unions, who wish to check on the financial prospects of the business
- the tax authorities, who will wish to see that tax due by the business on profits and for Value Added Tax has been paid
- competitors, who wish to assess the profitability of the business
- potential investors in the business
- the local community and national interest groups, who may be seeking to influence business policy
- government and official bodies, eg Companies House who need to see the financial statements of limited companies

Clearly not all of these will be interested in smaller businesses – such as those run by sole traders. However, a wider range of stakeholders has an interest in the activities of companies.

Accounting Terms

In the course of this chapter a number of specific accounting terms have been introduced. You should now study this section closely to ensure that you are clear about these definitions:

accounts financial records, where business transactions are entered

journals books of prime entry of a business

ledger the set of accounts of a business

assets items owned by a business

liabilities items owed by a business

capital the amount of the owner's stake in the business

purchases goods bought – whether on credit or for cash – which are intended to be resold later

credit purchases goods bought, with payment to be made at a later date

cash purchases goods bought, with immediate payment made in cash, by cheque, by debit card, by credit card, or by bank transfer

sales the sale of goods – whether on credit or for cash – in which the business trades

credit sales goods sold, with payment to be received at an agreed date in the future

cash sales goods sold, with immediate payment received in cash, by cheque, by debit card, by credit card, or by bank transfer

trade receivables individuals or businesses who owe money in respect of goods or services supplied by the business

trade payables individuals or businesses to whom money is owed by the business

revenue the total of sales, both cash and credit, for a particular time period

sales returns goods returned by customers; also known as returns inwards

purchases returns goods returned by the business to suppliers; also known as returns outwards

CHAPTER SUMMARY

- Accounting is known as 'the language of business'.
- The accounting system comprises a number of specific stages of recording and presenting business transactions:
  - source documents
  - books of prime entry
  - double-entry system of ledgers
  - trial balance
  - financial statements
- Accounting records call for the development of skills of accuracy and neatness.
- The statement of financial position uses the accounting equation:
  Assets – Liabilities = Capital

- Two basic accounting concepts which apply to all aspects of accounting are:
  - business entity
  - money measurement

- Financial reports are used both by the owner and managers of the business and also by outside bodies.

- Accounting involves the use of very specific terminology which should be learned.

In the next chapter we will look at some transactions that are to be found in most financial accounts. By studying these we will begin to understand the principles of double-entry bookkeeping.

QUESTIONS

visit **www.osbornebooks.co.uk** to take an online test

An asterisk (*) after the question number means that the answer is given at the end of this book.

1.1* Fill in the missing words from the following sentences:

(a) The set of double-entry accounts of a business is called the ....

(b) A .... is a person who owes you money when you sell on credit.

(c) A .... is a person to whom you owe money when you buy on credit.

(d) The .... is a list of sales made, compiled from invoices issued.

(e) The business' record of bank account and amount of cash held is kept in the ....

(f) Accounts such as sales, purchases, expenses are kept in the ....

(g) The accounting equation is:
.... minus ....equals ....

(h) Accounts record and report on the financial transactions of a particular business: this is the application of the .... concept.

1.2 State three purposes of accounting.

1.3 Describe the main stages in the financial accounting system. State five pieces of information that can be found from the accounting system that will be of interest to the owner of the business.

1.4 As well as the owner and managers of the business, other stakeholders have an interest in the accounting information. Select any *four* of these other stakeholders, and briefly explain the interest they will have.

1.5 Explain the accounting concepts of:

(a) Business entity.

(b) Money measurement.

1.6 Distinguish between:

- assets and liabilities
- trade receivables and trade payables
- purchases and sales
- credit purchases and cash purchases

1.7 Show the dual aspect, as it affects the accounting equation (assets – liabilities = capital), of the following transactions for a particular business:

- owner starts in business with capital of £8,000 in the bank
- buys a computer for £4,000 for use in the office, paying by bank transfer
- obtains a loan of £3,000 by cheque from a friend
- buys a van for £6,000, paying by cheque

1.8* Fill in the missing figures:

Assets	Liabilities	Capital
£	£	£
20,000	0	....
15,000	5,000	....
16,400	....	8,850
....	3,850	10,250
25,380	....	6,950
....	7,910	13,250

1.9* The table below sets out account balances from the books of a business. The columns (a) to (f) show the account balances resulting from a series of transactions that have taken place over time.

You are to compare each set of adjacent columns, ie (a) with (b), (b) with (c), and so on and state, with figures, what accounting transactions have taken place in each case.

	(a)	(b)	(c)	(d)	(e)	(f)
	£	£	£	£	£	£
Assets						
Office equipment	–	2,000	2,000	2,000	2,000	2,000
Van	–	–	–	10,000	10,000	10,000
Bank	10,000	8,000	14,000	4,000	6,000	3,000
Liabilities						
Loan	–	–	6,000	6,000	6,000	3,000
Capital	10,000	10,000	10,000	10,000	12,000	12,000

2 DOUBLE-ENTRY BOOKKEEPING: FIRST PRINCIPLES

As we have seen in Chapter 1, bookkeeping is the basic recording of business transactions in financial terms. Before studying financial accounting in detail it is important to study the principles of double-entry bookkeeping, as these form the basis of much that we shall be doing in the rest of the book.

In the previous chapter we looked briefly at the dual aspect of accounting – each time there is a business transaction there are two effects on the accounting equation. This chapter shows how the dual aspect is used in the principles of bookkeeping. In particular, we shall be looking at accounts for:

- bank
- cash
- capital
- non-current assets
- expenses
- income
- drawings
- loans

LEDGER ACCOUNTS

Double-entry bookkeeping, as its name suggests, recognises that each transaction has a dual aspect. Once the dual aspect of each transaction has been identified, the two bookkeeping entries can be made in the ledger accounts of the accounting system. An account is kept in the ledger to record each different type of transaction. In a handwritten bookkeeping system, the ledger will consist either of a bound book, or a series of separate sheets of paper – each account in the ledger will occupy a separate page; in a computerised system, the ledger will consist of a computer file, divided into separate accounts. Whether a handwritten or computerised system is being used, the principles remain the same.

A commonly-used layout for an account is set out on the next page. Entries in ledger accounts always include dates. Please note that dates used in this book, for the sake of simplicity, are often expressed as 20-8, 20-9, etc, unlike in a real business where the actual year date is shown (ie 2018, 2019, etc). Occasionally in this book 20-9 is followed by 20-0, ie when the decade changes from 2019 to 2020.

Debit (Dr)		Name of the account, eg Wages Account					Credit (Cr)
Date	**Details**	**Reference**	**£ p**	**Date**	**Details**	**Reference**	**£ p**
date of the trans-action	name of the other account	page or reference number of the other account	amount of the trans-action	date of the trans-action	name of the other account	page or reference number of the other account	amount of the trans-action

Note the following points about the layout of this account:

- the name of the account is written at the top
- the account is divided into two identical halves, separated by a central double vertical line
- the left-hand side is called the debit (or Dr) side
- the right-hand side is called the credit (or Cr) side
- the date, details and amount of the transaction are entered in the account
- in the details column is entered the name of the other account involved in the bookkeeping transaction
- the reference column is used as a cross-referencing system to the other entry of the double-entry bookkeeping transaction

In practice, each account would occupy a whole page in a handwritten bookkeeping system but, to save space when doing exercises, it is usual to put several accounts on a page. In future, in this book, the account layout will be simplified to give more clarity as follows:

Dr	**Wages Account**		Cr
20-1	£	20-1	£

This layout is often known in accounting jargon as a 'T' account; it will be used extensively in this book because it separates in a simple way the two sides – debit and credit – of the account. An alternative style of account has three money columns: debit, credit and balance. This type of account is commonly used for bank statements and computer accounting statements. Because the balance of the account is calculated after every transaction, it is known as a running balance account (see page 24).

DEBITS AND CREDITS

The principle of double-entry bookkeeping is that for every business transaction:

- one account is debited, and
- one account is credited

Debit entries are on the left-hand side of the appropriate account, while credit entries are on the right. The rules for debits and credits are:

- **debit entry** – the account which gains value, or records an asset, or an expense
- **credit entry** – the account which gives value, or records a liability, or an income item

This is illustrated as follows:

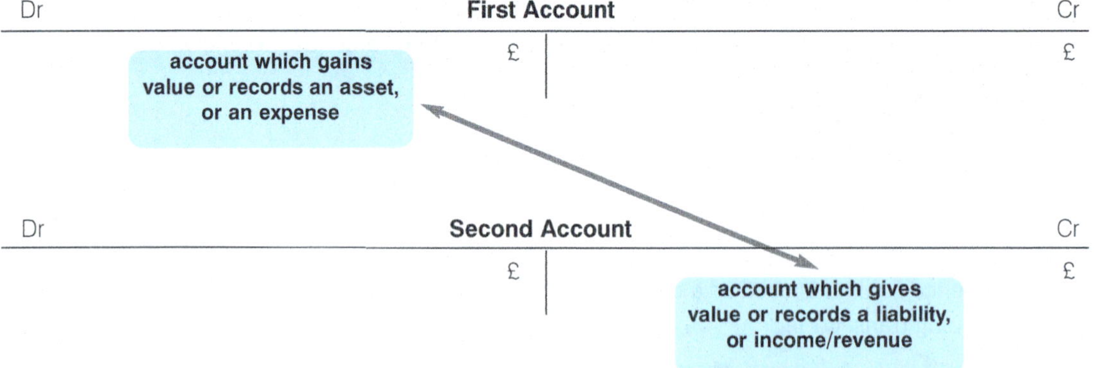

When one entry has been identified as a debit or credit, the other entry will be on the opposite side of the other account.

EXAMPLE TRANSACTIONS

In order to put the theory of double-entry bookkeeping into practice, we will look at some financial transactions undertaken by a new business which has just been set up by Jayne Hampson in 20-1:

1 September	Started in business with capital of £5,000, a cheque paid into the bank
4 September	Bought office equipment £2,500, paying by bank transfer
7 September	Paid rent of office £500, by cheque
10 September	Received commission of £100, by cheque
12 September	Withdrew £250 from the bank for own use (drawings)
16 September	Received a loan of £1,000 from James Henderson by cheque

All of these transactions involve the bank, and the business will enter them in its bank account. The bank account records money in the form of bank receipts and payments, ie cheques, standing orders, direct debits, bank transfers, credit card transactions, and debit card transactions. Many businesses use a separate cash account to record transactions which involve money in the form of cash and, in practice, the separate bank account and cash account are brought together in the cash book – see Chapter 7.

With both bank account and cash account, the rules for debit and credit are:

- money in is recorded on the debit side
- money out is recorded on the credit side

Using these rules, the bank account of Jayne Hampson's business, after entering the transactions listed on the previous page, appears as:

Dr		**Bank Account**			Cr
20-1		£	20-1		£
1 Sep	Capital	5,000	4 Sep	Office equipment	2,500
10 Sep	Commission	100	7 Sep	Rent paid	500
16 Sep	J Henderson: loan	1,000	12 Sep	Drawings	250
		Money in	Money out		

Note: the bank account shows the firm's record of how much has been paid into, and drawn out of, the bank – it is not exactly the same as the record of receipts and payments kept by the bank (we will compare the two in the form of a bank reconciliation statement in Chapter 8).

To complete the double-entry bookkeeping transactions we need to:

- identify on which side of the bank account the transaction has been recorded – debit (money in), or credit (money out)
- record the other double-entry transaction on the opposite side of the appropriate account
- note that business transactions involving cash will be entered in the cash account

The other accounts involved can now be recorded, and over the next few pages we shall look at the principles involved for each transaction of Jayne Hampson's business.

CAPITAL

Capital is the amount of money invested in the business by the owner. The amount is owed by the business back to the owner, although it is unlikely to be repaid immediately as the business would cease to exist. A capital account is used to record the amount paid into the business; the bookkeeping entries are:

- **capital introduced**
  - debit bank account, as in the case of Jayne Hampson, (or cash account, or a non-current asset account, where cash or non-current assets have been introduced by the owner as part of the capital)
  - credit capital account

Example transaction

1 Sep 20-1 Started in business with capital of £5,000, a cheque paid into the bank

Dr		**Capital Account**			Cr
20-1		£	20-1		£
			1 Sep	Bank	5,000

Note: the dual aspect is that bank account has gained value and has been debited (see account on page 19); capital account records a liability (an amount owed to the owner) and is credited. Remember that the business is a separate entity (see Chapter 1, page 10), and this bookkeeping entry looks at the transaction from the point of view of the business. The introduction of capital into a business is often the very first business transaction entered into the books of account.

Non-Current Assets

Non-current assets are items purchased by a business for use on a long-term basis. Examples are premises, motor vehicles, machinery and office equipment. All of these are bought by a business with the intention that they will be used over a long period of time. Without non-current assets, it would be difficult to continue in business, eg without machinery it would prove difficult to run a factory; without delivery vans and lorries it would be difficult to transport the firm's products to its customers.

When a business buys non-current assets, the expenditure is referred to as **capital expenditure**. This means that items have been bought for use in the business for some years to come. By contrast, **revenue expenditure** is where the items bought will be used by the business quite quickly. For example, the purchase of a car is capital expenditure, while the cost of fuel for the car is revenue expenditure.

non-current assets and double-entry bookkeeping

When non-current assets are bought, a separate account for each type of non-current asset is used, eg premises account, motor vehicles account, machinery account, etc. The bookkeeping entries are:

- **purchase of a non-current asset**
  - debit non-current asset account (using the appropriate account)
  - credit bank account (or cash account)

Example transaction

4 Sep 20-1 Bought office equipment £2,500, paying by bank transfer

Dr		Office Equipment Account			Cr
20-1		£	20-1		£
4 Sep	Bank	2,500			

The other part of the dual aspect of this transaction is a credit to bank account: this has been entered already (see account on page 19).

Expenses

Businesses pay various running expenses (overheads), such as rent, wages, electricity, telephone, and vehicle running expenses. These day-to-day expenses of running the business are termed **revenue expenditure**. A separate account is used in the accounting system for each main class of revenue expenditure, eg rent account, wages account, and so on.

The bookkeeping entries are:

- **payment of an expense**
  - debit expense account (using the appropriate account)
  - credit bank account (or cash account)

Example transaction

7 Sep 20-1 Paid rent of office £500, by cheque

Dr		Rent Paid Account			Cr
20-1		£	20-1		£
7 Sep	Bank	500			

Note: the accounting rules followed are that we have debited the account which has gained value (rent paid – the business has had the use and benefit of the office for a certain period of time). The account which has given value (bank) has already been credited (see page 19).

INCOME

From time-to-time a business may receive amounts of income, eg rent, commission, or fees. These are recorded in separate accounts for each category of income, eg rent income account, commission income account. The bookkeeping entries are:

- **receipt of income**
  - debit bank account (or cash account)
  - credit income account (using the appropriate account)

Example transaction

10 September 20-1 Received commission of £100, by cheque

Commission Income Account

Dr					Cr
20-1		£	20-1		£
			10 Sep	Bank	100

Note: We have already debited the account which has gained value (bank – see page 19) and credited the account which has given value (commission income).

OWNER'S DRAWINGS

Drawings is the term used when the owner takes money, in cash or by cheque (or sometimes goods), from the business for personal use. A drawings account is used to record such amounts; the bookkeeping entries for withdrawal of money are:

- **owner's drawings**
  - debit drawings account
  - credit bank account (or cash account)

Example transaction

12 Sep 20-1 Withdrew £250 from the bank for own use

Drawings Account

Dr					Cr
20-1		£	20-1		£
12 Sep	Bank	250			

The other part of the dual aspect of this transaction is a credit to bank account: this has been entered already (see page 19).

Loans

When a business receives a loan, eg from a relative or the bank, it is the cash account or bank account which gains value, while a loan account (in the name of the lender) records the liability.

- **loan received**
  - debit bank account (or cash account)
  - credit loan account (in name of the lender)

Example transaction

16 September 20-1 Received a loan of £1,000 from James Henderson by cheque

Dr		James Henderson: Loan Account			Cr
20-1		£	20-1		£
			16 Sep	Bank	1,000

The debit entry has already been made in bank account (see page 19).

Further Transactions

Using the accounts which we have seen already, here are some further transactions:

- **loan repayment**
  - debit loan account
  - credit bank account (or cash account)
- **disposal (sale) of a non-current asset**
  - debit bank account (or cash account)
  - credit non-current asset account

Note: accounting for the disposal of non-current assets is dealt with fully in Chapter 15.

- **withdrawal of cash from the bank for use in the business**
  - debit cash account
  - credit bank account
- **payment of cash into the bank**
  - debit bank account
  - credit cash account

Running Balance Accounts

The layout of accounts that we have used has a debit side and a credit side. Although this layout is very useful when learning the principles of bookkeeping, it is not always appropriate for practical business use. Most 'real-life' accounts have three money columns: debit transactions, credit transactions, and balance. A familiar example of this type of account is a bank statement. With a three-column account, the balance is calculated after each transaction has been entered – hence the name running balance accounts. For handwritten accounts, it would be rather tedious to calculate the balance after each transaction (and a potential source of errors) but, using computer accounting, the calculation is carried out automatically.

The following is the bank account used earlier in this chapter (page 19), set out in 'traditional' format:

Dr		Bank Account			Cr
20-1		£	20-1		£
1 Sep	Capital	5,000	4 Sep	Office equipment	2,500
10 Sep	Commission income	100	7 Sep	Rent paid	500
16 Sep	J Henderson: loan	1,000	12 Sep	Drawings	250

The account does not show the balance, and would need to be balanced (see Chapter 5).

In 'running balance' layout, the account appears as:

Bank Account

20-1		Debit	Credit	Balance
		£	£	£
1 Sep	Capital	5,000		5,000 Dr
4 Sep	Office equipment		2,500	2,500 Dr
7 Sep	Rent paid		500	2,000 Dr
10 Sep	Commission income	100		2,100 Dr
12 Sep	Drawings		250	1,850 Dr
16 Sep	J Henderson: loan	1,000		2,850 Dr

With a running balance account, it is necessary to state after each transaction whether the balance is debit (Dr) or credit (Cr). Note that the bank account in the books of this business has a debit balance, ie there is money in the bank, an asset.

In your studies you will normally use the traditional 'T' account format.

CHAPTER SUMMARY

- Every business transaction has a dual aspect.

- Business transactions are recorded in ledger accounts using double-entry bookkeeping principles.

- Each double-entry bookkeeping transaction involves a debit entry and a credit entry.

- Entries in the bank account and cash account are:
  - debit money in
  - credit money out

- Capital is the amount of money invested in the business by the owner. Capital introduced is recorded as:
  - debit bank account or cash account (or an asset account if an asset is introduced)
  - credit capital account

- Non-current assets are items purchased by a business for use on a long-term basis, eg premises, motor vehicles, machinery and office equipment. The purchase of such items is called capital expenditure.

- The purchase of non-current assets is recorded in the business accounts as:
  - debit non-current asset account
  - credit bank account (or cash account)

- Running expenses or overheads of a business, such as rent paid, wages, electricity, etc are called revenue expenditure.

- Expenses are recorded in the business accounts as:
  - debit expense account
  - credit bank account (or cash account)

- Receipt of income, eg rent received, commission income, fee income, is recorded as:
  - debit bank account (or cash account)
  - credit income account

- Drawings is where the owner takes money (or goods) from the business for personal use. The withdrawal of money is recorded as:
  - debit drawings account
  - credit bank account (or cash account)

- When a business receives a loan, it is recorded as:
  - debit bank account (or cash account)
  - credit loan account in the name of the lender

In the next chapter we will continue with double-entry bookkeeping and look at regular business transactions for purchases, sales and returns.

QUESTIONS

visit
www.osbornebooks.co.uk
to take an online test

An asterisk (*) after the question number means that the answer is given at the end of this book.

2.1 James Anderson has kept his bank account up-to-date, but has not got around to the other double-entry bookkeeping entries. Rule up the other 'T' accounts for him, and make the appropriate entries.

Dr				**Bank Account**	Cr
20-1		£	20-1		£
1 Feb	Capital	7,500	6 Feb	Computer	2,000
14 Feb	Bank loan	2,500	8 Feb	Rent paid	750
20 Feb	Commission income	145	12 Feb	Wages	425
			23 Feb	Drawings	200
			25 Feb	Wages	380
			28 Feb	Van	6,000

2.2* The following are the business transactions of Tony Long for the month of May 20-2:

20-2

1 May	Started a business with capital of £6,000 in the bank
4 May	Bought a machine for £3,500, paying by bank transfer
6 May	Bought office equipment for £2,000, paying by bank transfer
10 May	Paid rent £350, by cheque
12 May	Obtained a loan of £1,000 from a friend, Lucy Warner, and paid her cheque into the bank
15 May	Paid wages £250, by bank transfer
17 May	Received commission £150, by cheque
20 May	Drawings £85, by cheque
25 May	Paid wages £135, by bank transfer

Required:

(a) Write up Tony Long's bank account in 'T' account format.

(b) Complete the double-entry bookkeeping transactions using 'T' accounts.

2.3 Enter the following transactions into the double-entry bookkeeping accounts of Jean Lacey:

20-5

1 Aug	Started in business with capital of £5,000 in the bank
3 Aug	Bought a computer for £1,800, paying by bank transfer
7 Aug	Paid rent £100, by cheque
10 Aug	Received commission £200, in cash

12 Aug	Bought office fittings £2,000, paying by bank transfer
15 Aug	Received a loan, £1,000 by cheque, from a friend, Sally Orton
17 Aug	Drawings £100, in cash
20 Aug	Returned some of the office fittings (unsuitable) and received a refund cheque of £250
25 Aug	Received commission £150, by cheque
27 Aug	Made a loan repayment to Sally Orton of £150, by cheque

2.4* Tom Griffiths has recently set up in business. He has made some errors in writing up his bank account. You are to set out the bank account as it should appear, rule up the other accounts for him, and make the appropriate entries.

Dr		**Bank Account**			Cr
20-2		£	20-2		£
4 Mar	Office equipment	1,000	1 Mar	Capital	6,500
12 Mar	Drawings	175	5 Mar	Bank loan	2,500
			7 Mar	Wages	250
			8 Mar	Commission income	150
			10 Mar	Rent paid	200
			15 Mar	Van	6,000

2.5 Enter the following transactions into the double-entry bookkeeping accounts of Caroline Yates:

20-7

1 Nov	Started in business with capital of £75,000 in the bank
3 Nov	Bought a photocopier for £2,500, paying by bank transfer
7 Nov	Received a bank loan of £70,000
10 Nov	Bought office premises £130,000, paying by bank transfer
12 Nov	Paid business rates of £3,000, by cheque
14 Nov	Bought office fittings £1,500, paying by bank transfer
15 Nov	Received commission of £300, in cash
18 Nov	Drawings in cash £125
20 Nov	Paid wages £250, by bank transfer
23 Nov	Paid £100 of cash into the bank
25 Nov	Returned some of the office fittings (unsuitable) and received a refund cheque for £200
28 Nov	Received commission £200, by cheque

2.6 Write up the bank account from Question 2.5 in the form of a 'running balance' account.

2.7 You are the bookkeeper at Wyvern Electronics. A trainee has just joined the firm and is helping you with the recording of business transactions. Write down the guidance you will give her which explains the principles of double-entry bookkeeping.

3 DOUBLE-ENTRY BOOKKEEPING: FURTHER TRANSACTIONS

This chapter continues with the principles of double-entry bookkeeping and builds on the skills established in the previous chapter. We shall be looking at the dual aspect and the bookkeeping required for the business transactions of:

- cash purchases
- cash sales
- credit purchases
- credit sales
- returns
- carriage inwards and outwards

PURCHASES AND SALES

Common business transactions are to buy and sell goods. These transactions are recorded in purchases account and sales account respectively. It is important to remember that these two accounts are used to record the purchase and sale of the goods in which the business trades. For example, a shoe shop buys shoes from the manufacturer and records this in purchases account; as shoes are sold, the transactions are recorded in sales account. Note that the bookkeeping system does not use a 'goods account' – instead, when buying goods, a purchases account is used; when selling goods, a sales account is used. In this way, a business knows the amount of its purchases and sales.

The normal entry on a purchases account is on the debit side – the account has gained value, ie the business has bought goods for resale. The normal entry on a sales account is on the credit side – the account has given value, ie the business has sold goods.

When a business buys an item for use in the business, eg a computer, this is debited to a separate account, because a non-current asset – see Chapter 2, page 20 – has been purchased. Likewise, when a non-current asset is sold or disposed of, it is not entered in the sales account.

WORKED EXAMPLE: PURCHASES AND SALES

In order to put the theory of double-entry bookkeeping for purchases and sales into practice, we will use as an illustration some financial transactions undertaken by Temeside Traders, a business which started trading on 1 October 20-1:

1 October	Started in business with capital of £7,000 paid into the bank
2 October	Bought goods for £5,000, paying by bank transfer
3 October	Sold some of the goods for £3,000, a cheque being received
5 October	Bought computer for use in the business for £700, paying by cheque
10 October	Bought goods for £2,800, paying by bank transfer
12 October	Sold some of the goods for £5,000, a bank transfer being received
15 October	Paid rent £150, by cheque

These transactions are entered into the bookkeeping system of Temeside Traders as follows:

Bank Account

Dr					Cr
20-1		£	20-1		£
1 Oct	Capital	7,000	2 Oct	Purchases	5,000
3 Oct	Sales	3,000	5 Oct	Computer	700
12 Oct	Sales	5,000	10 Oct	Purchases	2,800
			15 Oct	Rent paid	150

Capital Account

Dr					Cr
20-1		£	20-1		£
			1 Oct	Bank	7,000

Purchases Account

Dr					Cr
20-1		£	20-1		£
2 Oct	Bank	5,000			
10 Oct	Bank	2,800			

Sales Account

Dr					Cr
20-1		£	20-1		£
			3 Oct	Bank	3,000
			12 Oct	Bank	5,000

Computer Account

Dr					Cr
20-1		£	20-1		£
5 Oct	Bank	700			

Rent Paid Account

Dr					Cr
20-1		£	20-1		£
15 Oct	Bank	150			

notes to worked example

- Only one purchases account and one sales account is used to record the purchases and sales of the goods in which a business trades.
- The computer is a non-current asset, so its purchase is entered to a separate computer account.
- The purchases and sales made in the transactions above are called cash purchases and cash sales, because payment is immediate.

CREDIT TRANSACTIONS

In the previous section, we looked at the bookkeeping for cash purchases and cash sales (here 'cash' means 'where payment is made immediately' – involving either notes and coins or bank payments). However, in business, many transactions for purchases and sales are made on credit, ie the goods are bought or sold now, with payment to be made at a later date in cash or by cheque/bank transfer. It is an important aspect of double-entry bookkeeping to record the credit transaction as a purchase or a sale, and then record the second entry in an account in the name of the trade payable (recording the amount owing by the firm to a trade payable), or trade receivable (recording the amount owing to the firm by trade receivable).

Note that the term 'credit transactions' does not refer to the side of an account. Instead, it means the type of transaction where money is not paid at the time of making the sale but will be made at a later date.

credit purchases

Credit purchases are goods or services obtained from a supplier, with payment to take place at a later date. From the buyer's viewpoint, the supplier is a trade payable.

The bookkeeping entries are:

- **credit purchase**
  - debit purchases account
  - credit trade payable's (supplier's) account

When payment is made to the trade payable the bookkeeping entries are:

- **payment made to trade payable**
  - debit trade payable's account
  - credit bank account or cash account

credit sales

With credit sales, goods or services are sold to a customer who is allowed to settle the account at a later date. From the seller's viewpoint, the customer is a trade receivable.

The bookkeeping entries are:

- **credit sale**
  - debit trade receivable's (customer's) account
  - credit sales account

When payment is received from the customer the bookkeeping entries are:

- **payment received from trade receivable**
  - debit bank account or cash account
  - credit trade receivable's account

WORKED EXAMPLE: CREDIT TRANSACTIONS

A local business, Wyvern Wholesalers, has the following transactions in the year 20-1:

18 Sep	Bought goods, £250, on credit from Malvern Manufacturing Co, with payment to be made in 30 days' time
20 Sep	Sold goods, £175, on credit to Strensham Stores, payment to be made in 30 days' time
18 Oct	Paid £250 by bank transfer to Malvern Manufacturing Co
20 Oct	Received a bank transfer for £175 from Strensham Stores

These transactions will be recorded in the bookkeeping system of Wyvern Wholesalers as follows:

Dr — Purchases Account — Cr

20-1		£	20-1		£
18 Sep	Malvern Manufacturing Co	250			

Dr — Sales Account — Cr

20-1		£	20-1		£
			20 Sep	Strensham Stores	175

Dr — Malvern Manufacturing Co — Cr

20-1		£	20-1		£
18 Oct	Bank	250	18 Sep	Purchases	250

Dr		Strensham Stores			Cr
20-1		£	20-1		£
20 Sep	Sales	175	20 Oct	Bank	175

Dr		Bank Account			Cr
20-1		£	20-1		£
20 Oct	Strensham Stores	175	18 Oct	Malvern Manufacturing Co	250

Note: the name of the other account involved has been used in the details column as a description.

balancing off accounts

In the example above, after the transactions have been recorded in the books of Wyvern Wholesalers, the accounts of Malvern Manufacturing Co and Strensham Stores have the same amount entered on both debit and credit side. This means that nothing is owing to Wyvern Wholesalers, or is owed by it, ie the accounts have a 'nil' balance. In practice, as a business trades, there will be a number of entries on both sides of such accounts, and we shall see in Chapter 5 how accounts are 'balanced off' at regular intervals.

non-current assets bought on credit

Non-current assets are often purchased on credit terms. As with the purchase of goods for resale, an account is opened in the name of the trade payable, as follows:

- **purchase of a non-current asset on credit**
  - debit non-current asset account, eg computer account
  - credit trade payable's (supplier's) account

When payment is made to the trade payable the bookkeeping entries are:

- **payment made to a trade payable**
  - debit trade payable's account
  - credit bank account or cash account

Note that some businesses will use an 'other payables' account for this type of transaction.

PURCHASES RETURNS AND SALES RETURNS

From time-to-time goods in which the business trades are returned, perhaps because the wrong items have been supplied (eg wrong type, size or colour), or because the goods are unsatisfactory. We will now see the bookkeeping entries for returned goods.

- **Purchases returns** (or returns outwards) is where a business returns goods to a trade payable (supplier).

  The bookkeeping entries are:

  – debit trade payable's (supplier's) account

  – credit purchases returns (or returns outwards) account

  Purchases returns are kept separate from purchases, ie they are entered in a separate purchases returns account rather than being credited to purchases account.

- **Sales returns** (or returns inwards) is where a trade receivable (customer) returns goods to the business.

  The bookkeeping entries are:

  – debit sales returns (or returns inwards) account

  – credit trade receivable's (customer's) account

Sales returns are kept separate from sales, ie they are entered in a separate sales returns account rather than being debited to sales account.

WORKED EXAMPLE: PURCHASES RETURNS AND SALES RETURNS

Hightown Stores has the following transactions during the year 20-1:

7 October	Bought goods, £280, on credit from B Lewis Ltd
10 October	Returned unsatisfactory goods, £30, to B Lewis Ltd
11 October	Sold goods, £125, on credit to A Holmes
17 October	A Holmes returned goods, £25
26 October	Paid the amount owing to B Lewis Ltd by bank transfer
29 October	A Holmes paid the amount owing in cash

The transactions will be recorded in the bookkeeping system of Hightown Stores as follows:

Dr — Purchases Account — Cr

20-1		£	20-1		£
7 Oct	B Lewis Ltd	280			

Dr — B Lewis Ltd — Cr

20-1		£	20-1		£
10 Oct	Purchases returns	30	7 Oct	Purchases	280
26 Oct	Bank	250			

Dr		Purchases Returns Account			Cr
20-1		£	20-1		£
			10 Oct	B Lewis Ltd	30

Dr		Sales Account			Cr
20-1		£	20-1		£
			11 Oct	A Holmes	125

Dr		A Holmes			Cr
20-1		£	20-1		£
11 Oct	Sales	125	17 Oct	Sales returns	25
			29 Oct	Cash	100

Dr		Sales Returns Account			Cr
20-1		£	20-1		£
17 Oct	A Holmes	25			

Dr		Bank Account			Cr
20-1		£	20-1		£
			26 Oct	B Lewis Ltd	250

Dr		Cash Account			Cr
20-1		£	20-1		£
29 Oct	A Holmes	100			

Carriage Inwards and Carriage Outwards

When goods are bought and sold, the cost of transporting the goods is referred to as 'carriage'.

Carriage inwards is where the buyer pays the carriage cost of purchases, eg an item is purchased by an internet order, and the buyer has to pay the additional cost of delivery.

Carriage outwards is where the seller pays the carriage charge, eg an item is sold to the customer and described as 'delivery free'.

Both carriage inwards and carriage outwards are expenses and their cost is debited to two separate accounts, carriage inwards account and carriage outwards account respectively.

- The bookkeeping entries for carriage inwards are:
  - debit carriage inwards account — *the cost of carriage on purchases*
  - credit bank account — *paid by the buyer*
- The bookkeeping entries for carriage outwards are:
  - debit carriage outwards account — *the cost of carriage on sales*
  - credit bank account — *paid by the seller*

General Principles of Debits and Credits

By now you should have a good idea of the principles of debits and credits. From the transactions we have considered in this and the previous chapter, the 'rules' can be summarised as follows:

Debits include:

- purchases of goods for resale
- sales returns (or returns inwards) when goods previously sold are returned to the business
- purchase of non-current assets for use in the business
- expenses and overheads incurred by the business
- trade receivables where money is owed to the business
- money received into the business through cash account or bank account
- drawings made by the owner of the business
- loan repayment, where a loan liability is reduced/repaid

Credits include:

- sales of goods by the business
- purchases returns (or returns outwards) of goods previously bought by the business
- sale of non-current assets
- income received by the business

- trade payables where money is owed by the business
- money paid out by the business through cash account or bank account
- capital introduced into the business by the owner
- loan received by the business

It is important to ensure, at an early stage, that you are clear about the principles of debits and credits. They are important for an understanding of bookkeeping, and are essential for your later studies in financial accounting.

To summarise the double-entry bookkeeping 'rules':

- **debit entry** – the account which gains value, or records an asset, or an expense
- **credit entry** – the account which gives value, or records a liability, or an income item

Types of Account

Within a bookkeeping system there are different types of account: a distinction is made between personal and impersonal accounts. Personal accounts are in the names of people or businesses, eg the accounts for trade receivables and trade payables. Impersonal accounts are the other accounts; these are usually divided between those accounts which represent things such as cash, bank, computers, vehicles, inventory, etc, and those accounts which record income and expenses such as sales, purchases, wages, etc.

These distinctions are shown in the diagram below.

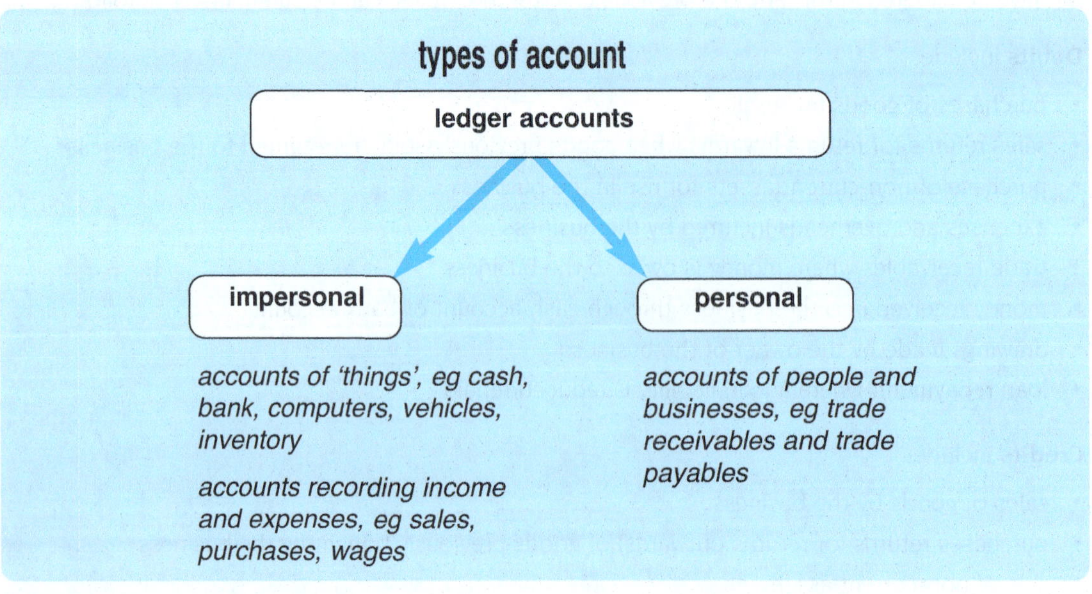

CHAPTER SUMMARY

- Purchases account is used to record the purchase of goods in which the business trades: the normal entry is on the debit side.

- Sales account is used to record the sale of goods in which the business trades: the normal entry is on the credit side.

- The purchase of goods is recorded as:
  - debit purchases account
  - credit bank/cash account or, if bought on credit, trade payable's account

- The sale of goods is recorded as:
  - debit bank/cash account or, if sold on credit, trade receivable's account
  - credit sales account

- Purchases returns (or returns outwards) are recorded as:
  - debit trade payable's account
  - credit purchases returns (or returns outwards) account

- Sales returns (or returns inwards) are recorded as:
  - debit sales returns (or returns inwards) account
  - credit trade receivable's account

- 'Carriage' is the expense of transporting goods:
  - carriage inwards is the cost of carriage paid on purchases
  - carriage outwards is the cost of carriage paid on sales

- Accounts are divided between personal (the accounts of people, firms, eg trade receivables and trade payables; also capital account), and impersonal accounts (the accounts of things and the accounts of income and expenses).

In the next chapter we will look at the business documents used when goods are sold to another business.

QUESTIONS

visit
www.osbornebooks.co.uk
to take an online test

An asterisk (*) after the question number means that the answer is given at the end of this book.

3.1 The following are the business transactions of Evesham Enterprises for the month of October 20-2:

1 Oct	Started in business with capital of £2,500 in the bank
2 Oct	Bought goods, £200, paying by bank transfer
4 Oct	Sold goods, £150, a cheque being received
6 Oct	Bought goods, £90, paying by cheque
8 Oct	Sold goods, £125, a cheque being received
12 Oct	Received a loan of £2,000 from J Smithson by bank transfer
14 Oct	Bought goods, £250, paying by bank transfer
18 Oct	Sold goods, £155, a cheque being received
22 Oct	Bought a second-hand delivery van for use in the business, £4,000, paying by bank transfer
25 Oct	Paid wages, £375, by bank transfer
30 Oct	Sold goods, £110, a cheque being received

You are to:

(a) Write up the firm's bank account.

(b) Complete the double-entry bookkeeping transactions.

3.2* The following are the business transactions of Oxford Trading Company for the month of February 20-1:

1 Feb	Started in business with capital of £3,000 in the bank
2 Feb	Sold goods, £250, a cheque being received
3 Feb	Bought goods, £100, paying by cheque
5 Feb	Paid wages, £150, by bank transfer
7 Feb	Sold goods, £300, a cheque being received
12 Feb	Bought goods, £200, paying by cheque
15 Feb	Received a loan of £1,000 from James Walters by bank transfer
20 Feb	Bought a computer for use in the business for £1,950, paying by bank transfer
25 Feb	Sold goods, £150, a cheque being received
27 Feb	Paid wages, £125, by bank transfer

You are to:

(a) Write up the firm's bank account.

(b) Complete the double-entry bookkeeping transactions.

3.3* Write up the bank account from Question 3.2 in the form of a 'running balance' account.

3.4* The following are the business transactions of Pershore Packaging for the month of January 20-1:

4 Jan	Bought goods, £250, on credit from AB Supplies Ltd
5 Jan	Sold goods, £195, a cheque being received
7 Jan	Sold goods, £150, cash being received
10 Jan	Received a loan of £1,000 from J Johnson by bank transfer
15 Jan	Paid £250 to AB Supplies Ltd by cheque
17 Jan	Sold goods, £145, on credit to L Lewis
20 Jan	Bought goods, £225, paying by bank transfer
22 Jan	Paid wages, £125, in cash
26 Jan	Bought office equipment for use in the business, £160, on credit from Mercia Office Supplies Ltd
29 Jan	Received a cheque for £145 from L Lewis
31 Jan	Paid the amount owing to Mercia Office Supplies Ltd by bank transfer

You are to record the transactions in the books of account.

3.5 The following are the business transactions for April 20-2 of William King, who runs a food wholesaling business:

2 Apr	Bought goods, £200, on credit from Wyvern Producers Ltd
4 Apr	Bought goods, £250, on credit from A Larsen
5 Apr	Sold goods, £150, on credit to Pershore Patisserie
7 Apr	Sold goods, £175, a cheque being received
9 Apr	Returned goods, £50, to Wyvern Producers Ltd
12 Apr	Sold goods, £110, a cheque being received
15 Apr	Pershore Patisserie returned goods, £25
17 Apr	Bought a weighing machine for use in the business £250, on credit from Amery Scales Limited
20 Apr	Paid Wyvern Producers Ltd £150, by bank transfer
22 Apr	Pershore Patisserie paid the amount owing by cheque
26 Apr	Returned goods, £45, to A Larsen
28 Apr	Sold goods, £100, cash received
29 Apr	Paid wages in cash, £90
30 Apr	Paid the amount owing to Amery Scales Ltd by bank transfer

You are to record the transactions in the books of account.

3.6 The following are the business transactions for June 20-3 of Helen Smith who trades as 'Fashion Frocks':

2 Jun	Bought goods, £350, on credit from Designs Ltd
4 Jun	Sold goods, £220, a cheque being received
5 Jun	Sold goods, £115, cash received
6 Jun	Returned goods, £100, to Designs Ltd
7 Jun	Bought goods, £400, on credit from Mercia Knitwear Ltd
10 Jun	Sold goods, £350, on credit to Wyvern Trade Supplies
12 Jun	Sold goods, £175, a cheque being received
15 Jun	Wyvern Trade Supplies returned goods, £50
17 Jun	Returned goods, £80, to Mercia Knitwear Ltd
18 Jun	Paid the amount owing to Designs Ltd by bank transfer
20 Jun	Sold goods, £180, cash received
23 Jun	Bought goods, £285, on credit from Designs Ltd
26 Jun	Paid rent in cash, £125
28 Jun	Received a bank transfer from Wyvern Trade Supplies for the amount owing

You are to record the transactions in the books of account.

3.7 For each transaction below, complete the table on the next page to show the names of the accounts which will be debited and credited:

(a) Bought goods, paying by bank transfer

(b) Bank transfer received for sales

(c) Bought goods on credit from Teme Traders

(d) Sold goods on credit to L Harris

(e) Returned unsatisfactory goods to Teme Traders

(f) L Harris returns unsatisfactory goods

(g) Received a loan from D Perkins, by cheque

(h) Withdrew cash from the bank for use in the business

Transaction	Account debited	Account credited
(a)	....	....
(b)	....	....
(c)	....	....
(d)	....	....
(e)	....	....
(f)	....	....
(g)	....	....
(h)	....	....

3.8 You are the bookkeeper at Wyvern Electronics. Today your trainee has been working on recording sales and purchases transactions in the double-entry system. She asks you to explain the following points:

- Why do we use separate accounts for purchases and sales? Surely a combined account – called 'goods' – would be better?
- I can't see why purchases should go on the debit side and sales on the credit side of their respective accounts.
- Why can't I record the purchase of a new delivery van for use in the business in purchases account?
- I can't see the logic of purchases returns and sales returns.
- Why do I need separate accounts for carriage inwards and carriage outwards? Surely an account called 'carriage' would do just as well?

Write the answers you will give to the trainee.

4 BUSINESS DOCUMENTS

In this chapter we look at the main business documents which are used when goods are bought and sold. Two of these documents are 'source documents' which are used to update the bookkeeping records. We cover the following:

- purchase order
- delivery note
- invoice (a source document)
- credit note (a source document)
- statement of account
- other source documents

We will also see how cash discount – an allowance off the invoice price for prompt payment – is recorded in the bookkeeping system.

DOCUMENTS FOR A CREDIT TRANSACTION

You will see that the documents to be explained involve credit transactions, ie selling or buying with payment to be made at a later date. The normal stages in a credit transaction are:

1 buyer prepares
   - purchase order

2 seller prepares
   - delivery note
   - invoice
   - statement of account

3 buyer sends payment by
   - cheque, or
   - bank transfer

If some or all of the goods are unsatisfactory and are returned, the seller prepares a credit note.

The flow of these documents is shown in the diagram on the next page.

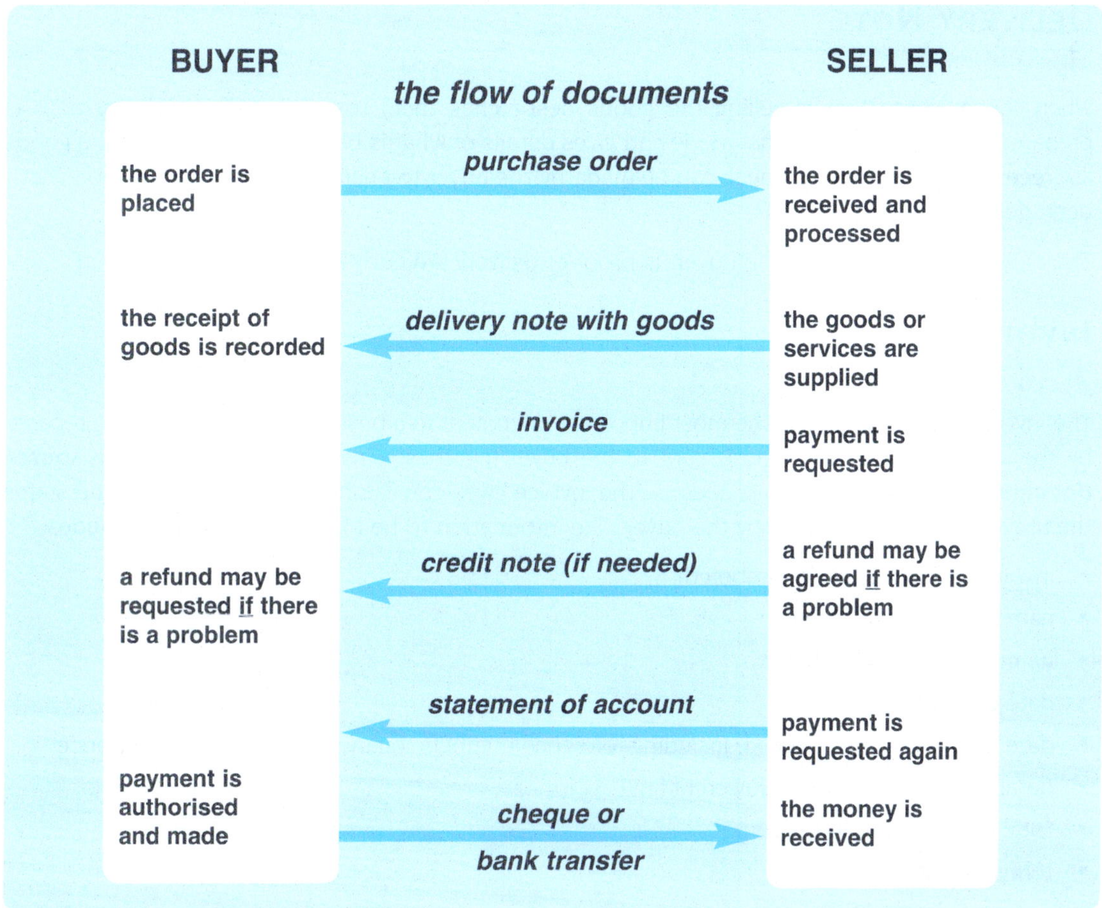

Purchase Order

A purchase order is prepared by the buyer, and is sent to the seller. Details normally found on a purchase order include:

- reference number of purchase order
- name and address of buyer
- name and address of seller
- full description of the goods, reference numbers, quantity required and unit price
- date of issue
- signature of person authorised to issue the order

In order to keep control over purchases many businesses authorise certain people as buyers. In this way, purchases are controlled so that duplicate or unauthorised goods are not ordered.

Delivery Note

When the business that is selling the goods despatches them to the buyer, a delivery note is prepared. This accompanies the goods and gives details of what is being delivered. When the goods are received by the buyer, a check can be made by the buyer to ensure that the correct goods have been delivered.

The delivery note, signed by the buyer, is proof of delivery – a copy is retained by the carrier.

Invoice

The invoice (see next page) is the most important document in a business transaction. It is prepared by the seller (sales invoice) and is sent to the buyer (purchases invoice) who uses it as a **source document** for bookkeeping transactions. The invoice gives details of the goods supplied, and states the money amount to be paid by the buyer. The information to be found on an invoice includes:

- invoice number (serially numbered)
- name and address of seller
- name and address of buyer
- date of sale
- date that goods are supplied, including reference numbers, quantity supplied and unit price
- details of trade discount allowed (if any)
- total amount of money due
- terms of trade

value added tax

Where the seller is registered for Value Added Tax (VAT), tax must be charged at the appropriate rate on all sales subject to VAT.

terms of trade

The terms of trade are stated on an invoice to indicate the date by which the invoice amount is to be paid. The term 'net' on an invoice means that the invoice total is the amount to be paid; 'net 30 days' means that the amount is payable within 30 days of the invoice date.

trade discount

Trade discount is the amount sometimes allowed as a reduction in price:

- to businesses, often in the same trade (but not normally to the general public)
- for buying in bulk, ie large quantities (this discount is also known as bulk discount)
- by wholesalers as a discount to retailers off list prices

INVOICE

TREND FASHION DESIGNS LIMITED

Unit 45 Elgar Estate, Broadfield, BR7 4ER
Tel 01908 765314 Fax 01908 765951

invoice to

Zing Fashions
4 Friar Street
Broadfield
BR1 3RF

invoice no	**787923**
account	**3993**
your reference	**47609**

deliver to

as above

date	**01 10 -5**

product code	description	quantity	unit price £	unit	total £	trade discount %	net £
45B	**Trend tops (black)**	**40**	**12.50**	**each**	**500.00**	**10**	**450.00**

TOTAL	**450.00**

terms
Net 30 days

In the invoice shown above, trade discount of 10%, amounting to £50, is allowed on clothes supplied to Zing Fashions, a shop. Note that trade discount is never shown in the accounts – only the amount after deduction of trade discount is recorded. Here this amount is £450.

cash discount

Cash discount (also known as settlement discount) is an allowance off the invoice amount for prompt payment. When it applies, it is indicated on the invoice, eg 2% cash discount for settlement within seven days. The buyer can choose whether to take up the cash discount by paying promptly, or whether to take longer to pay, perhaps thirty days from the invoice date, without cash discount. When cash discount is taken, it needs to be recorded in the accounts – see page 52.

Compare the amounts to be paid in the following example where the terms of trade are "2% cash discount for full settlement within seven days, otherwise net 30 days".

	No cash discount taken – full settlement between 8 and 30 days	Cash discount of 2% taken – full settlement within 7 days
	£	£
Invoice amount	1,000	1,000
Cash discount at 2%	–	20
Amount paid	1,000	980

format of invoices

Invoices (like other business documents) can be handwritten or typed on printed forms, or input and printed out on a computer. Invoicing is an ideal function for computerised accounting and, for this purpose, pre-printed invoices are available, either in the form of continuous stationery or as separate sheets. Also, increasingly nowadays, invoices can be sent electronically as part of the paperless EDI (electronic data interchange) system which integrates the ordering, invoicing and payment processes.

Credit Note

If a buyer returns goods for some reason (eg faulty goods supplied), or requires a reduction in the amount owed (the buyer may have been overcharged) the seller prepares a credit note (see next page) to record the amount of the allowance made to the buyer. The credit note is the **source document** for recording returned goods in the bookkeeping system.

Statement of Account

At regular intervals, often at the end of each month, the seller issues a statement of account (see page 48) to each trade receivable. This gives a summary of the transactions that have taken place since the previous statement and shows how much is currently owed. The details on a statement are:

CREDIT NOTE

TREND FASHION DESIGNS LIMITED

Unit 45 Elgar Estate, Broadfield, BR7 4ER
Tel 01908 765314 Fax 01908 765951

to

Zing Fashions
4 Friar Street
Broadfield
BR1 3RF

credit note no	**12157**
account	**3993**
your reference	**47609**
our invoice	**787923**
date	**10 10 -5**

product code	description	quantity	unit price £	unit	total £	trade discount %	net £
45B	**Trend tops (black)**	**2**	**12.50**	**each**	**25.00**	**10**	**22.50**

Reason for credit
2 tops received damaged

TOTAL	**22.50**

- name and address of seller
- name and address of the trade receivable (buyer)
- date of the statement
- details of transactions, eg invoices, debit notes, credit notes, payments
- balance currently due

Most statements have three money columns: debit, credit and balance, just like a bank statement.

The debit column is used to record the money amount of invoices and debit notes sent to the trade receivable; the credit column is for payments received and credit notes issued; the balance column shows the amount due, and is prepared on the 'running balance' (see page 24) basis, ie a new balance is shown after each transaction. The balance is usually a debit balance, which indicates that the buyer is a trade receivable in the seller's accounting records.

Some statements of account also incorporate a remittance advice as a tear-off slip; this is returned to the seller together with the payment.

STATEMENT OF ACCOUNT

TREND FASHION DESIGNS LIMITED

Unit 45 Elgar Estate, Broadfield, BR7 4ER
Tel 01908 765314 Fax 01908 765951

TO

Zing Fashions
4 Friar Street
Broadfield
BR1 3RF

account **3993**

date **31 10 -5**

date	details	debit £	credit £	balance £
01 10 -5	**Invoice 787923**	**450.00**		**450.00**
10 10 -5	**Credit note 12157**		**22.50**	**427.50**

AMOUNT NOW DUE **427.50**

PAYMENT

Before payment is made to the seller, the buyer must check that the goods have been received and are as ordered. The payment can then be authorised by an appointed employee and made by means of either a cheque (sent by post) or a bank transfer which passes the money from the buyer's bank account to the seller's account. Bank transfers are made either by Bacs (Bacs Payment Schemes) transfer or by direct transfer between bank accounts using internet banking. If a cheque is posted to the seller, it is sent with a remittance advice, which shows the amount of the payment, and the transactions to which it relates. If a payment is sent by bank transfer, a separate remittance advice will be mailed or emailed.

Other Source Documents

cash receipts

Often when payment is made to the seller, a receipt is given; this can take the form of a machine-produced receipt, such as is given in a shop, or a handwritten receipt. The copy of these receipts – in the form of a **till roll/till summary** and **receipt book** – form the **source documents** for the seller. The originals are the **source documents** for the buyer. Look at these examples:

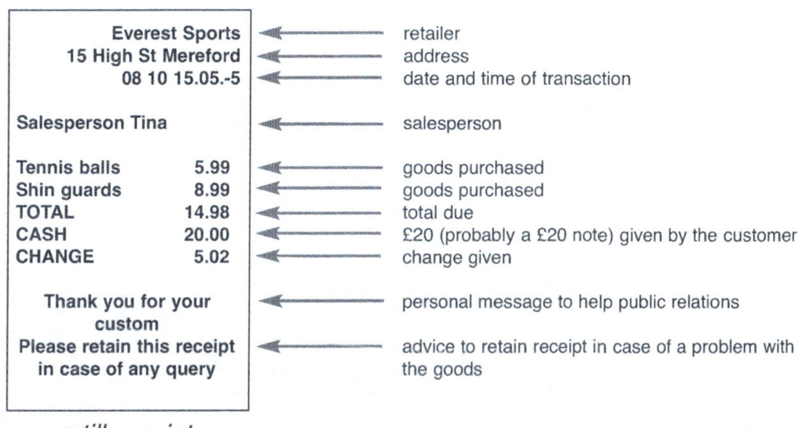
Everest Sports
15 High St Mereford
08 10 15.05.-5

Salesperson Tina

Tennis balls	5.99
Shin guards	8.99
TOTAL	14.98
CASH	20.00
CHANGE	5.02

Thank you for your custom
Please retain this receipt in case of any query

a till receipt

ENIGMA MUSIC LIMITED **receipt** 958

13 High Street, Mereford MR1 2TF

Customer *R V Williams* date *3 Oct 20-5*

'Golden Oldies' by J Moore	*£20.00*
Total	*£20.00*

a hand-written receipt

Note that, although the above documents are often described as 'cash receipts', they are issued whatever payment method is used – cash, cheque, credit card, debit card.

banking documents

Most businesses have a bank account into which they pay money using a paying-in slip, and make payments by cheque and bank transfers. The **paying-in slip counterfoils** (below) and **cheque counterfoils** (on the next page) form **source documents** for the accounting system. At regular intervals a bank issues a **statement of account** to its customers – the statement, which is a **source document** may show other receipts and payments, standing orders, direct debits, credit transfers, dishonoured cheques, debit card transactions, direct bank transfers and bank charges.

We will be looking further at bank statements and banking transactions in Chapters 7 and 8 when we deal with the cash book and prepare bank reconciliation statements.

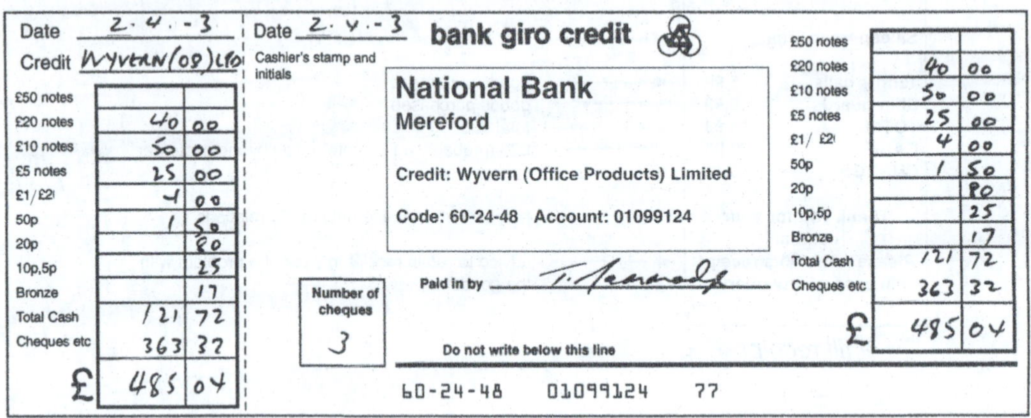

Counterfoil:

Date 2.4.-3
Credit WYVERN (OP) LTD

	£	p
£50 notes		
£20 notes	40	00
£10 notes	50	00
£5 notes	25	00
£1/£2	4	00
50p	1	50
20p		80
10p,5p		25
Bronze		17
Total Cash	121	72
Cheques etc	363	32
£	485	04

Paying-in slip:

Date 2.4.-3
Cashier's stamp and initials

bank giro credit

National Bank
Mereford

Credit: Wyvern (Office Products) Limited

Code: 60-24-48 Account: 01099124

Number of cheques 3

Paid in by T. [signature]

Do not write below this line

60-24-48 01099124 77

	£	p
£50 notes		
£20 notes	40	00
£10 notes	50	00
£5 notes	25	00
£1/£2	4	00
50p	1	50
20p		80
10p,5p		25
Bronze		17
Total Cash	121	72
Cheques etc	363	32
£	485	04

counterfoil *paying-in slip (front)*

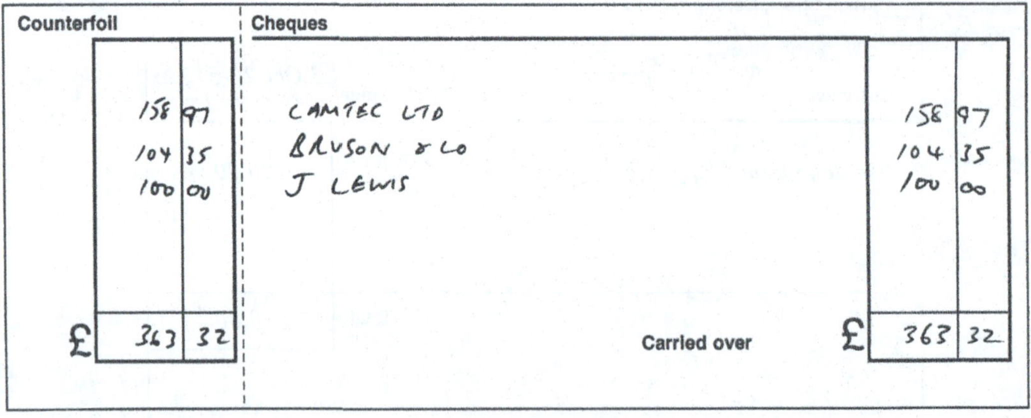

Counterfoil:

£	p
158	97
104	35
100	00
£ 363	32

Cheques:

	£	p
CAMTEC LTD	158	97
BRUSON & CO	104	35
J LEWIS	100	00
Carried over	£ 363	32

counterfoil *paying-in slip (back)*

paying-in slip counterfoils

In a paying-in book, which is issued by the bank to business customers, the counterfoil is the part that is retained by the customer and stamped as a receipt by the bank cashier for the amount being paid in. A completed paying-in slip and counterfoil is illustrated above.

cheque counterfoils

In cheque books the counterfoil is the part retained by the payer when the cheque is sent off to the payee (the person who is being paid). The counterfoil gives information as to the date of the cheque, the payee, and the amount being paid; it also has the cheque number printed along the bottom. A completed cheque and counterfoil are illustrated below.

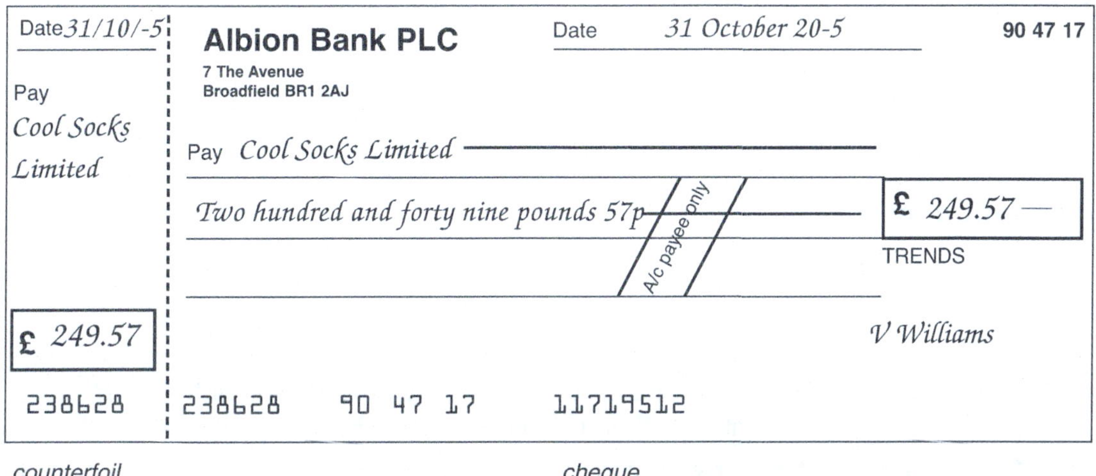

Date 31/10/-5
Pay
Cool Socks Limited
£ 249.57
238628

Albion Bank PLC
7 The Avenue
Broadfield BR1 2AJ
Date 31 October 20-5
90 47 17
Pay Cool Socks Limited
Two hundred and forty nine pounds 57p
A/c payee only
£ 249.57 —
TRENDS
V Williams
238628 90 47 17 11719512

counterfoil

cheque

bank statements

A bank sends statements – or they are available electronically – to its customers in the same way that a business issues statements of account to its customers. In addition to entries for cheques paid in and out, a bank statement shows a number of other receipts and payments which need to be recorded in the bookkeeping system:

- standing orders, for regular payments – eg hire purchase – made automatically by the bank on the instructions of the customer
- direct debits, for fixed or variable amounts – eg telephone bills – where the payment is requested by the receiver (beneficiary) of the payment through the banking system
- credit transfers, where money has been received through the banking system by Bacs and credited to a seller's account, eg where the seller's customers have paid the amounts they owe
- dishonoured cheques, where the payer has instructed the bank to 'stop' the cheque, or when the payer has insufficient money in the bank to meet the cheque
- debit card transactions, where the bank customer has made payments using the card
- direct bank transfers, where payments have been made directly between bank accounts using internet banking
- bank charges, where the bank makes a charge for providing banking services; the charge may be calculated by reference to the number of transactions that have taken place on the bank account

These items are explained in more detail in Chapter 7, pages 102-103.

Recording Cash Discount in the Bookkeeping System

We saw earlier (page 46) that cash discount (or settlement discount) is an allowance deducted from the invoice amount for prompt payment, eg 2% cash discount for settlement within seven days. A business can be involved with cash discount in two ways:

- discount allowed to trade receivables
- discount received from trade payables

Note that, although the terms 'discount allowed' and 'discount received' do not use the word 'cash', they do refer to cash discount.

discount allowed

When cash discount is taken by a trade receivable it is entered into the accounts as shown by the following transactions:

10 October 20-2	Sold goods, £100, on credit to P Henry, allowing her a cash discount of 2% for settlement within seven days
15 October 20-2	P Henry pays £98 by bank transfer

Sales Account (Dr / Cr)

Dr 20-2		£	Cr 20-2		£
			10 Oct	P Henry	100

P Henry (Dr / Cr)

Dr 20-2		£	Cr 20-2		£
10 Oct	Sales	100	15 Oct	Bank	98
			15 Oct	Discount allowed	2
		100			100

Bank Account (Dr / Cr)

Dr 20-2		£	Cr 20-2		£
15 Oct	P Henry	98			

Discount Allowed Account (Dr / Cr)

Dr 20-2		£	Cr 20-2		£
15 Oct	P Henry	2			

Notes

- The amount of the payment received from the trade receivable is entered in the bank account.
- The amount of discount allowed is entered in both the trade receivable's account and discount allowed account:
  - debit discount allowed account
  - credit trade receivable's account
- Discount allowed is an expense of the business, because it represents the cost of collecting payments more speedily from the trade receivables.
- The account of P Henry has been totalled to show that both the debit and credit money columns are the same – thus her account now has a nil balance (the method of balancing accounts is looked at in the next chapter).

discount received

With cash discount received, a business is offered cash discount for prompt payment by its trade payables. The following transactions give an example of this:

20 October 20-2	Bought goods, £200, on credit from B Lewis Ltd; 2.5% cash discount is offered for settlement by the end of October
30 October 20-2	Paid B Lewis Ltd £195 by bank transfer

Purchases Account

Dr			Cr		
20-2		£	20-2		£
20 Oct	B Lewis Ltd	200			

B Lewis Ltd

Dr			Cr		
20-2		£	20-2		£
30 Oct	Bank	195	20 Oct	Purchases	200
30 Oct	Discount received	5			
		200			200

Bank Account

Dr			Cr		
20-2		£	20-2		£
			30 Oct	B Lewis Ltd	195

Discount Received Account

Dr			Cr		
20-2		£	20-2		£
			30 Oct	B Lewis Ltd	5

Notes

- The business is receiving cash discount from its trade payable, and the amount is entered as:
  - debit trade payable's account
  - credit discount received account
- Discount received account is an income account.
- The money columns of the account of B Lewis Ltd have been totalled to show that the account now has a nil balance.

revision summary

- Cash discount – when taken – is recorded in the trade receivables' and trade payables' accounts.
- Both discount allowed (an expenses account) and discount received (an income account) store up information until the end of the financial year, when it is used in the firm's income statement – see Chapter 9.
- The cash book (see Chapter 7) is usually used for listing the amounts of discount received and allowed – transfers are then made at the end of each month to the discount accounts.
- Trade discount is never recorded in the double-entry accounts; only the net amount of an invoice is recorded after trade discount has been deducted.

CHAPTER SUMMARY

- Correct documentation is important for businesses to be able to record accurately buying and selling transactions.
- There are a number of documents involved – the two most important source documents for bookkeeping transactions are the invoice and the credit note.
- An invoice is a source document prepared by the seller and sent to the buyer – it states the value of goods sold and the amount to be paid by the buyer.
- Trade discount is often deducted when goods are sold to other businesses.
- Bulk discount may be given for buying in large quantities.
- Cash discount (or settlement discount) is an allowance off the invoice amount for prompt payment.
- A credit note is a source document which shows that the buyer is entitled to a reduction in the amount charged by the seller; it is used, for example, if:
  - some of the goods delivered were faulty, or incorrectly supplied
  - the price charged on the invoice was too high
- Statements of account are issued regularly to each trade receivable of a business to show the amount currently due.
- Other source documents include cash receipts, till rolls, cheque counterfoils, paying-in slip counterfoils, bank statements.

- Information from bank statements gives details of standing orders, direct debits, credit transfers, dishonoured cheques, debit card transactions, direct bank transfers and bank charges.
- Cash discount allowed is entered in the accounts as:
  - debit discount allowed account
  - credit trade receivable's account
- Cash discount received is entered as:
  - debit trade payable's account
  - credit discount received account

This chapter has explained business documents; the next chapter concentrates on double-entry bookkeeping and shows how accounts are balanced, and a trial balance is extracted.

QUESTIONS

visit
www.osbornebooks.co.uk
to take an online test

An asterisk (*) after the question number means that the answer is given at the end of this book.

free download from website www.osbornebooks.co.uk
Blank financial documents for use in these questions are available for free download from the Products and Resources section of the Osborne Books website.

4.1* Fill in the missing words from the following sentences:

(a) A .... is prepared by the buyer and sent to the seller and describes the goods to be supplied.

(b) The seller prepares the ...., which gives details of the goods supplied, and states the money amount to be paid by the buyer.

(c) .... is a deduction made in the price if the purchaser pays within a stated time.

(d) When the purchaser is in business, an amount of ....

.... is sometimes allowed as a reduction in the price.

(e) The term .... on an invoice means that the invoice total is the amount to be paid.

(f) If a buyer returns goods, the seller prepares a ....

(g) At regular intervals the seller sends a summary of transactions to the buyer in the

form of a ....

4.2 You work for Jane Smith, a wholesaler of fashionwear, who trades from Unit 21, Eastern Industrial Estate, Wyvern, Wyvernshire, WY1 3XJ. A customer, Excel Fashions of 49 Highland Street, Longtown, Mercia, LT3 2XL, orders the following:

5 dresses at £30 each

3 suits at £45.50 each

4 coats at £51.50 each

A 2.5 per cent cash discount is offered for full settlement within 14 days.

You are to prepare invoice number 2451, under today's date, to be sent to the customer. What amount will be paid by Excel Fashions if they pay the invoice in full within 14 days?

4.3 You work for Deansway Trading Company, a wholesaler of office stationery, which trades from The Model Office, Deansway, Rowcester, RW1 2EJ. A customer, The Card Shop of 126 The Cornbow, Teamington Spa, Wyvernshire, WY33 0EG, orders the following:

5 boxes of assorted rubbers at £5 per box

100 shorthand notebooks at £4 for 10

250 ring binders at 50p each

A 2.5 per cent cash discount is offered for full settlement within 14 days.

You are to prepare invoice number 8234, under today's date, to be sent to the customer. What amount will be paid by The Card Shop if they pay the invoice in full within 14 days?

4.4 Enter the following transactions into the double-entry bookkeeping accounts of Sonya Smith:

20-4	
2 Feb	Bought goods £200, on credit from G Lewis
4 Feb	Sold goods £150, on credit to L Jarvis
7 Feb	Sold goods £240, on credit to G Patel
10 Feb	Paid G Lewis the amount owing by bank transfer, after deducting a cash discount of 5%
12 Feb	L Jarvis pays the amount owing by cheque, after deducting a cash discount of 2%
16 Feb	Bought goods £160, on credit from G Lewis
20 Feb	G Patel pays the amount owing by cheque, after deducting a cash discount of 2.5%
24 Feb	Paid G Lewis the amount owing by bank transfer, after deducting a cash discount of 5%

4.5 Trend Fashion Designs Limited has partially prepared the following invoice from a delivery note:

INVOICE

TREND FASHION DESIGNS LIMITED

Unit 45 Elgar Estate, Broadfield, BR7 4ER
Tel 01908 765314 Fax 01908 765951

invoice to

Fashion Shop
48 High Street
Wyvern
WV1 2AJ

invoice no	**7878106**
account	**2667**
your reference	**54208**
date	**10 11 -5**

deliver to

as above

product code	description	quantity	unit price £	unit	total £	trade discount %	net £
45B	**Trend tops (black)**	**30**	**12.50**	**each**		**10**	
35W	**Trend trousers (white)**	**20**	**25.00**	**each**		**10**	

terms
5% cash discount for full settlement within 7 days
Net 30 days

TOTAL	

Required:

(a) Complete the invoice to show the total amount due.

(b) Explain the following terms:
- trade discount
- cash discount

(c) What amount will be paid by the Fashion Shop if they pay the invoice in full within seven days?

4.6* Kingston Traders is seeking to attract new customers and has decided to offer trade and cash discounts.

Required:

(a) Explain the circumstances under which they would give:

(i) Trade discount

(ii) Cash discount

(b) Kingston Traders supply goods to a customer, Queenstown Retail, on the following terms:

Selling price	£500
Trade discount	20%
Cash discount	5% (for full settlement within 14 days)

Calculate the total of the invoice for these goods. Show your workings.

(c) What amount will be paid by Queenstown Retail if they pay the invoice in full within 14 days?

4.7 (a) What is meant by the term source documents?

(b) Describe the purpose of (i) an invoice, and (ii) a credit note, as source documents.

(c) State *three* further source documents used in bookkeeping.

4.8 You work in the accounts department of Alpha Office Furniture Limited. Part of your job involves checking invoices before they are sent to customers.

The invoice, shown on the next page, to Wyvern Products Limited, has been prepared by a new member of staff. The purchase order, number 5915, from Wyvern Products Limited to Alpha Office Furniture Limited was for the following:

- 5 computer desks, product code CD, at £65 each
- 10 office chairs, product code OC, at £20 each

The terms of trade offered to Wyvern Products Limited are for 10% trade discount, and 5% cash discount for full settlement within 14 days, otherwise net 30 days.

Today's date is 6 April 20-5.

INVOICE

ALPHA OFFICE FURNITURE LIMITED

Unit 1, Ashtree Estate, Mereford, MR3 7JG
Tel 01907 334482 Fax 01907 334493

invoice to

Wyvern Products Limited
Wyvern Business Park
Wyvern
WV1 8TQ

deliver to

as above

invoice no	**234061**
account	**3571**
your reference	**5915**
date	**06 04 20-5**

product code	description	quantity	unit price £	unit	total £	trade discount %	net £
CD	**Computer desks**	**10**	**70.00**	**each**	**350.00**	**10**	**350.00**
OC	**Office chairs**	**5**	**20.00**	**each**	**200.00**	**10**	**20.00**

terms
5% cash discount for full settlement within 14 days
Net 30 days

TOTAL	**370.00**

Required:

(a) Check the invoice using the information available to you, and list any errors that you find.

(b) Prepare a corrected invoice.

(c) What amount will be paid by Wyvern Products Limited if they pay the invoice in full within 14 days?

5 BALANCING ACCOUNTS – THE TRIAL BALANCE

With the 'traditional' form of account – a 'T' account – that we have used so far, it is necessary to calculate the balance of each account from time-to-time, according to the needs of the business, and at the end of each financial year.

The balance of an account is the total of that account to date, eg the amount of wages paid, the amount of sales made. In this chapter we shall see how this balancing of accounts is carried out.

We shall then use the balances from each account in order to check the double-entry bookkeeping by extracting a trial balance, which is a list of the balances of ledger accounts.

Balancing the Accounts

At regular intervals, often at the end of each month, accounts are balanced in order to show the amounts, for example:

- owing to each trade payable
- owing by each trade receivable
- of sales
- of purchases
- of sales returns (returns inwards)
- of purchases returns (returns outwards)
- of expenses incurred by the business
- of non-current assets, eg premises, machinery, etc owned by the business
- of capital and drawings of the owner of the business
- of other liabilities, eg loans

We have already noted earlier that, where running balance accounts (see page 24) are used, there is no need to balance each account, because the balance is already calculated – either manually or by computer – after each transaction.

METHOD OF BALANCING ACCOUNTS

Set out below is an example of an account which has been balanced at the month-end:

Dr		Bank Account			Cr
20-1		£	20-1		£
1 Sep	Capital	5,000	2 Sep	Computer	1,800
5 Sep	J Jackson: loan	2,500	6 Sep	Purchases	500
10 Sep	Sales	750	12 Sep	Drawings	100
			15 Sep	Wages	200
			30 Sep	Balance c/d	5,650
		8,250			8,250
1 Oct	Balance b/d	5,650			

The steps involved in balancing accounts are:

Step 1

The entries in the debit and credit money columns are subtotalled and either recorded on the account, or noted on a separate piece of paper. In the example above, the debit side totals £8,250, while the credit side is £2,600.

Step 2

The difference between the two totals is the balance of the account and this is entered on the account:

- on the side of the smaller total
- on the next available line
- with the date of balancing (often the last day of the month)
- with the description 'balance c/d', or 'balance carried down'

In the bank account above, the balance carried down is £8,250 – £2,600 = £5,650, entered in the credit column.

Step 3

Both sides of the account are now totalled, including the balance carried down which has just been entered, and the totals (the same on both sides) are entered on the same line in the appropriate column, and bold or double underlined. The bold underline indicates that the account has been balanced at this point using the figures above the total: the figures above the underline should not be added in to anything below the underline.

In the bank account above, the totals on each side of the account are £8,250.

Step 4

As we are using double-entry bookkeeping, there must be an opposite entry to the 'balance c/d' calculated in Step 2. The same money amount is entered on the other side of the account below the bold underlined totals entered in Step 3. We have now completed both the debit and credit entry. The date is usually recorded as the next day after 'balance c/d', ie often the first day of the following month, and the description can be 'balance b/d' or 'balance brought down'.

In the example on the previous page, the balance brought down on the bank account on 1 October 20-1 is £5,650 debit; this means that, according to the firm's accounting records, there is £5,650 in the bank.

a practical point

When balancing accounts, use a pen and not a pencil. If any errors are made, cross them through neatly with a single line, and write the corrected version on the line below. Use correcting fluid in moderation; at best it conceals errors, at worst it conceals fraudulent transactions.

Further Examples of Balancing Accounts

Wages Account

Dr					Cr
20-1		£	20-1		£
9 Apr	Bank	750	30 Apr	Balance c/d	2,250
16 Apr	Bank	800			
23 Apr	Bank	700			
		2,250			**2,250**
1 May	Balance b/d	2,250			

The above wages account has transactions on one side only, but is still balanced in the same way. This account shows that the total amount paid for wages is £2,250.

B Lewis Ltd

Dr					Cr
20-1		£	20-1		£
10 Apr	Purchases returns	30	7 Apr	Purchases	280
26 Apr	Bank	250			
		280			**280**

This account in the name of a trade payable has a 'nil' balance after the transactions for April have taken place. The two sides of the account are totalled and, as both debit and credit side are the same amount, there is nothing further to do, apart from entering the bold or double underlined total.

Dr			A Holmes		Cr
20-1		£	20-1		£
1 Apr	Balance b/d	105	10 Apr	Bank	105
11 Apr	Sales	125	11 Apr	Sales returns	25
			30 Apr	Balance c/d	100
		230			230
1 May	Balance b/d	100			

This is the account of a trade receivable and, at the start of the month, there was a debit balance of £105 brought down from March showing A Holmes owed £105 at the beginning of April. After the various transactions for April, there remains a debit balance of £100 owing at 1 May.

Dr			Office Equipment Account		Cr
20-1		£	20-1		£
12 Apr	Bank	2,000			

This non-current asset account has just the one transaction and, in practice, there is no need to balance it. It should be clear that the account has a debit balance of £2,000, which is represented by the asset of office equipment.

Dr			Malvern Manufacturing Co		Cr
20-1		£	20-1		£
29 Apr	Bank	250	18 Apr	Purchases	250

This trade payable's account has a 'nil' balance, with just one transaction on each side. All that is needed here is to bold or double underline the amount on both sides.

Extracting a Trial Balance

The bookkeeper extracts a trial balance from the accounting records in order to check the arithmetical accuracy of the double-entry bookkeeping, ie that the debit entries equal the credit entries.

A trial balance is a list of the balances of every account forming the ledger, distinguishing between those accounts which have debit balances and those which have credit balances.

A trial balance is extracted at regular intervals – often at the end of each month.

example of a trial balance

Trial balance of A-Z Suppliers as at 31 January 20-1

	Dr	*Cr*
Name of account	£	£
Purchases	750	
Sales (Revenue)		1,600
Sales returns	25	
Purchases returns		50
J Brown (trade receivable)	155	
T Sweet (trade payable)		110
Rent paid	100	
Wages	150	
Heating and lighting	125	
Office equipment	500	
Machinery	1,000	
Cash	50	
Bank	455	
J Williams – loan		800
Capital		1,000
Drawings	250	
	3,560	3,560

Notes

- The debit and credit columns have been totalled and are the same amount. Thus the trial balance proves that the accounting records are arithmetically correct. (A trial balance does not prove the complete accuracy of the accounting records – see page 66.)
- The heading for a trial balance gives the name of the business whose accounts have been listed and the date it was extracted, ie the end of the accounting period.
- The balance for each account transferred to the trial balance is the figure brought down after the accounts have been balanced.
- As well as the name of each account, it is quite usual to show in the trial balance the account number. Most accounting systems give numbers to accounts and these can be listed in a separate reference column.

Debit and Credit Balances – Guidelines

Certain accounts always have a debit balance, while others always have a credit balance. You should already know these, but the lists set out below will act as a revision guide, and will also help in your understanding of trial balances.

debit balances include:

- cash account
- purchases account
- sales returns account (returns inwards)
- non-current asset accounts, eg premises, vehicles, machinery, office equipment, etc
- expenses and overheads accounts, eg wages, telephone, rent paid, carriage outwards, carriage inwards, discount allowed
- drawings account
- trade receivables' accounts (often, for the purposes of a trial balance, the balances of individual trade receivables' accounts are totalled, and the total is entered in the trial balance as trade receivables)

credit balances include:

- sales account – referred to as 'revenue' in the trial balance
- purchases returns account (returns outwards)
- income accounts, eg rent income, commission income, discount received
- capital account
- loan account
- trade payables' accounts (often a total is entered in the trial balance, rather than the individual balances of each account)

Note: bank account can be either debit or credit – it will be debit when the business has money in the bank, and credit when it is overdrawn.

If the Trial Balance Doesn't Balance . . .

If the trial balance fails to balance, ie the two totals are different, there is an error (or errors):

- either in the addition of the trial balance
- and/or in the double-entry bookkeeping, such as partial omission, transposition of figures (ie reversal of figures) and unequal posting

The procedure for finding the error(s) is as follows:

- check the addition of the trial balance

- check that the balance of each account has been correctly entered in the trial balance, and under the correct heading, ie debit or credit
- check that the balance of every account in the ledger has been included in the trial balance
- check the calculation of the balance on each account
- calculate the amount that the trial balance is wrong, and then look in the accounts for a transaction for this amount: if one is found, check that the double-entry bookkeeping has been carried out correctly
- halve the amount by which the trial balance is wrong, and look for a transaction for this amount: if it is found, check the double-entry bookkeeping
- if the amount by which the trial balance is wrong is divisible by nine, then the error may be a transposition (reversal) of figures, eg £65 entered as £56, or £45 entered as £54
- if the trial balance is wrong by a round amount, eg £10, £100, £1,000, the error is likely to be in the calculation of the account balances
- if the error(s) is still not found, it is necessary to check the bookkeeping transactions since the date of the last trial balance, by going back to the source documents and the subsidiary books

Errors not shown by a Trial Balance

As mentioned earlier, a trial balance does not prove the complete accuracy of the accounting records. There are six types of errors that are not shown by a trial balance.

error of omission

Here a business transaction has been completely omitted from the accounting records, ie both the debit and credit entries have not been made.

reversal of entries

With this error, the debit and credit entries have been made in the accounts but on the wrong side of the two accounts concerned. For example, a cash sale has been entered wrongly as debit sales account, credit cash account – this should have been entered as a debit to cash account, and a credit to sales account.

mispost/error of commission

Here, a transaction is entered to the wrong person's account. For example, a sale of goods on credit to A T Hughes has been entered as debit A J Hughes' account, credit sales account. Here, double-entry bookkeeping has been completed but, when A J Hughes receives a statement of account, he or she will soon complain about being debited with goods not ordered or received.

error of principle

This is when a transaction has been entered in the wrong type of account. For example, the cost of fuel for vehicles has been entered as debit vehicles account, credit bank account. The error is that motor vehicles account represents non-current assets, and the transaction should have been debited to the expense account for vehicle running expenses.

error of original entry (or transcription)

Here, the correct accounts have been used, and the correct sides: what is wrong is that the amount has been entered incorrectly in both accounts. This could be caused by a 'bad figure' on an invoice or a cheque, or it could be caused by a 'reversal of figures', eg an amount of £45 being entered in both accounts as £54. Note that both debit and credit entries need to be made incorrectly for the trial balance still to balance; if one entry has been made incorrectly and the other is correct, then the error will be shown.

compensating error

This is where two errors cancel each other out. For example, if the balance of purchases account is calculated wrongly at £10 too much, and a similar error has occurred in calculating the balance of sales account, then the two errors will compensate each other, and the trial balance will not show the errors.

Correction of errors is covered fully in Chapter 10.

Importance of the Trial Balance

A business will extract a trial balance on a regular basis to check the arithmetic accuracy of the bookkeeping. However, the trial balance is also used as the starting point in the production of the financial statements of a business. These financial statements, which are produced once a year (often more frequently) comprise:

- **income statement**
- **statement of financial position**

The financial statements show the owner how profitable the business has been, what the business owns, and how the business is financed. The preparation of financial statements is an important aspect of your studies and one which we shall be coming to in later chapters. For the moment, we can say that extraction of a trial balance is an important exercise in the accounting process: it proves the bookkeeper's accuracy, and also lists the account balances which form the basis for the financial statements of a business.

CHAPTER SUMMARY

- The traditional 'T' account needs to be balanced at regular intervals – often at the month-end.
- When balancing accounts, the bookkeeper must adhere strictly to the rules of double-entry bookkeeping.
- When each account in the ledger has been balanced, a trial balance can be extracted.
- A trial balance is a list of the balances of every account forming the ledger, distinguishing between those accounts which have debit balances and those which have credit balances.
- If a trial balance fails to balance, errors could be:
  - in the addition of the trial balance
  - in the double-entry bookkeeping, such as partial omission, transposition of figures (ie reversal of figures), and unequal posting
- A trial balance does not prove the complete accuracy of the accounting records; errors not shown by a trial balance are:
  - error of omission
  - reversal of entries
  - mispost/error of commission
  - error of principle
  - error of original entry
  - compensating error
- The trial balance is used as the starting point for the preparation of a business' financial statements.

In the next chapter we will look at the division of the ledger into manageable sections, and we will see how an expanding accounting system uses books of prime entry to cope with large numbers of routine transactions.

QUESTIONS

visit www.osbornebooks.co.uk to take an online test

An asterisk (*) after the question number means that the answer is given at the end of this book.

5.1 The following are the business transactions of Andrew Johnstone, a retailer of computer software, for the months of January and February 20-9:

Transactions for January

1 Jan	Started in business with £10,000 in the bank
4 Jan	Paid rent on premises £500, by cheque
5 Jan	Bought shop fittings for use in the business £1,500, by cheque
7 Jan	Bought computer software £5,000, on credit from Comp Supplies Limited
11 Jan	Software sales £1,000 paid into bank

12 Jan	Software sales £1,250 paid into bank
16 Jan	Software sales £850 on credit to Rowcester College
20 Jan	Paid Comp Supplies Limited £5,000 by cheque
22 Jan	Software sales £1,450 paid into bank
25 Jan	Bought software £6,500 on credit from Comp Supplies Limited
27 Jan	Rowcester College returns software £100

Transactions for February

2 Feb	Paid rent on premises £500 by cheque
4 Feb	Software sales £1,550 paid into bank
5 Feb	Returned faulty software, £150 to Comp Supplies Limited
10 Feb	Software sales £1,300 paid into bank
12 Feb	Rowcester College pays the amount owing by cheque
15 Feb	Bought shop fittings for use in the business £850 by cheque
19 Feb	Software sales £1,600 paid into bank
22 Feb	Paid Comp Supplies Limited the amount owing by cheque
24 Feb	Bought software £5,500 on credit from Comp Supplies Limited
25 Feb	Software sales £1,100 paid into bank
26 Feb	Software sales £1,050 on credit to Rowcester College

You are to:

(a) Record the January transactions in the books of account, and balance each account at 31 January 20-9.

(b) Draw up a trial balance at 31 January 20-9.

(c) Record the February transactions in the books of account, and balance each account at 28 February 20-9.

(d) Draw up a trial balance at 28 February 20-9.

5.2 Produce the trial balance of Jane Greenwell as at 28 February 20-1. She has omitted to open a capital account.

	£
Bank overdraft	1,250
Purchases	850
Cash	48
Sales (Revenue)	730
Purchases returns	144
Trade payables	1,442
Equipment	2,704
Van	3,200
Sales returns	90
Trade receivables	1,174
Wages	1,500
Capital	?

5.3* The bookkeeper of Lorna Fox has extracted the following list of balances as at 31 March 20-2:

	£
Purchases	96,250
Sales (Revenue)	146,390
Sales returns	8,500
Administration expenses	10,240
Wages	28,980
Telephone	3,020
Interest paid	2,350
Travel expenses	1,045
Premises	125,000
Machinery	40,000
Trade receivables	10,390
Bank overdraft	1,050
Cash	150
Trade payables	12,495
Loan from bank	20,000
Drawings	9,450
Capital	155,440

You are to:

(a) Produce the trial balance at 31 March 20-2.

(b) Take any three debit balances and any three credit balances and explain to someone who does not understand accounting why they are listed as such, and what this means to the business.

5.4* Fill in the missing words from the following sentences:

(a) "You made an error of .... when you debited the cost of fuel for the van to vans account."

(b) "I've had the bookkeeper from D Jones Limited on the telephone concerning the statements of account that we sent out the other day. She says that there is a sales invoice charged that she knows nothing about. I wonder if we have done a .... and it should be for T Jones' account?"

(c) "There is a 'bad figure' on a purchases invoice – we have read it as £35 when it should be £55. It has gone through our accounts wrongly so we have an error of .... to put right."

(d) "Although the trial balance balanced last week, I've since found an error of £100 in the calculation of the balance of sales account. We will need to check the other balances as I think we may have a .... error."

(e) "Who was in charge of that trainee last week? He has entered the payment for the electricity bill on the debit side of the bank and on the credit side of electricity – a .... of ...."

(f) "I found this purchase invoice from last week in amongst the copy letters. As we haven't put it through the accounts we have an error of ...."

5.5 *"A trial balance does not prove the complete accuracy of the accounting records."*

You are to describe *four* types of error that are not shown by a trial balance.

Give an example of each type of error.

5.6* The purchase of a non-current asset has been debited to purchases account.

What is this type of error called?

A	Principle	
B	Omission	
C	Commission	
D	Original entry	

6 DIVISION OF THE LEDGER – THE USE OF BOOKS OF PRIME ENTRY

As we saw in Chapter 1, the double-entry system involves the recording of transactions in accounts in the ledger. In this chapter we will learn how, in order to cope with an expanding bookkeeping system, the ledger is divided into separate sections. This is called the division of the ledger.

We will also examine how a business makes use of books of prime entry to summarise business transactions before they are entered into the double-entry system.

Division of the Ledger

Double-entry bookkeeping involves, as we have seen, making two entries in the ledger accounts for each business transaction. The traditional meaning of a ledger is a weighty leather-bound volume into which each account was entered on a separate page. With such a hand-written bookkeeping system, as more and more accounts were opened, the point was reached where another ledger book was needed. Finally, in order to sort the accounts into a logical order, the accounting system was divided into main sections or divisions, and this practice continues today:

- sales ledger (or receivables ledger), containing the accounts of trade receivables
- purchases ledger (or payables ledger), containing the accounts of trade payables
- general ledger (or nominal ledger), containing the accounts of income and expenses, etc and the accounts of things, non-current assets, cash, bank, etc

These three divisions comprise the ledger, and are illustrated in full on the opposite page. Most computer accounting programs use these divisions of the ledger.

Use of the Divisions of the Ledger

To understand how the divisions of the ledger are used, we will examine a number of business transactions and see which ledgers are used and in which accounts the transactions are recorded:

purchase of goods on credit

- general ledger – debit purchases account
- purchases ledger – credit the account of the trade payable (supplier)

continued on page 74

DIVISION OF THE LEDGER

sales ledger (or receivables ledger)

Sales ledger contains the accounts of trade receivables, and records:

- sales made on credit to customers of the business
- sales returns (returns inwards) by customers
- payments received from trade receivables
- cash discount allowed for prompt payment
- irrecoverable debts written off (see page 217)

Sales ledger does not record cash sales.

Sales ledger contains an account for each trade receivable and records the transactions with that trade receivable. A sales ledger control account (see Chapter 11) is often used to summarise the transactions on the accounts of trade receivables.

purchases ledger (or payables ledger)

Purchases ledger contains the accounts of trade payables, and records:

- purchases made on credit from suppliers of the business
- purchases returns (returns outwards) made by the business
- payments made to trade payables
- cash discount received for prompt payment

Purchases ledger does not record cash purchases.

Purchases ledger contains an account for each trade payable and records the transactions with that trade payable. A purchases ledger control account (see Chapter 11) may be used to summarise the trade payable account transactions.

general ledger (or nominal ledger)

The general (nominal) ledger contains the other accounts of the business:

Accounts of income and expenses

- sales account (cash and credit sales), sales returns
- purchases account (cash and credit purchases), purchases returns
- expenses and income, loans, capital, drawings
- income statement

Accounts of things

- non-current assets, eg computers, vehicles
- cash book*, which records all transactions for bank account and cash account
- inventory

* note that in some accounting systems the cash book is kept as a separate division of the ledger

purchase of goods by cheque

- general ledger – debit purchases account
- general ledger – credit bank account

sale of goods on credit

- sales ledger – debit the account of the trade receivable (customer)
- general ledger – credit sales account

sale of goods for cash

- general ledger – debit cash account
- general ledger – credit sales account

purchase of a computer for use in the business, paying by cheque

- general ledger – debit computer account (non-current asset)
- general ledger – credit bank account

Note that in some accounting systems the main cash book is kept as a separate division of the ledger.

BOOKS OF PRIME ENTRY

The place where a business transaction is recorded for the first time, prior to entry in the ledger, is known as the book of prime entry. These comprise:

- sales journal
- purchases journal
- sales returns, or returns inwards, journal
- purchases returns, or returns outwards journal
- cash book (see Chapter 7)
- general journal (see Chapter 10)

In the rest of this chapter we will see how the first four of these journals fit into the accounting system. The other two books of prime entry will be looked at in more detail in later chapters. We have already used cash account and bank account which, together, make up a business' cash book. In the next chapter (Chapter 7), we will see how these two accounts are brought together in the cash book. Cash book is the book of prime entry for receipts and payments in the forms of cash or cheque/bank transfer. General journal (often known more simply as the journal) is covered in Chapter 10.

SALES JOURNAL

The sales journal (also known as the sales day book) is used by businesses that have a lot of separate sales transactions. The journal is simply a list of transactions, the total of which, at the end of the day, week, or month, is transferred to sales account. Note that the journal is not part of double-entry bookkeeping, but is used as a book of prime entry to give a total which is then entered into the accounts. By using a journal for a large number of transactions in this way, there are fewer transactions passing through the double-entry accounts. Also, the work of the accounts department can be divided up – one person can be given the task of maintaining the journal, while another can concentrate on keeping the ledger up-to-date.

The most common use of a sales journal is to record credit sales from invoices issued.

example transactions

3 Jan 20-1	Sold goods, £80, on credit to E Doyle, invoice no 901
8 Jan 20-1	Sold goods, £200, on credit to A Sparkes, invoice no 902
12 Jan 20-1	Sold goods, £80, on credit to T Young, invoice no 903
18 Jan 20-1	Sold goods, £120, on credit to A Sparkes, invoice no 904

The sales journal is written up as follows:

Sales Journal				
Date	Details	Invoice	Reference	Amount
20-1				£
3 Jan	E Doyle	901	SL 58	80
8 Jan	A Sparkes	902	SL 127	200
12 Jan	T Young	903	SL 179	80
18 Jan	A Sparkes	904	SL 127	120
31 Jan	Total for month			480

Notes

- Total credit sales for the month are £480, and this amount is credited to sales account in the general ledger.
- The credit sales transactions are debited in the personal accounts of the firm's trade receivables in the sales ledger (or receivables ledger).

- The sales journal incorporates a reference column which cross-references each transaction to the personal account of each trade receivable. In this way, an audit trail is created so that a particular transaction can be traced from source document (invoice), through the book of prime entry (sales journal), to the trade receivable's ledger account.
- Where control accounts are in use (see Chapter 11), the total for the month, £480, is debited to the sales ledger control account.
- When businesses are registered for Value Added Tax (VAT), they incorporate a VAT money column into their sales – and other – journals and operate a VAT account.

The accounts to record the above transactions are:

GENERAL LEDGER

Dr **Sales Account** Cr

20-1		£	20-1		£
			31 Jan	Sales journal	480

SALES (RECEIVABLES) LEDGER

Dr **E Doyle (account no 58)** Cr

20-1		£	20-1		£
3 Jan	Sales	80			

Dr **A Sparkes (account no 127)** Cr

20-1		£	20-1		£
8 Jan	Sales	200			
18 Jan	Sales	120			

Dr **T Young (account no 179)** Cr

20-1		£	20-1		£
12 Jan	Sales	80			

revision summary

Sales journal fits into the accounting system in the following way:

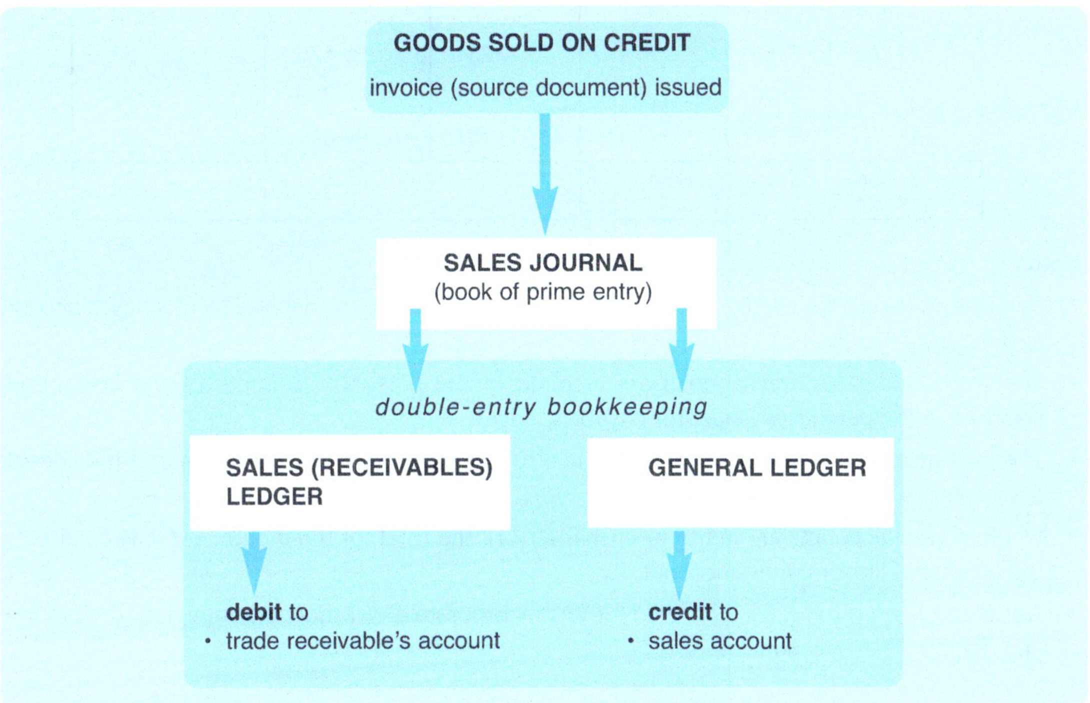

Purchases Journal

This book of prime entry (also known as the purchases day book) is used by businesses that have a lot of separate purchases transactions. The purchases journal lists the transactions for credit purchases from invoices received and, at the end of the day, week or month, the total is transferred to purchases account.

example transactions

2 Jan 20-1	Bought goods, £80, on credit from P Bond, his invoice no 1234
11 Jan 20-1	Bought goods, £120, on credit from D Webster, her invoice no A373
16 Jan 20-1	Bought goods, £160, on credit from P Bond, his invoice no 1247

The purchases journal is written up as follows:

Purchases Journal				
Date	Details	Invoice	Reference	Amount
20-1				£
2 Jan	P Bond	1234	PL 525	80
11 Jan	D Webster	A373	PL 730	120
16 Jan	P Bond	1247	PL 525	160
31 Jan	Total for month			360

Notes

- Total credit purchases for the month are £360, and this amount is debited to purchases account in the general ledger.
- The credit purchases transactions are credited in the personal accounts of the firm's trade payables in the purchases ledger (or payables ledger).
- The reference column gives a cross-reference to the trade payables' accounts and provides an audit trail.
- Where control accounts are in use (see Chapter 11), the total for the month, £360, is credited to the purchases ledger control account.
- As noted earlier, businesses registered for VAT incorporate a VAT money column into their journal and operate a VAT account.

The accounts to record the above transactions are:

GENERAL LEDGER

Purchases Account

Dr		£	Cr		£
20-1			20-1		
31 Jan	Purchases journal	360			

PURCHASES (PAYABLES) LEDGER

P Bond (account no 525)

Dr		£	Cr		£
20-1			20-1		
			2 Jan	Purchases	80
			16 Jan	Purchases	160

D Webster (account no 730)

Dr		£	Cr		£
20-1			20-1		
			11 Jan	Purchases	120

revision summary

Purchases journal fits into the accounting system in the following way:

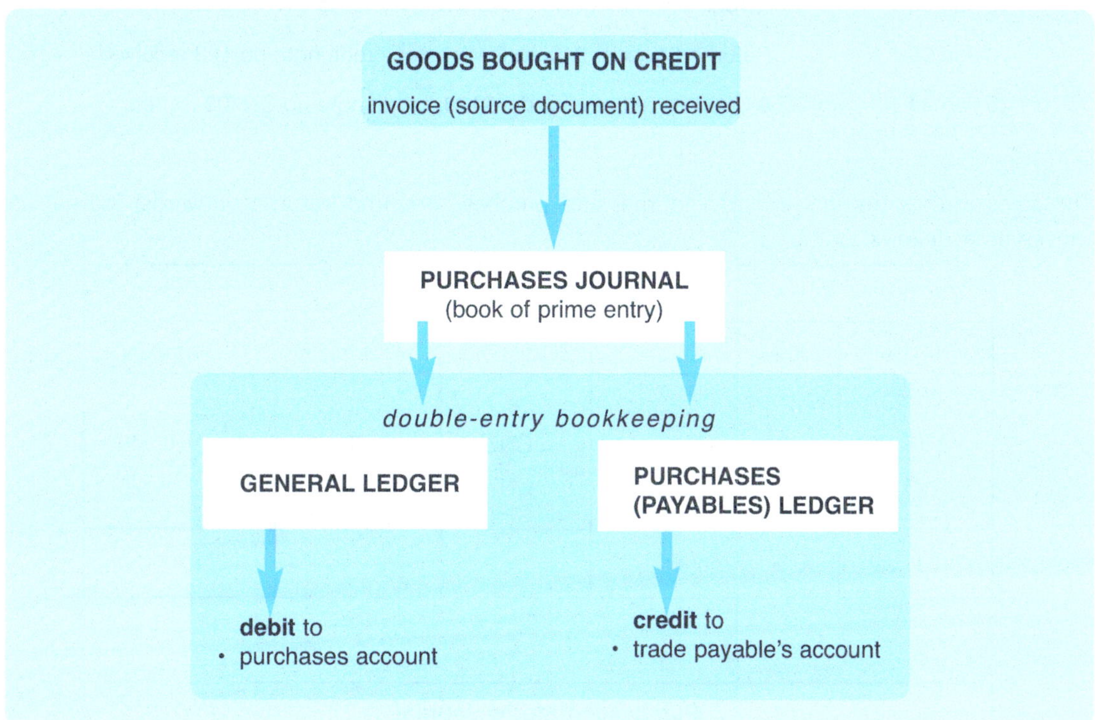

RETURNS JOURNALS

Where a business has a sufficient number of sales returns and purchases returns each day, week or month, it will make use of the two returns journals:

- **sales returns (or returns inwards) journal** – for goods previously sold on credit and now being returned to the business by its customers
- **purchases returns (or returns outwards) journal** – for goods purchased on credit by the business, and now being returned to the suppliers

The two returns journals operate in a similar way to the other journals: they are used to store information about returns until such time as it is transferred to the appropriate returns account. Note that, like all journals, the transactions are recorded from source documents (credit notes issued for sales returns, and credit notes received for purchases returns). The returns journals are books of prime entry and do not form part of the double-entry bookkeeping system: the information from the journal must be transferred to the appropriate accounts in the ledger.

example transactions

6 Jan 20-1	Returned goods, £40, to P Bond, credit note no 406 received
15 Jan 20-1	T Young returns goods, £40, credit note no CN702 issued
20 Jan 20-1	Returned goods, £40, to D Webster, credit note no 123 received
25 Jan 20-1	A Sparkes returns goods, £120, credit note no CN703 issued

The sales returns (returns inwards) journal and purchases returns (returns outwards) journal are written up as follows:

Sales Returns Journal

Date	Details	Credit note	Reference	Amount
20-1				£
15 Jan	T Young	CN702	SL 179	40
25 Jan	A Sparkes	CN703	SL 127	120
31 Jan	Total for month			160

Purchases Returns Journal

Date	Details	Credit note	Reference	Amount
20-1				£
6 Jan	P Bond	406	PL 525	40
20 Jan	D Webster	123	PL 730	40
31 Jan	Total for month			80

Notes

- Total sales returns and purchases returns are debited to the sales returns account and credited to the purchases returns account respectively in the general ledger.
- The amounts of sales returns are credited to the trade receivables' personal accounts in the sales ledger (or receivables ledger); purchases returns are debited to the trade payables' accounts in the purchases ledger (or payables ledger).
- Where control accounts are in use (see Chapter 11), the total for the month of sales returns, £160, is credited to sales ledger control account, and the total for the month of purchases returns, £80, is debited to purchases ledger control account.

- As noted earlier, businesses registered for VAT incorporate a VAT money column into their journals and operate a VAT account.

The accounts to record the above transactions (including any other transactions already recorded on these accounts) are:

GENERAL LEDGER

Sales Returns Account

Dr					Cr
20-1		£	20-1		£
31 Jan	Sales returns journal	160			

Purchases Returns Account

Dr					Cr
20-1		£	20-1		£
			31 Jan	Purchases returns journal	80

SALES (RECEIVABLES) LEDGER

A Sparkes (account no 127)

Dr					Cr
20-1		£	20-1		£
8 Jan	Sales	200	25 Jan	Sales returns	120
18 Jan	Sales	120			

T Young (account no 179)

Dr					Cr
20-1		£	20-1		£
12 Jan	Sales	80	15 Jan	Sales returns	40

PURCHASES (PAYABLES) LEDGER

P Bond (account no 525)

Dr					Cr
20-1		£	20-1		£
6 Jan	Purchases returns	40	2 Jan	Purchases	80
			16 Jan	Purchases	160

D Webster (account no 730)

Dr					Cr
20-1		£	20-1		£
20 Jan	Purchases returns	40	11 Jan	Purchases	120

revision summary

The two returns journals fit into the accounting system as follows:

GOODS RETURNED BY THE CUSTOMER

credit note (source document) issued to the customer

↓

SALES RETURNS JOURNAL
(book of prime entry)

↓ ↓

double-entry bookkeeping

GENERAL LEDGER

↓

debit to
- sales returns account

SALES (RECEIVABLES) LEDGER

↓

credit to
- trade receivable's account

GOODS RETURNED TO THE SUPPLIER

credit note (source document) received from supplier

↓

PURCHASES RETURNS JOURNAL
(book of prime entry)

↓ ↓

double-entry bookkeeping

PURCHASES (PAYABLES) LEDGER

↓

debit to
- trade payable's account

GENERAL LEDGER

↓

credit to
- purchases returns account

Analysed Journals

An analysed journal is used whenever a business needs to split its purchases, sales or returns between different categories of products, between different departments, or between different geographical areas, eg southern division, northern division.

For example, a paint and wallpaper shop may decide to write up its purchases journal as follows:

Purchases Journal						
Date	Details	Invoice	Reference	Paint	Wallpaper	Total
20-1				£	£	£
8 Jan	DIY Wholesalers Ltd	5478	PL 210	75	125	200
12 Jan	Luxor Paints Ltd	A869	PL 360	120	-	120
16 Jan	Bond Supplies	9740	PL 150	180	100	280
22 Jan	Southern Manufacturing Co	2162	PL 450	60	100	160
31 Jan	Totals for month			435	325	760

By using analysed journals, a business can keep track of the purchases, sales, etc between different products, departments, geographical areas, and assess their performance.

CHAPTER SUMMARY

- Division of the ledger means that the accounts are divided between three sections:
  - sales ledger (or receivables ledger)
  - purchases ledger (or payables ledger)
  - general ledger (or nominal ledger)

  In some accounting systems the cash book is kept as a separate division of the ledger.

- Books of prime entry include:
  - sales journal
  - purchases journal
  - sales returns, or returns inwards, journal
  - purchases returns, or returns outwards, journal
  - cash book
  - general journal

- A journal is a listing device which is used to take pressure off the main double-entry bookkeeping system, and also allows the work of the accounts department to be split up amongst staff.
- Most businesses use sales, purchases, sales returns and purchases returns journals for credit transactions only.
- An analysed journal is used when a business needs to know the purchases, sales, etc made by different products, departments, or geographical areas of the business.

In the next chapter, we will look at the cash book – which is the book of prime entry for all cash and bank transactions.

QUESTIONS

visit **www.osbornebooks.co.uk** to take an online test

An asterisk (*) after the question number means that the answer is given at the end of this book.

6.1* Lucinda Lamille operates a clothes wholesaling business. During February 20-6, the following credit transactions took place:

20-6	
1 Feb	Purchased goods from Flair Clothing Co for £520
2 Feb	Sold goods to Wyvern Fashions for £200
4 Feb	Purchased goods from Modernwear for £240
10 Feb	Sold goods to Zandra Smith for £160
15 Feb	Sold goods to Just Jean for £120
18 Feb	Purchased goods from Quality Clothing for £800
23 Feb	Sold goods to Zandra Smith for £320
24 Feb	Sold goods to Wyvern Fashions for £80
26 Feb	Sold goods to Mercian Models for £320
28 Feb	Purchased goods from Flair Clothing Co for £200

You are to:

(a) Enter the above transactions in Lucinda Lamille's books of prime entry, and total the columns for the month.

(b) Record the accounting entries in Lucinda Lamille's purchases (payables) ledger, sales (receivables) ledger and general ledger.

6.2 James Scriven started in business as a furniture wholesaler on 1 February 20-2. During the first month of business, the following credit transactions took place:

1 Feb	Purchased furniture for resale and received invoice no 961 from Softseat Ltd, £320
2 Feb	Purchased furniture for resale and received invoice no 068 from PRK Ltd, £80
8 Feb	Sold furniture and issued invoice no 001 to High Street Stores, £440
14 Feb	Sold furniture and issued invoice no 002 to Peter Lounds Ltd, £120
15 Feb	Purchased furniture for resale and received invoice no 529 from Quality Furnishings, £160
18 Feb	Sold furniture and issued invoice no 003 to Carpminster College, £320
19 Feb	Purchased furniture for resale and received invoice no 984 from Softseat Ltd, £160
25 Feb	Sold furniture and issued invoice no 004 to High Street Stores, £200

You are to:

(a) Enter the above transactions in James Scriven's books of prime entry, and total the columns for the month.

(b) Record the accounting entries in James Scriven's purchases (payables) ledger, sales (receivables) ledger and general ledger.

6.3 Anne Green owns a shop selling paint and decorating materials. She has two suppliers, Wyper Ltd (account no 301) and M Roper & Sons (account no 302). During the month of May 20-2 Anne received the following source documents from her suppliers:

2 May	Invoice no 562 from M Roper & Sons for £190
4 May	Invoice no 82 from Wyper Ltd for £200
10 May	Invoice no 86 from Wyper Ltd for £210
18 May	Invoice no 580 from M Roper & Sons for £180
18 May	Credit note no 82 from M Roper & Sons for £30
21 May	Invoice no 91 from Wyper Ltd for £240
23 May	Credit note no 6 from Wyper Ltd for £40
25 May	Invoice no 589 from M Roper & Sons for £98
28 May	Credit note no 84 from M Roper & Sons for £38

You are to:

(a) Enter the above transactions in the appropriate journals which are to be totalled at the end of May.

(b) Enter the transactions in the appropriate accounts in Anne Green's ledgers. (The credit balances of Wyper Ltd and M Roper & Sons at the beginning of the month were £100 and £85 respectively.)

(c) Balance each account and bring down a balance on 1 June 20-2.

6.4* Lorna Pratt runs a computer software business, specialising in supplies to educational establishments. At the beginning of January 20-2 the balances in her ledgers were as follows:

Sales (Receivables) ledger	Mereford College (account no 201)	£705.35 debit
	Carpminster College (account no 202)	£801.97 debit
Purchases (Payables) ledger	Macstrad plc (account no 101)	£1,050.75 credit
	Amtosh plc (account no 102)	£2,750.83 credit

During the course of the month the following source documents are issued:

2 Jan	Invoice from Macstrad plc, M1529	£2,900.00
3 Jan	Invoice from Amtosh plc, A7095	£7,500.00
5 Jan	Invoice to Mereford College, 1093	£3,900.00
7 Jan	Invoice to Carpminster College, 1094	£8,500.00
10 Jan	Credit note from Macstrad plc, MC105	£319.75
12 Jan	Credit note from Amtosh plc, AC730	£750.18
13 Jan	Credit note to Mereford College, CN109	£850.73
14 Jan	Invoice to Carpminster College, 1095	£1,800.50
14 Jan	Invoice to Mereford College, 1096	£2,950.75
18 Jan	Invoice from Macstrad plc, M2070	£1,750.00
19 Jan	Invoice from Amtosh plc, A7519	£5,500.00
20 Jan	Invoice to Carpminster College, 1097	£3,900.75
22 Jan	Invoice to Mereford College, 1098	£1,597.85
23 Jan	Credit note from Macstrad plc, MC120	£953.07
27 Jan	Credit note to Mereford College, CN110	£593.81

You are to:

(a) Enter the above transactions in the appropriate journals which are to be totalled at the end of January.

(b) Record the accounting entries in Lorna Pratt's sales (receivables) ledger, purchases (payables) ledger and general ledger.

6.5 Malik Importers has partially prepared the following invoice from the delivery note.

INVOICE

MALIK IMPORTERS

Unit 2B, Brookside Estate, Wyvern, WV3 8PT
Tel 01927 493841 Fax 01927 493822

invoice to

Flair Fashions
18B Retail Arcade
Porthperran
TR10 0BX

invoice no	**45762**
account no	**F28**
your order no	**0347**
delivery note no	**0175**
date	**15 March 20-7**

product code	quantity	details	unit price (£)	unit	total amount (£)
X24	**96**	**Trend tops**	**8.50**	**each**	
Y36	**20**	**Jeans**	**15**	**each**	
				trade discount 20%	
				total	

terms
5% cash discount for full settlement within 7 days
Net 30 days

question continued on the next page . . .

question continued from the previous page . . .

Required:

(a) Complete the total amount column of the invoice.

(b) This invoice will be used as a source document by both Flair Fashions and Malik Importers. Which book of prime entry will be used for the entry:

(i) in the books of Flair Fashions? ....

....

(ii) in the books of Malik Importers? ....

....

(c) Explain the terms:

(i) trade discount ....

....

....

....

(ii) cash discount ....

....

....

....

....

6.6* In the catalogue of Wyvern Plumbers Merchants is part number B321 which has a list price of £50.00, less a trade discount of 20%.

Russell The Plumber, a customer, who is allowed trade discount and a cash discount of 5% for payment in 7 days, returned 8 units of part B321, which were faulty.

Required:

(a) What document will Wyvern Plumbers Merchants prepare and send to Russell The Plumber?

....

(b) Calculate the amount to be recorded on the document, clearly showing your calculations.

....

....

....

....

....

....

....

(c) State the book of prime entry that is used by Wyvern Plumbers Merchants for the returned parts and show the amount to be entered.

....

6.7* A business has issued a credit note.

What entries will be made in the business's ledger accounts?

	Account debited	**Account credited**	
A	Purchases returns	Trade payables	
B	Trade payables	Purchases returns	
C	Sales returns	Trade receivables	
D	Trade receivables	Sales returns	

6.8* Complete the following table by giving the source document and the book of prime entry to be used for the transactions.

Transaction	Source document	Book of prime entry
(a) Goods purchased on credit from a supplier		
(b) Goods sold on credit to a customer		
(c) Faulty goods returned to a supplier		
(d) Payment made by cheque to a supplier		
(e) Purchase on credit of a new machine for use in the factory		
(f) Faulty goods returned by a customer		
(g) Bank transfer received from a customer		

6.9 Complete the following table by giving for each source document:

- the book of prime entry
- the account to be debited
- the account to be credited

	Source document	Book of prime entry	Account to be debited	Account to be credited
(a)	Invoice for goods sold on credit to V Singh			
(b)	Invoice received for goods bought on credit from Okara Limited			
(c)	Credit note issued to S Johnson			
(d)	Credit note received from Roper & Company			

6.10* For each transaction shown below, state

- the source document
- the book of prime entry
- the account to be debited
- the account to be credited

(a) purchased goods on credit from A Cotton

(b) sold goods on credit to D Law

(c) cheque received for cash sales

(d) returned damaged goods to A Cotton

(e) paid gas bill by bank transfer

(f) D Law returns damaged goods

Set up your answer in the form of a table.

6.11* A business has sold goods in which it trades on credit to a customer.

How should the sale of the goods be recorded in the accounting system of the business?

	Book of prime entry	Debit	Credit	
A	Sales journal	Bank	Sales	
B	Sales journal	Sales	Customer	
C	Sales journal	Sales	Bank	
D	Sales journal	Customer	Sales	

6.12* A business has bought goods for resale on credit from a supplier. The goods are faulty and are returned to the supplier.

How should the return of the goods be recorded in the accounting system of the business?

	Book of prime entry	Debit	Credit	
A	Purchases returns journal	Supplier	Purchases returns	
B	Purchases journal	Supplier	Purchases returns	
C	Purchases returns journal	Purchases returns	Supplier	
D	Purchases journal	Purchases	Suppler	

6.13 Kasha Bialas owns a retail business. Her bookkeeper has been preparing the business's accounting records for May 20-4, but the following has not yet been recorded:

Date 20-4	**Source document**	**Details**
23 May	Sales invoice	M Gonzalez for goods with a list price of £2,400 less a trade discount of 20%.
25 May	Bank statement	T Pitman settled the amount due on 1 May by bank transfer, less a 5% cash discount.
26 May	Credit note	Sent to M Gonzalez as one-third of the goods sold on 23 May were not as ordered.
27 May	Paying-in slip counterfoil	Cheque from P Lewis in settlement of the amount currently due, less a 2% cash discount.
29 May	Sales invoice	T Pitman for goods with a list price of £1,500 less a trade discount of 15%.

(a) **Record** the transactions above in the business's books of prime entry shown below.

BOOKS OF PRIME ENTRY

SALES JOURNAL		
20-4		£

SALES RETURNS JOURNAL		
20-4		£

BANK ACCOUNT					
20-4		£	20-4		£
			1 May	Balance b/d	1,027

(b) **Record** the transactions above in the business's sales (receivables) ledger shown below at 23 May.

SALES (RECEIVABLES) LEDGER

M GONZALEZ ACCOUNT					
20-4		£	20-4		£

T PITMAN ACCOUNT					
20-4		£	20-4		£
1 May	Balance b/d	320			

P LEWIS ACCOUNT					
20-4		£	20-4		£
1 May	Balance b/d	550	10 May	Sales returns journal	150

(c) **Record** the relevant transactions above in the business's discount allowed account shown below.

DISCOUNT ALLOWED ACCOUNT					
20-4		£	20-4		£

7 THE CASH BOOK

The cash book brings together the separate cash and bank transactions of a business into one 'book'.

The cash book is used to record the bookkeeping transactions which involve the receipt and payment of money, for example cash, cheques and bank transfers.

The cash book forms part of the double-entry system.

Control of cash and money in the bank is very important for all businesses. A shortage of money may mean that wages and other day-to-day running expenses cannot be paid as they fall due. This could lead to the failure of the business.

THE CASH BOOK IN THE ACCOUNTING SYSTEM

For most businesses, control of cash takes place in the cash book which records:

- receipts and payments in cash
- receipts and payments by cheque and bank transfer

The cash book combines the roles of a book of prime entry and double-entry bookkeeping. The cash book is:

- a book of prime entry for cash and bank transactions
- the double-entry accounts for cash and bank

Within the division of the ledger (Chapter 6), the cash book is usually located in the general ledger. However, in some accounting systems, the cash book is kept as a separate division of the ledger.

Note that, as well as the cash book, businesses often have a petty cash book which is used for low-value expense payments. However, the A-level course does not require you to study the petty cash book.

Uses of the Cash Book

We have already used a separate cash account and bank account for double-entry bookkeeping transactions. These two accounts are, in practice, brought together into one book under the title of the cash book. This cash book is, therefore, used to record the money side of bookkeeping transactions and is part of the double-entry system. The cash book is used for:

- **cash transactions**
  - all receipts in cash
  - most payments for cash, except for low-value expense payments
- **bank transactions**
  - all receipts by cheque and bank transfer (or payment of cash into the bank)
  - all payments by cheque or bank transfer (or withdrawal of cash from the bank)

The cash book is usually controlled by a **cashier** who:

- records receipts and payments by cheque, by bank transfer and in cash
- makes cash payments, and prepares cheques and bank transfer payments for signature and/or authorisation
- pays cash and cheques received into the bank
- has control over the firm's cash, either in a cash till or cash box
- checks the accuracy of the cash and bank balances at regular intervals

It is important to note that transactions passing through the cash book must be supported by **source documents**. In this way an audit trail is established which provides a link that can be checked and followed through the accounting system:

- source document
- book of prime entry
- double-entry accounts

Such an audit trail is required both as a security feature within the business (to help to ensure that fraudulent transactions cannot be made), and also for taxation purposes.

The **cashier** has an important role to play within the accounting function of a business – most business activities will, at some point, involve cash or bank transactions. Thus the cash book and the cashier are at the hub of the accounting system. In particular, the cashier is responsible for:

- issuing receipts for cash (and sometimes cheques) received
- making authorised payments in cash, by cheque and by bank transfer against documents received (such as invoices and statements) showing the amounts due

At all times, payments can only be made by the cashier when authorised to do so by the appropriate person within the business, eg the accountant or the purchasing manager.

With so many transactions passing through the cash book, accounting procedures must include:

- security – of cash and cheque books, correct authorisation of bank payments
- confidentiality – that all cash/bank transactions, including cash and bank balances, are kept confidential

If the cashier has any queries about any transactions, he or she should refer them to the accounts supervisor.

LAYOUT OF THE CASH BOOK

Although a cash book can be set out in many formats to suit the requirements of a particular business, a common format is the three column cash book. This is set out like other double-entry accounts, with debit and credit sides, but there may be several money columns on each side. An example of a three column cash book (three money columns on each side) is shown below:

Dr				Cash Book							Cr
Date	Details	Ref	Discount allowed	Cash	Bank	Date	Details	Ref	Discount received	Cash	Bank
			£	£	£				£	£	£

Note the following points:

- The debit side is used for receipts.
- The credit side is used for payments.
- On both the debit and credit sides there are separate money columns for cash receipts/payments and bank receipts/payments.
- A third money column on each side is used to record cash discount (that is, an allowance offered for prompt payment of the amount due, eg 2% cash discount for settlement within seven days).
- The discount column on the debit side is for discount allowed to customers.
- The discount column on the credit side is for discount received from suppliers.
- The discount columns are not part of the double-entry bookkeeping system – they are used in the cash book as a listing device or memorandum column. As we will see in the worked example which follows, the discount columns are totalled at the end of the week or month, and the totals are then transferred into the double-entry system.
- The reference column is used to cross-reference to the other entry in the ledger system.

WORKED EXAMPLE: TRANSACTIONS IN THE CASH BOOK

We will now look at some example transactions and then see how the three column cash book is balanced at the month-end. The year is 20-7.

The transactions to be entered in the cash book are:

1 April	Balances at start of month: cash £300, bank £550
4 April	Received a bank transfer from S Wright for £98 – we have allowed her £2 cash discount
7 April	Paid a cheque to J Crane for £145 – he has allowed £5 cash discount
11 April	Paid wages in cash £275
14 April	Paid by bank transfer the account of T Lewis £120, deducting 2.5% cash discount
17 April	J Jones settles in cash her account of £80, deducting 5% cash discount
21 April	Withdrew £100 in cash from the bank for use in the business
23 April	Received a cheque for £45 from D Whiteman in full settlement of her account of £48
28 April	Paid cash of £70 to S Ford in full settlement of our account of £75

All cheques are banked on the day of receipt.

The cash book records these transactions (as shown below) and, after they have been entered, is balanced on 30 April. (The other part of each double-entry bookkeeping transaction is not shown here, but has to be carried out in order to record the transactions correctly.)

Cash Book (Dr / Cr)

Date	Details	Ref	Discount allowed	Cash	Bank	Date	Details	Ref	Discount received	Cash	Bank
			£	£	£				£	£	£
20-7						20-7					
1 Apr	Balances b/d			300	550	7 Apr	J Crane		5		145
4 Apr	S Wright		2		98	11 Apr	Wages			275	
17 Apr	J Jones		4	76		14 Apr	T Lewis		3		117
21 Apr	Bank	C		100		21 Apr	Cash	C			100
23 Apr	D Whiteman		3		45	28 Apr	S Ford		5	70	
						30 Apr	Balances c/d			131	331
			9	476	693				13	476	693
1 May	Balances b/d			131	331						

Note that the transaction on 21 April (£100 withdrawn from the bank for use in the business) involves a transfer of money between cash and bank. As each transaction is both a receipt and a payment within the cash book, it is usual to indicate both of them in the reference column with a 'C' – this stands for 'contra' and shows that both parts of the transaction are in the same book.

BALANCING THE CASH BOOK

We saw in Chapter 5 how accounts are balanced. The cash book is the ledger for cash account and bank account, and the procedure for balancing these is exactly the same as for other ledger accounts.

The cash book in the worked example on the previous page is balanced in the following way:

- subtotal the two cash columns (ie £476 in the debit column, and £345 in the credit column)
- deduct the lower total from the higher (payments from receipts) to give the balance of cash remaining (£476 – £345 = £131)
- the higher total is recorded at the bottom of both cash columns in a totals 'box' (£476)
- the balance of cash remaining (£131) is entered as a balancing item above the totals box (on the credit side), and is brought down underneath the total on the debit side as the opening balance for next month (£131)
- the two bank columns are dealt with in the same way (£693 – £362 = £331)

Notice that, in the cash book shown on the previous page, the cash and bank balances have been brought down on the debit side. It may happen that the balance at bank is brought down on the credit side: this occurs when payments exceed receipts, and indicates a bank overdraft. It is very important to appreciate that the bank columns of the cash book represent the firm's own records of bank transactions and the balance at bank – the bank statement may well show different figures (see the next chapter, Chapter 8).

A cash balance can only be brought down on the debit side, indicating the amount of cash held.

At the end of the month, each discount column is totalled separately – no attempt should be made to balance them. At this point, amounts recorded in the columns and the totals are not part of the double-entry system. However, the two totals are transferred to the double-entry system as follows:

- the total on the debit side (£9 in the example) is debited to discount allowed account in the general ledger
- the total on the credit side (£13 in the example) is credited to discount received account, also in the general ledger

The opposite bookkeeping entries will have already been entered in the trade receivables' and trade payables' accounts respectively (see Chapter 4). The accounts appear as follows:

Dr		**Discount Allowed Account**			Cr
20-7		£	20-7		£
30 Apr	Cash book	9			

Dr		**Discount Received Account**			Cr
20-7		£	20-7		£
			30 Apr	Cash book	13

The two discount accounts represent an expense and income respectively and, at the end of the firm's financial year, the totals of the two accounts will be used in the calculation of profit. Where control accounts (see Chapter 11) are in use, the total of discount allowed is credited to the sales ledger (receivables) control account, while the total of discount received is debited to the purchases ledger (payables) control account.

THE CASH BOOK AS A BOOK OF PRIME ENTRY

The cash book performs two functions within the accounting system:

- it is a book of prime entry for cash/bank transactions
- it forms part of the double-entry bookkeeping system

The diagram below shows the flow involving:

- source documents – cash and bank receipts and payments
- the cash book as a book of prime entry
- double-entry bookkeeping, involving cash book and other ledgers (note that the cash book is located in the general ledger)

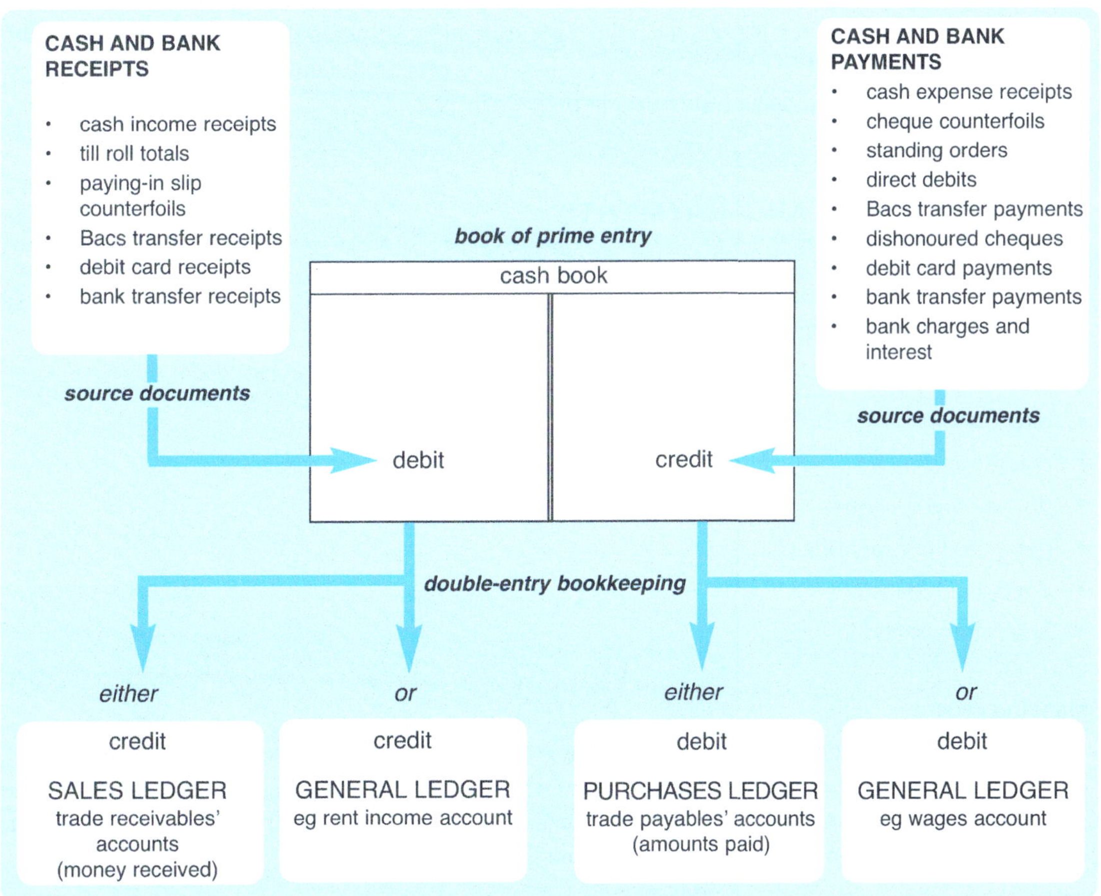

CHECKING THE CASH BOOK

As the cash book forms such an integral part of a firm's bookkeeping system, it is essential that transactions are recorded accurately and that balances are calculated correctly at regular intervals, eg weekly or monthly – depending on the needs of the business. How can the cash book be checked for accuracy?

cash columns

To check the cash columns is easy. It is simply a matter of counting the cash in the cash till or box, and agreeing it with the balance shown by the cash book. In the example in the worked example on page 99, there should be £131 in the firm's cash till at 30 April 20-7. If the cash cannot be agreed in this way, the discrepancy needs to be investigated urgently.

bank columns

How are these to be checked? We could compare with the bank statement, however, the balance of the account at the bank may well not agree with that shown by the bank columns of the cash book. There are several reasons why there may be a difference: for example, a cheque that has been written out recently to pay a bill may not yet have been recorded on the bank statement, ie it has been entered in the cash book, but is not yet on the bank statement. To agree the bank statement and the bank columns of the cash book, it is usually necessary to prepare a bank reconciliation statement, and this topic is dealt with fully in the next chapter, Chapter 8.

BANK RECEIPTS AND PAYMENTS

In writing up the receipts and payments columns of the cash book we come across a number of banking terms that are commonly used. These are:

- standing orders
- direct debits
- credit transfers
- dishonoured cheques
- debit card transactions
- direct bank transfers
- bank charges and interest

standing orders

There are regular payments – eg monthly, weekly – made from the bank account (ie they are on the credit side of the cash book, in the bank column). The payments are for the same amount each time and are made by the bank on behalf of the customer and on the written instructions of the customer. Rent payments and loan repayments are often made by standing order.

direct debits

These are payments (ie credit side of the cash book, in the bank column) made from the bank for the customer. It is the payee, or beneficiary, who originates the payment on the written instructions of the customer. Direct debits are often used where money amounts to be paid vary, and where the payments dates alter. Electricity/gas bills and business rates are often paid by direct debit.

credit transfers

These can be either receipts or payments – ie the debit and credit side of the cash book (bank columns) respectively. Receipts are from customers who have paid the amount due, through the banking system, directly into the bank account of the payee. Payments are to suppliers, or to employees for wages, and go into the bank account of the payees. Most credit transfers are made by Bacs (Bacs Payment Schemes) computer transfer. In order to make these payments, it is necessary to have the bank account details – account number, sort code of the bank branch – of the payee.

dishonoured cheques

These are cheques received by a business and paid into the bank but which are dishonoured by the payer's bank because:

- the cheque has been 'stopped' by the payer
- there are technical problems with the cheque, eg it is not signed
- the payer's bank account has insufficient money to meet payment of the cheque

debit card transactions

These are payments made by a bank customer using a debit card. The payments can be for both small amounts (eg for a cup of coffee) and for large amounts (eg buying a car). Payments can be made by means of a card machine – with the bank customer keying in the pin code for the card, or using 'tap-and-go' for small transactions – and to make payments over the internet confirming the card with the three digit security code on the reverse of the card. Some transactions need to be verified to the card issuer by means of a password.

For all debit card transactions, there must be money in the bank account to meet the payment, which will be shown on the bank statement a day or so afterwards. Remember that a debit card is not a credit card, and is a means of paying for goods and services from the bank account.

direct bank transfers

These are where payments are made directly between bank accounts using internet banking. They are often used to pay suppliers and other regular payees. The payee's details – sort code of the bank branch and account number – need to be set up in advance using online banking. Payments can then be made by logging onto the bank account – which requires various security steps – and then the payee can be selected and the amount to be paid completed. Confirming the details and amount sends the payment directly to the recipient, with the money being received usually the same working day.

It is especially important for a business to maintain high security around access to its bank account and internet banking – only authorised staff, eg the cashier, can have access and all direct bank transfers must be authorised by the appropriate manager.

bank charges and interest

Bank charges are made by the bank for services provided. Charges are usually calculated in relation to the number of transactions – eg cheques written, amounts paid in – during the period. As a payment from the bank account, bank charges are on the credit side of the cash book.

In addition to bank charges, a bank will make a separate charge for interest on overdrafts and loans which have been provided to the customer.

The source document for bank charges and interest is the bank statement.

CHAPTER SUMMARY

- The cash book records receipts (debits) and payments (credits) both in cash (except for low-value expense payments) and by cheque.
- A basic layout for a cash book has money columns for cash transactions and bank transactions on both the debit and credit sides, together with a further column on each side for discounts.
- In the discount columns are recorded cash discounts: discounts allowed (to customers) on the debit side, and discounts received (from suppliers) on the payments side.
- Banking terms commonly used are: standing orders, direct debits, credit transfers, dishonoured cheques, debit card transactions, direct bank transfers and bank charges.

In the next chapter we will see how bank reconciliation statements are prepared in order to agree the balance of the bank columns in the cash book with the bank statement balance.

QUESTIONS

visit
www.osbornebooks.co.uk
to take an online test

An asterisk (*) after the question number means that the answer is given at the end of this book.

7.1* You work as the cashier for Wyvern Publishing, a company which publishes a wide range of travel and historical books. As the cashier, your main responsibility is for the firm's cash book. Explain to a friend what your job involves and the qualities required of a cashier.

7.2* Walter Harrison is a sole trader who records his cash and bank transactions in a three column cash book. The following are the transactions for June 20-2:

1 June	Balances: cash £280; bank overdraft £2,240
3 June	Received a bank transfer from G Wheaton for £195, in full settlement of a debt of £200
5 June	Received cash of £53 from T Francis, in full settlement of a debt of £55
8 June	Paid the amount owing to F Lloyd by cheque: the total amount due is £400 and Harrison takes advantage of a 2.5% per cent cash discount
10 June	Paid wages in cash £165
12 June	Paid A Morris in cash, £100 less 3 per cent cash discount
16 June	Withdrew £200 in cash from the bank for use in the business
18 June	Received a cheque for £640 from H Watson in full settlement of a debt of £670
20 June	Paid R Marks £78 by bank transfer
24 June	Paid D Farr £65 by cheque, in full settlement of a debt of £67
26 June	Paid telephone account £105 in cash
28 June	Received a cheque from M Perry in settlement of his account of £240 – he has deducted 2.5% per cent cash discount
30 June	Received cash £45 from K Willis

All cheques are banked on the day of receipt.

Required:

(a) Enter the above transactions in Walter Harrison's three column cash book, balance the cash and bank columns, and carry the balances down to 1 July.

(b) Total the two discount columns and transfer them to the appropriate accounts.

7.3 On 1 August 20-7, the balances in the cash book of Metro Trading Company were:

Cash	£276 debit
Bank	£4,928 debit

Transactions for the month were:

1 Aug	Received a cheque from Wild & Sons Limited, £398
5 Aug	Paid T Hall Limited a cheque for £541 in full settlement of a debt of £565
8 Aug	Paid wages in cash £254
11 Aug	Withdrew £500 in cash from the bank for use in the business
12 Aug	Received a cheque for £1,755 from A Lewis Limited in full settlement of their account of £1,775
18 Aug	Paid F Jarvis £457 by cheque
21 Aug	Received a bank transfer for £261 from Harvey & Sons Limited
22 Aug	Paid wages in cash £436
25 Aug	Paid J Jones a cheque for £628 in full settlement of a debt of £661
27 Aug	Paid salaries by cheque £2,043
28 Aug	Paid telephone account by bank transfer £276
29 Aug	Received a cheque for £595 from Wild & Sons Limited in full settlement of their account of £610
29 Aug	Withdrew £275 in cash from the bank for use in the business

All cheques are banked on the day of receipt.

Required:

- Enter the above transactions in the three column cash book of Metro Trading Company.
- Balance the cash and bank columns at 31 August, and carry the balances down to 1 September.
- Total the two discount columns.

7.4 Tom Singh keeps a three column cash book for his business. The following information relates to the month of March 20-5:

20-5	
1 March	Balances of cash and bank were £106 and £3,214 respectively
2 March	Paid rent by cheque £250
3 March	Sales £1,050. Banked £950 of this on the same day
5 March	Paid cleaning expenses of £35 from cash
8 March	Sales banked £1,680
9 March	Payment by bank transfer for purchases costing £1,200
11 March	Drew cheque for £150, to replenish cash
13 March	Sales banked £1,800
16 March	Paid postage of £50 from cash
18 March	Drew cheque for £168, to pay a telephone bill
20 March	Paid stationery of £128 from cash
22 March	Drew cheque for £150, to replenish cash
25 March	Sales banked £2,108
26 March	Paid miscellaneous expenses of £70 from cash
27 March	Paid wages by bank transfer £2,000
29 March	Sales £2,200. Banked £2,000 of this on the same day
30 March	Drew cheque for £106, to pay an electricity bill
31 March	Payment by bank transfer of £855 to Evans & Co, in settlement of a debt of £900
31 March	Drew cheque for £494 payable to A Bennett, in settlement of a debt of £520
31 March	Received cheque for £720 from Hobbs Ltd, in settlement of an amount of £750
31 March	Received a bank transfer for £1,160 from Pratley & Co, in settlement of an amount of £1,210

All cheques are banked on the day of receipt.

Required:

Write up the three column cash book, and carry the balances down to 1 April 20-5.

7.5* The following items have yet to be recorded in the cash book of Andrew Lim for the first week in April 20-3:

		£	
1 April	Balance of cash	100.00	
1 April	Overdrawn bank balance	633.86	
	Cheque counterfoils show:	£	
2 April	A-Z Ltd (cash discount taken – £5.00)	195.00	cheque amount
3 April	Teme Traders	256.22	cheque amount
4 April	Akhtar Ltd (cash discount taken – £4.25)	146.13	cheque amount
6 April	Wyvern Wares Ltd	208.25	cheque amount
	Paying-in counterfoils show:		
4 April	Southern Stores Ltd	476.82	amount banked
6 April	O Parry (cash discount taken – £3.45)	223.89	amount banked

The following additional items should also be recorded in the cash book:

	£
The bank statement dated 7 April shows:	£
Direct debit payment City Council	176.50
Bank transfer received from Frobisher & Co	361.28
Bank charges	33.47
Bank interest paid	62.35
The week's till rolls show:	
Cash receipts total of	968.27
There were cash payments of:	
Part time wages	124.50
Office stationery	26.32

It is the business's policy to retain a cash float of £100 at the end of each week and pay the rest of the cash into the bank. This was done on 7 April 20-3.

Required:

Record this information in the cash book on the next page and balance the cash book at 7 April 20-3.

Dr | Andrew Lim Cash Book | Cr

Date 20-3	Details	Discount allowed £	Cash £	Bank £	Date 20-3	Details	Discount rec'd £	Cash £	Bank £

7.6 Explain the meaning of the following items which have been found in the bank statement received by Nick Evans for his business and give the ledger entries for them.

(i) Standing order payment for rent

Explanation ....

....

....

....

Account to be debited ....

Account to be credited ....

(ii) Bank transfer payment received from a trade receivable

Explanation ....

....

....

....

Account to be debited ....

Account to be credited ....

(iii) Dishonoured cheque from a trade receivable

Explanation ....

....

....

....

Account to be debited ....

Account to be credited ....

7.7*

Complete the following table by filling in the blank boxes.

	Source document	**Book of prime entry**	**Ledger account to be debited**	**Ledger account to be credited**
Sold goods on credit to a customer				
Faulty goods returned to the supplier		Purchases returns journal	Trade payables/Purchases ledger control account*	Purchases returns
Cash sales paid into the bank		Cash book		
Standing order payment for rent		Cash book		
Purchase of office stationery, paid by bank transfer				

*see Chapter 11

7.8 Sally Johnson uses a three column cash book as part of her double-entry bookkeeping system. The following details relate to March 20-3.

March		£
1	Balance in cash account	100
	Overdrawn bank balance	852
2	Bank transfer made to A-Z Supplies in settlement of an invoice for £200	195
6	Cheque from J Jones paid into bank	623
11	Paid rent by cheque	500
13	Cheque from A Patel paid into bank. Discount of £6 had been taken by the customer	294
14	Cash sales	458
27	Paid wages of part-time employee in cash	165
28	Cash sales	428

A bank statement received on 28 March revealed the following additional items.

20	Direct debit to Southern Electricity	155
21	Interest charged by bank	55
24	Bank transfer from Ogden & Co Ltd	347

On 31 March, all cash, except a float of £100, was paid into the bank.

Required:

(a) Write up the cash book, on the next page, for the month of March 20-3 from the information provided above.

(b) Balance the cash book at the end of the month, and carry down the balances to 1 April 20-3.

(c) Transfer the discounts to the general ledger accounts shown on the next page.

Dr		Sally Johnson Cash Book							Cr
Date 20-3	Details	Discount £	Cash £	Bank £	Date 20-3	Details	Discount £	Cash £	Bank £

Dr	Discount Allowed Account				Cr
Date 20-3	Details	£	Date 20-3	Details	£

Dr	Discount Received Account				Cr
Date 20-3	Details	£	Date 20-3	Details	£

7.9* Which **one** of the following transactions will not be recorded on the payments side of cash book?

A	Purchase of a vehicle for £10,000 paid for by cheque	
B	Cash purchase for £150	
C	Bank transfer from a trade receivable for £1,350	
D	Bacs transfer to a trade payable for £2,200	

7.10* Which **one** of the following transactions will not be recorded on the receipts side of cash book?

A	Cheque to a trade payable for £870	
B	Bank transfer from a trade receivable for £3,250	
C	Debit card payment by a customer for £580	
D	Cash sales of £195	

8 BANK RECONCILIATION STATEMENTS

Bank reconciliation statements are part of the verification process of the double-entry records. They form the link between the balance at bank shown in the cash book of a business's bookkeeping system and the balance shown on the bank statement received from the bank.

The reasons why the cash book and bank statement may differ are because:

- there are timing differences caused by:
  - unpresented cheques, ie the time delay between writing out (drawing) a cheque and recording it in the cash book, and the cheque being banked by the payee and being recorded on the bank statement
  - amounts not yet credited, ie amounts paid into the bank, but not yet recorded on the bank statement
- the cash book has not been updated with items which appear on the bank statement and which should also appear in the cash book, eg bank charges

Assuming that there are no errors, both cash book and bank statement are correct, but need to be reconciled with each other, ie the closing balances need to be agreed.

TIMING DIFFERENCES

The two main timing differences between the bank columns of the cash book and the bank statement are:

- **unpresented cheques**, ie cheques issued, not yet recorded on the bank statement
- **amounts not yet credited**, ie amounts paid into the bank, not yet recorded on the bank statement

The first of these – unpresented cheques – is caused because, when a cheque is written out, it is immediately entered on the payments side of the cash book, even though it may be some days before the cheque is banked by the payee, passes through the banking system and is recorded on the bank statement. Therefore, for a few days at least, the cash book shows a lower balance than the bank statement in respect of this cheque. When the cheque is recorded on the bank statement, the difference will disappear. We have looked at only one cheque here, but a business will often be issuing many cheques each day, and the difference between the cash book balance and the bank statement balance may be considerable.

With the second timing difference – amounts not yet credited – the firm's cashier will record a receipt in the cash book as he or she prepares the bank paying-in slip. However, the receipt may not be recorded by the bank on the bank statement for a day or so, particularly if it is paid in late in the day (when the bank will put it into the next day's work), or if it is paid in at a bank branch other than the one at which the account is maintained. Until the receipt is recorded by the bank the cash book will show a higher bank account balance than the bank statement. Once the receipt is entered on the bank statement, the difference will disappear.

These two timing differences are involved in the calculation known as the bank reconciliation statement. The business cash book must not be altered for these because, as we have seen, they will correct themselves on the bank statement as time goes by.

Updating the Cash Book

Besides the timing differences described above, there may be other differences between the bank columns of the cash book and the bank statement, and these do need to be entered in the cash book to bring it up-to-date. For example, the bank might make an automatic standing order payment on behalf of a business – such an item is correctly debited by the bank, and it might be that the bank statement acts as a reminder to the business cashier of the payment: it should then be entered in the cash book.

Examples of items that show in the bank statement and need to be entered in the cash book include:

receipts

- credit transfers and bank transfers received by the bank, eg payments from trade receivables
- debit card receipts from customers
- interest credited by the bank, if any

payments

- standing order and direct debit payments
- debit card payments
- bank transfers made
- bank charges and interest
- dishonoured cheques debited by the bank (ie cheques from trade receivables paid in by the business which have 'bounced' and are returned by the bank marked 'refer to drawer')

For each of these items, the cashier needs to check to see if they have been entered in the cash book; if not, they need to be recorded (provided that the bank has not made an error). If the bank has made an error, it must be notified as soon as possible and the incorrect transactions reversed by the bank in its own accounting records.

THE BANK RECONCILIATION STATEMENT

This forms the link between the balances shown in the cash book and the bank statement.

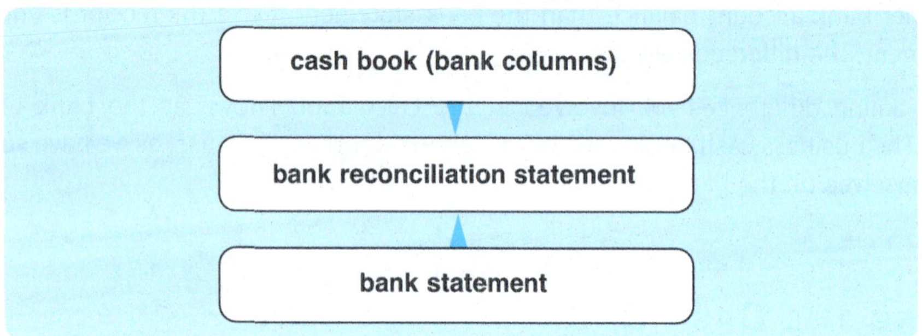

Upon receipt of a bank statement, reconciliation of the two balances is carried out in the following way:

- tick off the items that appear in both cash book and bank statement
- the unticked items on the bank statement are entered into the bank columns of the cash book to bring it up-to-date (provided none are errors made by the bank)
- the bank columns of the cash book are now balanced to find the revised figure
- the remaining unticked items from the cash book will be the timing differences
- the timing differences are used to prepare the bank reconciliation statement, which takes the following format (with example figures):

XYZ TRADING LTD

Bank Reconciliation Statement as at 31 October 20-1

			£	£
Balance at bank as per cash book				525
Add: unpresented cheques				
	J Lewis	cheque no. 0012378	60	
	ABC Ltd	cheque no. 0012392	100	
	Eastern Oil Company	cheque no. 0012407	80	
				240
				765
Less: amounts not yet credited			220	
			300	
				520
Balance at bank as per bank statement				245

Notes:

- The layout shown on the opposite page starts from the cash book balance, and works towards the bank statement balance. A common variation of this layout is to start with the bank statement balance and to work towards the cash book balance (see page 122).
- If a bank overdraft is involved, brackets should be used around the numbers to indicate this for the cash book or bank statement balance. The timing differences are still added or deducted, as appropriate.
- Once the bank reconciliation statement agrees, it should be filed because it proves that the cash book (bank columns) and bank statement were reconciled at a particular date. If, next time it is prepared, it fails to agree, the previous statement is proof that reconciliation was reached at that time.

WORKED EXAMPLE: BANK RECONCILIATION STATEMENT

The cashier of Severn Trading Co has written up the firm's cash book for the month of February 20-2, as follows (the cheque number is shown against payments):

Dr				Cash Book					Cr
Date	Details		Cash	Bank	Date	Details		Cash	Bank
20-2			£	£	20-2			£	£
1 Feb	Balances b/d		250.75	1,340.50	3 Feb	Appleton Ltd 123456			675.25
7 Feb	A Abbott			208.50	5 Feb	Wages		58.60	
10 Feb	Sales		145.25		12 Feb	Rent 123457			125.00
13 Feb	Sales		278.30		14 Feb	Transfer to bank	C	500.00	
14 Feb	Transfer from cash	C		500.00	17 Feb	D Smith & Co 123458			421.80
20 Feb	Sales		204.35		24 Feb	Stationery		75.50	
21 Feb	D Richards Limited			162.30	25 Feb	G Christie 123459			797.55
26 Feb	Sales		353.95		27 Feb	Transfer to bank	C	500.00	
27 Feb	Transfer from cash	C		500.00	28 Feb	Balances c/d		98.50	954.00
28 Feb	P Paul Limited			262.30					
			1,232.60	2,973.60				1,232.60	2,973.60
1 Mar	Balances b/d		98.50	954.00					

The cash balance of £98.50 shown by the cash columns on 1 March has been agreed with the cash held in the firm's cash box.

The bank statement for February 20-2 is shown on the next page.

National Bank plc

Branch Bartown

TITLE OF ACCOUNT Severn Trading Company

ACCOUNT NUMBER 67812318

STATEMENT NUMBER 45

DATE	PARTICULARS	PAYMENTS	RECEIPTS	BALANCE
20-2		£	£	£
1 Feb	Balance brought forward			1340.50 CR
8 Feb	Credit		208.50	1549.00 CR
10 Feb	Cheque no. 123456	675.25		873.75 CR
17 Feb	Credit		500.00	1373.75 CR
17 Feb	Cheque no. 123457	125.00		1248.75 CR
24 Feb	Credit		162.30	1411.05 CR
24 Feb	Bacs credit: J Jarvis Ltd		100.00	1511.05 CR
26 Feb	Cheque no. 123458	421.80		1089.25 CR
26 Feb	Direct debit: A-Z Finance	150.00		939.25 CR
28 Feb	Credit		500.00	1439.25 CR
28 Feb	Bank charges	10.00		1429.25 CR

Note that the bank statement is prepared from the bank's viewpoint: thus a credit balance shows that the customer is a liability of the bank, ie the bank owes the balance to the customer. In the customer's own cash book, the bank is shown as a debit balance, ie an asset.

As the month-end balance at bank shown by the cash book, £954.00, is not the same as that shown by the bank statement, £1,429.25, it is necessary to prepare a bank reconciliation statement. The steps are:

1 Tick off the items that appear in both cash book and bank statement.

2 The unticked items on the bank statement are entered into the bank columns of the cash book to bring it up-to-date. These are:

• receipt	24 Feb	Bacs credit, J Jarvis Limited £100.00
• payments	26 Feb	Direct debit, A-Z Finance £150.00
	28 Feb	Bank Charges, £10.00

In double-entry bookkeeping, the other part of the transaction will need to be recorded in the accounts, eg in J Jarvis Ltd's account in the sales ledger, etc.

3 The cash book is now balanced to find the revised balance:

Dr		**Cash Book (bank columns)**			Cr
20-2		£	20-2		£
	Balance b/d	954.00	26 Feb	A-Z Finance	150.00
24 Feb	J Jarvis Ltd	100.00	28 Feb	Bank Charges	10.00
			28 Feb	Balance c/d	894.00
		1,054.00			1,054.00
1 Mar	Balance b/d	894.00			

4 The remaining unticked items from the cash book are used in the bank reconciliation statement:

- receipt 28 Feb – P Paul Limited £262.30
- payment 25 Feb – G Christie (cheque no 123459) £797.55

These items are timing differences, which should appear on next month's bank statement.

5 The bank reconciliation statement is now prepared, starting with the re-calculated cash book balance of £894.00.

SEVERN TRADING CO.

Bank Reconciliation Statement as at 28 February 20-2

	£
Balance at bank as per cash book	894.00
Add: unpresented cheque, no. 123459	797.55
	1,691.55
Less: amount not yet credited, P Paul Limited	262.30
Balance at bank as per bank statement	1,429.25

With the above, a statement has been produced which starts with the amended balance from the cash book, and finishes with the bank statement balance, ie the two figures are reconciled.

Notes:

- The unpresented cheque is added back to the cash book balance because, until it is recorded by the bank, the cash book shows a lower balance than the bank statement.
- The amount not yet credited is deducted from the cash book balance because, until it is recorded by the bank, the cash book shows a higher balance than the bank statement.

Preparing a Bank Reconciliation Statement

In order to help you with the questions at the end of the chapter, here is a step-by-step summary of the procedure. Reconciliation of the cash book balance with that shown in the bank statement should be carried out in the following way:

1 From the bank columns of the cash book tick off, in both cash book and bank statement, the receipts that appear in both.

2 From the bank columns of the cash book tick off, in both cash book and bank statement, the payments that appear in both.

3 Identify the items that are unticked on the bank statement and enter them in the cash book on the debit or credit side, as appropriate. If, however, the bank has made a mistake and debited or credited an amount in error, this should not be entered in the cash book, but should be notified to the bank for them to make the correction. The amount will need to be entered on the bank reconciliation statement – see section below, dealing with unusual items on bank statements: bank errors.

4 The bank columns of the cash book are now balanced to find the up-to-date balance.

5 Start the bank reconciliation statement with the balance brought down figure shown in the cash book.

6 In the bank reconciliation statement add the unticked payments shown in the cash book – these will be unpresented cheques.

7 In the bank reconciliation statement, deduct the unticked receipts shown in the cash book – these are amounts not yet credited.

8 The resultant money amount on the bank reconciliation statement is the balance of the bank statement.

Alternative Layout of Bank Reconciliation Statements

The layout which is often used for the bank reconciliation statement is that shown on page 118. The layout starts with the cash book balance and finishes with the bank statement balance. However, there is no reason why it should not commence with the bank statement balance and finish with the cash book balance. With this layout it is necessary to:

- deduct unpresented cheques
- add amounts not yet credited

The bank reconciliation statement of Severn Trading Company (see previous page) would then appear as:

SEVERN TRADING COMPANY
Bank Reconciliation Statement as at 28 February 20-2

	£
Balance at bank as per bank statement	1,429.25
Less: unpresented cheque, no 123459	797.55
	631.70
Add: amount not yet credited, P Paul Limited	262.30
Balance at bank as per cash book	894.00

Dealing with Unusual Items on Bank Statements

The following are some of the unusual features that may occur on bank statements. As with other accounting discrepancies and queries, where they cannot be resolved they should be referred to a supervisor for guidance.

out-of-date cheques

These are cheques that are more than six months' old. Where a business has a number of out-of-date – or 'stale' – cheques which have not been debited on the bank statement, they will continue to appear on the bank reconciliation statement. As the bank will not pay these cheques, they can be written back in the cash book, ie debit cash book (and credit the other double-entry account involved).

dishonoured cheques

A cheque received by a business is entered as a receipt in the cash book and then paid into the bank, but it may be returned ('bounced') by the payer's bank because:

- the payer has instructed the bank to 'stop' the cheque
- the cheque has been returned by the bank, either because the payer has no money or because there is a technical problem with the cheque, eg it is not signed

A cheque returned ('bounced') in this way should be entered in the bookkeeping system:

- as a payment in the cash book on the credit side
- as a debit to the trade receivable's account in the sales ledger (if it is a credit sale), or sales account (if it is a cash sale)

bank errors

Errors made by the bank can include:

- A cheque deducted from the bank account which has not been issued by the business – look for a cheque number on the bank statement that is different from the current cheque series. Care should be taken, however, as it could be a cheque from an old cheque book.
- A Bacs or bank transfer receipt shown on the bank statement for which the business is not the correct recipient. If in doubt, the bank will be able to give further details of the sender of the credit.
- Standing orders and direct debits paid at the wrong time or for the wrong amounts. A copy of all standing order and direct debit mandates sent to the bank should be kept by the business for reference purposes.

When an error is found, it should be queried immediately with the bank. The item and amount should not be entered in the firm's cash book until the issue has been resolved. If, in the meantime, a bank reconciliation statement is to be prepared, the bank error should be shown separately:

- if working from the cash book balance to the bank statement balance, deduct payments and add receipts that the bank has applied to the account incorrectly
- if working from the bank statement balance to the cash book balance, add payments and deduct receipts that the bank has applied to the account incorrectly

bank charges and interest

From time-to-time the bank will debit business customers' accounts with an amount for:

- service charges, ie the cost of operating the bank account
- interest, ie the borrowing cost when the business is overdrawn

Banks usually notify customers in writing before debiting the account.

reconciliation of opening cash book and bank statement balances

If you look back to the example on page 119, you will see that both the cash book (bank columns) and the bank statement balance both started the month with the same balance: 1 February 20-2 £1,340.50.

In reality, it is unlikely that the opening cash book and bank statement balances will be the same. It will be necessary, in these circumstances, to prepare an opening bank reconciliation statement in order to prove that there are no errors between cash book and bank statement at the start of the month.

This is set out in the same format as the end-of-month bank reconciliation statement, and is best prepared immediately after ticking off the items that appear in both cash book and bank statement. The earliest unpresented cheques drawn and amounts not yet credited will comprise the opening bank reconciliation statement. Of course, where last month's bank reconciliation statement is available, such as in business, there is no need to prepare an opening reconciliation.

In the A-level examinations there will be no need to prepare a formal opening bank reconciliation statement, unless the question calls for one. Any discrepancy in opening balances can be resolved quickly by checking the bank statement for the earliest receipts and payments.

Importance of Bank Reconciliation Statements

- A bank reconciliation statement is important because, in its preparation, the transactions in the bank columns of the cash book are compared with those recorded on the bank statement. In this way, any errors in the cash book or bank statement will be found and can be corrected (or advised to the bank, if the bank statement is wrong).
- The bank statement is an independent accounting record, therefore it will assist in deterring fraud by providing a means of verifying the cash book balance.
- By writing the cash book up-to-date, the business has an amended figure for the bank balance to be shown in the trial balance.
- Unpresented cheques over six months old – out-of-date cheques – can be identified and written back in the cash book (any cheque dated more than six months' ago will not be paid by the bank).
- It is good practice to prepare a bank reconciliation statement on a regular basis. The reconciliation statement should be prepared as quickly as possible so that any queries – either with the bank statement or in the firm's cash book – can be resolved. Many businesses will specify to their accounting staff the timescales for preparing bank reconciliation statements – as a guideline, for a weekly bank statement the reconciliation statement should be prepared within three or four working days.

CHAPTER SUMMARY

- A bank reconciliation statement is used to agree the balance shown by the bank columns of the cash book with that shown by the bank statement.

- Certain differences between the two are timing differences. The main timing differences are:
  - unpresented cheques
  - amounts not yet credited

  These differences will be corrected by time and, most probably, will be recorded on the next bank statement.

- Certain differences appearing on the bank statement need to be entered in the cash book to bring it up-to-date. These include:

  Receipts
  - credit transfer and bank transfer amounts received by the bank
  - debit card receipts from customers
  - interest credited by the bank, if any

  Payments
  - standing order and direct debit payments
  - debit card payments
  - bank charges and interest
  - dishonoured cheques debited by the bank

- The bank reconciliation statement makes use of the timing differences.

- Once prepared, a bank reconciliation statement is proof that the bank statement and the cash book (bank columns) were agreed at a particular date.

In the next chapter we take an introductory look at how businesses prepare their year-end financial statements.

QUESTIONS

visit **www.osbornebooks.co.uk** to take an online test

An asterisk (*) after the question number means that the answer is given at the end of this book.

8.1* Upon receipt of a bank statement, which **one** of the following must be written into the firm's cash book?

A	Payment debited in error by the bank	
B	Unpresented cheques	
C	Bank transfers from trade receivables	
D	Amounts not yet credited	

8.2* A firm's bank statement shows an overdraft of £600. Unpresented cheques total £250; outstanding lodgements total £1,000. What is the balance at bank shown by the cash book?

A	£150 debit	
B	£650 debit	
C	£250 credit	
D	£150 credit	

8.3* The bank columns of Tom Reid's cash book for December 20-7 are as follows:

20-7	*Receipts*	*£*	*20-7*	*Payments*		*£*
1 Dec	Balance b/d	280	9 Dec	W Smith	345123	40
12 Dec	P Jones	30	12 Dec	Rent	345124	50
18 Dec	H Homer	72	18 Dec	Wages	345125	85
29 Dec	J Hill	13	19 Dec	B Kay	345126	20
			31 Dec	Balance c/d		200
		395				395

His bank statement for the same period was as follows:

BANK STATEMENT		Payments	Receipts	Balance
20-7		£	£	£
1 Dec	Balance brought forward			280 CR
12 Dec	Credit		30	310 CR
15 Dec	Cheque no. 345123	40		270 CR
17 Dec	Cheque no. 345124	50		220 CR
22 Dec	Credit		72	292 CR
23 Dec	Cheque no. 345125	85		207 CR

You are to prepare a bank reconciliation statement which agrees with the bank statement balance.

8.4 The bank columns of P Gerrard's cash book for January 20-7 are as follows:

20-7	*Receipts*	*£*	*20-7*	*Payments*		*£*
1 Jan	Balance b/d	800.50	2 Jan	A Arthur Ltd	001351	100.00
6 Jan	J Baker	495.60	10 Jan	C Curtis	001352	398.50
31 Jan	G Shotton Ltd	335.75	13 Jan	Donald & Co	001353	229.70
			14 Jan	Bryant & Sons	001354	312.00
			23 Jan	P Reid	001355	176.50
			31 Jan	Balance c/d		415.15
		1,631.85				1,631.85

His bank statement for the same period was as follows:

BANK STATEMENT		Payments	Receipts	Balance
20-7		£	£	£
1 Jan	Balance brought forward			800.50 CR
6 Jan	Cheque no. 001351	100.00		700.50 CR
6 Jan	Credit		495.60	1,196.10 CR
13 Jan	Bacs credit: T K Supplies		716.50	1,912.60 CR
20 Jan	Cheque no. 001352	398.50		1,514.10 CR
23 Jan	Direct debit: Omni Finance	207.95		1,306.15 CR
24 Jan	Cheque no. 001353	229.70		1,076.45 CR

You are to:

(a) Write the cash book up-to-date at 31 January 20-7.

(b) Prepare a bank reconciliation statement at 31 January 20-7.

8.5 The bank columns of Jane Doyle's cash book for May 20-7 are as follows:

20-7	*Receipts*	*£*	*20-7*	*Payments*		*£*
1 May	Balance b/d	300	2 May	P Stone	867714	28
7 May	Cash	162	14 May	Alpha Ltd	867715	50
16 May	C Brewster	89	29 May	E Deakin	867716	110
23 May	Cash	60				
30 May	Cash	40				

Her bank statement for the same period was as follows:

BANK STATEMENT

		Payments	*Receipts*	*Balance*
20-7		£	£	£
1 May	Balance brought forward			400 CR
2 May	Cheque no 867713	100		300 CR
5 May	Cheque no. 867714	28		272 CR
7 May	Credit		162	434 CR
16 May	Standing order: A-Z Insurance	25		409 CR
19 May	Credit		89	498 CR
20 May	Cheque no. 867715	50		448 CR
26 May	Credit		60	508 CR
31 May	Bank charges	10		498 CR

You are to:

(a) Write the cash book up-to-date at 31 May 20-7.

(b) Prepare a bank reconciliation statement at 31 May 20-7.

8.6* The bank statement of Milestone Motors for May 20-4 was as follows:

BANK STATEMENT		Paid out	Paid in	Balance
20-4		£	£	£
1 May	Balance brought forward			3,652 C
10 May	Cheque no 451762	751		2,901 C
11 May	Cheque no 451763	268		2,633 C
13 May	Cheque no 451765	1,045		1,588 C
14 May	Bacs credit: Perran Taxis		2,596	4,184 C
18 May	Direct debit: Wyvern Council	198		3,986 C
20 May	Direct debit: A1 Insurance	1,005		2,981 C
25 May	Direct debit: Okaro and Company	254		2,727 C
25 May	Bank charges	20		2,707 C
D = Debit C = Credit				

The cash book of Milestone Motors as at 31 May 20-4 is shown below:

CASH BOOK

Date	Details	Bank	Date	Cheque no	Details	Bank
20-4		£	20-4			£
1 May	Balance b/f	3,652	4 May	451762	Smith and Company	751
26 May	J Ackland	832	4 May	451763	Bryant Limited	268
28 May	Stamp Limited	1,119	7 May	451764	Curtis Cars	1,895
			7 May	451765	Parts Supplies	1,045

You are to:

(a) Check the items on the bank statement against the items in the cash book.

(b) Update the cash book as needed.

(c) Total the cash book and show clearly the balance carried down at 31 May and brought down at 1 June.

(d) Prepare a bank reconciliation statement as at 31 May 20-4.

8.7* Blenheim Builders received a bank statement showing the following transactions in their account for April 20-3.

Bank Statement

Date	Details	Dr £	Cr £	Balance £
Apr 1	Balance			2,620 Cr
5	Durning Supplies (Cheque no 100186)	1,320		1,300 Cr
6	Cash and cheques paid in		2,410	3,710 Cr
10	Wyvern Finance (Direct debit)	245		3,465 Cr
14	L Dove (Bacs)		455	3,920 Cr
18	Cash and cheques paid in		1,240	5,160 Cr
20	Central Cement Co (Cheque no 100187)	850		4,310 Cr
25	Bank charges	45		4,265 Cr
28	Aydee Traders (dishonoured cheque)	340		3,925 Cr

Required:

(a) Update the cash book below with the relevant items from the bank statement, and bring down the balance at the end of the month.

Dr **Cash Book** Cr

Date	Details	£	Date	Details	£
Apr 1	Balance b/d	2,620	Apr 2	Durning Supplies	1,320
4	Sales banked	2,410	16	Central Cement Co	850
16	Sales banked	1,240	28	Abbott & Co	390
30	Sales banked	1,030	29	Wages	1,280

(b) Prepare a bank reconciliation statement as at 30 April 20-3.

(c) Explain the term 'dishonoured cheque' shown in the bank statement.

8.8 Francis trades as the 'Village Stores'. On 31 August 20-6 the business' cash book for the month of August was as follows:

Cash Book (bank columns)

Dr					Cr
20-6		£	20-6		£
Aug 1	Balance b/f	1,520	Aug 5	Rent (SO)	750
10	Sales	875	7	Food Supplies (cheque 247384)	1,042
19	Sales	1,233	16	Eastern Electricity (DD)	326
30	Sales	628	22	Drawings (cheque 247385)	154
			24	Lindum Council (DD)	315
			28	Food Supplies (cheque 247386)	822
			31	Balance c/d	847
		4,256			4,256
Sep 1	Balance b/d	847			

The business' bank statement for the same period was as follows:

Bank Statement

Date	Details	Dr £	Cr £	Balance £
August 1	Balance			1,955 Cr
3	247383	435		1,520 Cr
5	SO Lindum Lettings	750		770 Cr
12	Sundries		875	1,645 Cr
13	247384	1,042		603 Cr
16	DD Eastern Electricity	326		277 Cr
18	Bacs Interest from PQR Ltd		25	302 Cr
19	DD Midlands Finance	1,160		858 Dr
22	Sundries		1,233	375 Cr
24	Lindum Council	315		60 Cr
26	Cheque 247385	145		85 Dr
30	Charges	55		140 Dr

Note: SO = Standing Order; DD = Direct Debit; BACS = Bankers Automated Clearing Services

Additional information:

Francis realises he made an error in recording the amount for cheque 247385 in his cash book.

(a) Update the cash book on 31 August 20-6.

Dr	Cash Book (bank columns)				Cr
20-6		£	20-6		£

(b) Prepare a bank reconciliation statement as at 31 August 20-6.

9 INTRODUCTION TO FINANCIAL STATEMENTS

For most businesses, the financial statements, which are produced at the end of each financial year, comprise:

- income statement, which shows profit or loss of the business for the year
- statement of financial position, which shows the assets and liabilities of the business at the year-end

This chapter provides an introduction to financial statements, explaining how they fit in with the double-entry bookkeeping system. Financial statements will be studied further in subsequent chapters.

FINANCIAL STATEMENTS AND THE TRIAL BALANCE

So far we have described the format of financial accounts and the recording of different types of transactions. All that we have covered is usually carried out by the bookkeeper. We will now explain how the accountant takes to a further stage the information prepared by the bookkeeper. The accountant will use the information from the accounting system, which is summarised in the trial balance (see Chapter 5), in order to produce the financial statements of a business.

The financial statements can be produced more often than once a year in order to give information to the owner on how the business is progressing. However, it is customary to produce annual financial statements for the benefit of the tax authorities, the bank and other stakeholders.

The starting point for preparing financial statements is the trial balance prepared by the bookkeeper. All the figures recorded on the trial balance are used in the financial statements. The income statement is an 'account' in terms of double-entry bookkeeping. This means that amounts recorded in this account must also be recorded elsewhere in the bookkeeping system. By contrast, the statement of financial position is not an account, but is simply a statement of account's balances remaining after the income statement has been prepared.

To help us with the preparation of financial statements we will use the trial balance, shown on the next page, of Wyvern Wholesalers, a sole trader business. This has been produced by the bookkeeper at the end of the financial year of the business.

TRIAL BALANCE OF WYVERN WHOLESALERS AS AT 31 DECEMBER 20-1

	Dr	Cr
	£	£
Revenue (Sales)		250,000
Purchases	156,000	
Sales returns	5,400	
Purchases returns		7,200
Discount received		2,500
Discount allowed	3,700	
Inventory at 1 January 20-1	12,350	
Salaries	46,000	
Electricity and gas	3,000	
Rent and business rates	2,000	
Sundry expenses	4,700	
Property at cost	100,000	
Equipment at cost	30,000	
Trade receivables	23,850	
Bank overdraft		851
Cash	125	
Trade payables		12,041
Capital		113,475
Drawings	10,442	
Long-term loan		11,500
	397,567	397,567

Note: inventory at 31 December 20-1 is valued at £16,300

You will see that the trial balance includes the inventory value at the start of the year, while the end-of-year valuation is noted after the trial balance. For the purposes of financial accounting, the inventory of goods for resale are valued by the business (and may be verified by an auditor who checks the accounts) at the end of each financial year, and the valuation is entered into the bookkeeping system (see page 144). We will set out the financial statements:

- before adjustments for items such as accruals and prepayments of expenses, income due and received in advance, depreciation charges of non-current assets, and irrecoverable debts (each of which will be dealt with in Chapter 12 and 15)
- in vertical presentation, ie in columnar form

On pages 144-146 we will illustrate the double-entry bookkeeping for amounts entered in the income statement.

INCOME STATEMENT

calculation of gross profit

The main activity of a trading business is to buy goods at one price and then to sell the same goods at a higher price. The difference between the two prices represents a profit known as **gross profit**. Instead of calculating the gross profit on each item bought and sold, we have seen how the bookkeeping system stores up the totals of transactions for the year in either purchases account or sales account. Further, any goods returned are recorded in either purchases returns account or sales returns account.

At the end of the financial year (which can end at any date – it does not have to be the calendar year) the totals of purchases and sales accounts, together with purchases returns and sales returns, are used to calculate gross profit. It is also necessary to take note of the value of inventories – goods for resale held at the beginning and end of the financial year.

The trading section of the income statement to show gross profit is set out in a columnar form as follows:

INCOME STATEMENT OF WYVERN WHOLESALERS
FOR THE YEAR ENDED 31 DECEMBER 20-1

	£	£	£
Revenue (Sales)			250,000
Less Sales returns			5,400
Net revenue (or turnover)			244,600
Opening inventory (1 January 20-1)		12,350	
Purchases	156,000		
Carriage in	–		
Less Purchases returns	7,200		
Net purchases		148,800	
		161,150	
Less Closing inventory (31 December 20-1)		16,300	
Cost of sales			144,850
Gross profit			99,750

*Note that, when using the columnar form, the right-hand column is the total column. Other columns are for showing figures used in sub-totals – these other columns do **not** represent debit and credit.*

Note the following:

- **Revenue** is the term used in trial balances and income statements to refer to sales, or net sales.
- **Sales and purchases** only include items in which the business trades – items to be kept for use in the business, such as machinery, are not included in sales and purchases but are classified as non-current assets.
- **Adjustments** are made for the value of inventory in the store or warehouse at the beginning and end of the financial year. The opening inventory is added to the purchases because it has been

sold during the year. The closing inventory is deducted from purchases because it has not been sold; it will form the opening inventory for the next financial year, when it will be added to next year's figure for purchases.

- The figure for **cost of sales** (or cost of goods sold) represents the cost to the business of the goods which have been sold in this financial year. Cost of sales is:

  opening inventory
  + purchases
  + carriage in (see below)
  – purchases returns
  – closing inventory
  = cost of sales (or cost of goods sold)

- **Gross profit** is calculated as:

  revenue (sales)
  – sales returns
  = net revenue
  – cost of sales
  = gross profit

  If cost of sales is greater than net revenue, the business has made a *gross loss*.

- **Carriage in** is the expense to the business of having purchases delivered (eg if you buy from a mail order company, you often have to pay the post and packing – this is the 'carriage in' cost). The cost of carriage in is added to purchases.

- **Net revenue** (often described as turnover) is:

  revenue (sales)
  – sales returns
  = net revenue

- **Net purchases** is:

  purchases
  + carriage in
  – purchases returns
  = net purchases

calculation of profit for the year

The income statement continues by listing the various expenses (overheads) of running the business. The total of expenses is deducted from gross profit to give **profit for the year**. Profit for the year is an important figure: it shows the profitability of the business after all expenses, and how much has been earned by the business for the owner. It is on this profit, after certain adjustments, that the tax liability will be based.

The calculation of profit for the year is set out as follows:

INCOME STATEMENT OF WYVERN WHOLESALERS
FOR THE YEAR ENDED 31 DECEMBER 20-1

	£	£	£
Gross profit			99,750
Add Discount received			2,500
			102,250
Less expenses:			
Discount allowed		3,700	
Salaries		46,000	
Electricity and gas		3,000	
Rent and business rates		2,000	
Sundry expenses		4,700	
			59,400
Profit for the year			42,850

Notes:

- The various expenses (overheads) shown in the income statement can be listed to suit the needs of a particular business: the headings used here are for illustrative purposes only.
- Amounts of income are also included in the income statement, eg discount received in the example; these are added to gross profit.
- Profit for the year is the amount the business earned for the owner(s); it is important to note that this is not the amount by which the cash/bank balance has increased during the year.
- If the total of expenses exceeds gross profit (and other income), the business has made a loss for the year.
- Drawings by the owner are not listed as an overhead in the income statement – instead, they are deducted from capital (see statement of financial position on page 140).
- If the owner of the business has taken goods for his or her own use, the amount should be deducted from purchases and added to drawings.

The two parts of the income statement are combined together, as shown at the top of the next page.

The income statement forms part of the double-entry bookkeeping system (see pages 144-146).

service sector businesses

You should note that when preparing the financial statements of a service sector business – such as a secretarial agency, a firm of solicitors, an estate agency, a doctors' practice – a gross profit figure will not be calculated because, instead of trading in goods, the business supplies services. The income statement, instead of calculating gross profit, will commence with the revenue from the business activity, such as 'fee income', 'income from clients', 'charges', 'work done'. Other items of revenue, such as discount received, are added, and the expenses are then listed and deducted to give the profit, or loss, for the year. An example is shown at the bottom of the next page.

INCOME STATEMENT OF WYVERN WHOLESALERS

FOR THE YEAR ENDED 31 DECEMBER 20-1

	£	£	£
Revenue (Sales)			250,000
Less Sales returns			5,400
Net revenue (or turnover)			244,600
Opening inventory (1 January 20-1)		12,350	
Purchases	156,000		
Carriage in	–		
Less Purchases returns	7,200		
Net purchases		148,800	
		161,150	
Less Closing inventory (31 December 20-1)		16,300	
Cost of sales			144,850
Gross profit			99,750
Add Discount received			2,500
			102,250
Less expenses:			
Discount allowed		3,700	
Salaries		46,000	
Electricity and gas		3,000	
Rent and business rates		2,000	
Sundry expenses		4,700	
			59,400
Profit for the year			42,850

INCOME STATEMENT OF WYVERN SECRETARIAL AGENCY

FOR THE YEAR ENDED 31 DECEMBER 20-1

	£	£
Revenue from clients		110,000
Less expenses:		
Salaries	64,000	
Heating and lighting	2,000	
Telephone	2,000	
Rent and business rates	6,000	
Sundry expenses	3,000	
		77,000
Profit for the year		33,000

STATEMENT OF FINANCIAL POSITION

The income statement shows two types of profit – gross profit and profit for the year (or such other time period as may be chosen by the business). A statement of financial position, by contrast, shows the state of the business at one moment in time. It lists the assets and the liabilities at a particular date, but is not part of the double-entry bookkeeping system.

The statement of financial position of Wyvern Wholesalers, using the figures from the trial balance on page 135, is as follows:

STATEMENT OF FINANCIAL POSITION OF WYVERN WHOLESALERS AS AT 31 DECEMBER 20-1

	£	£	£
Non-current Assets			
Property at cost			100,000
Equipment at cost			30,000
			130,000
Current Assets			
Inventory		16,300	
Trade receivables		23,850	
Cash		125	
		40,275	
Less Current Liabilities			
Trade payables	12,041		
Bank overdraft	851		
		12,892	
Net Current Assets or Working Capital			27,383
			157,383
Less Non-current Liabilities			
Loan			11,500
NET ASSETS			145,883
FINANCED BY			
Capital			
Opening capital			113,475
Add Profit for the year			42,850
			156,325
Less Drawings			10,442
			145,883

notes on the statement of financial position

- **assets**

  Assets are items or amounts owned or owed to the business, and are normally listed in increasing order of liquidity, ie the most permanent assets are listed first.

  Non-current assets are long-term assets purchased for use in the business and used over a long period (more than 12 months) to generate profits. They are divided between tangible non-current assets, which have material substance such as property, equipment, machinery, vehicles, and intangible non-current assets, such as goodwill (see below).

  Current assets are short-term assets held for less than 12 months. They change from day-to-day, such as inventory (which will be sold and replaced with new inventory), trade receivables (who will pay the amounts due and will be replaced by further amounts as credit sales are made), bank – if not overdrawn – and cash (note that bank and cash are often referred to as 'cash and cash equivalents' in limited company statements of financial position).

- **intangible non-current assets**

  Intangible non-current assets (not shown in the statement above) will appear on some statements of financial position, and are listed before the tangible non-current assets. An intangible asset does not have material substance, but belongs to the business and has value. A common example of an intangible non-current asset is goodwill, which is where a business has bought another business and paid an agreed amount for the existing reputation and customer connections (the goodwill).

- **liabilities**

  Liabilities are items or amounts owed by the business.

  Current liabilities are amounts owing at the date of the statement of financial position and due for repayment within 12 months or less (eg trade payables, bank overdraft).

  Non-current liabilities are where repayment is due in more than 12 months (eg loans, bank loans).

- **capital**

  Capital is money owed by the business to the owner. It is usual practice to show on the statement of financial position the owner's investment at the start of the year plus profit for the year less drawings for the year; this equals the owner's investment at the end of the year, ie at the date of the statement of financial position.

- **net current assets**

  Net current assets – often referred to as working capital – is the excess of current assets over current liabilities. Without net current assets, a business cannot continue to operate.

significance of the statement of financial position

The statement of financial position shows the assets used by the business and how they have been financed:

	Non-current assets
plus	Net current assets
less	Non-current liabilities
equals	Net assets
equals	Capital

The columnar presentation statement of financial position agrees the figure for net assets (£145,883), with capital.

Note that there are alternative columnar layouts for the statement of financial position, for example:

	Non-current assets
plus	Current assets
equals	Total assets

which balances against

	Capital
plus	Non-current liabilities
plus	Current liabilities
equals	Capital and liabilities

Preparation of Financial Statements from a Trial Balance

The trial balance contains the basic figures necessary to prepare the financial statements but, as we shall see in the next section, the figures are transferred from the double-entry accounts of the business. Nevertheless, the trial balance is a suitable summary from which to prepare the financial statements. The information needed for the preparation of the financial statements needs to be picked out from the trial balance in the following way:

- go through the trial balance and write against the items the financial statement in which each appears
- 'tick' each figure as it is used – each item from the trial balance appears in the financial statements once only

- the year-end (closing) inventory figure is not listed in the trial balance, but is shown as a note; the closing inventory appears twice in the financial statements – firstly in the income statement, and secondly in the statement of financial position (as a current asset).

If this routine is followed with the trial balance of Wyvern Wholesalers, it then appears as follows:

TRIAL BALANCE OF WYVERN WHOLESALERS AS AT 31 DECEMBER 20-1

	Dr £	Cr £		
Revenue (Sales)		250,000	IS	✔
Purchases	156,000		IS	✔
Sales returns	5,400		IS	✔
Purchases returns		7,200	IS	✔
Discount received		2,500	IS *(income)*	✔
Discount allowed	3,700		IS *(expense)*	✔
Inventory 1 January 20-1	12,350		IS	✔
Salaries	46,000		IS *(expense)*	✔
Electricity and gas	3,000		IS *(expense)*	✔
Rent and business rates	2,000		IS *(expense)*	✔
Sundry expenses	4,700		IS *(expense)*	✔
Property at cost	100,000		SOFP *(non-current asset)*	✔
Equipment at cost	30,000		SOFP *(non-current asset)*	✔
Trade receivables	23,850		SOFP *(current asset)*	✔
Bank overdraft		851	SOFP *(current liability)*	✔
Cash	125		SOFP *(current asset)*	✔
Trade payables		12,041	SOFP *(current liability)*	✔
Capital		113,475	SOFP *(capital)*	✔
Drawings	10,442		SOFP *(capital deduction)*	✔
Long-term loan		11,500	SOFP *(non-current liability)*	✔
	397,567	397,567		
Inventory at 31 December 20-1 is valued at £16,300			IS	✔
			SOFP *(current asset)*	✔

Note: IS = income statement; SOFP = statement of financial position

DOUBLE-ENTRY BOOKKEEPING AND THE FINANCIAL STATEMENTS

We have already noted earlier in this chapter that the income statement forms part of the double-entry bookkeeping system. Therefore, each amount recorded in the income statement must have an opposite entry elsewhere in the accounting system. In preparing the income statement we are, in effect, emptying each account that has been storing up a record of the transactions of the business during the course of the financial year and transferring it to the income statement.

sales, purchases and inventory accounts

In the income statement of Wyvern Wholesalers the balance of purchases account is transferred as follows (debit income statement; credit purchases account):

Dr **Purchases Account** Cr

20-1		£	20-1		£
31 Dec	Balance b/d (ie total for year)	156,000	31 Dec	Income statement	156,000

The account now has a nil balance and is ready to receive the transactions for next year.

The balances of sales, sales returns, and purchases returns accounts are cleared to nil in a similar way and the amounts transferred to the income statement, as debits or credits as appropriate.

Inventory account, however, is dealt with differently. Inventory is valued for financial accounting purposes at the end of each year (it is also likely to be valued more regularly in order to provide management information). Only the annual inventory valuation is recorded in inventory account, and the account is not used at any other time. After the bookkeeper has extracted the trial balance, but before preparation of the income statement, the inventory account appears as follows:

Dr **Inventory Account** Cr

20-1		£	20-1		£
31 Dec	Balance b/d	12,350			

This balance, which is the opening inventory valuation for the year, is transferred to the income statement to leave a nil balance, as follows (debit income statement; credit inventory account):

Dr **Inventory Account** Cr

20-1		£	20-1		£
31 Dec	Balance b/d	12,350	31 Dec	Income statement	12,350

The closing inventory valuation for the year is now recorded on the account as an asset (debit inventory account; credit income statement):

Dr		Inventory Account			Cr
20-1		£	20-1		£
31 Dec	Balance b/d	12,350	31 Dec	Income statement	12,350
31 Dec	Income statement	16,300	31 Dec	Balance c/d	16,300
20-2					
1 Jan	Balance b/d	16,300			

The closing inventory figure is shown on the statement of financial position as a current asset, and will be the opening inventory in next year's income statement.

expenses and income accounts

Expenses (overheads) and income items are transferred from the double-entry accounts to the income statement. For example, the salaries account of Wyvern Wholesalers has been storing up information during the year and, at the end of the year, the total is transferred to income statement (debit income statement; credit salaries account):

Dr		Salaries Account			Cr
20-1		£	20-1		£
31 Dec	Balance b/d (ie total for year)	46,000	31 Dec	Income statement	46,000

The salaries account now has a nil balance and is ready to receive transactions for 20-2, the next financial year.

profit for the year

After the income statement has been completed, the amount of profit (or loss) for the year is transferred to the owner's capital account. The bookkeeping entries are:

- **profit for the year**
  - debit income statement
  - credit capital account

- **loss for the year**
  - debit capital account
  - credit income statement

Profit increases the owner's stake in the business by adding to capital account, while a loss decreases the owner's stake.

drawings

At the same time the account for drawings, which has been storing up the amount of drawings during the year is also transferred to capital account:

- debit capital account
- credit drawings account

Thus the total of drawings for the year is debited to capital account.

capital account

When these transactions are completed, the capital account for Wyvern Wholesalers appears as:

Dr		Capital Account			Cr
20-1		£	20-1		£
31 Dec	Drawings for year	10,442	31 Dec	Balance b/d	113,475
31 Dec	Balance c/d	145,883	31 Dec	Income statement (profit for year)	42,850
		156,325			156,325
20-2			20-2		
			1 Jan	Balance b/d	145,883

Note: It is the balance of capital account at the end of the year, ie £145,883, which forms the total for the capital section of the statement of financial position. Whilst this figure could be shown by itself, it is usual to show capital at the start of the year, with profit for the year added, and drawings for the year deducted. In this way, the capital account is summarised on the statement of financial position.

statement of financial position

Unlike the income statement, the statement of financial position is not part of the double-entry accounts. The statement of financial position is made up of those accounts which remain with balances after the income statement transfers have been made. Thus it consists of asset and liability accounts, including capital.

A 'Pro-forma' Layout of Financial Statements

Many students studying financial statements for the first time find it helpful to be able to follow a set layout, or pro-forma – certainly in the early stages. A sample layout for financial statements is available as a free download from the Products and Resources section at www.osbornebooks.co.uk. Note that there are some items included in these financial statement layouts that will be covered in the later chapters of this book.

CHAPTER SUMMARY

- The financial statements of a business comprise:
  - income statement, which shows profit (or loss) for the year
  - statement of financial position, which shows the assets and liabilities of the business at the year-end

- The starting point for the preparation of financial statements is the summary of the information from the accounting records contained in the bookkeeper's trial balance.

- Each item from the trial balance is entered into the financial statements once only.

- Any notes to the trial balance, such as the closing inventory, affect the financial statements in two places.

- The income statement forms part of the double-entry bookkeeping system – amounts entered must be recorded elsewhere in the accounts.

- The statement of financial position is not part of the double-entry system; it lists the assets, liabilities and capital at a particular date.

There is more material in connection with financial statements later in this book:

- adjustments to the accounts: accruals and prepayments of expenses, income due and received in advance, depreciation charges of non-current assets, irrecoverable debts and provision for doubtful debts (Chapters 12 and 15)
- accounting concepts (Chapter 14)
- financial statements of limited companies (Chapter 17)
- the analysis and interpretation of financial statements – which gives the user information about the financial state of the business (Chapter 18)

In the next chapter we will see how the general journal is used as a book of prime entry to record transfers to the financial statements, and for the correction of errors.

QUESTIONS

visit **www.osbornebooks.co.uk** to take an online test

An asterisk (*) after the question number means that the answer is given at the end of this book.

9.1* The following information has been extracted from the business accounts of Matthew Lloyd for his first year of trading which ended on 31 December 20-8:

	£
Purchases	94,350
Revenue (Sales)	125,890
Inventory at 31 December 20-8	5,950
Office rent	4,850
Heating and lighting	2,120
Wages and salaries	10,350
Office equipment	8,500
Vehicles	10,750
Trade receivables	3,950
Bank balance	4,225
Cash	95
Trade payables	1,750
Capital at start of year	20,000
Drawings for year	8,450

You are to prepare the income statement of Matthew Lloyd for the year ended 31 December 20-8, together with his statement of financial position at that date.

9.2 Complete the table below for each item (a) to (g) indicating with a tick:

- whether the item would normally appear in the debit or credit column of the trial balance
- in which financial statement the item would appear at the end of the accounting period and whether as a debit or credit

	TRIAL BALANCE		FINANCIAL STATEMENTS			
			INCOME STATEMENT		FINANCIAL POSITION	
	Debit	Credit	Debit	Credit	Debit	Credit
(a) Salaries						
(b) Purchases						
(c) Trade receivables						
(d) Sales returns						
(e) Discount received						
(f) Vehicle						
(g) Capital						

9.3* You are to fill in the missing figures for the following businesses:

	Revenue (Sales)	Opening inventory	Purchases	Closing inventory	Gross profit	Expenses	Profit/(Loss)* for the year
	£	£	£	£	£	£	£
Business A	20 000	5 000	10 000	3 000	....	4 000	....
Business B	35 000	8 000	15 000	5 000	....	....	10 000
Business C	....	6 500	18 750	7 250	18 500	11 750	....
Business D	45 250	9 500	....	10 500	20 750	....	10 950
Business E	71 250	....	49 250	9 100	22 750	24 450	....
Business F	25 650	4 950	13 750	....	11 550	....	(3 450)

* Note: a loss for the year is indicated in brackets

9.4* The following trial balance has been extracted by the bookkeeper of John Adams at 31 December 20-7:

	Dr £	Cr £
Inventory at 1 January 20-7	14,350	
Purchases	114,472	
Revenue (Sales)		259,688
Office rent	13,718	
Heating and lighting	12,540	
Wages and salaries	42,614	
Vehicle expenses	5,817	
Advertising	6,341	
Property	75,000	
Office equipment	33,000	
Vehicles	21,500	
Trade receivables	23,854	
Bank	1,235	
Cash	125	
Capital at 1 January 20-7		62,500
Drawings	9,903	
Loan from bank		35,000
Trade payables		17,281
	374,469	374,469

Inventory at 31 December 20-7 is valued at £16,280.

You are to prepare the income statement of John Adams for the year ended 31 December 20-7, together with his statement of financial position at that date.

9.5 The following trial balance has been extracted by the bookkeeper of Clare Lewis at 31 December 20-4:

	Dr £	Cr £
Trade receivables	18,600	
Trade payables		12,140
Bank overdraft		5,820
Capital at 1 January 20-4		25,250
Revenue (Sales)		144,810
Purchases	96,318	
Inventory at 1 January 20-4	16,010	
Salaries	18,465	
Heating and lighting	1,820	
Rent and business rates	5,647	
Vehicles	9,820	
Office equipment	5,500	
Sundry expenses	845	
Vehicle expenses	1,684	
Drawings	13,311	
	188,020	188,020

Inventory at 31 December 20-4 is valued at £13,735.

You are to prepare the income statement of Clare Lewis for the year ended 31 December 20-4, together with her statement of financial position at that date.

9.6* The following balances have been taken from the books of Gina Campbell showing totals for the year ended 31 December 20-4.

	£
Revenue (Sales)	125,642
Purchases	55,261
Sales returns	1,347
Purchases returns	2,105
Carriage inwards	622

Carriage outwards	1,233
Inventory at 1 January 20-4	8,220
Inventory at 31 December 20-4	9,156
Wages	40,112
Other expenses	10,397

Required:

Prepare the income statement of Gina Campbell for the year ended 31 December 20-4.

9.7* The following information was provided by a sole trader for the year ended 30 September 20-7.

	£
Capital 1 October 20-6	83,000
Capital 30 September 20-7	79,000
Drawings	14,000

What was the business's profit or loss for the year ended 30 September 20-7?

A	Profit £4,000	
B	Profit £10,000	
C	Loss £4,000	
D	Loss £10,000	

9.8 The books of prime entry of Western Trading show the following totals for the month of June 20-4.

Totals for the month	**Amount**
	£
Sales journal	6,055
Sales returns journal	226
Purchases journal	4,123
Purchases returns journal	187

The balances in the general ledger, made up of the totals for April and May 20-4, are:

	£
Sales account	14,592
Sales returns account	468
Purchases account	7,317
Purchases returns account	429

The following information is also given:

	£
Inventory on 1 April 20-4	3,054
Inventory on 30 June 20-4	3,962
Carriage inwards for the three months	221

You are to complete the income statement as far as gross profit for the three months ended 30 June 20-4.

10 THE GENERAL JOURNAL AND CORRECTION OF ERRORS

The general journal – or journal – is the book of prime entry for non-regular transactions, eg opening entries at the start of a business, purchase and sale of non-current assets on credit, correction of errors and end-of-year ledger transfers.

As a book of prime entry, the general journal is not part of double-entry bookkeeping; instead the journal is used to list transactions before they are entered into the accounts. In this way, the journal completes the accounting system by providing the book of prime entry for non-regular transactions.

Uses of the General Journal

The general journal – or journal – completes the accounting system by providing the book of prime entry for non-regular transactions, which are not recorded in any other book of prime entry. The categories of such non-regular transactions include:

- opening entries at the start of a business
- purchase and sale of non-current assets on credit
- correction of errors
- year-end ledger transfers

The reasons for using a journal are:

- to provide a book of prime entry for non-regular transactions
- to eliminate the need for remembering why non-regular transactions were put through the accounts – the journal acts as a notebook
- to reduce the risk of fraud, by making it difficult for unauthorised transactions to be entered in the accounting system
- to reduce the risk of errors, by listing the transactions that are to be put into the double-entry accounts
- to ensure that entries can be traced back to a source document, thus providing an audit trail for non-regular transactions

The General Journal – a Book of Prime Entry

The general journal is a book of prime entry; it is used to record the transactions that will be entered into the double-entry bookkeeping system. The accounting system for non-regular transactions is as follows:

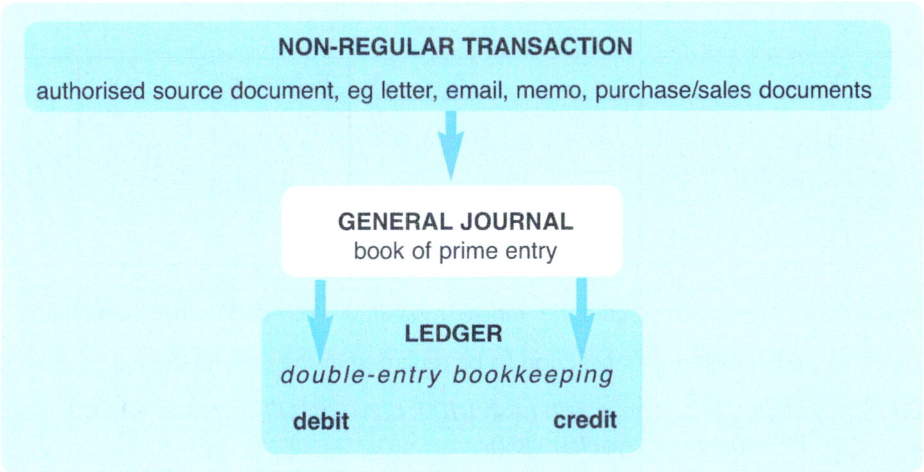

Study the way the general journal is set out with a sample transaction, and then read the notes that follow.

Date	Details	Reference	Dr	Cr
20-1			£	£
1 Jan	Bank	GL	10,000	
	Capital	GL		10,000
	Opening capital introduced			

- the names of the accounts to be debited and credited in the bookkeeping system are written in the details column; it is customary to show the debit transaction first
- the money amount of each debit and credit is stated in the appropriate columns
- the reference column cross-references to the division of the ledger where each account will be found – general ledger (GL), sales ledger (SL), purchases ledger (PL); an account number can also be included (note that the cash book – containing bank account – is in the general ledger)
- a journal entry always balances, ie debit and credit entries are for the same amount or total
- it is usual to include a brief narrative explaining why the transaction is being carried out, and making reference to the source document whenever possible (when answering questions you should always include a narrative unless specifically told otherwise)
- each journal entry is complete in itself and is ruled off to separate it from the next entry

Opening Entries

These are the transactions which open the accounts at the start of a new business. For example, a first business transaction is:

1 Jan 20-1 *Started in business with £10,000 in the bank*

This non-regular transaction is entered in the general journal as follows:

Date	Details	Reference	Dr	Cr
20-1			£	£
1 Jan	Bank	GL	10,000	
	Capital	GL		10,000
	Opening capital introduced			

After the journal entry has been made, the transaction can be recorded in the double-entry accounts.

Here is another opening entries transaction to be recorded in the general journal:

1 Feb 20-2 *Started in business with cash £100, bank £5,000, inventory £1,000, machinery £2,500, trade payables £850*

The journal entry is:

Date	Details	Reference	Dr	Cr
20-2			£	£
1 Feb	Cash	GL	100	
	Bank	GL	5,000	
	Inventory	GL	1,000	
	Machinery	GL	2,500	
	Trade payables	PL		850
	Capital	GL		7,750
			8,600	8,600
	Assets and liabilities at the start of business			

Notes:

- Capital is in this example the balancing figure, ie assets minus liabilities.
- The journal is the book of prime entry for all opening entries, including cash and bank; however the normal book of prime entry for other cash/bank transactions is the cash book.
- The amounts from the journal entry will now need to be recorded in the double-entry accounts.

Purchase and Sale of Non-Current Assets on Credit

The purchase and sale of non-current assets are non-regular business transactions which are recorded in the journal as the book of prime entry. Only credit transactions are entered in the journal (because cash/bank transactions are recorded in the cash book as the book of prime entry). However, a business (or an examination question) may choose to journalise cash entries: strictly, though, this is incorrect as two books of prime entry are being used.

15 Apr 20-3 *Bought a machine for £1,000 on credit from Machinery Supplies Limited, purchase order no 2341.*

Date	Details	Reference	Dr	Cr
20-3			£	£
15 Apr	Machinery	GL	1,000	
	Machinery Supplies Limited*	PL		1,000
	Purchase of machine, purchase order 2341			

20 May 20-4 *Car sold for £2,500 on credit to Wyvern Motors Limited.*

Date	Details	Reference	Dr	Cr
20-4			£	£
20 May	Wyvern Motors Limited*	SL	2,500	
	Disposals**	GL		2,500
	Sale of car, registration no VU64 XXX			

When a business has bought non-current assets for use in the business from a supplier and the assets are returned – for example, because they are faulty – a journal entry is needed to record this non-regular transaction. For example:

16 June 20-6 *A computer for use in the business and bought on credit from Computer Supplies Limited for £750 is faulty and is returned to the supplier*

Date	Details	Reference	Dr	Cr
20-6			£	£
16 June	Computer Supplies Limited*	PL	750	
	Computer	GL		750
	Return of faulty computer, returns note 347			

* Instead of entering these transactions in the purchases ledger and sales ledger, an alternative treatment would be to open general ledger accounts as 'other payables' (Machinery Supplies Limited and Computer Supplies Limited) and 'other receivables' (Wyvern Motors Limited). This would avoid confusion with trade payables (in the purchases ledger) and trade receivables (in the sales ledger).

** Accounting for the disposal of non-current assets is dealt with in Chapter 13.

Correction of Errors

In any bookkeeping system there is always the possibility of an error. Ways to avoid errors, or ways to reveal them sooner, include:

- division of the accounting function between a number of people
- regular circulation of statements to trade receivables, who will check the transactions on their accounts and advise any discrepancies
- checking statements received from trade payables
- extraction of a trial balance at regular intervals
- the preparation of bank reconciliation statements (see Chapter 8)
- checking cash balances against cash held
- the use of control accounts (see Chapter 11)
- the use of a computer accounting program

Despite all these precautions, errors will still occur from time-to-time. In this chapter we will describe:

- correction of errors not shown by a trial balance
- correction of errors shown by a trial balance, using a suspense account
- the effect of correcting errors on profit for the year and the statement of financial position

errors not shown by a trial balance

In Chapter 5, page 66, we have already seen that some types of errors in a bookkeeping system are not revealed by a trial balance. These are:

- error of omission
- reversal of entries
- mispost/error of commission
- error of principle
- error of original entry (or transcription)
- compensating error

Although these errors are not shown by a trial balance, they are likely to come to light if the procedures suggested above are followed. For example, a trade receivable will soon let you know if her account has been debited with goods she did not buy. When an error is found, it needs to be corrected by means of a journal entry which shows the bookkeeping entries that have been made.

We will now look at an example of each of the errors not shown by a trial balance, and will see how it is corrected by means of a general journal entry. (A practical hint which may help in correcting errors is to write out the 'T' accounts as they appear with the error; then write in the correcting entries and see if the result has achieved what was intended.) Note that the journal narrative includes document details.

Error of Omission

Credit sale of goods, £200 on invoice 4967 to H Jarvis completely omitted from the accounting system; the error is corrected on 12 May 20-8

Date	Details	Reference	Dr	Cr
20-8			£	£
12 May	H Jarvis	SL	200	
	Sales	GL		200
	Correction of error of omission: invoice 4967 omitted from the accounts			

This type of error can happen in a very small business – often where the bookkeeping is done by one person. For example, an invoice, when typed out, is 'lost' down the back of a filing cabinet. In a large business, particularly one using a computer accounting system, it should be impossible for this error to occur. Also, if documents are numbered serially, then none should be mislaid.

Reversal of Entries

A payment, on 3 May 20-8 by bank transfer of £50 to a trade payable, S Wright, has been debited in the cash book and credited to Wright's account; this is corrected on 12 May 20-8

Date	Details	Reference	Dr	Cr
20-8			£	£
12 May	S Wright	PL	50	
	Bank	GL		50
	S Wright	PL	50	
	Bank	GL		50
			100	100
	Correction of reversal of entries: bank transfer for £50 dated 3 May 20-8			

To correct this type of error it is best to reverse the entries that have been made incorrectly (the first two journal entries), and then to put through the correct entries. This is preferable to debiting Wright £100 and crediting £100 to bank account: this is because there was never a transaction for £100 – the original transaction was for £50.

As noted earlier, it is often an idea to write out the 'T' accounts, complete with the error, and then to write in the correcting entries. As an example, the two accounts involved in this last error are shown with the error made on 3 May, and the corrections made on 12 May indicated by the shading (the opening credit balance of S Wright's account is shown as £50):

Dr		S Wright			Cr
20-8		£	20-8		£
12 May	Bank	50	1 May	Balance b/d	50
12 May	Bank	50	3 May	Bank	50
		100			100

Dr		Cash Book (bank columns)			Cr
20-8		£	20-8		£
3 May	S Wright	50	12 May	S Wright	50
			12 May	S Wright	50

The accounts now show a net debit transaction of £50 on S Wright's account, and a net credit transaction of £50 on bank account, which is how this payment to a trade payable should have been recorded in order to clear the balance on the account.

Mispost/Error of Commission

Credit sale of goods £47 on invoice 5327 have been debited to the account of J Adams, instead of the account of J Adams Ltd; the error is corrected on 15 May 20-8

Date	Details	Reference	Dr	Cr
20-8			£	£
15 May	J Adams Ltd	SL	47	
	J Adams	SL		47
	Correction of error of commission:			
	mispost of invoice 5327			

This type of error can be avoided, to some extent, by the use of account numbers, and by persuading the customer to quote the account number or reference on each transaction.

Error of Principle

The cost of fuel, £30, has been debited to vehicles account; the error is corrected on 20 May 20-8

Date	Details	Reference	Dr	Cr
20-8			£	£
20 May	Vehicle expenses	GL	30	
	Vehicles	GL		30
	Correction of error of principle:			
	fuel debited to vehicles account in error			

This type of error is similar to a mispost except that, instead of the wrong person's account being used, it is the wrong class of account. In this example, the vehicle expenses must be kept separate from the cost of the asset (the vehicle), otherwise the expense and asset accounts will be incorrect, leading to profit for the year being overstated and the non-current asset being shown in the statement of financial position at too high a figure.

Error of Original Entry (or Transcription)

Postages of £45 paid by debit card entered in the accounts as £54; the error is corrected on 27 May 20-8

Date	Details	Reference	Dr	Cr
20-8			£	£
27 May	Bank	GL	54	
	Postages	GL		54
	Postages	GL	45	
	Bank	GL		45
			99	99
	Correction of error original entry: postages of £45			
	entered into the accounts as £54			

This error could have been corrected by debiting bank and crediting postages with £9, being the difference between the two amounts. However, there was no original transaction for this amount, and it is better to reverse the wrong transaction and put through the correct one. A reversal of figures either has a difference of nine (as above), or an amount divisible by nine. An error of original entry can also be a 'bad' figure on a business document, entered wrongly into both accounts.

COMPENSATING ERROR

Rent paid account is added up by £100 more than it should be (ie it is overadded or overcast); sales account is also overcast by the same amount; the error is corrected on 31 May 20-8

Date	Details	Reference	Dr	Cr
20-8			£	£
31 May	Sales	GL	100	
	Rent paid	GL		100
	Correction of compensating error: overcast on rent paid account and sales account			

Here, an account with a debit balance – rent paid – has been overcast; this is compensated by an overcast on an account with a credit balance – sales. There are several permutations on this theme, eg two debit balances, one overcast, one undercast; a debit balance undercast, a credit balance undercast.

important notes to remember

We have just looked at several journal entries in connection with the correction of errors. Remember that:

- The general journal is the book of prime entry for non-regular transactions. The journal entries must then be recorded in the bookkeeping system.
- When a business uses control accounts (see Chapter 11), the transactions from the journal must be recorded in the sales ledger control account or purchase ledger control account as well as in the sales ledger or purchases ledger accounts of trade receivables or trade payables.

TRIAL BALANCE ERRORS: USE OF SUSPENSE ACCOUNT

There are many types of errors revealed by a trial balance. Included amongst these are:

- omission of one part of the double-entry transaction
- recording two debits or two credits for a transaction
- recording a different amount for a transaction on the debit side from the credit side
- errors in the calculation of balances (not compensated by other errors)
- error in transferring the balance of an account to the trial balance
- error of addition in the trial balance

When errors are shown, the trial balance is 'balanced' by recording the difference in a suspense account, as shown in the worked example on the next page.

WORKED EXAMPLE: SUSPENSE ACCOUNT

The bookkeeper of a business is unable to balance the trial balance on 31 December 20-1. As the error or errors cannot be found quickly the trial balance is balanced by recording the difference in a suspense account, as follows:

	Dr	Cr
	£	£
Trial balance totals	100,000	99,850
Suspense account		150
	100,000	100,000

A suspense account is opened in the general ledger with, in this case, a credit balance of £150:

Dr		**Suspense Account**			Cr
20-1	£	20-1			£
		31 Dec	Trial balance difference		150

A detailed examination of the bookkeeping system is now made in order to find the errors. As errors are found, they are corrected by means of a journal entry. The journal entries will balance, with one part of the entry being either a debit or credit to suspense account. In this way, the balance on suspense account is eliminated by bookkeeping transactions. Using the above suspense account, the following errors are found and corrected on 15 January 20-2:

- sales account is undercast by £100
- a bank transfer to a trade payable, A Wilson, for £65, has been recorded in the bank as £56
- telephone expenses of £55 paid by direct debit have not been entered in the expenses account
- stationery expenses £48 paid by debit card have been debited to both the stationery account and the bank account

These errors are corrected by general journal entries shown on the next page. Note that the journal narrative includes details of dates taken from the records of the business.

Date	Details	Reference	Dr	Cr
20-2			£	£
15 Jan	Suspense	GL	100	
	Sales	GL		100
	Undercast on 23 December 20-1 now corrected			
15 Jan	Bank	GL	56	
	Suspense	GL		56
	Suspense	GL	65	
	Bank	GL		65
			121	121
	Bank transfer to A Wilson for £65 on 30 December 20-1 entered in bank as £56 in error			
15 Jan	Telephone expenses	GL	55	
	Suspense	GL		55
	Omission of entry in expenses account			
15 Jan	Suspense	GL	48	
	Bank	GL		48
	Suspense	GL	48	
	Bank	GL		48
			96	96
	Payment of stationery expenses debited in error to bank account			

After these journal entries have been recorded in the accounts, suspense account appears as:

Suspense Account

Dr		£		Cr	£
20-2		£	20-1		£
15 Jan	Sales	100	31 Dec	Trial balance difference	150
15 Jan	Bank	65	20-2		
15 Jan	Bank	48	15 Jan	Bank	56
15 Jan	Bank	48	15 Jan	Telephone expenses	55
		261			261

Thus all the errors have now been found, and suspense account has a nil balance.

Note that if financial statements have to be prepared after creating a suspense account but before the errors are found, the balance of suspense account is shown, depending on the balance, as either a current asset (debit balance) or a current liability (credit balance) on the statement of financial position. Nevertheless, the error must be found at a later date and suspense account eliminated.

EFFECT ON PROFIT FOR THE YEAR AND THE STATEMENT OF FINANCIAL POSITION

The correction of errors, whether shown by a trial balance or not, often has an effect on the profit for the year figure calculated before the errors were found. For example, an undercast of sales account, when corrected, will increase gross profit and profit for the year and, of course, the profit figure shown in the statement of financial position. Some errors, however, only affect the statement of financial position, eg errors involving trade receivables' and trade payables' accounts. The diagram that follows shows the effect of errors when corrected on gross profit, profit for the year and the statement of financial position.

INCOME STATEMENT

Correction of error	Gross profit	Profit for the year	Statement of FP
sales undercast/understated	increase	increase	profit increase
sales overcast/overstated	decrease	decrease	profit decrease
purchases undercast/understated	decrease	decrease	profit decrease
purchases overcast/overstated	increase	increase	profit increase
opening inventory undervalued	decrease	decrease	profit decrease
opening inventory overvalued	increase	increase	profit increase
closing inventory undervalued	increase	increase	profit increase inventory increase
closing inventory overvalued	decrease	decrease	profit decrease inventory decrease
expense undercast/understated	-	decrease	profit decrease
expense overcast/overstated	-	increase	profit increase
income undercast/understated	-	increase	profit increase
income overcast/overstated	-	decrease	profit decrease

STATEMENT OF FINANCIAL POSITION

Correction of error	Gross profit	Profit for the year	Statement of FP
asset undercast/understated	-	-	increase asset
asset overcast/overstated	-	-	decrease asset
liability undercast/understated	-	-	increase liability
liability overcast/overstated	-	-	decrease liability

Some examination questions on correction of errors require the preparation of a statement showing the amended profit for the year after errors have been corrected. We will look at the errors shown on page 163 and see how their correction affects the profit for the year (assume the profit before adjustments is £10,000).

Statement of corrected profit for the year ended 31 December 20-1

	£
Profit for the year (unadjusted)	10,000
Add sales undercast	100
	10,100
Less additional telephone expenses	55
Adjusted profit for the year	10,045

Note: the other two errors do not affect profit.

The effect on the statement of financial position of correcting the errors is:

- profit for the year increases £45
- bank balance reduces £105 (+£56, –£65, –£48, –£48)
- the credit balance of £150 in suspense account (shown as a current liability) is eliminated

The statement of financial position will now balance without the need for a suspense account – the errors have been found and corrected.

YEAR-END LEDGER TRANSFERS

Any other non-regular transactions or adjustments need to be recorded in the general journal. These usually take place at the end of the financial year and are concerned with:

- transfers to the income statement
- expenses charged to the owner's drawings
- goods for the owner's use
- irrecoverable debts written off

transfers to income statement

As we have seen in the previous chapter, the income statement forms part of double-entry bookkeeping. Therefore, each amount recorded in income statement must have an opposite entry in another account: such transfers are recorded in the general journal as the book of prime entry, as shown by the entries which follow.

31 Dec 20-1 *Balance of sales account at the year end, £155,000, transferred to the income statement (debit sales account; credit income statement)*

Date	Details	Reference	Dr	Cr
20-1			£	£
31 Dec	Sales	GL	155,000	
	Income statement	GL		155,000
	Transfer to income statement of sales for the year			

31 Dec 20-1 *Balance of purchases account at the year-end, £105,000, transferred to the income statement (debit income statement; credit purchases account)*

Date	Details	Reference	Dr	Cr
20-1			£	£
31 Dec	Income statement	GL	105,000	
	Purchases	GL		105,000
	Transfer to income statement of purchases for the year			

31 Dec 20-1 *Closing inventory has been valued at £12,500 and is to be entered into the accounts*

Date	Details	Reference	Dr	Cr
20-1			£	£
31 Dec	Inventory	GL	12,500	
	Income statement	GL		12,500
	Inventory valuation at 31 December 20-1 transferred to income statement			

Remember that the closing inventory valuation for the year is recorded in inventory account as an asset (*debit* inventory account; *credit* income statement).

31 Dec 20-1 *Balance of wages account, £23,500, transferred to income statement (debit income statement; credit wages account)*

Date	Details	Reference	Dr	Cr
20-1			£	£
31 Dec	Income statement	GL	23,500	
	Wages	GL		23,500
	Transfer to income statement of expenditure for the year			

expenses charged to owner's drawings

Sometimes the owner of a business uses business facilities for private use, eg telephone, or car. The owner will agree that part of the expense shall be charged to him or her as drawings, while the other part represents a business expense. The bookkeeping entry to record the private use adjustment is:

- debit drawings account
- credit expense account, eg telephone

31 Dec 20-1 *The balance of telephone account is £600; one-quarter of this is the estimated cost of the owner's private usage*

The journal entry is:

Date	Details	Reference	Dr	Cr
20-1			£	£
31 Dec	Drawings	GL	150	
	Telephone	GL		150
	Transfer of private expenses to drawings account			

goods for the owner's use

When the owner of a business takes some of the goods in which the business trades for his or her own use, the double-entry bookkeeping is:

- debit drawings account
- credit purchases account

15 Oct 20-1 *Owner of the business takes goods for own use, £105*

The journal entry is:

Date	Details	Reference	Dr	Cr
20-1			£	£
15 Oct	Drawings	GL	105	
	Purchases	GL		105
	Goods taken for own use by the owner			

irrecoverable debts written off

An irrecoverable debt is a debt owing to a business which it considers will never be paid.

One of the problems of selling goods and services on credit terms is that, from time-to-time, some customers will not pay. As a consequence, the balances of such trade receivables' accounts have to be written off when they become uncollectable. This happens when all reasonable efforts to recover the amounts owing have been exhausted, ie statements and letters have been sent to the trade receivable requesting payment, and legal action – where appropriate – or the threat of legal action has failed to obtain payment.

In writing off a trade receivable's account as irrecoverable, the business is bearing the cost of the amount due. The trade receivable's account is written off as irrecoverable and the amount (or amounts where a number of accounts are dealt with in this way) is debited to irrecoverable debts written off account.

Towards the financial year-end it is good practice to go through the trade receivables' accounts to see if any need to be written off. The bookkeeping entries for this are:

- debit irrecoverable debts written off account
- credit trade receivable's account

15 Dec 20-1 Write off the account of T Hughes, which has a balance of £25, as an irrecoverable debt

The journal entry is:

Date	Details	Reference	Dr	Cr
20-1			£	£
15 Dec	Irrecoverable debts written off	GL	25	
	T Hughes	SL		25
	Account written off as an irrecoverable debt – see memo dated 14 December 20-1			

Note that in Chapter 12 we will see how irrecoverable debts are dealt with in the financial statements.

Making Journal Entries

As we have seen in this chapter, the general journal is the book of prime entry for non-regular transactions. Because of the irregular nature of journal transactions, it is important that they are correctly authorised by the appropriate person – such as the accounts supervisor, the administration manager, the owner of the business. The authorisation will, ideally, be a source document – eg letter, memo, email or other document – but may well be verbal – eg "make the year-end ledger transfers to income statement", or "find the errors and put them right".

It is good practice to ensure that journal entries are checked by an appropriate person before they are entered into the double-entry bookkeeping system. It is all too easy to get a journal entry the wrong way round resulting in an error becoming twice as much as it was in the first place!

CHAPTER SUMMARY

- The general journal is used to list non-regular transactions.
- The general journal is a book of prime entry – it is not a double-entry account.
- The general journal is used for:
  - opening entries at the start of a business
  - purchase and sale of non-current assets on credit
  - correction of errors
  - year-end ledger transfers
- Correction of errors is always a difficult topic to put into practice: it tests knowledge of bookkeeping procedures and it is all too easy to make the error worse than it was in the first place! The secret of dealing with this topic well is to write down – in account format – what has gone wrong. It should then be relatively easy to see what has to be done to put the error right.
- Errors not shown by a trial balance: error of omission, reversal of entries, mispost/error of commission, error of principle, error of original entry (or transcription), compensating error.
- Errors shown by a trial balance include: omission of one part of the bookkeeping transaction, recording two debits/credits for a transaction, recording different amounts in the two accounts, calculating balances, transferring balances to the trial balance.
- All errors are non-regular transactions and need to be corrected by means of a general journal entry: the bookkeeper then needs to record the correcting transactions in the accounts.
- When error(s) are shown by a trial balance, the amount is placed into a suspense account. As the errors are found, journal entries are made which 'clear out' the suspense account.
- Correction of errors may have an effect on gross profit and profit for the year, and on the figures in the statement of financial position. It may be necessary to restate profit and to adjust the statement of financial position.

In the next chapter we look at the use of control accounts which are used as a checking device for a section of the ledgers.

QUESTIONS

visit
www.osbornebooks.co.uk
to take an online test

An asterisk (*) after the question number means that the answer is given at the end of this book.

10.1* Lucy Wallis started in business on 1 May 20-8 with the following assets and liabilities:

	£
Vehicle	6,500
Fixtures and fittings	2,800
Opening inventory	4,100
Cash	150
Loan from husband	5,000

You are to prepare Lucy's opening general journal entry, showing clearly her capital at 1 May 20-8.

10.2 Show the general journal entries for the following transfers which relate to Trish Hall's business for the year ended 31 December 20-8:

(a) Closing inventory is to be recorded in the accounts at a valuation of £22,600.

(b) Telephone expenses for the year, amounting to £890, are to be transferred to the income statement.

(c) Vehicle expenses account shows a balance of £800; one-quarter of this is for Trish Hall's private expenses; three-quarters is to be transferred to the income statement.

(d) Trish has taken goods for her own use of £175.

(e) The sales ledger account of N Marshall, which has a debit balance of £125, is to be written off as an irrecoverable debt.

10.3* Henry Lewis's business sells office stationery. He uses the following books of prime entry:

- general journal
- sales journal
- purchases journal
- sales returns journal
- purchases returns journal
- cash book

The following business transactions take place:

(a) He receives an invoice from Temeside Traders for £956 for goods supplied on credit.

(b) He issues an invoice to Malvern Models for £176 of goods.

(c) He buys a computer for use in his business for £2,000 on credit from A-Z Computers Limited.

(d) He issues a credit note to Johnson Brothers for £55 of goods.

(e) A trade receivable, Melanie Fisher, settles the balance of her account, £107, by bank transfer.

(f) He makes cash sales of £25.

(g) Henry Lewis withdraws cash £100 for his own use.

(h) He pays a trade payable, Stationery Supplies Limited, the balance of the account, £298, by bank transfer.

(i) A trade receivable, Jim Bowen, with an account balance of £35 is to be written off as an irrecoverable debt.

(j) A credit note for £80 is received from a trade payable, Ian Johnson.

You are to take each business transaction in turn and state:

- the name of the book of prime entry
- the name of the account to be debited
- the name of the account to be credited

10.4

The trial balance of Thomas Wilson balanced. However, a number of errors have been found in the bookkeeping system:

(a) Credit sale of £150 to J Rigby has not been entered in the accounts.

(b) A bank transfer for £125 to H Price Limited, a trade payable, has been recorded in the account of H Prince.

(c) The cost of a new delivery van, £10,000, has been entered to vehicle expenses account.

(d) Postages of £55, paid by debit card, have been entered on the wrong sides of both accounts.

(e) The totals of the purchases journal and the purchases returns journal have both been undercast by £100.

(f) A bank transfer for £89 from L Johnson, a trade receivable, has been entered in the accounts as £98.

You are to take each error in turn and:

- state the type of error
- show the correcting general journal entry

10.5*

Jeremy Johnson extracts a trial balance from his bookkeeping records on 30 September 20-8. Unfortunately the trial balance fails to balance and the difference, £19 debit, is placed to a suspense account pending further investigation.

The following errors are later found:

(a) A bank transfer of £85 for office expenses has been entered in the cash book but no entry has been made in the office expenses account.

(b) Photocopying of £87, paid by debit card, has been correctly entered in the cash book, but is shown as £78 in the photocopying account.

(c) The sales returns journal has been overcast by £100.

(d) Commission income of £25 has been entered twice in the account.

You are to:

- make general journal entries to correct the errors
- show the suspense account after the errors have been corrected

10.6* A business bought a computer for use in the business on credit from a supplier. The computer was delivered damaged and is returned to the supplier.

How should the return of the computer be recorded in the accounting system of the business?

	Book of prime entry	Debit	Credit	
A	General journal	Computer	Supplier	
B	Purchases returns journal	Supplier	Purchases returns	
C	General journal	Supplier	Computer	
D	Purchases returns journal	Purchases returns	Supplier	

10.7* A payment for computer repairs has been entered in the computers account.

Which of the following correctly describes the type of error and corrections to be made?

	Type of error	Entries to correct the error		
		Debit	Credit	
A	Principle	Computers	Computer repairs	
B	Commission	Computers	Computer repairs	
C	Principle	Computer repairs	Computers	
D	Commission	Computer repairs	Computers	

10.8* A trial balance failed to balance. The debit column totalled £154,896 and the credit column totalled £155,279. What entry would be made in the suspense account to balance the trial balance?

A	£766 debit	
B	£383 debit	
C	£383 credit	
D	£766 credit	

10.9* A trial balance fails to agree by £75 and the difference is placed in a suspense account. Later it is found that a cash sale for this amount has not been entered in the sales account. Which one of the following general journal entries is correct?

A	Debit suspense account £75; credit sales account £75	
B	Debit suspense account £150; credit sales account £150	
C	Debit sales account £75; credit suspense account £75	
D	Credit sales account £75	

10.10 Lisa Lanyon has drawn up a suspense account at 31 December 20-1 following the discovery of errors in her accounting system.

Required:

(a) Name two accounting techniques which may have been used to detect the presence of errors in the accounting system.

....

....

(b) Show the entries in the general journal below to correct the following errors (narratives are not required):

(1) The purchases journal has been undercast by £200.

(2) The balance of sales return account has been recorded as £320; it should be £230.

(3) Discount received of £110 has been recorded in the cash book but omitted from discount received account.

(4) A bank payment to T Smith, a trade payable, for £210 has been entered in the account of J Smith in error.

GENERAL JOURNAL

Account	Debit £	Credit £

10.11* The totals of Fran Smith's trial balance on 30 June 20-3 did not agree.

The totals were:

Debit £76,335 Credit £76,550

She entered the difference in a suspense account. On checking the books, she discovered the following errors.

1. Purchases account was overcast by £250.
2. Rent paid of £650, entered in the cash book, had been omitted from the expense account.
3. Wages of £580 paid for the week ended 30 June 20-3 had been recorded as £850 in wages account.
4. Discount allowed of £85 had been recorded in the cash book but omitted from discount allowed account.

Required:

(a) Enter the trial balance difference in the suspense account below. Make the entries necessary to correct the errors.

Dr **Suspense Account** **Cr**

Date 20-3	Details	£	Date 20-3	Details	£

(b) Explain clearly, using an example, why some types of error are not revealed by a trial balance.

11 CONTROL ACCOUNTS

Control accounts are 'master' accounts which are part of the verification process of the double-entry records. They control a number of ledger accounts (see the diagram below).

A control account (also known as a totals account) is used to record the totals of transactions passing through the ledger accounts.

In this way, the balance of the control account will always be equal (unless an error has occurred) to the total balances of the ledger accounts.

Two commonly-used control accounts are:

- sales ledger control account – the total of the trade receivables
- purchases ledger control account – the total of the trade payables

In this chapter we look at:

- the concept of control accounts
- the layout of sales ledger and purchases ledger control accounts
- the use of control accounts as an aid to the management of a business

The Concept of Control Accounts

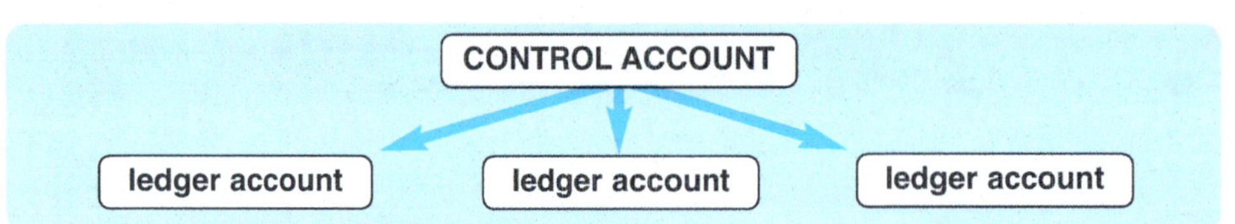

The illustration above shows how a control account acts as a master account for a number of ledger accounts. The principle is that, if the total of the opening balances for the ledger accounts is known, together with the total of amounts increasing these balances, and the total of amounts decreasing these balances, then the total of the closing balances for the ledger accounts can be calculated.

For example:

	£
Total of opening balances	50,000
Add increases	10,000
	60,000
Less decreases	12,000
Total of closing balances	48,000

The total of the closing balances can now be checked against a separate listing of the ledger accounts to ensure that the two figures agree. If so, it proves that the ledgers within the section are correct (subject to any errors such as misposts and compensating errors). Let us now apply this concept to one of the divisions of the ledger – sales ledger.

The diagram on the next page shows the personal accounts which form the entire sales ledger of a particular business (in practice there would, of course, be more than four accounts involved). The sales ledger control account acts as a total account, which records totals of the transactions passing through the individual accounts which it controls. Notice that transactions appear in the control account on the same side as they appear in the individual accounts. It follows that the control account acts as a checking device for the individual accounts which it controls. Thus, control accounts act as an aid to locating errors: if the control account and the ledger accounts agree, then the error is likely to lie elsewhere. In this way the control account acts as an intermediate checking device – proving the arithmetical accuracy of the ledger section.

Normally the whole of a ledger section is controlled by one control account, eg sales ledger control account and purchases ledger control account. However, it is also possible to have a number of separate control accounts for subdivisions of the sales ledger and purchases ledger, eg sales ledger control account A-K, purchases ledger control account S-Z, etc. It is for a business – the user of the accounting system – to decide what is most suitable, taking into account the number of accounts in the sales and purchases ledger, together with the type of bookkeeping system – manual or computerised.

In the diagram on the next page the balances on the sales ledger control account and the sales ledger accounts are reconciled at the beginning and end of the month, as follows:

Reconciliation of sales ledger control account with trade receivable balances

	1 January 20-1	31 January 20-1
	£	£
A Ackroyd	100	150
B Barnes	200	200
C Cox	50	180
D Douglas	150	150
Sales ledger control account	500	680

Note: The business will decide how often to reconcile the control account with the ledger accounts – weekly, monthly, quarterly or annually. Any discrepancy should be investigated immediately and the error(s) traced.

Dr			SALES LEDGER CONTROL ACCOUNT		Cr
20-1		£	20-1		£
1 Jan	Balance b/d	500	31 Jan	Bank	443
31 Jan	Sales	700	31 Jan	Discount allowed	7
			31 Jan	Sales returns	70
			31 Jan	Balance c/d	680
		1,200			1,200
1 Feb	Balance b/d	680			

Dr			A Ackroyd		Cr
20-1		£	20-1		£
1 Jan	Balance b/d	100	10 Jan	Bank	98
6 Jan	Sales	150	10 Jan	Discount allowed	2
			31 Jan	Balance c/d	150
		250			250
1 Feb	Balance b/d	150			

Dr			B Barnes		Cr
20-1		£	20-1		£
1 Jan	Balance b/d	200	13 Jan	Bank	195
6 Jan	Sales	250	13 Jan	Discount allowed	5
			27 Jan	Sales returns	50
			31 Jan	Balance c/d	200
		450			450
1 Feb	Balance b/d	200			

Dr			C Cox		Cr
20-1		£	20-1		£
1 Jan	Balance b/d	50	20 Jan	Bank	50
15 Jan	Sales	200	29 Jan	Sales returns	20
			31 Jan	Balance c/d	180
		250			250
1 Feb	Balance b/d	180			

Dr			D Douglas		Cr
20-1		£	20-1		£
1 Jan	Balance b/d	150	30 Jan	Bank	100
20 Jan	Sales	100	31 Jan	Balance c/d	150
		250			250
1 Feb	Balance b/d	150			

Sales Ledger Control Account

The layout of a sales ledger control account (or trade receivables' control account) is shown below. Study the layout carefully and then read the text which explains the additional items.

Dr	Sales Ledger Control Account		Cr
	£		£
Balance b/d		Cash/cheques received from trade receivables	
Credit sales		Cash discount allowed	
Dishonoured cheques		Sales returns	
Interest charged to trade receivables		Irrecoverable debts written off	
		Set-off/contra entries	
		Balance c/d	
Balance b/d			

- **Balance b/d**

The figure for balance b/d on the debit side of the control account represents the total of the balances of the individual trade receivables' accounts in the sales ledger. This principle is illustrated in the diagram on the opposite page. Remember that, at the end of the month (or other period covered by the control account), the account must be balanced and carried down (on the credit side) on the last day of the month, and then brought down (on the debit side) on the first day of the next month.

Note that it is possible for a trade receivable's account to have a credit balance, instead of the usual debit balance – see page 186. This may come about, for example, because the trade receivable has paid for goods and then returned them, or has overpaid in error: the business owes the amount due, ie the trade receivable has a credit balance for the time being.

- **Credit sales**

Only credit sales – and not cash sales – are entered in the control account because it is this transaction that is recorded in the trade receivables' accounts. The total revenue of the business will comprise both credit and cash sales.

- **Dishonoured cheques**

If a trade receivable's cheque is returned dishonoured by the bank, ie the cheque has 'bounced', then entries have to be made in the bookkeeping system to record this. These entries are:

– debit trade receivable's account

– credit cash book (bank columns)

As a transaction has been made in a trade receivable's account, then the amount must also be recorded in the sales ledger control account – on the debit side.

Interest charged to trade receivables

Sometimes a business will charge a trade receivable for slow payment of an account. The entries are:

– debit trade receivable's account

– credit interest income account

As a debit transaction has been made in the trade receivable's account, so a debit entry must be recorded in the control account.

Irrecoverable debts written off

The bookkeeping entries for writing off an irrecoverable debt (see Chapter 10) are:

– debit irrecoverable debts written off account

– credit trade receivable's account

As you can see, a credit transaction is entered in a trade receivable's account. The control account 'masters' the sales ledger and so the transaction must also be recorded as a credit transaction in the control account.

Set-off/contra entries

See page 185.

Purchases Ledger Control Account

The layout of a purchases ledger control account (or trade payables' control account) is shown below. Study the format and read the notes which follow.

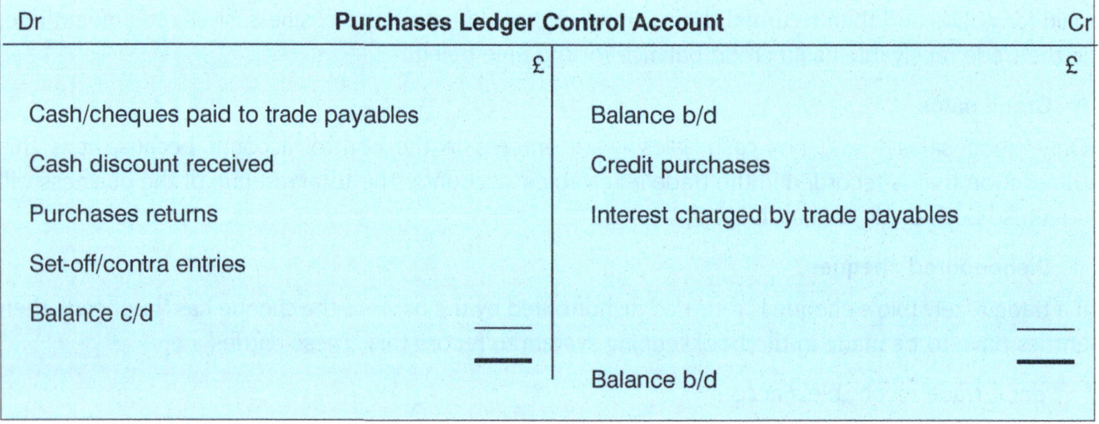

Dr	Purchases Ledger Control Account		Cr
	£		£
Cash/cheques paid to trade payables		Balance b/d	
Cash discount received		Credit purchases	
Purchases returns		Interest charged by trade payables	
Set-off/contra entries			
Balance c/d			
		Balance b/d	

Balance b/d

The figure for balance b/d on the credit side of the control account represents the total of the balances of the individual trade payables' accounts in the purchases ledger. This principle is illustrated in the diagram on the next page.

Note that it is possible for a trade payable's account to have a debit balance, instead of the usual credit balance – see page 187. This may come about, for example, if the trade payable has been paid and then goods are returned, or if the trade payable has been overpaid.

Credit purchases

Only credit purchases – and not cash purchases – are entered in the control account. However, the total purchases of the business will comprise both credit and cash purchases.

Interest charged by trade payables

If trade payables charge interest because of slow payment, this must be recorded on both the trade payable's account and the control account.

Set-off/contra entries

See page 185.

reconciliation of purchases ledger control account

The diagram on the next page shows how a purchases ledger control account acts as a totals account for the trade payables of a business.

Reconciliation of the balances on the purchases ledger control account and the purchases ledger accounts is made as follows:

Reconciliation of purchases ledger control account with trade payable balances

	1 January 20-1	31 January 20-1
	£	£
F Francis	100	200
G Gold	200	350
H Harris	300	500
I Ingram	400	900
Purchases ledger control account	1,000	1,950

PURCHASES LEDGER CONTROL ACCOUNT

Dr					Cr
20-1		£	20-1		£
31 Jan	Purchases returns	150	1 Jan	Balances b/d	1,000
31 Jan	Bank	594	31 Jan	Purchases	1,700
31 Jan	Discount received	6			
31 Jan	Balance c/d	1,950			
		2,700			2,700
			1 Feb	Balance b/d	1,950

F Francis

Dr					Cr
20-1		£	20-1		£
17 Jan	Bank	98	1 Jan	Balance b/d	100
17 Jan	Discount received	2	3 Jan	Purchases	200
31 Jan	Balance c/d	200			
		300			300
			1 Feb	Balance b/d	200

G Gold

Dr					Cr
20-1		£	20-1		£
15 Jan	Purchases returns	50	1 Jan	Balance b/d	200
28 Jan	Bank	100	9 Jan	Purchases	300
31 Jan	Balance c/d	350			
		500			500
			1 Feb	Balance b/d	350

H Harris

Dr					Cr
20-1		£	20-1		£
28 Jan	Purchases returns	100	1 Jan	Balance b/d	300
30 Jan	Bank	200	17 Jan	Purchases	500
31 Jan	Balance c/d	500			
		800			800
			1 Feb	Balance b/d	500

I Ingram

Dr					Cr
20-1		£	20-1		£
22 Jan	Bank	196	1 Jan	Balance b/d	400
22 Jan	Discount received	4	27 Jan	Purchases	700
31 Jan	Balance c/d	900			
		1,100			1,100
			1 Feb	Balance b/d	900

Set-off/Contra Entries

These entries occur when the same person or business has an account in both sales ledger and purchases ledger, ie they are both buying from, and selling to, the business whose accounts we are preparing. For example, M Patel Ltd has the following accounts in the sales and purchases ledgers:

SALES LEDGER

Dr	**A Smith**		Cr
	£		£
Balance b/d	200		

PURCHASES LEDGER

Dr	**A Smith**		Cr
	£		£
		Balance b/d	300

From these accounts we can see that:

- A Smith owes M Patel Ltd £200 (sales ledger)
- M Patel Ltd owes A Smith £300 (purchases ledger)

To save each having to make a payment and send it to the other, it is possible (with A Smith's agreement) to set-off one account as a contra against the other, so that they can settle their net indebtedness with one payment. The bookkeeping entries for this contra transaction in M Patel's books will be:

– debit A Smith (purchases ledger) £200

– credit A Smith (sales ledger) £200

The accounts will now appear as:

SALES LEDGER

Dr	**A Smith**		Cr
	£		£
Balance b/d	200	Contra: purchases ledger	200

PURCHASES LEDGER

Dr	**A Smith**		Cr
	£		£
Contra: sales ledger	200	Balance b/d	300

The net result is that M Patel Ltd owes A Smith £100. The important point to note is that, because transactions have been recorded in the personal accounts, an entry needs to be made in the two control accounts:

- debit purchases ledger control account with the contra amount
- credit sales ledger control account with the contra amount

Contra or set-off transactions should be appropriately documented with a general journal entry authorised by the accounts supervisor.

Sales Ledger Credit Balances and Purchases Ledger Debit Balances

sales ledger

The normal account balance of trade receivables in the sales ledger is debit, ie the amount is owing to the business by the trade receivables. As noted earlier in the chapter (page 181), it can sometimes happen that a trade receivable's account has a credit balance. This comes about, for example, when a trade receivable has paid for goods and then returns them, or has overpaid in error.

The following example shows a trade receivable's account with a credit balance at the end of the month:

SALES LEDGER

Dr **S Johnson** Cr

20-1		£	20-1		£
1 Jan	Balance b/d	100	20 Jan	Bank	300
3 Jan	Sales	200	30 Jan	Sales returns	200
31 Jan	Balance c/d	200			
		500			500
			1 Feb	Balance b/d	200

This trade receivable's account has a credit balance at the end of January – not what we would expect to find on an account in sales ledger. Assuming that this is the only such balance, for sales ledger control account the credit balance is shown on the same side as in the trade receivable's account:

Dr **Sales Ledger Control Account** Cr

20-1		£	20-1		£
		⋮			⋮
31 Jan	Balance c/d	200			
			1 Feb	Balance b/d	200

All other aspects of the sales ledger control account are the same as before. If there is more than one such credit balance in sales ledger, then they will be added together for the control account. Also note that, in a trial balance, any such credit balances must be shown on the credit side, ie separate from the main debit balances of sales ledger.

purchases ledger

In purchases ledger the normal account balance of trade payables is credit, ie the amount the business owes to its trade payables. As noted on page 183, it is possible for a trade payable's account to have a debit balance – for example, if a trade payable has been paid and then goods are returned, or if the trade payable has been overpaid.

The following example shows a trade payable's account with a debit balance at the end of the month.

PURCHASES LEDGER

T Singh

Dr					Cr
20-1		£	20-1		£
10 Jan	Bank	300	1 Jan	Balance b/d	200
20 Jan	Purchases returns	100	4 Jan	Purchases	100
			31 Jan	Balance c/d	100
		400			400
1 Feb	Balance b/d	100			

The debit balance on a trade payable's account in purchases ledger is shown in purchases ledger control account as it appears on the account (assuming that this is the only such balance at the end of January):

Purchases Ledger Control Account

Dr					Cr
20-1		£	20-1		£
		⋮			⋮
			31 Jan	Balance c/d	100
1 Feb	Balance b/d	100			

All other aspects of purchases ledger control account are the same as before. If there is more than one such debit balance, then they will be added together for the control account. Note that, in a trial balance, any such debit balances must be shown on the debit side, ie separate from the main credit balances of purchases ledger.

Sources of Information for Control Accounts

Control accounts use totals (remember that their other name is totals accounts) for the week, month, quarter or year – depending on what time period is decided upon by the business. The totals come from a number of sources in the accounting system:

sales ledger control account

- total credit sales – from the sales journal
- total sales returns – from the sales returns journal
- total cash/bank payments received from trade receivables – from the cash book
- dishonoured cheques – from the cash book
- total discount allowed – from the discount allowed column of the cash book, or from discount allowed account
- irrecoverable debts – from the general journal, or irrecoverable debts written off account
- set-off/contra entries – from the general journal

purchases ledger control account

- total credit purchases – from the purchases journal
- total purchases returns – from the purchases returns journal
- total cash/bank payments paid to trade payables – from the cash book
- total discount received – from the discount received column of the cash book, or from discount received account
- set-off/contra entries – from the general journal

Note that when using a computer accounting system, relevant transactions are automatically recorded on the control account

Control Accounts as an Aid to Management

- **instant information**

  When the manager of a business needs to know the figure for trade receivables or trade payables – important information for the manager – the balance of the appropriate control account will give the information immediately. There is no need to add up the balances of all the trade receivables' or trade payables' accounts. With a computer accounting system, the control accounts can be printed at any time.

- **prevention of fraud**

  The use of a control account makes fraud more difficult – particularly in a manual accounting system. If a fraudulent transaction is to be recorded on a personal account, the transaction must also be entered in the control account. As the control account will be either maintained by the accounts supervisor, and/or checked regularly by the manager, the control account adds another level of security within the accounting system.

- **location of errors**

  We have already seen in this chapter how control accounts can help in locating errors. However, a control account can only indicate that there is an error within a ledger section – it will not pinpoint where the error has occurred. Also, a control account only demonstrates the arithmetical accuracy of the accounts which it controls – there could still be errors, such as misposts and compensating errors, within the ledger section.

- **preparation of financial statements**

  A further use of control accounts is to help with the preparation of financial statements when a business has not kept double-entry accounts and a trial balance cannot be extracted. This aspect of accounting is known as 'incomplete records'.

- **limitation of control accounts**

  Whilst control accounts can help in locating errors, they do have the limitation that not all errors will be revealed by them. As noted above, such errors include:

  - omission, where a transaction has been completely omitted from the accounting records
  - mispost/error of commission, where a transaction is entered in the wrong person's account, but within the same ledger section
  - original entry, where the wrong money amount has been entered into the accounting system, eg a 'bad' figure on a cheque received from a trade receivable is entered wrongly in both cash book and sales ledger
  - compensating error, where one error is cancelled out by another error within the same ledger section, eg the balance of one account in purchases ledger is calculated at £1,000 too much, while another account in the same ledger is calculated at £1,000 too little

Control Accounts and Bookkeeping

A business must decide how to use control accounts in its bookkeeping system. One way of doing this is to keep the control accounts as memorandum records only, ie they are not part of the double-entry system.

The control accounts, therefore, do not form part of the double-entry system, but are used as a 'checking device' for the ledger section which they control. The personal accounts of trade receivables and trade payables – in the sales ledger and purchases ledger respectively – continue to be part of the double-entry system. From time-to-time, the balances of the memorandum control accounts are agreed with the balances of the personal accounts in the sales ledger and purchases ledger.

The diagrams on the next two pages show how the sales ledger control account and the purchases ledger control account are kept as memorandum accounts, while the personal accounts of trade receivables and trade payables are part of the double-entry system – in the sales ledger and purchases ledger.

continued on page 192

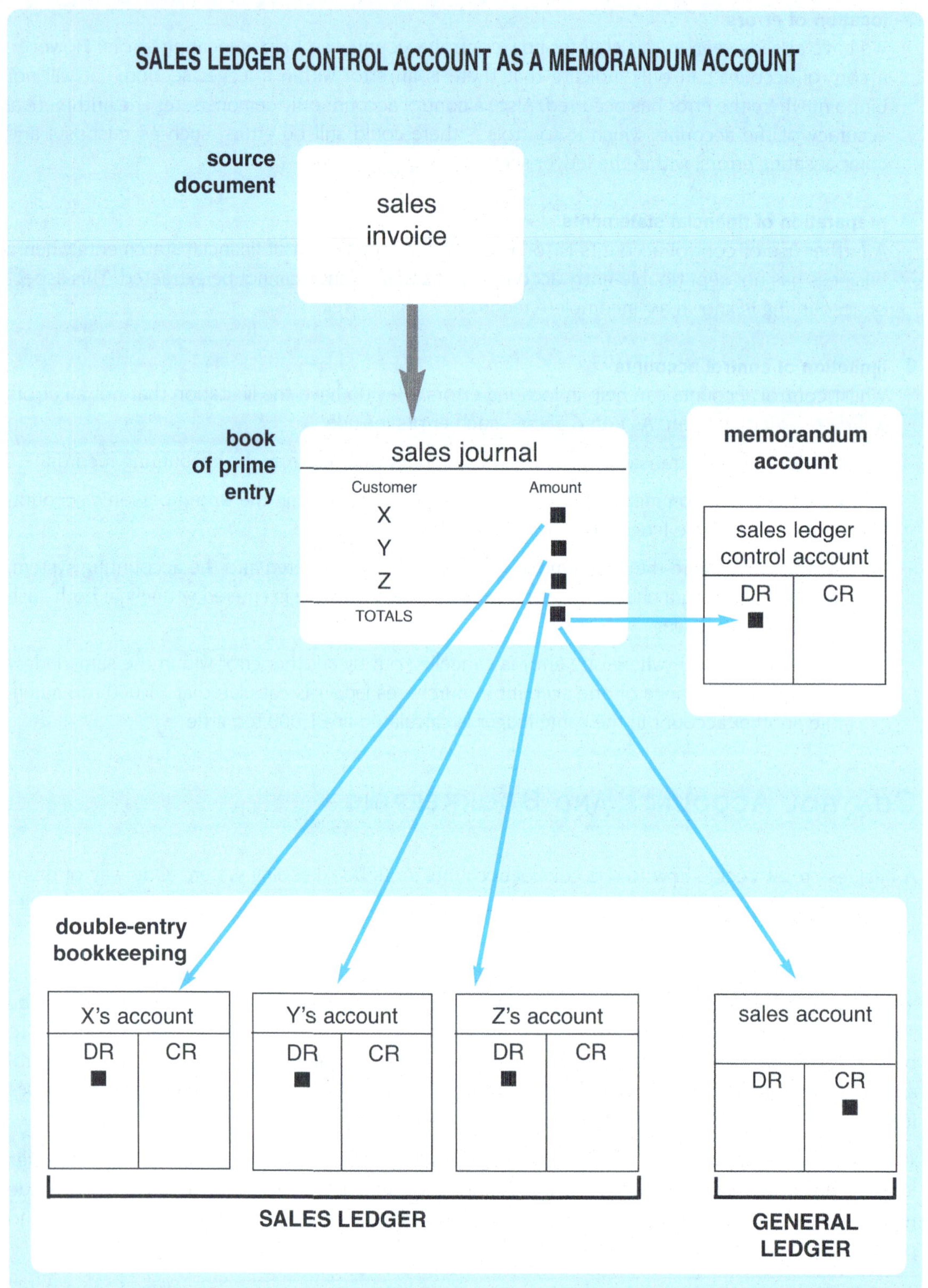
SALES LEDGER CONTROL ACCOUNT AS A MEMORANDUM ACCOUNT
source document
sales invoice
book of prime entry
sales journal
Customer
Amount
X
Y
Z
TOTALS
memorandum account
sales ledger control account
DR
CR
double-entry bookkeeping
X's account
DR
CR
Y's account
DR
CR
Z's account
DR
CR
sales account
DR
CR
SALES LEDGER
GENERAL LEDGER

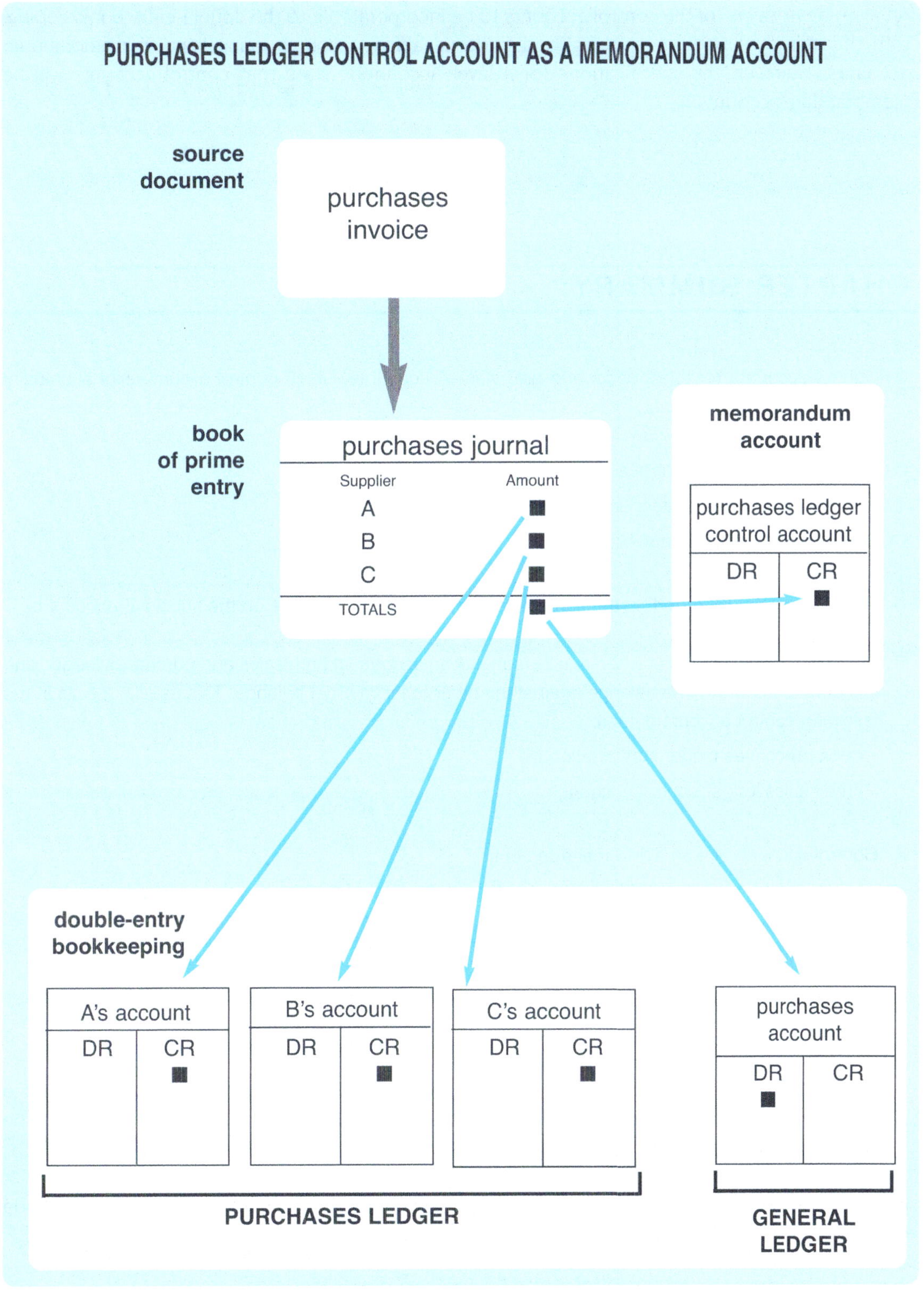
PURCHASES LEDGER CONTROL ACCOUNT AS A MEMORANDUM ACCOUNT
source document
purchases invoice
book of prime entry
purchases journal
Supplier
Amount
A
B
C
TOTALS
memorandum account
purchases ledger control account
DR
CR
double-entry bookkeeping
A's account
DR
CR
B's account
DR
CR
C's account
DR
CR
purchases account
DR
CR
PURCHASES LEDGER
GENERAL LEDGER

An alternative way is for the control accounts to be incorporated into the double-entry bookkeeping, with the individual trade receivables' and trade payables' accounts being kept as memorandum accounts. However, the specifications for A-level Accounting state that control accounts will be memorandum accounts.

CHAPTER SUMMARY

- Control accounts (or totals accounts) are 'master' accounts, which control a number of subsidiary accounts.

- Two commonly used control accounts are:
  - sales ledger control account
  - purchases ledger control account

- Transactions are recorded on the same side of the control account as on the subsidiary accounts.

- Set-off/contra entries occur when one person has an account in both sales and purchases ledger, and it is agreed to contra one balance against the other to leave a net balance. This usually results in the following control account entries:

  – debit purchases ledger control account

  – credit sales ledger control account

- Control accounts are an aid to management:
  - in giving immediate, up-to-date information on the total of trade receivables or trade payables
  - by making fraud more difficult
  - in helping to locate errors
  - in assisting with the preparation of financial statements when a business has not kept double-entry accounts

- Control accounts may be kept as memorandum records only, or they can be incorporated into the double-entry system. (The specifications for A-level Accounting state that control accounts will be memorandum accounts.)

In the next chapter we return to financial statements and consider year-end adjustments which are made in order to show a more relevant and reliable view of the state of the business.

QUESTIONS

visit
www.osbornebooks.co.uk
to take an online test

An asterisk (*) after the question number means that the answer is given at the end of this book.

11.1* Prepare a sales ledger control account for the month of June 20-1 from the following information:

20-1		£
1 Jun	Sales ledger balances	17,491
30 Jun	Credit sales for month	42,591
	Sales returns	1,045
	Payments received from trade receivables	39,024
	Cash discount allowed	593
	Irrecoverable debts written off	296

The trade receivables figure at 30 June is to be entered as the balancing figure.

11.2* Prepare a purchases ledger control account for the month of April 20-2 from the following information:

20-2		£
1 Apr	Purchases ledger balances	14,275
30 Apr	Credit purchases for month	36,592
	Purchases returns	653
	Payments made to trade payables	31,074
	Cash discount received	1,048
	Contra transfer of credit balances to sales ledger	597

The trade payables figure at 30 April is to be entered as the balancing figure.

11.3 The sales ledger of Rowcester Traders contains the following accounts on 1 February 20-8:

Arrow Valley Retailers	balance £826.40 debit
B Brick (Builders) Limited	balance £59.28 debit
Mereford Manufacturing Company	balance £293.49 debit
Redgrove Restorations	balance £724.86 debit
Wyvern Warehouse Limited	balance £108.40 debit

The following transactions took place during February:

3 Feb	Sold goods on credit to Arrow Valley Retailers £338.59, and to Mereford Manufacturing Company £127.48
7 Feb	Redgrove Restorations returned goods £165.38
15 Feb	Received a bank transfer from Wyvern Warehouse Limited for the balance of the account after deduction of 2.5% cash discount
17 Feb	Sold goods on credit to Redgrove Restorations £394.78, and to Wyvern Warehouse Limited £427.91
20 Feb	Arrow Valley Retailers settled an invoice for £826.40 by bank transfer after deducting 2.5% cash discount
24 Feb	Mereford Manufacturing Company returned goods £56.29
28 Feb	Set-off the balance of Mereford Manufacturing Company's account to the company's account in the purchases ledger
28 Feb	Wrote off the account of B Brick (Builders) Limited as irrecoverable

You are to:

(a) Write up the personal accounts in the sales ledger of Rowcester Traders for February 20-8, balancing them at the end of the month.

(b) Prepare a sales ledger control account for February 20-8, balancing it at the end of the month.

(c) Reconcile the control account balance with the trade receivables' accounts at 1 February and 28 February 20-8.

Note: journals are not required.

11.4* You have the following information:

- opening supplier balances at start of month £15,300
- credit purchases for month £18,100
- purchases returns for month £200
- payments made to trade payables £10,000

What is the figure for closing supplier balances at the end of the month?

A	£7,000	
B	£7,400	
C	£23,200	
D	£23,600	

11.5* You work as an accounts assistant for Shire Traders. Today you are working on the sales ledger control account and sales ledger.

A summary of transactions with credit customers during June 20-5 is shown below.

	£
Goods sold on credit	118,600
Money received from credit customers	96,214
Discount allowed	300
Goods returned by credit customers	650
Irrecoverable debt written off	350

The balance of customer accounts at 1 June 20-5 was £180,824.

Required:

Prepare the sales ledger control account for the month of June 20-5 from the above details. Show clearly the balance carried down at 30 June 20-5.

Date 20-5	Details	Amount £	Date 20-5	Details	Amount £

11.6* (a) State **two** benefits to a business of using control accounts.

Benefit 1 ....

....

Benefit 2 ....

....

The sales ledger control account of Zelah Supplies for the month ended 30 September 20-6 did not agree with the sales ledger balances list total.

The following errors have been discovered.

1. The sales journal was undercast by £220.
2. The sales returns journal includes £150 which is, in fact, purchases returns.
3. A discount allowed of £16 has been omitted from the accounts completely.
4. A bank payment received from Tingwall & Co for £645 was entered in the account of Dingwall Ltd in error.
5. The opening balance brought down should have been £15,450.

(b) Enter the appropriate corrections in the sales ledger control account and then balance the account.

Dr		**Sales Ledger Control Account**			Cr
20-6		£	20-6		£
30 Sep	Balance b/d	15,540			

11.7 The following figures have been drawn from the accounting records of Ling Trading for the month ended 30 September 20-3:

	£
Balances at 1 September 20-3:	
Credit balances in the purchases ledger	18,471
Debit balances in the purchases ledger	229
Balances at 30 September 20-3:	
Purchases on credit for the month	88,765
Returns to suppliers of credit purchases	2,173
Cash purchases	3,496
Purchase ledger balances set off contra sales ledger balances	641
Payments made to suppliers	79,417
Discount received	1,512
Cash refunds from credit suppliers	56
Debit balance in the purchases ledger	296
Credit balances in the purchases ledger	?

Required:

From the above information, complete the purchases ledger control account for the month ended 30 September 20-3 and calculate the credit balance at that date.

Dr		**Purchases Ledger Control Account**			Cr
Date 20-3	Details	£	Date 20-3	Details	£

11.8 The following is the sales ledger control account of Wyvern Supplies for January 20-5:

Dr		**Sales Ledger Control Account**			Cr
20-5		£	20-5		£
1 Jan	Balance b/d	44,359	31 Jan	Bank	23,045
31 Jan	Sales	26,632	31 Jan	Discount allowed	1,126
31 Jan	Dishonoured cheque	275	31 Jan	Sales returns	2,347
			31 Jan	Balance c/d	44,748
		71,266			71,266
1 Feb	Balance b/d	44,748			

The following errors have been discovered.

1. The sales journal total has been undercast by £1,000.
2. The sales returns journal total should be £2,964.
3. A contra entry with the purchases ledger of £247 has been omitted.
4. A bank transfer for £685 received from a trade receivable, J Hampton, has been credited in error to the account of Hampton Limited.

You are to redraft the sales ledger control account making the entries necessary to show the correct balance to be brought down on 1 February 20-5.

12 ADJUSTMENTS TO FINANCIAL STATEMENTS

In Chapter 9 we prepared the financial statements – income statement, and statement of financial position. There are, however, a number of adjustments which are made to the financial statements at the year-end in order to show a more relevant and reliable view of the state of the business.

This chapter is concerned with adjustments for accruals and prepayments of expenses, depreciation and irrecoverable debts.

Also covered are the treatment of owner's private expenses and goods for owner's use, and the accounting entries when good are supplied on a sale or return bases.

The difference between income and expenditure accounting and receipts and payments accounting is discussed towards the end of the chapter.

INTRODUCTION TO ADJUSTMENTS TO FINANCIAL STATEMENTS

By making adjustments to financial statements we can improve the relevance and reliability of accounts in determining the income and expenditure, and showing the profit, and the assets and liabilities of the business.

The adjustments to financial statements covered in this chapter are as follows:

- **adjusting for accruals of expenses** – expenses due in an accounting period which have not been paid for at the end of that period (see page 201)
- **adjusting for prepayments of expenses** – payments of expenses made in advance of the accounting period to which they relate (see page 204)
- **depreciation of non-current assets** – writing down the value of non-current assets over their useful economic lives (see page 208)
- **irrecoverable debts written off** – removing from the sales ledger the accounts of trade receivables who will not pay, or cannot pay (see page 217)

The following adjustment to financial statements has been seen already (in Chapter 9).

- **closing inventory** – incorporating the value of inventory held at the financial year-end into the financial statements

Each of these adjustments is based on a number of accounting concepts – which we will look at in more detail in Chapter 14. For the moment, we can say that the two main accounting concepts which form the basis of these adjustments are:

- the **accruals concept** – which is the matching of expenses and income to the same goods or services and the same time period – applies to closing inventory, accruals, prepayments, depreciation
- the **prudence concept** – which requires that financial statements should always, where there is any doubt, report a conservative (lower) figure for profit or the valuation of assets – applies to depreciation and irrecoverable debts written off – ie profit is not deliberately overstated nor understated

To illustrate the effect of adjustments we shall be referring to the financial statements of Wyvern Wholesalers, a sole trader business, which are shown on the next two pages before adjustments (the trial balance – if you wish to refer to it – is on page 135).

Accrual of Expenses

An accrual is an amount due in an accounting period which is unpaid at the end of that period.

In the financial statements, accrued expenses are:

- added to the expense in the trial balance before listing it in the income statement
- shown as a current liability in the year-end statement of financial position

The reason for dealing with accruals in this way is to ensure that the income statement records the expense that has been incurred for the year, instead of simply the amount that has been paid. In other words, the expense is adjusted to relate to the time period covered by the income statement. The year-end statement of financial position shows a liability for the amount that is due, but unpaid.

example of an accrual expense

The trial balance of Wyvern Wholesalers (see page 135) shows a debit balance for electricity and gas of £3,000. Before preparing the financial statements, an electricity bill for £250 is received on 1st January 20-2, ie on the first day of the new financial year. As this bill is clearly for electricity used in 20-1, an adjustment needs to be made in the financial statements for 20-1 to record this accrued expense.

In the income statement, the total cost of £3,250 (ie £3,000 from the trial balance, plus £250 accrued) is recorded as an expense. In the statement of financial position, £250 is shown as a separate current liability of 'other payables'.

accruals – the bookkeeping records

In the double-entry records, accruals must be shown as an amount owing at the end of the financial year. Thus the account for electricity and gas in the records of Wyvern Wholesalers will appear as shown at the top of page 204.

continued on page 204

Financial Statements Before Adjustments

INCOME STATEMENT OF WYVERN WHOLESALERS
FOR THE YEAR ENDED 31 DECEMBER 20-1

	£	£	£
Revenue (Sales)			250,000
Less Sales returns			5,400
Net revenue (or turnover)			244,600
Opening inventory (1 January 20-1)		12,350	
Purchases	156,000		
Carriage in	–		
Less Purchases returns	7,200		
Net purchases		148,800	
		161,150	
Less Closing inventory (31 December 20-1)		16,300	
Cost of sales			144,850
Gross profit			99,750
Add Discount received			2,500
			102,250
Less expenses:			
Discount allowed		3,700	
Salaries		46,000	
Electricity and gas		3,000	
Rent and business rates		2,000	
Sundry expenses		4,700	
			59,400
Profit for the year			42,850

STATEMENT OF FINANCIAL POSITION OF WYVERN WHOLESALERS
AS AT 31 DECEMBER 20-1

	£	£	£
Non-current Assets			
Property at cost			100,000
Equipment at cost			30,000
			130,000
Current Assets			
Inventory		16,300	
Trade receivables		23,850	
Cash		125	
		40,275	
Less Current Liabilities			
Trade payables	12,041		
Bank overdraft	851		
		12,892	
Net Current Assets or Working Capital			27,383
			157,383
Less Non-current Liabilities			
Loan			11,500
NET ASSETS			145,883
FINANCED BY			
Capital			
Opening capital			113,475
Add Profit for the year			42,850
			156,325
Less Drawings			10,442
			145,883

Electricity and Gas Account

Dr					Cr
20-1		£	20-1		£
31 Dec	Balance b/d (trial balance total)	3,000	31 Dec	Income statement	3,250
31 Dec	Balance c/d	250			
		3,250			3,250
20-2			20-2		
			1 Jan	Balance b/d	250

Notes:

- The bookkeeper's trial balance showed the debit side balance brought down of £3,000
- As £250 is owing for electricity at the end of the year, the transfer to income statement is the expense that has been incurred for the year – this amounts to £3,250
- The balance remaining on the account – a credit balance of £250 – is the amount of the accrual, which is listed on the statement of financial position at 31 December 20-1 as a current liability (other payables)
- Later on, for example on 5 January, the electricity bill is paid and the account for 20-2 now appears as:

Electricity and Gas Account

Dr					Cr
20-2		£	20-2		£
5 Jan	Bank	250	1 Jan	Balance b/d	250

The effect of the payment on 5 January is that the account now has a 'nil' balance and the bill received on 1 January will not be recorded as an expense in the income statement drawn up at the end of 20-2.

effect on profit

Taking note of the accrual of an expense has the effect of reducing a previously reported profit for the year. As the expenses have been increased, profit is less (but there is no effect on gross profit). Thus, the profit for the year of Wyvern Wholesalers reduces by £250 from £42,850 to £42,600.

PREPAYMENT OF EXPENSES

A prepayment is a payment made in advance of the accounting period to which it relates.

A prepayment is, therefore, the opposite of an accrual: with a prepayment of expenses, some part of the expense has been paid in advance of the next accounting period.

In the financial statements, prepaid expenses are:

- deducted from the expense in the trial balance before listing it in the income statement
- shown as a current asset in the year-end statement of financial position

As with accruals, the reason for dealing with prepaid expenses in this way is to ensure that the income statement records the expense incurred for the year, and not the amount that has been paid – the income statement expense relates to the time period covered by the income statement. The year-end statement of financial position shows an asset for the amount that has been prepaid.

example of a prepaid expense

The owner of Wyvern Wholesalers tells you that the trial balance figure for rent and business rates of £2,000, includes £100 of rent paid in advance for January 20-2. An adjustment needs to be made in the financial statements for 20-1 to record this prepaid expense.

In the income statement, the cost of £1,900 (ie £2,000 from the trial balance, less £100 prepaid) is recorded as an expense. In the statement of financial position, £100 is shown as a separate current asset of 'other receivables'.

prepayments – the bookkeeping records

In the double-entry records, prepayments must be shown as an asset at the end of the financial year. Thus the account for rent and business rates in the records of Wyvern Wholesalers will appear as follows:

Dr **Rent and Business Rates Account** Cr

20-1		£	20-1		£
31 Dec	Balance b/d	2,000	31 Dec	Income statement	1,900
	(trial balance total)				
			31 Dec	Balance c/d	100
		2,000			2,000
20-2					
1 Jan	Balance b/d	100			

Notes:

- The trial balance total for rent and business rates is £2,000
- As £100 is prepaid at the end of the year, the transfer to income statement is the expense that has been incurred for the year of £1,900
- The balance remaining on the account – a debit balance of £100 – is the amount of the prepayment, which is listed on the statement of financial position at 31 December 20-1 as a current asset (other receivables)
- The debit balance of £100 on 1 January 20-2 will be included in the expenses for rent and business rates for the year and will be transferred to income statement account on 31 December 20-2

effect on profit

Taking note of the prepayment of an expense has the effect of increasing a previously reported profit for the year – expenses have been reduced, so profit is greater.

office supplies

At the end of a financial year most businesses hold quantities of office supplies which have been recorded as expenses during the year, such as stationery, postage stamps (or a balance held in a franking machine). Technically, at the end of each year, these items should be valued and treated as a prepayment for next year, so reducing the expense in the current year's income statement. However, in practice, this is done only when the value of such items is substantial enough to affect the financial statements in a material way. The firm's accountant will decide at what level the prepayment will apply.

To give an example of office supplies, the trial balance total for postages of a business at the year-end is £1,050; postage stamps held at the same date are £150. The business will record an expense of £900 (£1,050, less £150) in the income statement, while £150 is listed on the statement of financial position as a current asset for 'other receivables'.

ACCRUALS AND PREPAYMENTS IN THE FINANCIAL STATEMENTS

We have looked at the separate effect of dealing with accruals and prepayments of expenses. Let us now see how they are presented in the financial statements of Wyvern Wholesalers. Remember that we are taking note of the following items at 31 December 20-1:

- electricity accrued £250
- rent prepaid £100

income statement

There is no effect on gross profit, so the details of the first part of the income statement are not shown here. Note that the calculations for accruals and prepayments do not appear in the financial statements; they are presented here for illustrative purposes only.

INCOME STATEMENT OF WYVERN WHOLESALERS
FOR THE YEAR ENDED 31 DECEMBER 20-1

		£	£	£
Gross profit				99,750
Add Discount received				2,500
				102,250
Less overheads (expenses):				
Discount allowed			3,700	
Salaries			46,000	
Electricity and gas	3,000 + 250		3,250	
Rent and business rates	2,000 – 100		1,900	
Sundry expenses			4,700	
				59,550
Profit for the year				42,700

The effect of taking note of accruals and prepayments of expenses is to alter profit:

	£
Profit for the year (before adjustments)	42,850
Add rent prepaid	100
	42,950
Less electricity accrued	250
Profit for the year (after adjustments)	42,700

statement of financial position

The statement of financial position is shown below with the accruals and prepayments of expenses shaded for illustrative purposes. These items do appear in the financial statements, (but not the shading).

STATEMENT OF FINANCIAL POSITION OF WYVERN WHOLESALERS
AS AT 31 DECEMBER 20-1

	£	£	£
Non-current Assets			
Property			100,000
Equipment			30,000
			130,000
Current Assets			
Inventory		16,300	
Trade receivables		23,850	
Other receivables (Payment of expenses)		100	
Cash		125	
		40,375	
Less Current Liabilities			
Trade payables	12,041		
Other payables (Accrual of expenses)	250		
Bank	851		
		13,142	
Net Current Assets or Working Capital			27,233
			157,233
Less Non-current Liabilities			
Loan			11,500
NET ASSETS			145,733
FINANCED BY			
Capital			
Opening capital			113,475
Add Profit for the year			*42,700
			156,175
Less Drawings			10,442
			145,733

* see profit calculations at top of page

DEPRECIATION OF NON-CURRENT ASSETS

Depreciation is a measure of the amount of the fall in value of non-current assets over a time period.

Most non-current assets fall in value over time and, in accounting, it is necessary, in order to present a realistic view of the business, to measure the amount of the fall in value. This is done by showing an expense – called 'depreciation of non-current assets' – in the income statement, and recording the asset at a lower value than cost price in the statement of financial position. The expense of depreciation is an estimate of both the fall in value of the non-current asset and the time period; the estimate is linked usually to the cost price of the asset. Depreciation is an application of the accruals concept because we are recognising the timing difference between payment for the non-current asset and the asset's fall in value, and the prudence concept because we are estimating the fall in value of the asset and reporting a more reliable value for the asset on the statement of financial position.

The main factors which cause non-current assets to depreciate are:

- wearing out through use, eg vehicles, machinery, etc
- passage of time, eg the lease on a building
- using up, eg extraction of stone from a quarry
- economic reasons
  - obsolescence, eg a new design of machine which does the job better and faster makes the old machine obsolete
  - inadequacy, eg a machine no longer has the capacity to meet the demand for its goods

Non-current assets – even property – are depreciated over their useful economic life. The only exception is freehold land which, because it is a non-wasting asset, does not normally depreciate (unless it is a quarry or a mine, when it will have a limited useful economic life).

calculating depreciation

There are several different ways in which we can allow for the fall in value of non-current assets. All of these are estimates, and it is only when the asset is sold or scrapped that we will know the accuracy of the estimate, and adjustments can be made. The two most common methods of calculating depreciation are:

- straight-line method
- reducing balance method

For the calculation of depreciation amounts we will use the following data:

MACHINE	
Cost price on 1 January 20-1	£2,000
Estimated life	4 years
Estimated disposal value at end of four years	£400

straight-line method

At its most simple, with this method of calculating depreciation, a fixed percentage is written off the original cost of the asset each year. For example, if twenty-five per cent is written off an asset's cost each year by the straight-line method it gives a useful economic life of four years.

The depreciation percentage will be decided by a business on the basis of what it considers to be the useful economic life of the asset. Different classes of non-current assets are often depreciated at different rates, eg vehicles may be depreciated at a different rate from office equipment. It is important that, once a particular method and rate of depreciation has been selected, depreciation should be applied consistently, ie methods and rates are not changed from year-to-year without good reason.

The method of calculating straight-line depreciation, taking into account the asset's estimated disposal proceeds at the end of its useful economic life, is:

$$\frac{\text{cost of asset} - \text{estimated disposal (scrap or salvage) proceeds}}{\text{number of years' expected use of asset}}$$

For example, the machine on the previous page is expected to have a disposal (scrap or salvage) value of £400, so the depreciation amount will be:

$$\frac{£2{,}000 - £400}{4 \text{ years}} = £400 \text{ per year}$$

reducing balance method

With this method, a fixed percentage is written off the reduced balance each year. The reduced balance is cost of the asset less depreciation to date. For example, the machine on the previous page is to be depreciated by 33.3% (one-third) each year, using the reducing balance method. The depreciation amounts for the four years of ownership are:

Original cost	£2,000
20-1 depreciation: 33.3% of £2,000	£667
Value at end of 20-1	£1,333
20-2 depreciation: 33.3% of £1,333	£444
Value at end of 20-2	£889
20-3 depreciation: 33.3% of £889	£296
Value at end of 20-3	£593
20-4 depreciation: 33.3% of £593	£193
Value at end of 20-4	£400

Note that the figures have been rounded to the nearest £, and year 4 depreciation has been adjusted by £5 to leave a residual value of £400.

straight-line and reducing balance methods compared

When selecting a method of depreciation, the main consideration must be how the value of the asset reduces within the business. For example, vehicles lose a large amount of their value in the first two years of ownership – therefore it is appropriate to use the reducing balance method of depreciation. The diagram on the next page makes a comparison between the two main methods of depreciation.

The following comparison tables use the depreciation amounts calculated above.

straight-line depreciation

Year	1 Original cost	2 Depreciation for year	3 Depreciation to date	4 Net book value (ie column 1-3)
	£	£	£	£
20-1	2,000	400	400	1,600
20-2	2,000	400	800	1,200
20-3	2,000	400	1,200	800
20-4	2,000	400	1,600	400

Note: Net book value (or carrying amount) is cost, less provision for depreciation, ie column 1, less column 3.

These calculations will be used in the financial statements as follows: taking 20-2 as an example, the income statement will be charged with £400 (column 2) as an expense, while the statement of financial position will record £1,200 (column 4) as the net book value (or carrying amount).

reducing balance depreciation

Year	1 Original cost	2 Depreciation for year	3 Depreciation to date	4 Net book value (ie column 1-3)
	£	£	£	£
20-1	2,000	667	667	1,333
20-2	2,000	444	1,111	889
20-3	2,000	296	1,407	593
20-4	2,000	193	1,600	400

In the financial statements, using 20-3 as an example, £296 (column 2) will be charged as an expense in income statement, while £593 (column 4) is the net book value (or carrying amount) that will be shown in the statement of financial position.

Using these tables, we will now see how the two methods compare:

	straight-line method	reducing balance method
depreciation amount	Same money amount each year – see chart below	Different money amounts each year: more than straight-line in early years, less in later years – see chart below
depreciation percentage	Lower depreciation percentage required to achieve same residual value	Higher depreciation percentage required to achieve same residual value – but can never reach a nil value
suitability	Best used for non-current assets likely to be kept for the whole of their expected lives, eg machinery, office equipment, fixtures and fittings	Best used for non-current assets which depreciate more in early years and which are not kept for the whole of expected lives, eg vehicles

The year-by-year depreciation amounts of the machine in the example are shown on the following bar chart:

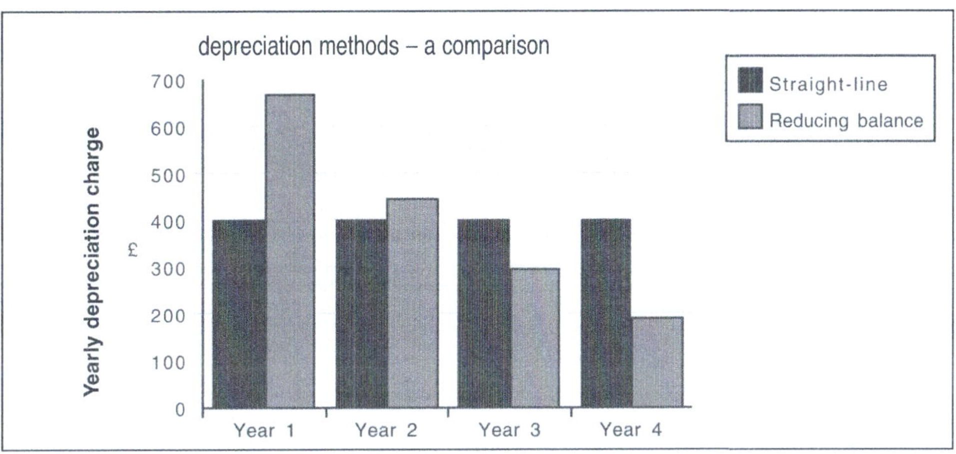

accounting entries for depreciation

Once the amounts of depreciation have been calculated, they can be recorded in the accounting system. The procedure is to use two accounts for each class of non-current assets:

- non-current asset account, which records the cost price of the asset
- provision for depreciation account, which records the depreciation to date for the asset

example accounting entries

A machine is purchased for £2,000 on 1 January 20-1. It is decided to depreciate it at twenty per cent each year, using the straight-line method. The firm's financial year runs from 1 January to 31 December. The accounting records for the first four years will be:

Machinery Account

Dr					Cr
20-1		£	20-1		£
1 Jan	Bank	2,000			

This account remains with the balance of £2,000, which is the cost price of the machine. The other transaction on 1 January 20-1 is to bank account – this has not been shown.

The double-entry bookkeeping for each year's depreciation is:

- debit income statement
- credit provision for depreciation account

Provision for Depreciation Account – Machinery

Dr					Cr
20-1		£	20-1		£
31 Dec	Balance c/d	400	31 Dec	Income statement	400
20-2			20-2		
31 Dec	Balance c/d	800	1 Jan	Balance b/d	400
			31 Dec	Income statement	400
		800			800
20-3			20-3		
31 Dec	Balance c/d	1,200	1 Jan	Balance b/d	800
			31 Dec	Income statement	400
		1,200			1,200
20-4			20-4		
31 Dec	Balance c/d	1,600	1 Jan	Balance b/d	1,200
			31 Dec	Income statement	400
		1,600			1,600
20-5			20-5		
			1 Jan	Balance b/d	1,600

The provision for depreciation account stores up the amounts of depreciation year by year. Notice that, while the asset account of machinery has a debit balance, provision for depreciation has a credit balance. The difference between the two balances at any time will tell us the net book value (or carrying amount) of the asset, ie what it is worth according to our accounting records. For example, at 31 December 20-3, the net book value of the machine is £800 (£2,000 cost, less £1,200 depreciation to date).

When a business owns several non-current assets of the same class, eg several machines, it is usual practice to maintain only one asset account and one provision for depreciation account for that class. This does mean that the calculation of amounts of depreciation can become quite complex – particularly when assets are bought and sold during the year. It may be helpful, in an examination or assessment, to calculate the separate depreciation amount for each asset, before amalgamating the figures as the year's depreciation charge. In order to keep a record of non-current assets, many businesses make use of a **non-current asset register** which separates out each class of non-current asset and records details of each asset owned, original cost, depreciation rate and amount each year, and disposal proceeds. A non-current asset register can be kept manually or on computer.

We will look at how to deal with the accounting for the sale of an asset in Chapter 15.

In the financial statements depreciation is shown as follows:

income statement

The depreciation amount calculated for each class of asset is listed amongst the expenses. For example, for the machine being depreciated by the straight-line method, the income statement will show 'depreciation: machinery £400' as an expense for each of the years 20-1 to 20-4. If the machine is being depreciated by the reducing balance method, the income statement for 20-1 will show 'depreciation: machinery £667' as an expense. In subsequent years the amounts will be £444 in 20-2, £296 in 20-3, and £193 in 20-4.

statement of financial position

Each class of non-current asset is shown at cost price, less the amount of provision for depreciation to date (ie this year's depreciation, plus depreciation from previous years if any). The resulting figure is the net book value of the non-current asset.

The usual way of setting these out in a statement of financial position (using the first year figures for the machine being depreciated by the straight-line method) is:

Statement of financial position (extract) as at 31 December 20-1

	£	£	£
	Cost	Depreciation	Net book value
Non-current Assets			
Machinery	2,000	400	1,600
Vehicles, etc	x	x	x
	x	x	x

Note that the figures for the statement of financial position come from columns 1, 3 and 4 from the table on page 210. Where there is only one class of non-current asset, eg machinery, the figures can be set out in a simpler layout, as follows:

Statement of financial position (extract) as at 31 December 20-1

	£
Non-current Assets	
Machinery at cost	2,000
Less depreciation	400
Net book value	1,600

At the end of the second year, the machine is shown as follows:

Statement of financial position (extract) .... as at 31 December 20-2

	£ Cost	£ Depreciation	£ Net book value
Non-current Assets			
Machinery	2,000	800	1,200
Vehicles, etc	x	x	x
	x	x	x

Notice, from the above, how provision for depreciation increases with the addition of each further year's depreciation. At the same time, the net book value figure reduces – it is this net book value figure which is added to the other non-current assets to give a sub-total for this section of the statement of financial position.

depreciation policies of a business

In examination questions, information will be given – where it is needed – on the depreciation policies of the business whose financial statements you are preparing. In particular, the information will be given on what to do when a non-current asset is bought part of the way through a firm's financial year. The choices here will be to allocate depreciation for the part of the year that it is owned; alternatively the firm may choose to provide for depreciation for the whole year on assets held at the end of the year.

DEPRECIATION IN THE FINANCIAL STATEMENTS

We will now focus on how the depreciation amounts are shown in the income statement and statement of financial position of Wyvern Wholesalers (see pages 206 and 207) and include depreciation for the year of:

- property at cost: 2 per cent straight-line, ie £2,000 depreciation
- equipment at cost: 10 per cent straight-line, ie £3,000 depreciation

income statement

There is no effect on gross profit, so the details of the first part of the income statement are not shown here. The income statement appears as shown below, with the depreciation amounts for the year included amongst the expenses, where they are shaded for illustrative purposes. Note that it is usual to show the separate amount of depreciation for each class of non-current asset (as below), rather than the total amount of depreciation.

INCOME STATEMENT OF WYVERN WHOLESALERS
FOR THE YEAR ENDED 31 DECEMBER 20-1

	£	£	£
Gross profit			99,750
Add Discount received			2,500
			102,250
Less expenses:			
Discount allowed		3,700	
Salaries		46,000	
Electricity and gas		3,250	
Rent and business rates		1,900	
Sundry expenses		4,700	
Depreciation:			
premises		2,000	
equipment		3,000	
			64,550
Profit for the year			37,700

The effect of taking note of depreciation is to reduce profit:

	£	
Profit (before adjustment for depreciation)	42,700	(see page 207)
Less depreciation £2,000 + £3,000	5,000	
Profit for the year (after adjustment for depreciation)	37,700	

statement of financial position

The statement of financial position is shown on the next page with the depreciation amounts shaded for illustrative purposes. Note that the deduction is the amount of provision for depreciation to date (ie this year's depreciation, plus depreciation from previous years, if any). Cost, less depreciation, equals the net book value (or carrying amount) of the non-current asset. It is good practice when preparing statement of financial positions to total the first two columns and to sub-total the third, as illustrated on the next page.

STATEMENT OF FINANCIAL POSITION OF WYVERN WHOLESALERS AS AT 31 DECEMBER 20-1

	£	£	£
Non-current Assets	*Cost*	*Depreciation*	*Net book value*
Property	100,000	2,000	98,000
Equipment	30,000	3,000	27,000
	130,000	5,000	125,000
Current Assets			
Inventory		16,300	
Trade receivables		23,850	
Other receivables		100	
Cash		125	
		40,375	
Less Current Liabilities			
Trade payables	12,041		
Other payables	250		
Bank	851		
		13,142	
Net Current Assets or Working Capital			27,233
			152,233
Less Non-current Liabilities			
Loan			11,500
NET ASSETS			140,733
FINANCED BY			
Capital			
Opening capital			113,475
Add Profit for the year			*37,700
			151,175
Less Drawings			10,442
			140,733

* see profit calculations on previous page

depreciation: a non-cash expense

It is very important to realise that depreciation is a non-cash expense: unlike most of the other expenses in the income statement, no cheque is written out, or cash paid, for depreciation. In cash terms, depreciation causes no outflow of money. (The outflow of money occurs when the asset is purchased.) Nevertheless, it is correct, in the financial statements of a business, to show an allowance for depreciation in the income statement, and to reduce the value of the non-current asset in the statement of financial position. This is because the business has had the use of the asset, and needs to record the fall in value as an expense in order to present a true picture of its financial state. Thus we are led back to the definition of depreciation as 'a measure of the amount of the fall in value of non-current assets over a time period', ie it is an accounting adjustment. As depreciation is shown as an expense in income statement, it reduces profit – a lower profit figure may discourage the owner from drawing too much cash from the business. The non-cash effect of depreciation is shown in the diagram on the next page.

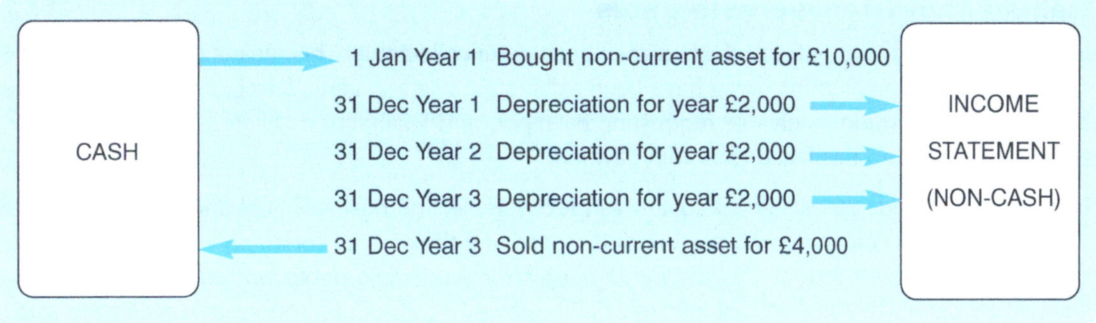

As depreciation is a non-cash expense, it should be noted that depreciation is not a method of providing a fund of cash which can be used to replace the asset at the end of its life.

Irrecoverable Debts

An irrecoverable debt is a debt owing to a business which it considers will never be paid.

Most businesses selling their goods and services to other businesses do not receive payment immediately. Instead, they often have to allow a period of credit and, until the payment is received, they have a current asset of trade receivables. Unfortunately, it is likely that not all trade receivables will eventually settle the amount they owe, ie the amounts are irrecoverable debts which have to be written off because the cost of their collection would be greater than the amount recovered.

Let us consider a business with trade receivables of £10,000. This total will, most probably, be made up of a number of trade receivables' accounts. At any one time, a few of these accounts will be uncollectable: these are irrecoverable debts, and they need to be written off, ie the business will give up trying to collect the debt and will accept the loss. The one thing the business with trade receivables of £10,000 cannot do is to show this amount as a current asset in the statement of financial position: to do so would be to imply that the full £10,000 is collectable. Instead, this gross trade receivables' figure might be reduced, for example, by writing off trade receivables' accounts with balances totalling £200.

Thus the trade receivables' figure becomes:

Gross trade receivables	£10,000
Less: irrecoverable debts	£200
Net trade receivables (recorded in statement of financial position)	£9,800

Irrecoverable debts is an application of the accounting concept of prudence. By reducing the trade receivables' figure, through the income statement and statement of financial position, a more reliable view is shown of the amount that the business can expect to receive.

treatment of irrecoverable debts

Irrecoverable debts are written off when they become uncollectable. This means that all reasonable efforts to collect the amount owing have been exhausted, ie statements, letters and emails etc have been sent to the trade receivable requesting payment, and legal action, where appropriate, or the threat of legal action has failed to obtain payment.

In writing off a trade receivable's account as irrecoverable, the business is bearing the cost of the amount due. The trade receivable's account is closed and the amount (or amounts, where a number of accounts are dealt with in this way) is debited to irrecoverable debts written off account. This account stores up the amounts of account balances written off during the year (in much the same way as an expense account). At the end of the financial year, the balance of the account is transferred to income statement, where it is described as irrecoverable debts written off.

In terms of bookkeeping, the transactions are:

- debit irrecoverable debts written off account
- credit trade receivable's account

with the amount of the irrecoverable debt written off.

At the end of the financial year, irrecoverable debts written off account is transferred to income statement:

- debit income statement
- credit irrecoverable debts written off account

with the total of irrecoverable debts written off for the year.

WORKED EXAMPLE: TREATMENT OF IRRECOVERABLE DEBTS

The following trade receivable's account is in the sales ledger:

Dr		**T Hughes**			Cr
20-1		£	20-1		£
5 Jan	Sales	55	8 May	Bank	25
			6 Jul	Cash	5

It is now 15 December 20-1 and you are reviewing the trade receivables' accounts before the end of the financial year on 31 December. Your business has sent statements and 'chaser' letters to T Hughes – the last letter was dated 30 September, and was returned marked 'gone away, not known at this address'. Nothing further has been heard from T Hughes. You take the decision to write off this account as an irrecoverable debt; the account will be closed off as follows:

Dr		T Hughes			Cr
20-1		£	20-1		£
5 Jan	Sales	55	8 May	Bank	25
			6 Jul	Cash	5
			15 Dec	Irrecoverable debts written off	25
		55			55

The balance is transferred to the 'holding' account, irrecoverable debts written off (in the general ledger), together with other trade receivables' accounts written off. At the end of the financial year, the total of this account is transferred to income statement:

Dr		Irrecoverable Debts Written Off Account			Cr
20-1		£	20-1		£
15 Dec	T Hughes	25	31 Dec	Income statement	200
15 Dec	A Lane	85			
15 Dec	A Harvey	90			
		200			200

In financial statements, the effect of writing off debts as irrecoverable is to reduce the previously reported profit – in the example above – by £200. Note that:

- If you are preparing financial statements and the figure for irrecoverable debts is shown in the trial balance (debit side), simply record the amount as an expense in income statement – the trade receivables' figure has been reduced already.
- If the irrecoverable debts figure is not already shown in the trial balance, and a note tells you to write off a certain debt as irrecoverable, you need to list the amount as an expense in income statement and reduce the trade receivables' figure for the statement of financial position.

Irrecoverable Debts in the Financial Statements

We will now focus on how the amounts for irrecoverable debts are shown in the income statement and statement of financial position. We will continue with the financial statements of Wyvern Wholesalers (see pages 215 and 216) where the owner tells you that there is £250 to be written off the trade receivables figures as irrecoverable debts.

income statement

There is no effect on gross profit, so the first part of the income statement is not shown here. The income statement appears as shown on the next page, with the irrecoverable debts written off amount for the year included amongst the expenses, where it is shaded for illustrative purposes.

INCOME STATEMENT OF WYVERN WHOLESALERS FOR THE YEAR ENDED 31 DECEMBER 20-1			
	£	£	£
Gross profit			99,750
Add Discount received			2,500
			102,250
Less expenses:			
Discount allowed		3,700	
Salaries		46,000	
Electricity and gas		3,250	
Rent and business rates		1,900	
Sundry expenses		4,700	
Depreciation:			
premises		2,000	
equipment		3,000	
Irrecoverable debts		250	
			64,800
Profit for the year			37,450

The effect of taking note of irrecoverable debts written off is to reduce profit:

Profit for the year (before adjustment for irrecoverable debts)	£37,700	(see page 215)
Less irrecoverable debts written off	£250	
Profit for the year (after adjustment for irrecoverable debts)	£37,450	

statement of financial position

The statement of financial position is shown on the next page with the trade receivables amount shaded for illustrative purposes. The amount of irrecoverable debts of £250 has been deducted before trade receivables are recorded, ie £23,850 – £250 written off = £23,600.

Private Expenses and Goods for Own Use

Adjustments also have to be made in the financial statements for the amount of any business facilities that are used by the owner for private purposes. These adjustments are for private expenses and goods for own use.

private expenses

Sometimes the owner of a business uses business facilities for private purposes, eg telephone, or car. The owner will agree that part of the expense shall be charged to him or her as drawings, while the other part represents a business expense.

STATEMENT OF FINANCIAL POSITION OF WYVERN WHOLESALERS
AS AT 31 DECEMBER 20-1

	£	£	£
Non-current Assets	*Cost*	*Depreciation*	*Net book value*
Property	100,000	2,000	98,000
Equipment	30,000	3,000	27,000
	130,000	5,000	125,000
Current Assets			
Inventory		16,300	
Trade receivables 23,850 – 250		23,600	
Other receivables		100	
Cash		125	
		40,125	
Less Current Liabilities			
Trade payables	12,041		
Other payables	250		
Bank	851		
		13,142	
Net Current Assets or Working Capital			26,983
			151,983
Less Non-current Liabilities			
Loan			11,500
NET ASSETS			140,483
FINANCED BY			
Capital			
Opening capital			113,475
Add Profit for the year			*37,450
			150,925
Less Drawings			10,442
			140,483

* see profit calculations on previous page

For example, telephone expenses for the year amount to £600, and the owner agrees that this should be split as one-quarter private use, and three-quarters to the business. This is recorded in the financial statements as:

- £450 (three-quarters) in income statement as a business expense
- £150 (one-quarter) is added to the owner's drawings

goods for own use

When the owner of a business takes some of the goods in which the business trades for his or her own use, the amount is:

- deducted from purchases
- added to the owner's drawings

The reason for reducing purchases is to ensure that only those purchases used in the business are recorded; these are then matched to the sales derived from them.

Goods on Sale or Return

Sale or return is where a business supplies goods to a customer on the basis that the customer will pay for the goods as and when they are sold. For example, newspapers and magazines are often supplied to shops by distributors on a sale or return basis. Until the goods are paid for by the customer they remain the property of the supplier and are included in the supplier's inventory. If the goods are not sold within an agreed time period the goods will be returned to the supplier. Usually the invoice issued for such goods will be marked clearly as 'sale or return'.

Accounting methods for sale or return vary. In the supplier's accounting records the following procedure is often used:

- supply of goods on sale or return to a customer
  - debit trade receivable's account
  - credit sales account
- payment received for some or all of the goods
  - debit bank account
  - credit trade receivable's account
- for unsold goods held by the customer at the financial year-end
  - debit sales account
  - credit trade receivable's account
- include the unsold goods in inventory at the cost to the supplier
- at the beginning of the next financial year for goods still held by the customer, reverse the end-of-year entry
  - debit trade receivable's account
  - credit sales account

In the customer's accounting, goods received from a supplier on a sale or return basis will not be recorded until they are sold. At this point the accounting records will show:

- the sale or return invoice
  - debit purchases account
  - credit trade payable's account
- the sale of the goods
  - debit bank account
  - credit sales account
- payment to the supplier
  - debit trade payable's account
  - credit bank account

From the customer's viewpoint, note the following:

- goods are not paid for until they are sold
- unsold goods may be returned to the supplier
- there is no liability to pay the supplier until the goods have been sold

- any inventory of sale or return goods held at the end of the financial year must not be included in the figures for purchases for the year and the closing inventory valuation

the legal position

With sale or return, the legal title to the goods is not transferred to the customer and so the customer cannot recognise their existence in law. In legal terms, the supplier has not transferred the 'risks and rewards of ownership' to the customer. The transfer of these risks and rewards – and the legal title – occurs when the customer sells on the goods.

INCOME AND EXPENDITURE ACCOUNTING

In this chapter we have made adjustments for accruals and prepayments to ensure that the income statement shows the correct amount of expenses for the financial year, ie what should have been paid, instead of what has actually been paid. In doing this we are adopting the principle of income and expenditure accounting. If we simply used the trial balance figures, we would be following the principle of receipts and payments (cash) accounting, ie comparing money coming in, with money going out: this would usually give a false view of the profit for the year.

The principle of income and expenditure accounting is applied in the same way to purchases and sales, although no adjustments are needed because of the way in which these two are handled in the accounting records. For purchases, the amount is entered into the accounts when the supplier's invoice is received, although the agreement to buy will be contained in the legal contract which exists between buyer and seller. From the accounting viewpoint, it is receipt of the supplier's invoice that causes an accounting entry to be made; the subsequent payment is handled as a different accounting transaction. A business could have bought goods, not paid for them yet, but will have a purchases figure to enter into the income statement. Doubtless the suppliers will soon be wanting payment!

Sales are recorded in a similar way – when the invoice for the goods is sent, rather than when payment is made. This applies the principle of income and expenditure accounting. In this way, a business could have made a large amount of sales, which will be entered in the income statement, but may not yet have received any payments from customers.

The way in which financial statements are adjusted to take note of adjustments such as expenses accruals and prepayments, depreciation of non-current assets, and irrecoverable debts, is formally recognised in the accruals (or matching) concept, which is discussed in more detail in Chapter 14.

CHAPTER SUMMARY

- Financial statements are prepared on the income and expenditure basis, rather than the receipts and payments (cash) basis.

- An adjustment should be made at the end of the financial year in respect of expense accruals and prepayments.

- In the financial statements, accrued expenses are:
  - added to the expense in the trial balance
  - shown as a current liability (other payables) in the statement of financial position

- In the financial statements, prepaid expenses are:
  - deducted from the expense in the trial balance
  - shown as a current asset (other receivables) in the statement of financial position
- Depreciation is a measure of the amount of the fall in value of non-current assets over a time period.
- Two common methods of calculating depreciation are the straight-line method and the reducing balance method.
- The depreciation amount for the year for each class of non-current asset is included amongst the expenses in income statement, while the asset is shown in the statement of financial position, reduced by the amount of provision for depreciation to date.
- Depreciation is a non-cash expense.
- An irrecoverable debt is a debt owing to a business which it considers will never be paid.
- In the income statement an irrecoverable debt written off is charged as an expense, and in the statement of financial position a net trade receivables' figure is shown.
- Adjustments also need to be made in the financial statements for:
  - private expenses
  - goods for own use
- Goods on sale or return is where a business supplies goods to a customer on the basis that they will be paid for when sold.

This chapter completes your introductory studies for financial accounting. In the next section of this book we move on to develop your knowledge and understanding of financial accounting.

QUESTIONS

visit www.osbornebooks.co.uk to take an online test

An asterisk (*) after the question number means that the answer is given at the end of this book.

12.1 Explain how the following would be dealt with in the income statement, and statement of financial position of a business with a financial year-end of 31 December 20-2:

(a) Wages and salaries paid to 31 December 20-2 amount to £55,640. However, at that date, £1,120 is owing: this amount is paid on 4 January 20-3.

(b) Business rates totalling £3,565 have been paid to cover the period 1 January 20-2 to 31 March 20-3.

(c) A computer is rented at a cost of £150 per month. The rental for January 20-3 was paid in December 20-2 and is included in the total payments during 20-2 which amount to £1,950.

12.2 The following information has been extracted from the accounts of Southtown Supplies, a wholesaling business, for the year-ended 31 December 20-9:

	£
Revenue (Sales)	420,000
Purchases	280,000
Inventory at 1 January 20-9	70,000
Inventory at 31 December 20-9	60,000
Rent and business rates	10,250
Electricity	3,100
Telephone	1,820
Salaries	35,600
Vehicle expenses	13,750

Notes: at 31 December 20-9:

- rent prepaid is £550
- salaries owing are £450

You are to prepare the income statement of Southtown Supplies for the year-ended 31 December 20-9.

12.3* Severn Services supplies goods to customers on a sale or return basis.

The following transactions with Jamal Stores take place in December 20-4:

20-4

10 Dec	Supplied Jamal Stores with 500 units of product AP on a sale or return invoice for £1,500
22 Dec	Jamal Stores pays for 400 units by bank transfer
31 Dec	Severn Services financial year ends

20-5

1 Jan	Severn Services financial year starts

You are to:

(a) Show the accounting entries of Severn Stores to record the sale or return transactions, including the year-end transfer from sales account to the income statement.

(b) Explain how Severn Services will treat the unsold inventory from these transactions in its year-end financial statements at 31 December 20-4, and give reasons for such treatment.

12.4* Susan Harper has produced a draft income statement for the year-ended 31 December 20-8. As yet no entries have been made in the income statement for the following information:

	£
Payments for business rates during the year	2,250
Payments for rent of premises during the year	5,300

Additional information	*Year ended 31 December 20-7*		*Year ended 31 December 20-8*	
		£		£
Payment for business rates	in advance	110	in arrears	150
Payment for rent of premises	in arrears	250	in advance	400

Required:

For each expense calculate the amounts to be entered in the income statement for the year ended 31 December 20-8. Indicate in the table below the amount and whether it should be subtracted from or added to the draft profit of the business. (Complete one box for each expense.)

	Amount to be subtracted from draft profit £	Amount to be added to draft profit £
Business rates		
Rent of premises		

12.5* The following trial balance has been extracted by the bookkeeper of Don Smith, who runs a wholesale stationery business, at 31 December 20-8:

	Dr	Cr
	£	£
Trade receivables	24,325	
Trade payables		19,684
Capital		30,000
Bank		1,083
Rent and business rates	10,862	
Electricity	2,054	
Telephone	1,695	
Salaries	55,891	
Vehicles	22,250	
Office equipment	7,500	
Vehicle expenses	10,855	
Drawings	15,275	
Discount allowed	478	
Discount received		591
Purchases	138,960	
Revenue (Sales)		257,258
Inventory at 1 January 20-8	18,471	
	308,616	308,616

Notes at 31 December 20-8:

- inventory is valued at £14,075
- business rates are prepaid £250
- electricity owing £110
- salaries are owing £365

Required:

(a) Prepare the rent and business rates, electricity and salaries accounts to record the balances shown by the above trial balance, the amounts to be transferred to the income statement and the balances to be carried forward to next year.

(b) Prepare the income statement of Don Smith for the year-ended 31 December 20-8, together with his statement of financial position at that date.

12.6* Martin Hough, sole owner of Juicyburger, a fast food shop, operating from leased premises in the town, is suspicious of his accountant, Mr S Harris, whom he claims doesn't really understand the food business. On the telephone he asks Mr Harris why depreciation is charged on a rigid formula, as surely no-one really knows how much his equipment is worth, and in fact he might not get anything for it. Draft a reply to Mr Hough from Mr Harris explaining the importance of depreciation and its application to financial statements.

12.7* David Evans started in business on 1 July 20-1 with a financial year-end of 30 June. On 1 July 20-1 he bought non-current assets at a cost of £50,000. The non-current assets have an expected useful life of 10 years at the end of which they will have a nil scrap value.

David has decided to use the straight-line method of depreciating his non-current assets at an annual rate of 10%.

David's profits for his first two years in business *before* depreciation of non-current assets were £18,700 for 20-2 and £33,100 for 20-3.

Required:

(a) Calculate David's profit after depreciation of non-current assets.

	year ended 30 June 20-2 £	year ended 30 June 20-3 £
Profit before depreciation	18,700	33,100
Depreciation of non-current assets	....	....
Profit after depreciation	....	....

(b) Prepare an extract of David's statement of financial position showing non-current assets after allowing for provision for depreciation.

	as at 30 June 20-2 £	as at 30 June 20-3 £
Non-current assets at cost	50,000	50,000
Less provision for depreciation to date	....	....
Net book value (carrying amount)	....	....

12.8 The following trial balance has been extracted by the bookkeeper of Hazel Harris at 31 December 20-4:

	Dr	Cr
	£	£
Bank loan		75,000
Capital		125,000
Purchases and Revenue (Sales)	465,000	614,000
Insurances	8,480	
Vehicles at cost	12,000	
Provision for depreciation on vehicles		2,400
Vehicle expenses	2,680	
Freehold land at cost	100,000	
Bank overdraft		2,000
Furniture and fittings at cost	25,000	
Provision for depreciation on furniture and fittings		2,500
Wages and salaries	86,060	
Discounts allowed and received	10,610	8,140
Drawings	24,000	
Business rates	6,070	
Trade receivables and payables	52,130	41,850
General expenses	15,860	
Inventory at 1 January 20-4	63,000	
	870,890	870,890

Notes at 31 December 20-4:

- Inventory is valued at £88,000
- Wages and salaries outstanding: £3,180
- Business rates paid in advance: £450
- Depreciate vehicles at 20 per cent per year using the reducing balance method
- Depreciate furniture and fittings at 10 per cent per year using the straight-line method
- The freehold land is not to be depreciated

Required:

You are to prepare the income statement of Hazel Harris for the year ended 31 December 20-4, together with her statement of financial position at that date.

12.9* You are the bookkeeper at Waterston Plant Hire. At 31 December 20-8, the end of the financial year, the business has gross trade receivables of £20,210. The owner decides to write off, as irrecoverable debts, the accounts of:

P Ross	£55
J Ball	£105
L Jones	£50

You are to:

(a) Show the irrecoverable debts written off account in the general ledger for the financial year.

(b) Explain the effect of this write off on the financial statements at the year-end.

12.10 The following trial balance has been extracted by the bookkeeper of Beth Davis, a solicitor, for the year ended 31 December 20-8.

	Dr	Cr
	£	£
Revenue: income from clients		95,374
Wages and salaries	55,217	
Heating and lighting	1,864	
Rent and business rates	5,273	
Advertising	2,246	
Irrecoverable debts written off	395	
Office expenses	13,959	
Office equipment at cost	10,000	
Provision for depreciation of office equipment		3,600
Trade receivables	23,641	
Trade payables		10,290
Bank		3,690
Cash	163	
Capital		17,000
Drawings	17,196	
	129,954	129,954

Notes at 31 December 20-8:

- rent prepaid £310
- accrued office expenses £85
- depreciate office equipment at 20% per year, using the reducing balance method

You are to prepare the income statement of Beth Davis for the year ended 31 December 20-8, together with her statement of financial position at that date.

12.11* The following information is available about motoring expenses for the year ended 30 September 20-4:

	£
Credit balance brought forward on 1 October 20-3	125
Payments during year ended 30 September 20-4	4,185
Credit balance brought down on 1 October 20-4	240

How much should be shown as the expense for motoring in the income statement for the year ended 30 September 20-4?

A	£4,550	
B	£4,070	
C	£4,425	
D	£4,300	

12.12 Brenda Azike has purchased a new computer system for her business at a cost of £8,000. She will use the system for four years and then replace it. At the end of the four years the system is expected to have a scrap value of £500.

Brenda will depreciate her computer system by using

either the straight-line method

or the reducing balance method using 50% per annum

She wishes to use the method that will increase her bank balance more over the four years.

Required:

(a) Calculate the depreciation charge to Brenda Azike's income statement for the two methods.

	Straight-line method £	Reducing balance method £
Year 1		
Year 2		
Year 3		
Year 4		

(b) Explain the effect of depreciation charges on Brenda's bank balance.

Financial Accounting

This section of the book develops your knowledge and understanding of financial accounting and introduces some of the ways in which financial accounting can provide valuable information for monitoring business performance. The following topics are covered:

- types of business organisation and their financing
- accounting concepts
- further aspects of the preparation of the financial statements of sole traders
- financial statements of limited companies for internal use
- financial ratios and the assessment of business performance

13 BUSINESS ORGANISATIONS AND FINANCING

In the first part of this book we have prepared the financial statements of sole traders. A sole trader is a person who sets up in business on his or her own.

In this chapter we look at two further types of business organisation – partnerships and limited companies – and compare the advantages of the three types of ownership.

The chapter also looks at the sources of finance available to business organisations.

PRIVATE SECTOR ORGANISATIONS

Sole traders, partnerships and limited companies are all private sector organisations – as distinct from public sector organisations (such as local authorities, central government, the National Health Service) and not-for-profit organisations (such as societies and charities). The following diagram illustrates the types of private sector organisations:

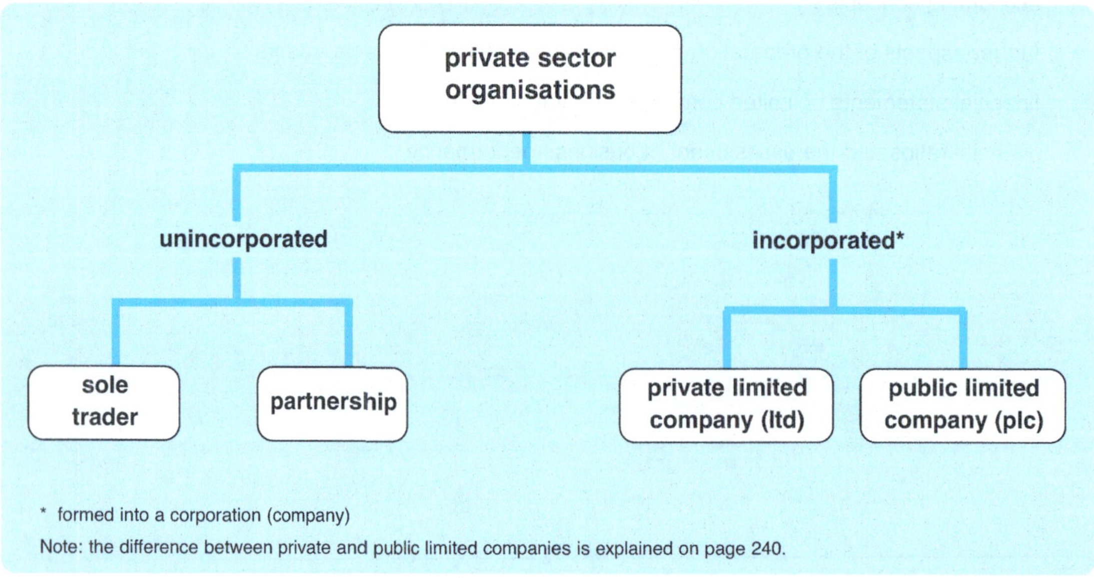

In terms of accounting, we have already prepared the financial statements of sole traders in earlier chapters. The transition from sole trader to partnership financial statements is not too big a step. In a partnership, instead of one person owning the business, there will be two or more owners.

The step from sole traders and partnerships to limited companies is rather greater, as a limited company is an incorporated business ('incorporated' means 'formed into a company'), where the owners are members (shareholders) of the company. The limited company financial statements you will study are for internal use by the owners and managers of the business – they are covered in Chapter 17.

Each of the three types of business organisation – sole trader, partnership, and limited company – is discussed in more detail in the rest of this chapter. The following table illustrates the key differences between them:

	sole trader	**partnership**	**limited company**
ownership	• owned by the sole trader	• owned by the partners	• owned by the shareholders
legal status	• the sole trader is the business	• the partners are the business	• separate legal entity from its owners
members	• one	• between 2 and 20 (normal maximum)	• minimum of one shareholder; no maximum
liability	• unlimited liability, for debts of business	• partners normally liable for entire partnership debt	• shareholders can lose their investment
legislation	• none	• Partnership Act 1890	• Companies Act 2006
regulation	• none	• written or oral partnership agreement	• Articles of Association
taxation	• as an individual on profit	• each partner as an individual on share of profit	• company pays tax on profit
management	• owner takes all decisions	• all partners normally take an active part	• directors and authorised employees
financial statements	• private – not available to the public	• private – not available to the public	• must be filed at Companies House where they are available to the public

SOLE TRADERS

A sole trader is a person who is in business on his or her own. Sole traders run shops, travel agencies, garages, local franchises, and so on. The businesses are generally small because the owner usually has a limited amount of capital to invest. All the profit belongs to the sole trader; some of it will be taken out as drawings and the rest ploughed back into expanding the business.

People set up as sole traders for various reasons:

- the owner has independence and can run the business, by and large without the need to involve others in decision-making
- in a small business with few, if any, employees, the owner is able to give personal service and supervise all areas of the business
- the business is easy to establish legally – either using the owner's name, or a trading name such as 'Wyvern Plumbing Services'

The disadvantages of a sole-trader business are:

- the owner has unlimited liability for the debts of the business – this means that if the sole trader should become bankrupt (unable to pay debts when they are due), the owner's personal assets may be sold to pay trade payables
- expansion is limited because it can be achieved only by the owner ploughing back profits, or by borrowing from a lender such as a bank
- the owner usually has to work long hours and it may be difficult to find time to take holidays; if the owner should become ill the work of the business may either slow down or stop altogether

financial statements of a sole trader

The financial statements of a sole trader comprise:

- income statement, which shows the profit or loss of the business
- statement of financial position, which shows the assets and liabilities of the business together with the owner's capital

These financial statements can be produced more often than once a year in order to give information to the owner on how the business is progressing. However, it is normal to produce annual statements for the benefit of HM Revenue & Customs (the tax authorities, who will wish to see that tax due – income tax and VAT – has been paid), providers of finance (such as the bank), and other stakeholders.

PARTNERSHIPS

The Partnership Act of 1890 defines a partnership as:

the relation which subsists between persons carrying on a business in common with a view of profit

Normally, partnerships consist of between two and twenty partners. Exceptions to this include large professional firms, eg solicitors and accountants, who often set up what are known as 'limited liability partnerships' (LLPs). Partnerships are often larger businesses than sole traders because, as there is more than one owner, there is likely to be more capital. A partnership may be formed to set up a new business or it may be the logical growth of a sole trader taking in partners to increase the capital.

advantages and disadvantages

Partnerships are cheap and easy to set up; their advantages are:

- there is the possibility of increased capital
- individual partners may be able to specialise in particular areas of the business
- with more people running the business, there is more cover for illness and holidays

The disadvantages are:

- as there is more than one owner, decisions may take longer because other partners may need to be consulted
- there may be disagreements amongst the partners
- each partner is liable in law for the dealings and business debts of the whole firm – unless it is a limited liability partnership (LLP) set up under the Limited Liability Partnerships Act 2000
- the retirement or death of one partner may adversely affect the running of the business

accounting requirements of a partnership

The accounting requirements of a partnership are:

- either to follow the rules set out in the Partnership Act 1890
- or – and more likely – for the partners to agree amongst themselves, by means of a partnership agreement, to follow different accounting rules

Unless the partners agree otherwise, the Partnership Act 1890 states the following accounting rules:

- profits and losses are to be shared equally between the partners
- no partner is entitled to a salary
- partners are not entitled to receive interest on their capital
- interest is not to be charged on partners' drawings
- when a partner contributes more capital than agreed, he or she is entitled to receive interest at five per cent per year on the excess

As noted above, the partners may well decide to follow different accounting rules – these will be set out in a partnership agreement:

- division of profits and losses between partners
- partners' salaries
- whether interest is to be allowed on capital and at what rate
- whether interest is to be charged on partners' drawings, and at what rate

partners' capital contributions

When forming a partnership, partners must agree how much capital each is to contribute – which may well not be in equal shares.

For example, a partnership business with three partners that requires a total capital of £240,000 could consider the following ratios:

	Partner A	Partner B	Partner C
Ratio of 1 : 1 : 1	£80,000	£80,000	£80,000
Ratio of 2 : 1 : 1	£120,000	£60,000	£60,000
Ratio of 1 : 2 : 3	£40,000	£80,000	£120,000

From the example above there are any number of capital variations – the important point is that the partners must agree how much each is to contribute.

financial statements of a partnership

A partnership prepares the same type of financial statements as a sole trader business:

- income statement
- statement of financial position

The main difference is that, immediately after the income statement, follows an appropriation section (often described as an appropriation account). This shows how the profit for the year from income statement is shared amongst the partners.

Limited Companies

A limited company is a separate legal entity, owned by shareholders and run by directors.

Many people in business as sole traders often consider converting to a limited company. Read the following Case Study about a sole trader business and the discussions that take place between the sole trader and her accountant:

Case Study: conversion to a limited company

Veta Bix has been trading very successfully for the last three years running her bodycare products business as a sole trader. At the moment she has three shops and an online business trading under the 'BodyZone' name. She has plans, as she says to her accountant:

'I've big plans for expansion and have identified suitable sites for new shops in the south east, nearer to London. My problem, though, is finance; I will need a lot more capital. As a sole trader, it is difficult to see how I can raise the money I will need. I am also concerned about my unlimited liability for the debts of the business.'

Veta's accountant suggests that she consider forming a private limited company which will enable her to issue shares to family, friends and to local investors. As the accountant says:

'We aren't talking about a company quoted on the Stock Exchange – although some small businesses have made it to that stage. Instead, forming a private limited company should enable you to raise the finance you need and you will still be able to retain control of the business.'

The accountant suggests she calls the company BodyZone Limited. He comments:

'Forming a company is a big change from a sole trader business as it must be registered at Companies House. The company will have to produce formal annual financial statements, which have to be filed at Companies House. The way you draw income from the company will also be different – a mix of salary and dividend payments. In terms of cost, it is quite an expensive option, but it would give you the added protection of limited liability.'

People choose to run a business as a limited company for a number of reasons:

limited liability

The shareholders (members) of a limited company can lose only the amount of their investment, being the money for shares paid already, together with any money unpaid on their shares (unpaid instalments on new share issues, for example). Thus, if the company became insolvent (went 'bust'), shareholders would have to pay any unpaid instalments to help pay the debts of the company. As this happens very rarely, shareholders are usually in a safe position: their personal assets are not available to pay the company's debts – ie they have **limited liability**.

separate legal entity

A limited company is a separate legal entity from its owners. Anyone taking legal action proceeds against the company and not the individual shareholders.

ability to raise finance

A limited company can raise funds from outside sources by the issue of shares:

- for the larger public company – from the public and investing institutions on the Stock Exchange or similar markets
- for the smaller company – privately from venture capital companies, relatives and friends

Companies can also raise finance by means of debentures, which are formal loan certificates issued by companies raising long-term finance from lenders and investors.

membership

A member of a limited company is a person who owns at least one share in that company. A member of a company is the same as a shareholder. All ordinary shareholders have voting rights, so a sole trader who has converted to limited company status may lose some control of the business if some of the shares are held by other investors.

other factors

A limited company may be a much larger business unit than a sole trader. This gives the company a higher standing and status in the business community, allowing it to benefit from economies of scale, and making it of sufficient size to employ specialists for functions such as production, marketing, finance and human resources.

On the negative side, there is more documentation – eg the preparation of formal Annual Accounts – for a company to produce than for a sole trader business. The costs of administering a company are higher than for a sole trader.

running the company

As noted in the definition, a limited company is owned by its shareholders but is run by the directors. Under the Companies Act 2006, the company's *Articles of Association* provides the constitution of the company, regulates the affairs of the company to the outside world, and sets out the rules for running the company – including the powers of directors and the holding of company meetings.

the Companies Act

Limited companies are regulated by the Companies Act 2006. Under the terms of the Act there are two main types of limited company: the larger **public limited company** (abbreviated to 'Plc') and the smaller company, traditionally known as a **private limited company** (abbreviated to 'Ltd'). A further type of company is limited by guarantee.

public limited company (Plc)

A company may become a public limited company if it has:

- issued share capital of over £50,000
- at least two members (shareholders) and at least two directors

A public limited company may raise capital from the public on the Stock Exchange or similar markets; however, a plc does not have to issue shares on the stock markets, and not all do so.

private limited company (Ltd)

The private limited company is the most common form of limited company and is defined by the Act as 'any company that is not a public company'. Many private limited companies are small companies, often in family ownership. A private limited company has:

- no minimum requirement for issued share capital
- at least one member (shareholder) and at least one director who may be the sole shareholder

The shares are not traded publicly, but are transferable between individuals, although valuation will be more difficult for shares not quoted on the stock markets.

company limited by guarantee

A company limited by guarantee does not have share capital, but relies on the guarantee of its members to pay a stated amount in the event of the company's insolvency. Examples of such companies include charities, and artistic and educational organisations.

financial statements of a limited company

For internal use, a limited company prepares the same type of financial statements as a sole trader and partnership business:

- income statement
- statement of financial position

The main difference is that a limited company follows the income statement with a **statement of changes in equity** which shows how the profit for the year has been distributed (including dividends paid to shareholders on the shares they own), and provides a link to the statement of financial position.

Every limited company has to produce annual financial statements which are also available for anyone to inspect if they so wish. Such Annual Accounts are those which are required to be produced under company law, and filed at Companies House (a Government Agency). The level of detail contained in the accounts is set out in company law and varies depending on the size of the company – for example, small and medium-sized private companies file modified accounts containing much less detail than public companies.

In Chapter 17 of this book we will prepare the financial statements of limited companies for internal use.

accounting personnel of a limited company

There are a number of different staff who may be involved in the accounting function. A large limited company, for example, may employ bookkeepers and ledger clerks, financial accountants, cost and management accountants, and internal and external auditors, as shown in the diagram below. A small limited company, on the other hand may have only a few employees carrying out these functions.

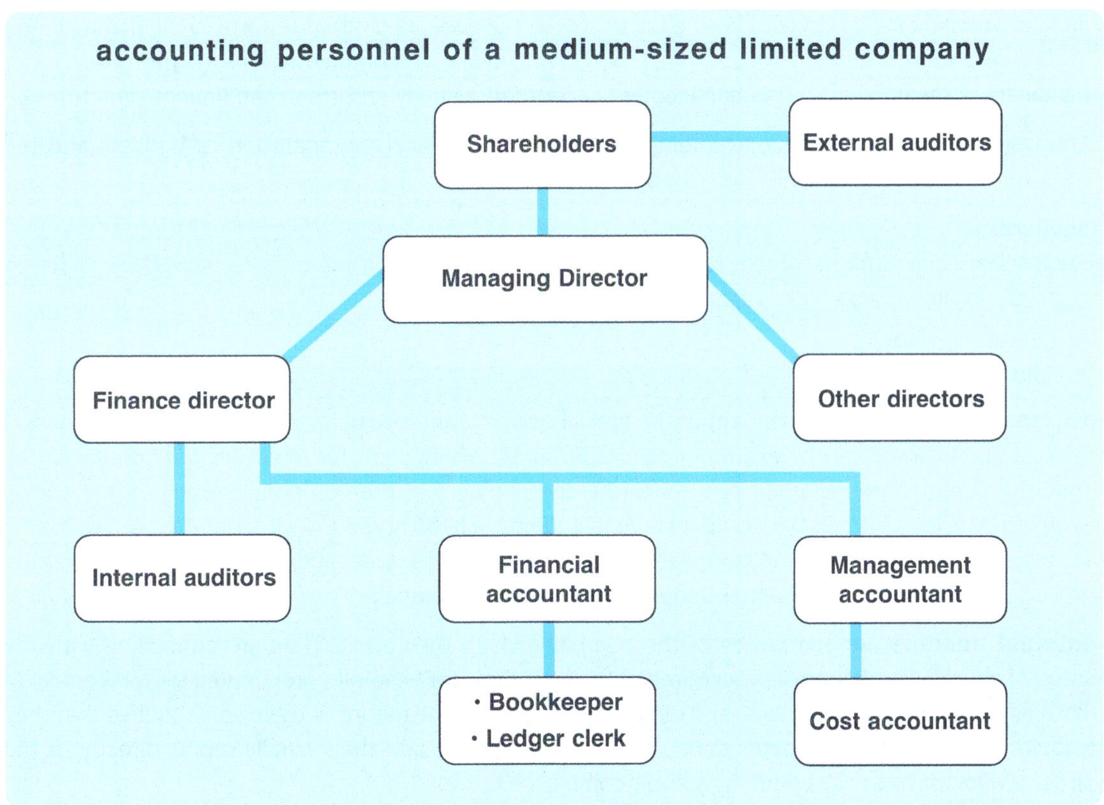

Bookkeepers and ledger clerks record the day-to-day transactions of the business, including:

- maintaining accounting records
- entering transactions in the books of prime entry (journals) and ledger accounts
- checking the accuracy of the bookkeeping

The bookkeeper will also be able to extract a trial balance.

financial accountant

The role of the financial accountant is to oversee the work of the bookkeepers and ledger clerks and to take further the information prepared by them. This includes the preparation of financial statements both for internal use, and published accounts which comply with the requirements of the Companies Act 2006. This Act requires the directors of a company to report annually to shareholders, with certain minimum financial accounting information being disclosed. In particular, the financial accountant will ensure that:

- accounting concepts are applied
- the financial statements show a true and fair view of the business

The financial accountant may be required to negotiate with the tax authorities on the amount of tax to be paid on the profits of the company. The financial accountant usually reports to the finance director.

cost and management accountants

The cost accountant obtains information about the recent costs of the company, eg raw materials and labour, and estimates costs for the future. Often the cost accountant reports to the management accountant who prepares budgets and reports, and makes recommendations to the directors or managers of the company. The management accountant usually reports to the finance director.

The work of the cost and management accountants includes the preparation of budgets and the exercise of budgetary control – see Chapter 19.

auditors

Auditors are accountants whose role is to check that accounting procedures have been followed correctly. There are two types of auditors:

- external auditors
- internal auditors

External auditors are independent of the firm whose accounts are being audited. The most common type of audit carried out by external auditors is the statutory audit for larger limited companies. In this, the auditors are reporting directly to the shareholders of the company, stating that the legal requirements laid down in the Companies Acts 2006 have been complied with, and that the accounts represent a 'true and fair view' of the state of the business. External auditors are usually appointed by the shareholders at the Annual General Meeting of the company.

Internal auditors are employees of the company which they audit. They are concerned with the internal checking and control procedures of the company: for example, procedures for the control of cash, authorisation of purchases, and disposal of property. The nature of their work requires that they should have a degree of independence within the company and they usually report directly to the finance director or to the company's audit committee.

Sources of Finance for Business

This section describes the different sources of finance available to business organisations, including:

- their features
- their advantages and risks

Note that, before a business considers any form of finance, it should look at methods of financing within the business. For example, before taking out a bank overdraft a business could consider:

- increasing sales
- reducing its inventory
- reducing the period of credit allowed to trade receivables
- increasing the period of credit taken from trade payables

It may not be possible to undertake all these, but there may be some measure of financing within the business.

Larger projects, such as the modernisation of a shop or a factory, are likely to require an amount of external finance.

The sources of finance and their suitability are:

- owner's capital – for sole traders
- partners' capital – for partnerships
- bank overdraft – for sole traders, partnerships and limited companies
- bank loan – for sole traders, partnerships and limited companies
- mortgage – for sole traders, partnerships and limited companies
- ordinary shares – for limited companies, both private and public
- debentures – for limited companies, both private and public

owner's and partners' capital

features

- Funds provided by the owner or partners – eg capital from savings.
- For an established business, funds generated from profits can be used to provide finance – eg new computers may be purchased using cash generated from profits made by the business.

advantages

- Very flexible – funds can be provided to the business when needed and taken out when not needed.
- No legal documents required to raise the finance.
- The owner or partners may decide not to charge interest to the business (although a partner contributing more capital than agreed is entitled to receive interest at five per cent per year on the excess).
- No security required from the owner or partners.

risks

- The owner or partners may not have any further cash to provide to the business.
- The business may not be able to repay any additional funds contributed.
- A business may not have sufficient funds generated from profits to provide finance for new assets.
- Using funds from profits as a source of finance reduces the amount that can be withdrawn from the business by the owner or partners.

bank overdraft

features

- A bank overdraft is a flexible arrangement with a bank which allows a customer to borrow money on a current account up to a certain limit, eg £50,000. An overdraft is used to cover the day-to-day net current asset (working capital) requirements of a business, eg purchase of inventory at times when funds are low.
- Interest is paid – normally at a variable rate in line with market rates.
- An overdraft limit is normally reviewed with the business every year.
- An overdraft is repayable on demand if the bank wants the borrowing repaid.
- Security, such as property, will be required from the business or business owner to safeguard the borrowing. A personal guarantee may also be required.

advantages

- A bank overdraft is very flexible: a business can borrow and repay whenever it likes.
- An overdraft can be economical to operate: interest is only payable when the business borrows, and is charged only the borrowed amount.

risks

- Interest rates for bank overdrafts can be higher than bank loan rates.
- If the business gets into financial difficulties the bank can ask for immediate repayment of an overdraft, which could cause further cash flow problems for the business.
- Security, including possibly the house of the business owner, is required for an overdraft. A personal guarantee may also be required.

bank loan

features

- A bank loan is finance provided by the banks for a specific purpose, often the purchase of an asset. Loan amounts can range from £1,000 to £100,000 or more.
- Interest is paid, either at a rate fixed at the beginning of the loan, or at a variable rate in line with market rates during the lifetime of the loan.
- A bank loan is for a set time period, normally between 1 and 25 years.
- The loan is often repaid in regular instalments, but this may be varied, for example with a 'repayment holiday' – this is where the borrower is allowed to

wait a year or so before starting to make repayments. Some loans can also be repaid in full at the end of the loan period rather than by instalments.

- Security, either the assets being purchased or the property of the business owner(s), is required for a bank loan.

advantages

- A bank loan is easy to budget for because the timing and the amount of the repayments is known.
- There may be flexibility in the repayment schedule, for example arranging to delay the early repayments (a 'repayment holiday').
- Favourable interest rates can be negotiated, often at a lower rate than an overdraft.

risks

- A business loan is a long-term financial commitment which will need to be serviced, ie interest and repayments.
- Security, including possibly the house of the business owner, is needed.

mortgage

features

- A mortgage is an arrangement in which property is used as security for borrowing. If the borrower defaults on the loan, the lender can sell the property to obtain the funds. Amounts range from £25,000 to £500,000 or more.
- Banks and other providers can offer finance for the purchase of commercial property, normally up to 70% of its market value. A commercial mortgage is basically the same for a business as it is for a house buyer.
- Interest is paid, either at a rate fixed at the beginning of the mortgage, or at a variable rate in line with market rates during the lifetime of the mortgage.
- A mortgage is for a set time period, normally up to 25 years.

advantages

- A mortgage is easy to budget for because the timing and the amount of the repayments is known.
- If a fixed rate mortgage is taken when rates are relatively low, the cost of borrowing is also relatively low.

risks

- A mortgage is a long-term financial commitment which will need to be serviced, ie interest and repayments. The property mortgaged is the security for the borrowing and, if repayments are not made, the lender will sell the property.

limited company ordinary shares

features

- When a limited company starts up for the first time, or expands its operations, it obtains finance by issuing ordinary shares to its owners and other investors who become its shareholders.
- Shares are issued in return for payment of a fixed amount per share and become the capital of the company.
- In return for investment in company ordinary shares the shareholders receive regular dividend payments, paid out of the profits of the company.

- It is possible to buy the shares of public limited companies (plc) on the Stock Exchange but the majority of limited companies are private limited companies (ltd), often started by sole trader or family businesses. Their shares are not for public sale.
- If a limited company wishes to raise finance by issuing more shares, it can do so either by issuing them to the existing owners and shareholders or by applying to a private equity firm for an issue to outside investors. These investors will provide the finance, but will also want an element of control over the company because they have in practice become new part-owners.

advantages

- A limited company making a share issue can potentially raise more finance than a sole trader or partnership because outside investors are able to buy shares in the company.
- A limited company making a share issue can also attract new management with valuable skills and expertise.
- Dividends on most ordinary shares vary according to the level of profits; therefore the cost of the finance is effectively variable and will not be such a burden if the business profits are lower.

risks

- If outside investors buy into the company by acquiring ordinary shares, they will have an element of control over the company which could prove disruptive for the existing management.
- With most shares, the finance is never 'paid off' as it is with a fixed term loan or overdraft because there will always be the need to pay dividends.
- If the company 'goes bust' the ordinary shareholders are normally the last people to get their money back – in fact they rarely get anything at all.

limited company debentures

features

- Debentures are a fixed interest, fixed repayment date investment – sometimes known as loan notes – issued by a limited company which represents debt owed by that company.
- Debentures only relate to loans made to the company and do not give any rights of ownership of the company in the way that ordinary shares do. They are sometimes secured on the company's assets.
- Debentures of larger companies can be traded on the stock markets.
- Debenture holders may require to have company assets charged as security.

advantages

- Debenture holders are unable to vote at shareholder meetings and so are unable to take part in the running of the company.
- Interest is paid at a fixed percentage rate – this makes budgeting easier for the company.

risks
- If the company does not make a profit, the interest (which ranks ahead of dividends) will always have to be paid at the fixed rate on the due date.
- Debentures often give the holders better rights than ordinary shareholders to obtain repayment if the company 'goes bust'.

CHAPTER SUMMARY

- Sole traders, partnerships and limited companies are private sector organisations.
- A sole trader is a person who is in business on his or her own.
- A partnership is formed when two or more (usually up to a maximum of twenty) people set up in business.
- The Partnership Act 1890 defines a partnership as 'the relation which subsists between persons carrying on a business in common with a view of profit'.
- The Partnership Act 1890 states certain accounting rules, principally that profits and losses must be shared equally.
- Many partnerships over-ride the accounting rules of the Act by making a partnership agreement which covers:
  - division of profits and losses between partners
  - partners' salaries
  - whether interest is to be allowed on capital, and at what rate
  - whether interest is to be charged on partners' drawings, and at what rate
- A limited company has a separate legal entity from its owners.
- A limited company is regulated by the Companies Act 2006, and is owned by shareholders and managed by directors.
- A limited company may be either a public limited company (plc) or a private limited company (ltd).
- The liability of shareholders is limited to the amount of their investment and any money unpaid on their shares.
- Sources of finance available to business organisations include:
  - owner's capital
  - partners' capital
  - bank overdraft
  - bank loan
  - mortgage
  - limited company ordinary shares
  - limited company debentures

QUESTIONS

visit
www.osbornebooks.co.uk
to take an online test

An asterisk (*) after the question number means that the answer is given at the end of this book.

13.1* Karen, a friend of yours, is keen to set up in business running a sandwich and coffee shop on her own. She will call the business 'Karen's Katering'. Point out to her the advantages and disadvantages of a sole trader business and indicate possible future developments in the business organisation that she might consider.

13.2 What financial statements are produced at the end of each financial year for a sole trader business? Explain the main sections contained within the financial statements.

13.3

(a) Define a partnership.

(b) State three accounting provisions from the Partnership Act 1890 which will apply to a partnership where no partnership agreement exists.

13.4* Ron, Sue and Tom are planning to form a partnership. Their business will require capital of £150,000.

The partners are considering three possible ratios in which to make their capital contributions.

Complete the table below with the amounts each partner will contribute based on each of the three ratios.

	Ron	Sue	Tom
Ratio of 1 : 1 : 1			
Ratio of 2 : 1 : 1			
Ratio of 1 : 2 : 2			

13.5* Wyvern Trading Ltd wishes to prepare a handout for new staff explaining some facts about limited companies.

Required:

(a) Who owns Wyvern Trading Ltd?

(b) Who is responsible for the day-to-day running of Wyvern Trading Ltd?

(c) What is the meaning of limited liability?

13.6 Prepare a five-minute talk on the types of companies and the advantages of forming a limited company. The talk is to form part of your local radio station's business programme entitled 'Business Matters'. To accompany your talk, prepare an information sheet which can be put on the station's website.

13.7 Describe the two types of limited company finance listed below. Include in your description the ways in which they differ as far as the payment of dividends or interest is concerned.

(a) Ordinary shares.

(b) Debentures.

13.8 Banks offer a number of sources of finance for business. You are to recommend the bank finance product which best fulfils the need of each of the three businesses described below. In each case you are to describe the main features of the product, give reasons for your choice and set out the advantages and disadvantages of the source of finance you have chosen for the business.

(a) Sajit is setting up a stationery shop and is looking for short-term finance which will see him through times when he is short of cash. For example, he will need to pay his suppliers for his inventory and the wages of his two assistants before the sales from his shop have become fully established.

(b) Rachel is setting up a business which will make and market organic yoghurt to the supermarket chains. In order to get going she needs to purchase substantial manufacturing and refrigeration equipment which she estimates will cost her £85,000.

(c) Basil, who has spent twenty years in the hotel trade, wants to buy a house in Torquay to convert into a hotel. The property will cost him £900,000 and he has £300,000 as a deposit. He is therefore looking for finance totalling £600,000 for the property purchase.

13.9 Tariq plans to set up a design consultancy business as a sole trader within the next six months. He will need total financing of £150,000 in addition to the money he is putting in himself (ie all his savings and available funds). His family have hinted that they might be willing to lend him money, interest-free, but he knows they will want to help him run the business, and he is not sure if this is a good idea.

He plans to rent an office and needs £80,000 for non-current assets such as furniture and computer equipment. The remaining £70,000 he will need for net current assets (working capital). He owns his house which has sufficient security value available for the finance.

Required:

Discuss alternative methods of raising the required finance for:

(a) The assets Tariq needs to purchase.

(b) The net current assets (working capital) he will need.

Your discussion should explain the options for Tariq's financial needs and come to a justified conclusion and firm recommendation in each case.

13.10* ChocsAway Limited is a small private company that makes and sells high-quality chocolates.

The company has an issued share capital of 200,000 £1 ordinary shares, all of which are owned by the three directors.

The company wishes to expand production of chocolates and would also like to purchase new factory premises. The directors seek your advice on two issues:

1. How to fund the increase in net current assets (working capital) that will be necessary as production is increased, creating short-term cash flow problems.

2. How to finance the purchase of new premises.

Issue 1

The finance director has prepared budgeted financial statements for the next six months, based upon an increase in production of 20%. The statements show that increases in inventory, trade receivables and trade payables would lead to an overdrawn bank balance of £25,000, instead of the present £4,000 of money in the bank at the end of the six month period.

The finance director advises that a bank overdraft facility should be arranged for twelve months – interest would be charged at a rate of 8% per annum. The alternative would be a bank short-term loan for twelve months at an interest rate of 6%.

Issue 2

Currently ChocsAway Limited rents its factory premises at a cost of £2,000 per month. New factory premises to purchase have been identified at a cost of £700,000. The finance director suggests that 50% of the cost could be financed through a commercial mortgage for 10 years at a rate of 4% per annum. The new factory premises are large enough to allow for future expansion of the company and, if the company buys them, it will give up the rented premises.

You are to evaluate potential sources of finance to:

(a) Solve the funding of the increased net current assets (working capital).

(b) Finance the purchase of new premises.

14 ACCOUNTING CONCEPTS AND INVENTORY VALUATION

In this chapter we will explain how accounting concepts – or principles – are applied when preparing financial statements. If the same concepts are followed, then comparisons can be made between the financial statements of different businesses.

Later in the chapter we see how the accounting concepts are applied to the valuation of the inventory of goods which a business holds for resale.

ACCOUNTING CONCEPTS

There are a number of generally applied **accounting concepts** – or principles of accounting – which underlie the preparation of financial statements. These concepts help to make financial statements relevant and reliable to stakeholders, and also enable them to be comparable and understandable.

The accounting concepts – which apply equally to sole trader, partnership and limited company businesses – are illustrated in the diagram below.

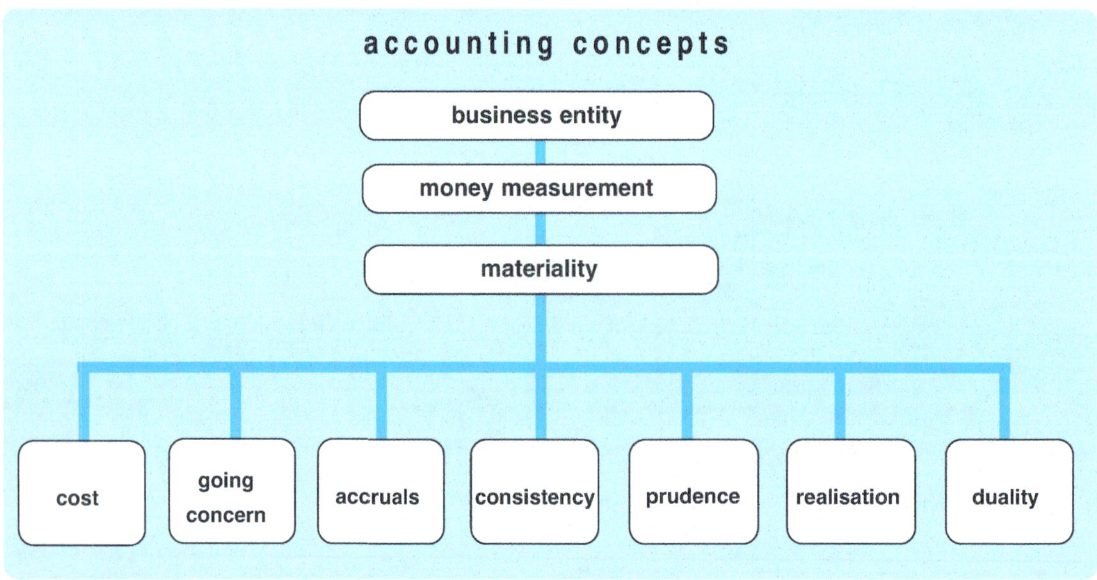

The 'gateway' concepts of business entity, money measurement and materiality apply to all aspects of financial statements – if information is not dealt with correctly under these three concepts it could have consequences for stakeholders who make decisions on the basis of the financial statements.

business entity

This refers to the fact that financial statements record and report on the activities of a particular business. They do not include the assets and liabilities of people who play a part in owning or running the business. For example, the personal assets and liabilities of the owner of a sole trader business are kept separate from those of the business, and personal expenses (eg a family holiday) cannot be paid for from the business bank account. The main links between the business and the owner's personal funds are capital and drawings.

money measurement

This concept refers to the fact that the accounting system uses money as the common denominator in recording and reporting all business transactions. Thus it is not possible to record, for example, the loyalty of a firm's workforce or the quantity of a product, because these cannot be reported in money terms.

materiality

Some items in accounts have such a low monetary (money) value that it is not worthwhile recording them separately, ie they are not 'material'. Examples of this include:

- Small expense items, such as donations to charities, the purchase of plants for the office, window cleaning, etc, may not justify their own separate expense account; instead they are grouped together in a sundry expenses account.
- End-of-year quantities of office stationery, eg paper clips, staples, photocopying paper, etc, are often not valued for the purpose of financial statements, because the amount is not material and does not justify the time and effort involved. This does mean, however, that the cost of all stationery purchased during the year is charged as an expense to income statement – this is technically wrong, but is not material enough to affect the financial statements significantly.
- Low-cost non-current assets are often charged as an expense in income statement, eg a stapler, waste-paper basket, etc. Theoretically, these should be treated as non-current assets and depreciated each year over their estimated life; in practice, because the amounts involved are not material, they are treated as income statement expenses.

Materiality depends very much on the size of the business. A large company may consider that items of less than £1,000 are not material; a smaller business will usually use a much lower figure. What is material and what is not becomes a matter of judgement and will vary from business to business.

cost

Assets and liabilities are recorded in the financial statements at historical cost, ie the actual amount of the transaction involved. The benefit of this is that the statement of financial position valuations are objective – there can be no dispute about the amounts shown. However, as time passes, historical cost valuations become out-of-date and some businesses do adopt a policy of regular revaluation of assets. For example, freehold land and property bought, say, 20 years ago will have a much higher value today than their cost price, so it makes sense for a business to carry out revaluations from time-to-time.

Generally, then, it can be said that the cost concept applies to all assets and liabilities unless there are sound reasons for using a different valuation.

going concern

This presumes that the business to which the financial statements relate will continue to trade in the foreseeable future. The income statement and statement of financial position are prepared on the basis that there is no intention to reduce significantly the size of the business or to liquidate the business. If the business was not a going concern, assets would have very different values, and the statement of financial position would be affected considerably. For example, a large, purpose-built factory has considerable value to a going concern business but, if the factory had to be sold, it is likely to have a limited use for other industries, and therefore will have a lower market value. The latter case is the opposite of the going concern concept and could be described as a 'gone concern'. Also, in a gone concern situation, extra depreciation would need to be charged as an expense to income statement to allow for the reduced value of non-current assets. Inventory valuation (see page 257), which is usually on a going concern basis, would normally be much lower on a gone concern basis.

accruals (or matching)

This means that expenses and income for goods and services are matched to the same time period. We have already put this concept into practice in Chapter 12, where expenses and income were adjusted to take note of prepayments and accruals. The income statement shows the amount of the expense that should have been incurred, and the amount of income that should have been received. This is the principle of income and expenditure accounting, rather than using receipts and payments as they are received and paid.

Further examples of the accruals concept in accounting are:

- trade receivables
- trade payables
- depreciation of non-current assets
- irrecoverable debts written off
- provision for doubtful debts (see Chapter 15)
- opening and closing inventory adjustments

consistency

This requires that, when a business adopts particular accounting policies, it should continue to use such policies consistently. For example, a business that decides to make a provision for depreciation on machinery at ten per cent a year, using the straight-line method, should continue to use that percentage and method for future financial statements for this asset. Of course, having once chosen a particular policy, a business is entitled to make changes provided there are good reasons for doing so, and a note to the financial statements would explain what has happened. By applying the consistency concept, direct comparison between the financial statements of different years can be made. Further examples of the use of the consistency concept are:

- inventory valuation (see page 257)
- provision for doubtful debts (see Chapter 15)
- the application of the materiality concept
- the treatment of capital and revenue expenditure

prudence

This concept requires that caution is exercised when making judgements under conditions of uncertainty. This means that, where there is any doubt, a conservative (lower) figure for profit and the valuation of assets should be reported. To this end, profits are not to be anticipated and should only be recognised when it is reasonably certain that they will be actually made; at the same time all known liabilities should be provided for.

It should be noted that application of the prudence concept requires careful judgement to be made when making estimates – caution is needed to ensure that assets and income are not overstated, while liabilities and expenses are not understated.

Examples of the use of the prudence concept are:

- accrual of expenses and income, where an estimate is made of the amount
- prepayment of expenses and income, where an estimate is made of the amount
- inventory valuation (see page 257)
- depreciation of non-current assets
- irrecoverable debts written off
- provision for doubtful debts (see Chapter 15)

realisation

This concept states that business transactions are recorded in the financial statements when the legal title (ownership in law) passes between buyer and seller. This may well not be at the same time as payment is made. For example, credit sales are recorded when the sale is made (which is when legal title passes to the buyer), but payment will be made at a later date. Likewise, goods on sale or return are invoiced to the customer when they are supplied, but will be either paid for or returned at a later date.

duality

This means that each financial transaction is recorded by means of two opposite accounting entries (debit and credit), but of equal values. In this way, double-entry bookkeeping is an example of the duality concept in practice.

application of accounting concepts

The diagram on the next page shows how the accounting concepts link to the adjustments which are made in order to improve the relevance and reliability of financial statements in showing the profit, assets and liabilities of the business.

The financial accountant of a business will ensure that accounting concepts are applied to the accounts – this will help the financial statements show a true and fair view of the business.

the application of accounting concepts

application \ concept	business entity	money measurement	materiality	cost	going concern	accruals (matching)	consistency	prudence	realisation	duality
accruals of expenses and income		✓				✓		✓		✓
prepayments of expenses and income		✓				✓		✓		✓
depreciation of non-current assets		✓	✓			✓	✓	✓		✓
irrecoverable debts written off		✓						✓	✓	✓
provision for doubtful debts		✓				✓	✓	✓		✓
inventory valuation		✓	✓		✓	✓	✓	✓		✓
asset valuation		✓	✓	✓	✓		✓	✓		✓
business will continue to trade		✓			✓					
financial statements prepared on same principles		✓					✓			
business separate from owner	✓									
capital and drawings	✓	✓								✓
goods for own use taken by owner	✓	✓								✓
goods on sale or return	✓	✓							✓	✓

Accounting Policies

Accounting policies are the methods used by an individual business to show the effect of transactions, and record assets and liabilities. For example, straight-line and reducing balance are two ways of recording depreciation: a business will select, as its accounting policy, a particular method for each class of non-current asset to be depreciated. A business selects its accounting policies to fit in with the objectives of:

- relevance – the financial information is useful to users of accounts
- reliability – the financial information can be depended upon by users
- comparability – financial information can be compared with that from previous accounting periods
- understandability – users can understand the financial information provided

Accounting Standards

Over the last fifty years, a number of accounting standards have been developed to provide a framework for accounting and to reduce the variety of accounting treatments. For companies this framework for accounting is represented by **International Financial Reporting Standards (IFRSs)**. The International Accounting Standards Board is the organisation responsible for these rules of accounting. Its aims are to establish and improve standards of financial accounting and reporting.

Valuation of Inventory

The control and valuation of inventory is an important aspect in the efficient management of a business. Manual or computer records are used to show the amount of inventory held and its value at any time during the year. However, at the end of the financial year it is essential for a business to make a physical inventory-count for use in the financial statements. This involves inventory control personnel going into the stores, the shop, or the warehouse and counting each item. The counted inventory for each type of inventory held is then valued as follows:

number of items held x inventory valuation per item = inventory value

The auditors of a business may make random checks to ensure that the inventory value is correct.

The value of inventory at the beginning and end of the financial year is used in the calculation for cost of sales. Therefore, the inventory value has an effect on profit for the year.

Inventory is valued at:

- either what it cost the business to buy* the inventory (including additional costs to bring the product or service to its present location and condition, such as delivery charges)

  *or to make the inventory: material + labour + overhead (expenses)

- or the net realisable value – the actual or estimated selling price (less any further costs, such as repairs and replacement parts, selling and distribution)

The inventory valuation is often described as being **at the lower of cost and net realisable value** and is an application of the **prudence concept**. It is illustrated as follows:

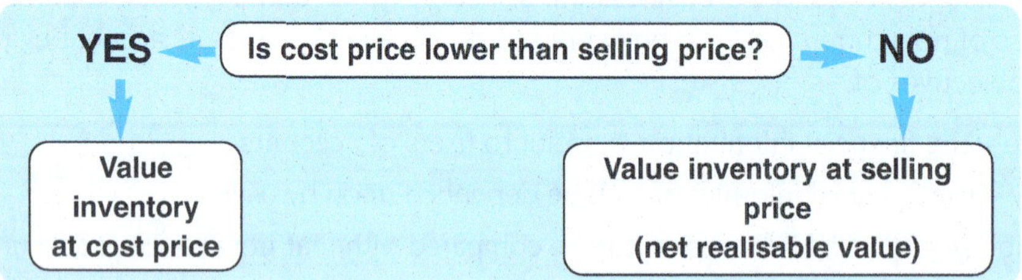

Thus two different inventory values are compared:

- cost, including additional costs such as delivery charges
- net realisable value, which is the selling price of the goods, less any expenses incurred in getting the inventory into a saleable condition, such as repairs and replacement parts, selling and distribution costs

Sometimes very large businesses use replacement cost – the cost of replacing inventory that has been sold – as a further inventory valuation. However, replacement cost applies only to raw materials, such as oil, that are traded on world markets. Unless you are told otherwise, the inventory valuation rule of the lower of cost and net realisable value should be used at all times.

WORKED EXAMPLE: INVENTORY VALUATION

situation

Andrew Williams runs an electrical shop. He asks for your advice on the valuation of the following items of inventory:

Item	cost £	net realisable value £	comments
washing machine	220	350	
dishwasher	300	280	the replacement cost is £290
TV	250	325	the case is badly scratched and will need to be replaced at a cost of £90 before the television can be sold
DVD player	75	125	the remote control has been lost; a new one will cost £20

You are to advise Andrew of the valuations for each item.

solution

The principle of lower of cost and net realisable value applies here as follows:

- **washing machine**
  - the cost price of £220 is used, being lower than the net realisable value of £350
- **dishwasher**
  - the net realisable value of £280 is used, being lower than cost price
  - replacement cost of £290 is not used as it does not apply to the inventory values of this type of business
- **TV**
  - replacement parts are needed before the item can be sold
  - the rule to follow is to deduct the cost of replacement parts/repairs from net realisable value, and then to compare with cost
  - here it is £325 – £90 = £235, compared with cost of £250
  - the net realisable value of £235 is used, being lower than cost price of £250
- **DVD player**
  - as with the television, money needs to be spent before this item can be sold
  - £125 – £20 = £105, compared with cost of £75
  - the cost price of £75 is used, being lower than the net realisable value less expenses, of £105

CHAPTER SUMMARY

- Accounting concepts – or principles – underlie the preparation of financial statements.
- Business entity concept – financial statements record and report on the activities of one particular business.
- Materiality concept – items with a low value are not worthwhile recording in the accounts separately.
- Cost concept – assets and liabilities are recorded in the financial statements at historical cost.
- Going concern concept – the presumption that the business to which the financial statements relate will continue to trade in the foreseeable future.
- Accruals concept – expenses and income for goods and services are matched to the same time period.
- Consistency concept – when a business adopts particular accounting policies, it should continue to use such policies consistently.
- Prudence concept – financial statements should always, where there is any doubt, report a conservative figure for profit or the valuation of assets.

- Realisation concept – business transactions are recorded in the financial statements when the legal title (ownership) passes between buyer and seller.
- Duality concept – each financial transaction is recorded by means of two opposite accounting entries.
- The usual valuation for inventory is at the lower of cost and net realisable value.
- Net realisable value is the selling price of the goods, less any expenses incurred in getting the inventory into a saleable condition.

In the next chapter we return to the preparation of the financial statements – income statement and statement of financial position – of sole traders. We will study further aspects including adjusting for accruals and prepayments of income, and making provision for doubtful debts.

QUESTIONS

visit
www.osbornebooks.co.uk
to take an online test

An asterisk (*) after the question number means that the answer is given at the end of this book.

14.1 The accounting concepts applied when preparing financial statements include:

- the going concern concept
- the accruals concept
- the materiality concept
- the business entity concept

You are to explain each of these concepts, giving in each case an example to illustrate an application of the concept.

14.2 When preparing the financial statements of a business, a number of accounting concepts are applied.

Required:

(a) Explain the concept of prudence.

....

....

....

....

(b) Explain, giving **one** example, how prudence is applied.

....

....

....

(c) Explain the concept of consistency.

....

....

....

(d) Explain, giving **one** example, how consistency is applied.

....

....

....

14.3* The owner of a sole trader business has paid for a new kitchen in the family house from the business bank account.

Which accounting concept has **not** been applied?

A	Money measurement	
B	Prudence	
C	Accruals	
D	Business entity	

14.4* When a business writes off debts as irrecoverable it applies a number of accounting concepts. Which **one** of the following pairs is applied?

A	Materiality; business entity	
B	Going concern; consistency	
C	Prudence; accruals	
D	Realisation; money measurement	

14.5* A discussion is taking place between Jane Smith, a sole trader, who owns a furniture shop, and her husband, John, who solely owns an engineering business. The following points are made:

(a) At the end of her financial year, Jane comments that the inventory of her shop had cost £10,000. She says that, as she normally adds 50 per cent to cost price to give the selling price, she intends to put a value of £15,000 for closing inventory in the financial statements.

(b) John's car is owned by his business but he keeps referring to it as my car. Jane reminds him that it does not belong to him, but to the firm. He replies that of course it belongs to him and, furthermore, if the firm went bankrupt, he would be able to keep the car.

(c) John's business has trade receivables of £30,000. He knows that, included in this figure is an irrecoverable debt of £2,500. He wants to show £30,000 as trade receivables in the year-end statement of financial position in order to have a high figure for current assets.

(d) On the last day of her financial year, Jane sold a large order of furniture, totalling £3,000, to a local hotel. The furniture was invoiced and delivered that day, before year-end inventory counting commenced. The payment was received early in the new financial year and Jane now asks John if she will be able to put this sale through the financial statements for the new year, instead of the old, but without altering the figures for purchases and closing inventory for the old year.

(e) John says that his accountant talks of preparing his financial statements on a going concern basis. John asks Jane if she knows of any other basis that can be used, and which it is usual to follow.

You are to take each of the points and state the correct accounting treatment, referring to appropriate accounting concepts.

14.6* A business has some closing inventory that has been damaged. The cost of the inventory was £5,400. It can be repaired at a cost of £500 and will then be sold for £6,500.

What is the value of this closing inventory?

A	£4,900	
B	£5,400	
C	£6,000	
D	£6,500	

14.7* The accountant of Wyvern Garden Centre has valued the year-end inventory at £35,500. The three items below have not been included in the inventory valuation and the accountant provides you with the following information:

item	cost	net realisable value	replacement cost
	£	£	£
lawnmower	220	430	200
conservatory	800	750	850
greenhouse	300	290	320

The accountant explains that he has not included the above items in the inventory valuation as he was not sure which value to use for each.

Required:

(a) You are to calculate the total value of Wyvern Garden Centre's inventory at the year-end.

(b) Which is the main accounting concept to be used in the valuation of the three items listed above?

(c) What is meant by the term 'net realisable value'?

14.8 Roger Dunn runs a clothes and accessories shop. He asks you for advice on the valuation of the following items of inventory:

item	cost	net realisable value	comments
	£	£	
jacket	40	75	the replacement cost is £35
shirt	30	25	
suit	80	150	there is a fault in the material, so Roger will sell the suit for £120
trousers	20	35	the stitching needs repairing at a cost of £10, after which the trousers will be sold for £25
electric trouser press	80	155	the electric plug and wiring is damaged and replacements will cost £15, after which the press will be sold for £130

Required:

(a) Advise Roger on the value of each item of inventory.

(b) How is the concept of prudence applied to inventory valuation and why is it necessary to apply it?

15 FURTHER ASPECTS OF FINANCIAL STATEMENTS

This chapter develops the preparation of financial statements of sole traders from what has been covered already in Chapters 9 and 12. In particular, in this chapter, we describe the further adjustments for:

- accruals and prepayments of income
- recovery of irrecoverable debts
- provision for doubtful debts
- the sale of non-current assets

The ledger entries for these adjustments will be shown, together with the way in which the financial statements are affected by each.

The next chapter continues the theme of these adjustments by applying them to a practical worked example of the financial statements of a sole trader.

INTRODUCTION TO FURTHER ASPECTS OF FINANCIAL STATEMENTS

In Chapter 12 we made a number of adjustments to financial statements in order to improve the relevance and reliability of the accounts. In this chapter we take those adjustments further as follows:

- **adjusting for accruals of income** – showing income due in an accounting period which has not been received at the end of that period (see page 265)
- **adjusting for prepayments of income** – showing income received in advance of the accounting period to which it relates (see page 265)
- **recovery of irrecoverable debts** – recording money received from a former trade receivable whose account has been previously written off as an irrecoverable debt (see page 269)
- **provision for doubtful debts** – making provisions for trade receivables who may not pay (see page 271)
- **the sale of non-current assets** – recording the accounting entries when non-current assets are sold (see page 277)

In the next chapter we will use a practical worked example of sole trader financial statements which applies these adjustments. This needs to be studied carefully before we move on to the financial statements of limited companies.

Accruals and Prepayments of Income

In Chapter 12 we saw how expenses can be accrued or prepaid at the end of a financial year. In the same way, income amounts – such as rent income and commission income – can also be accrued or prepaid. Note that sales, which is usually the main item of income for a business, are already dealt with on an accruals basis because sales are recorded when legal title passes to the buyer, whether or not payment has been received – this is the reason why we use accounts for trade receivables.

Amounts of income from sources other than sales are listed in the income statement where they are added to gross profit.

accrual of income

An accrual of income is an amount due in an accounting period which has not been received at the end of that period.

With accrual of income, an amount due to a business has not been received at the end of the financial year. For example, commission income might have been earned, but the payment is received after the end of the financial year to which it relates.

In the financial statements, accrual of income is:

- added to the income in the trial balance before listing it in the income statement
- shown as a current asset in the year-end statement of financial position (included in the section for 'other receivables')

prepayment of income

A prepayment of income is a payment received in advance of the accounting period to which it relates.

With prepayment of income, an amount of income of a business has been received in advance. For example, the rent income account for the financial year includes an advance payment received from a tenant in respect of the next financial year.

In the financial statements, prepayment of income is:

- deducted from the income in the trial balance before listing it in the income statement
- shown as a current liability in the year-end statement of financial position (included in the section for 'other payables')

The objective of taking note of accruals and prepayments of income is to ensure that the amount of income stated in the income statement relates to the period covered by that account. This is the application of the accruals concept.

WORKED EXAMPLE: ACCRUALS AND PREPAYMENTS OF INCOME

situation

The bookkeeper of Corley Carpets asks for your assistance in calculating the amount of income to show in the income statement for the year ended 31 December 20-8. The following information is available:

	£
Receipts from Zelah Limited for commission received during the year	700
Receipts received during the year from advertising board in shop window	320
Receipts received during the year from tenants for rent of the flats above the shop	15,720

Details of accruals and prepayments of income are:

	year ended 31 December 20-7		year ended 31 December 20-8	
		£		£
Commission income from Zelah Limited		–	in arrears	20
Income from advertising board		–	in advance	40
Income from tenants for rent	in advance	200	in advance	400
	in arrears	125	in arrears	75

solution

To calculate the correct amount for the income statement, we must take account of accruals and prepayments of income.

accrual of income – the bookkeeping records

In the double-entry records, accruals of income are shown as an amount due to the business at the end of the financial year. Thus the account for commission income in the records of Corley Carpets is as follows:

Dr		Commission Income Account			Cr
20-8		£	20-8		£
31 Dec	Income statement	720	31 Dec	Bank/Cash (receipts for year)	700
			31 Dec	Balance c/d (accrual of income)	20
		720			720
20-9			20-9		
1 Jan	Balance b/d (accrual of income)	20			

Notes:

- The amount of commission received during the year, £700, is shown on the credit side.
- As £20 of commission due to the business has not been received at the end of the year, the income transferred to income statement is the amount that should have been received during the year, ie £700 + £20 accrued income = £720.
- The balance remaining on the account – a debit balance of £20 – is the amount of the accrual of income, which is shown on the statement of financial position at 31 December 20-8 as a current asset (other receivables).
- Later on, for example on 10 January, the commission is paid by cheque and the account is as follows:

Commission Income Account

Dr			Cr		
20-9		£	20-9		£
1 Jan	Balance b/d	20	10 Jan	Bank	20

- Note that, applying the concept of prudence, accruals of income should be made only when the amount is expected to be received – if there is any doubt, then the accrual of income should not be made.
- The effect on profit of taking note of the accrual of income is to increase a previously reported profit – income has been increased, so profit is higher.

prepayment of income – the bookkeeping records

In the double-entry records, prepayments of income are shown as a liability of the business at the end of the financial year – in effect the business owes the amount back to the payer. Thus the account for income from the advertising board in the records of Corley Carpets is as follows:

Advertising Income Account

Dr			Cr		
20-8		£	20-8		£
31 Dec	Income statement	280	31 Dec	Bank/Cash	320
31 Dec	Balance c/d	40		(receipts for year)	
	(prepayment of income)				
		320			320
20-9			20-9		
			1 Jan	Balance b/d	40
				(prepayment of income)	

Notes:

- The amount of advertising received during the year, £320, is shown on the credit side.
- As £40 of advertising receipts is a prepayment, the income transferred to income statement is the amount due for the year, ie £320 – £40 prepayment of income = £280.
- The balance remaining on the account – a credit balance of £40 – is the amount of the prepayment of income, which is shown on the statement of financial position at 31 December 20-8 as a current liability (other payables).
- The credit balance of £40 on 1 January 20-9 will be included in the advertising income for 20-9 and will be transferred to income statement on 31 December 20-9.
- The effect on profit of taking note of the prepayment of income is to reduce a previously reported profit – income has been reduced, so profit is lower.

dealing with opening and closing balances

So far we have taken note of accruals and prepayments of income which take place at the end of a financial year. But what happens when there are also accruals and prepayments of income at the *beginning* of the year? In the Worked Example, this happens with the rent income from tenants of the flats above Corley Carpets' shop.

The rules for dealing with opening and closing balances in the income account are as follows:

received in year
+ prepayments at start of year
– accruals at start of year
– prepayments at end of year
+ accruals at end of year
= amount of income to income statement

For the rent income of Corley Carpets the calculations are:

	£
received in year	15,720
+ prepayment at start of year	200
– accrual at start of year	125
– prepayment at end of year	400
+ accrual at end of year	75
= amount of income to income statement	15,470

In the double-entry records of Corley Carpets, the account for rent income is as follows:

Dr		Rent Income Account			Cr
20-8		£	20-8		£
1 Jan	Balance b/d (accrual of income)	125	1 Jan	Balance b/d (prepayment of income)	200
31 Dec	Income statement	15,470	31 Dec	Bank/Cash (receipts for year)	15,720
31 Dec	Balance c/d (prepayment of income)	400	31 Dec	Balance c/d (accrual of income)	75
		15,995			15,995
20-9			20-9		
1 Jan	Balance b/d (accrual of income)	75	1 Jan	Balance b/d (prepayment of income)	400

The statement of financial position at 31 December 20-8 will show a current asset (other receivables) for the accrual of income of £75, and a current liability (other payables) for the prepayment of income of £400.

Note that the same principle for opening and closing balances applies to the expense accounts. For example, expenses paid in year £350 *minus* accrual at start of year £35, *plus* accrual at end of year £55, *equals* £370 expense to the income statement.

Recovery of Irrecoverable Debts

A recovery of irrecoverable debts happens when a former trade receivable, whose account has been written off as an irrecoverable debt, makes a payment.

In Chapter 12 we saw how irrecoverable debts can arise as a result of allowing customers a period of credit before they pay. An irrecoverable debt is a debt owing to a business which it considers will never be paid.

To recap, the bookkeeping entries to write off an irrecoverable debt are:

- debit irrecoverable debts written off account
- credit trade receivable's account

with the amount of the debt. At the end of the financial year, the balance of irrecoverable debts written off account is debited to the income statement as an expense, so reducing profit for the year.

From time-to-time, a former trade receivable whose account has been written off as irrecoverable may make a payment – either voluntarily, or as a result of debt collection procedures. For such an irrecoverable debt recovered the bookkeeping entries are:

- debit cash/bank account (with the amount of the recovery)
- credit recovery of irrecoverable debts account

The effect on financial statements is to record the amount of the recovery during the year as income – this is added below gross profit and described as 'recovery of irrecoverable debts'. Note that the payment received is debited to cash/bank account and credited to recovery of irrecoverable debts account; when preparing financial statements in an examination question, unless told otherwise, there will be no need to adjust cash/bank account.

Having recovered payment from a former trade receivable, if the customer now wishes to buy goods or services, it is prudent to insist on cash terms for some time to come!

WORKED EXAMPLE: RECOVERY OF IRRECOVERABLE DEBTS

situation

T Hughes is a former trade receivable of Pershore Packaging. The balance of £25 on T Hughes' account was written off as an irrecoverable debt on 15 December 20-1.

Today, on 15 April 20-3, T Hughes wishes to pay off the amount of the debt – with a cheque for £25.

solution

The bookkeeping entries to record the recovery of the irrecoverable debt on 15 April 20-3 are as follows:

Bank Account

Dr					Cr
20-3		£	20-3		£
15 Apr	Recovery of irrecoverable debts	25			

Recovery of Irrecoverable Debts Account

Dr					Cr
20-3		£	20-3		£
			15 Apr	Bank (T Hughes)	25

Recovery of irrecoverable debts account is a 'holding account' to which any other recoveries can be credited. At the end of the financial year, the total of the account is transferred to income statement:

Recovery of Irrecoverable Debts Account

Dr					Cr
20-3		£	20-3		£
31 Dec	Income statement	25	15 Apr	Bank (T Hughes)	25

In financial statements, the effect of recovery of irrecoverable debts is to increase the previously reported profit – by £25 in this case. It is recorded in the income statement (extract) as follows:

Income statement (extract) for the year ended 31 December 20-3

	£	£
Gross profit		x
Add income:		
Recovery of irrecoverable debt		25
		x
Less expenses:	x	
	x	
		x
Profit for the year		x

For the preparation of financial statements note that:

- if a figure for recovery of irrecoverable debts is shown in the trial balance (credit side), simply record the amount as income in the income statement, as above; do not alter the cash/bank account
- if there is no figure for recovery of irrecoverable debts shown in the trial balance, but a note says that an amount has recently been recovered but has not been recorded in the accounts, you need to increase cash/bank with the amount of the recovery and to record the income in the income statement

Provision for Doubtful Debts

A provision for doubtful debts is an estimate by a business of the likely percentage of its trade receivables which may become irrecoverable during any one accounting period.

Making a provision for doubtful debts is a further aspect of irrecoverable debts. However, it is different from writing off a debt because we are allowing for the possibility – not the certainty – of future irrecoverable debts. The trade receivables' figure (after irrecoverable debts, if any, have been written off) is reduced either by totalling the balances of the accounts that may not pay or, more likely, by applying a percentage to the total figure for trade receivables. The percentage chosen will be based on past experience and will vary from business to business – for example, a hire purchase company may well use a higher percentage than a bank. Note the difference between a *general provision* and a *specific provision*:

- a general provision for doubtful debts is an allowance applied to the total trade receivables (after writing off irrecoverable debts)
- a specific provision is an allowance applied to one or more specific doubtful debts where the risk of default is thought to be higher

The bookkeeping entries for doubtful debts make use of a **provision for doubtful debts account**, which records the accumulated total of the provision.

initial creation of a provision for doubtful debts

The procedure for the provision for doubtful debts comes after writing off irrecoverable debts (if any). The steps are:

1 A business, with trade receivables of £10,000 at the end of the financial year, estimates that five per cent of its trade receivables may become irrecoverable

2 The provision is calculated (eg £10,000 x 5% = £500)

3 The provision is recorded in the bookkeeping system:

   – debit income statement

   – credit provision for doubtful debts account

   The provision for doubtful debts account holds the total of the provision, which is deducted from trade receivables in the statement of financial position (see below), and represents the realistic estimate of trade receivables who may not pay

4 In the financial statements, the amount of the provision is:

   - listed in the income statement as an expense described as 'increase in provision for doubtful debts'
   - deducted from the trade receivables' figure in the current assets section of the statement of financial position, as here:

	£	£	£
Current Assets			
Inventory		X	
Trade receivables	10,000		
Less provision for doubtful debts	500		
		9,500	
Other receivables		X	
Bank		X	
Cash		X	
		X	

Note that, by creating a provision for doubtful debts, the business is following the accounting concept of prudence in the realistic estimate of its trade receivable position.

adjustments to provision for doubtful debts

Once a provision for doubtful debts has been created, the only adjustments that need to be made to the provision for doubtful debts are as a result of:

- a policy change in the provision, eg a decrease in the fixed percentage from 5% to 3%
- an arithmetic adjustment in the provision as a result of a change in the total of trade receivables, eg increase in trade receivables of £5,000 will require a higher provision

When either or both of these two situations arises, the adjustment to the existing provision will be:

- either upwards (increase in provision percentage, or increase in trade receivable figure)
- or downwards (decrease in provision percentage, or decrease in trade receivable figure)

An **increase in the provision** is recorded in the accounts as follows:

- debit income statement
- credit provision for doubtful debts account

with the amount of the increase

For the financial statements the amount of the increase is:

- listed in the income statement as an expense described as 'increase in provision for doubtful debts'
- shown in the statement of financial position where the amount of the increase is added to the existing provision to give a new higher figure for provision for doubtful debts (which is deducted from the trade receivables' figure)

A **decrease in the provision** is recorded in the accounts as follows:

- debit provision for doubtful debts account
- credit income statement

with the amount of the decrease

For the financial statements the amount of the decrease is:

- added after gross profit in the income statement as income, and described as 'reduction in provision for doubtful debts'
- shown in the statement of financial position at the lower amount, ie the existing provision less amount of decrease

Note that making a provision for doubtful debts is a completely separate adjustment from writing off an irrecoverable debt: the two should not be confused. It is quite usual to see in an income statement entries for both irrecoverable debts (written off) and provision for doubtful debts (the creation or adjustment of provision for bad debts).

WORKED EXAMPLE: PROVISION FOR DOUBTFUL DEBTS

situation

A business decides to create a provision for doubtful debts of five per cent of its trade receivables. After writing off irrecoverable debts, the trade receivables figures at the end of each of three years are:

20-1	£10,000
20-2	£15,000
20-3	£12,000

solution

Creating the provision (20-1)

- debit income statement
- credit provision for doubtful debts account

with £10,000 x 5% = £500

Increasing the provision (20-2)

- debit income statement
- credit provision for doubtful debts account

with £5,000 (increase in trade receivables) x 5% = £250

Decreasing the provision (20-3)

- debit provision for doubtful debts account
- credit income statement

with £3,000 (decrease in trade receivables) x 5% = £150

The provision for doubtful debts account is as follows:

Provision for Doubtful Debts Account

Dr		£			Cr £
20-1		£	20-1		£
31 Dec	Balance c/d	500	31 Dec	Income statement	500
20-2			20-2		
31 Dec	Balance c/d	750	1 Jan	Balance b/d	500
			31 Dec	Income statement (increase in provision)	250
		750			750
20-3			20-3		
31 Dec	Income statement (decrease in provision)	150	1 Jan	Balance b/d	750
31 Dec	Balance c/d	600			
		750			750
20-4			20-4		
			1 Jan	Balance b/d	600

the financial statements

The effect of the above transactions on the financial statements is shown in the following table:

Year	Income statement		Statement of financial position		
	Expense	Income	Trade receivables	Less provision for doubtful debts	Net trade receivables
	£	£	£	£	£
20-1	500	–	10,000	500	9,500
20-2	250	–	15,000	750	14,250
20-3	–	150	12,000	600	11,400

The income statement and statement of financial position extracts for each year are as follows:

20-1

Income statement (extract) for the year ended 31 December 20-1

	£	£
Gross profit		x
Less expenses:		
Provision for doubtful debts	500	

Statement of financial position (extract) as at 31 December 20-1

	£	£	£
Current Assets			
Inventory		x	
Trade receivables	10,000		
Less provision for doubtful debts	500		
		9,500	

20-2

Income statement (extract) for the year ended 31 December 20-2

	£	£
Gross profit		x
Less expenses:		
Increase in provision for doubtful debts	250	

Statement of financial position (extract) as at 31 December 20-2

	£	£	£
Current Assets			
Inventory		x	
Trade receivables	15,000		
Less provision for doubtful debts	750		
		14,250	

20-3

Income statement (extract) for the year ended 31 December 20-3

	£	£
Gross profit		x
Add income:		
Reduction in provision for doubtful debts		150

Statement of financial position (extract) as at 31 December 20-3

	£	£	£
Current Assets			
Inventory		x	
Trade receivables	12,000		
Less provision for doubtful debts	600		
		11,400	

Note:

When preparing financial statements in an examination question, there will be a note to the trial balance telling you to make an adjustment to the provision for doubtful debts. Sometimes you will be told a percentage figure, eg 'provision for doubtful debts is to be maintained at five per cent of trade receivables'; alternatively, you may be told the new provision figure (be careful of the wording – make sure you distinguish between 'increase the provision **to** £750' and 'increase the provision **by** £750').

Minimising the Risk of Irrecoverable Debts

Having studied the technicalities of accounting for irrecoverable debts in Chapter 12, and creating a provision for doubtful debts in this chapter, it is appropriate to look at ways in which businesses selling on credit can minimise the risks. The following are some of the procedures that can be followed:

- When first approached by an unknown business wishing to buy goods on credit, the seller should ask for references. One of these should be the buyer's bank, and the others should be from traders (at least two) with whom the buyer has previously done business.
- The seller, before supplying goods on credit, should take up the references and obtain satisfactory replies.
- Once satisfactory replies have been received, a credit limit for the customer should be established, and an account opened in the sales ledger. The amount of the credit limit will depend very much on the expected amount of future business – for example, £2,000 might be appropriate. The credit limit should not normally be exceeded – the firm's credit controller or financial accountant will approve any transactions above the limit.
- Invoices and month end statements of account should be sent out promptly; invoices should state the terms of trade and statements should analyse the balance to show how long it has been outstanding, eg 'over 30 days, over 60 days, over 90 days' – computer-produced statements can show this automatically.
- If a customer does not pay within a reasonable time, the firm should follow established procedures in order to chase up the debt promptly. These procedures are likely to include 'chaser' letters, emails and phone calls, the first of which points out that the account is overdue, and later threatening legal action. Whether or not legal action is taken will depend on the size of the debt – for a small amount the costs and time involved in taking legal action may outweigh the benefits of recovering the money.

the use of an aged schedule of trade receivables

To help with credit control, many firms produce an aged schedule of trade receivables at the end of each month. This analyses individual trade receivable balances into the time that the amount has been owing. Thus it shows the long outstanding debts that are, potentially, irrecoverable debts, against whom early action is necessary. An aged schedule is easily produced using a computer.

An aged schedule of trade receivables can also be used to calculate the provision for doubtful debts. For example, a business has the following schedule of trade receivables at the end of its financial year:

Days outstanding	**Trade receivables**
	£
Current (up to 30 days)	50,000
31 to 60	26,000
61 to 90	10,000
91 and over	4,000
	90,000

Provision for doubtful debts is to be calculated by providing for 25% on debts which have been outstanding for 91 days and over, 10% on debts outstanding for 61-90 days, and 2% on debts outstanding for 31-60 days. No provision is to be made on current debts.

Provision for doubtful debts is calculated as:

			£
Current	£50,000 (no provision)	=	nil
31-60 days	£26,000 x 2%	=	520
61-90 days	£10,000 x 10%	=	1,000
91 days and over	£4,000 x 25%	=	1,000
Provision for doubtful debts to be created (or adjusted) to			2,520

SALE OF NON-CURRENT ASSETS

When a non-current asset is sold or disposed, it is necessary to bring together:

- the original cost of the non-current asset
- provision for depreciation over the life of the non-current asset
- sale proceeds

These figures are transferred from the appropriate accounts to a disposals account (also known as a sale of assets account). The disposals account will enable us to calculate the 'profit' or 'loss' on sale of the asset (more correctly the terms are 'over-provision' and 'under-provision' of depreciation, respectively). The entries in the accounts are:

- **original cost of the asset**
  – debit disposals account
  – credit non-current asset account
  with the cost price of the non-current asset now sold

- **depreciation provided to date**
  – debit provision for depreciation account
  – credit disposals account
  with depreciation provided over the life of the asset
  Note that the amount of depreciation provided to date may need to be calculated for the correct period, eg if disposal takes place part of the way through a financial year and the firm's policy is to charge part-years.

- **sale proceeds**
  – debit bank/cash account
  – credit disposals account
  with the sale proceeds of the asset

- **loss on sale**
  – debit income statement
  – credit disposals account
  with the amount of under-provision of depreciation

- **profit on sale**
  – debit disposals account
  – credit income statement
  with the amount of over-provision of depreciation

Small adjustments for under- or over-provision of depreciation will usually be needed because it is impossible, at the start of an asset's life, to predict exactly what it will sell for in a number of years' time.

WORKED EXAMPLE: SALE OF A NON-CURRENT ASSET

situation

To illustrate the calculation of profit or loss on sale, we will use the machine purchased for £2,000 on 1 January 20-1, which is depreciated at twenty per cent each year, using the straight-line depreciation method. On 31 December 20-3, the machine is sold for £600; the company's accounting policy is to depreciate assets in the year of sale.

Tutorial note: take care with the year dates as there are three years from January 20-1 to 31 December 20-3.

solution

The calculations are:

		£
	original cost of machine	2,000
less	provision for depreciation to date	1,200
equals	net book value at date of sale	800
less	disposal proceeds (or part-exchange – see next page)	600
equals	loss on sale	200

The entries in the accounts (excluding bank account) are:

Machinery Account

Dr		£		Cr	£
20-1		£	20-3		£
1 Jan	Bank	2,000	31 Dec	Disposals	2,000

Provision for Depreciation Account – Machinery

Dr		£		Cr	£
20-1		£	20-1		£
31 Dec	Balance c/d	400	31 Dec	Income statement	400
20-2			20-2		
31 Dec	Balance c/d	800	1 Jan	Balance b/d	400
			31 Dec	Income statement	400
		800			800
20-3			20-3		
31 Dec	Disposals	1,200	1 Jan	Balance b/d	800
			31 Dec	Income statement	400
		1,200			1,200

Disposals Account – Machinery

Dr		£		Cr	£
20-3		£	20-3		£
31 Dec	Machinery	2,000	31 Dec	Provision for depreciation	1,200
			31 Dec	Bank	600
			31 Dec	Income statement (loss on sale)	200
		2,000			2,000

Income statement (extract) for the year ended 31 December 20-3

	£	£
Gross profit		x
Less expenses:		
Provision for depreciation: machinery	400	
Loss on sale of machinery	200	

Notes on these entries:

- In the machinery account, which is always kept 'at cost', the original price of the asset is transferred at the date of sale to disposals account. In this example, a nil balance remains on machinery account; however it is quite likely that the machinery account includes several machines, only one of which is being sold – in this case, there would be a balance on machinery account comprising the cost prices of the remaining machines.
- In provision for depreciation account, the amount of depreciation relating to the machine sold is transferred to disposals account. In this example, as only one machine is owned, the whole balance is transferred. However, if there were machines remaining, only part of the balance would be transferred – the amount remaining on the account relates to remaining machines.
- Disposals account would balance without the need for an income statement transfer if the depreciation rate used reflected exactly the fall in value of the machine. In practice, this is unlikely to happen, so a transfer to income statement must be made. In this example, it is an under-provision of depreciation (loss on sale), and the income statement lists an extra expense. If there had been an over-provision of depreciation (profit on sale), an item of additional income would be shown in income statement.

part-exchange of a non-current asset

Instead of selling a non-current asset for cash, it is quite common to part-exchange it for a new asset. This is exactly the same as if a person trades in an old car for a new (or newer) one. Once the part-exchange allowance has been agreed, the entries for disposal are as detailed earlier except that, instead of disposal proceeds, there will be entries for the part-exchange amount:

– debit non-current asset account

– credit disposals account

The remainder of the purchase cost of the new non-current asset paid from the bank is debited to non-current asset account and credited to bank account in the usual way.

For example, the machine referred to earlier in this section is part-exchanged on 31 December 20-3 at an agreed value of £600 for a new machine costing £2,500. The balance is paid from the bank. Machinery account will now be shown as:

Dr		Machinery Account			Cr
20-1		£	20-3		£
1 Jan	Bank	2,000	31 Dec	Disposals	2,000
20-3					
31 Dec	Disposals (part-exchange allowance)	600	31 Dec	Balance c/d	2,500
31 Dec	Bank (balance paid)	1,900			
		2,500			2,500
20-4					
1 Jan	Balance b/d	2,500			

Notes:

- This gives two debits (£600 and £1,900) in machinery account for a single machine.
- Disposals account will be unchanged, except that the description for the credit transaction of £600 will be machinery account, instead of bank.

CHAPTER SUMMARY

- An adjustment should be made at the end of the financial year to allow for accruals and prepayments of income.
- In the financial statements, accruals of income are:
  - added to the income in the trial balance
  - shown as a current asset (other receivables) in the statement of financial position
- In the financial statements, prepayments of income are:
  - deducted from the income in the trial balance
  - shown as a current liability (other payables) in the statement of financial position
- Recovery of an irrecoverable debt is when a former trade receivable, whose account has been written off as irrecoverable, makes a payment – either voluntarily, or as a result of debt collection procedures.
- Recovery of an irrecoverable debt is recorded as income, and the bookkeeping entries are:
  - debit cash/bank account
  - credit recovery of irrecoverable debts account

- In financial statements, the amount of any irrecoverable debts recovered during the year is recorded as income and added below the gross profit figure.
- A provision for doubtful debts is an estimate by a business of the likely percentage of its trade receivables which may become irrecoverable during any one accounting period.
- In the financial statements:
  - an increase or decrease in provision for doubtful debts is shown in the income statement
  - the provision for doubtful debts is deducted from the trade receivables' figure in the current assets section of the statement of financial position
- Having created a provision for doubtful debts, it will either be increased or decreased from year-to-year in line with the change in the level of provision and/or the level of trade receivables.
- When a non-current asset is sold, it is necessary to make an adjustment in respect of any under-provision (loss on sale) or over-provision (profit on sale) of depreciation during the life of the asset. The amount of profit or loss is calculated using a disposals account, and is then transferred to the income statement.
- Instead of selling a non-current asset for cash, it is quite common to part-exchange it for a new asset.

In the next chapter we continue the theme of these adjustments by applying them in a practical worked example of financial statements of a sole trader. We also see how, when preparing financial statements, it is important to distinguish between capital expenditure and revenue expenditure.

QUESTIONS

visit **www.osbornebooks.co.uk** to take an online test

An asterisk (*) after the question number means that the answer is given at the end of this book.

15.1* The following information is available about rent received for the year ended 30 June 20-7:

	£
Credit balance brought forward on 1 July 20-6	225
Receipts during year ended 30 June 20-7	4,150
Debit balance brought down on 1 July 20-7	350

How much should be shown as rent income in the income statement for the year ended 30 June 20-7?

A	£4,275	
B	£4,025	
C	£4,725	
D	£4,150	

15.2* Martin Ostrowski is about to prepare his financial statements for the year ended 31 December 20-8.

The flat above Martin's business premises is let to a tenant at a rent of £400 per calendar month. On 1 December 20-8 the tenant paid Martin £800 to cover the rent for December 20-8 and January 20-9.

You are to:

(a) State how Martin should treat the tenant's rent payment of £800 on 1 December 20-8 in his financial statements.

(b) Identify the accounting concept that should be applied in this situation.

15.3 You are the bookkeeper of Pershore Products. You are calculating the amount of income to be shown in the income statement for the year ended 31 December 20-7. The following information is available to you:

	£
Receipts from Aggie Surf Limited for commission during the year	1,250
Receipts from advertising on the company website received during the year	2,720
Receipts from tenants for rent of the flats owned by the business received during the year	18,290

Details of accruals and prepayments are:

	year ended 31 December 20-6		year ended 31 December 20-7	
		£		£
Commission income from Aggie Surf Limited	in arrears	100		–
Income from website advertisements	in arrears	150	in arrears	250
Income from tenants for rent	in advance	850	in arrears	120

You are to write up the accounts for:

- commission income
- advertising income
- rent income

to show the transfer to income statement for the year ended 31 December 20-7.

Dr		**Commission Income Account**	Cr
20-7	£	20-7	£

Dr		**Advertising Income Account**	Cr
20-7	£	20-7	£

Dr		**Rent Income Account**	Cr
20-7	£	20-7	£

15.4* The accounts supervisor at the firm where you work hands you a cheque for £50 received from a former trade receivable, James Abel, whose account was written off as irrecoverable last year. The cheque is in part settlement of the amount owed by James Abel.

You are to write up the following accounts using today's date for the transactions:

Dr	**Bank Account**		Cr
	£		£

Dr	**Recovery of Irrecoverable Debts Account**		Cr
	£		£

15.5 You are the bookkeeper of Wyvern Traders. At 31 December 20-9, the end of the financial year, the business has gross trade receivables of £40,420. The owner decides to:

- write off, as irrecoverable debts, the accounts of:

Webster Limited	£110
T Smith	£210
Khan and Company	£100

- make a provision for doubtful debts of 2.5% of trade receivables (after writing off the above irrecoverable debts)

You are to:

(a) Show the irrecoverable debts written off account in the general ledger for the financial year.

(b) Show the provision for doubtful debts account in the general ledger for the financial year.

(c) Explain the effect of these transactions on the financial statements at the end of the financial year.

15.6* Ross Engineering has an existing provision for doubtful debts of £300, based on 5 per cent of trade receivables. After writing off irrecoverable debts, the amounts of trade receivables at the end of the next two financial years are found to be:

30 June 20-1	£8,000
30 June 20-2	£7,000

The business continues to keep the provision for doubtful debts equal to 5 per cent of trade receivables.

As an accounts assistant at Ross Engineering, you are to show:

(a) The adjustments to the provision for doubtful debts at the end of the financial years ended 30 June 20-1 and 30 June 20-2.

(b) How the provision for doubtful debts will be recorded in the financial statements at the end of each of the two financial years.

15.7 You are the bookkeeper at Enterprise Trading Company. The following information is available for the financial years ending 31 December 20-5, 20-6, 20-7:

	£
• Trade receivable balances at 31 December 20-5, before writing off irrecoverable debts	105,200
• Irrecoverable debts written off on 31 December 20-5	1,800
• 2.5% provision for doubtful debts created at 31 December 20-5	
• Trade receivable balances at 31 December 20-6, before writing off irrecoverable debts	115,600
• Irrecoverable debts written off on 31 December 20-6	2,400
• 2.5% provision for doubtful debts adjusted in line with the change in the level of trade receivables at 31 December 20-6	
• Irrecoverable debt recovered on 15 June 20-7	150
• Trade receivable balances at 31 December 20-7, before writing off irrecoverable debts	110,200
• Irrecoverable debts written off on 31 December 20-7	1,400
• 2.5% provision for doubtful debts adjusted in line with the change in the level of trade receivables at 31 December 20-7	

You are to record the effect of these transactions in the appropriate columns of the following table:

YEAR	INCOME STATEMENT				STATEMENT OF FINANCIAL POSITION		
	Expense		Income				
	Irrecoverable debts written off	Increase in provision for doubtful debts	Recovery of irrecoverable debts	Decrease in provision for doubtful debts	Trade receivables (after irrecoverable debts written off)	Less prov for doubtful debts	Net trade receivables
	£	£	£	£	£	£	£
20-5							
20-6							
20-7							

15.8* The following balances were extracted from the accounting system of Arabella Amis on 30 September 20-4.

	Dr	Cr
	£	£
Provision for doubtful debts		450
Trade receivables	12,500	
Irrecoverable debts written off during the year	235	
Irrecoverable debts recovered during the year		115

Arabella's policy is to provide for doubtful debts at the rate of 4% on trade receivables outstanding at her financial year-end.
The profit earned in the year ended 30 September 20-4 was £21,060.
The profit has been arrived at *before* taking into account any irrecoverable debts, any recovery of irrecoverable debts and any adjustments to the provision for doubtful debts.

Required:

Using the above information, explain the changes to Arabella's:

(a) Profit for the year.

(b) Net current assets (working capital).

(c) Bank balance.

15.9* A debt which was written off as irrecoverable last year has been recovered this year. What effect will the recovery of an irrecoverable debt have on this year's profit, current assets, and capital of the business?

	Profit for the year	Current assets	Capital	
A	No effect	Decrease	Increase	
B	Increase	Increase	Increase	
C	Decrease	Increase	No effect	
D	Increase	No effect	Decrease	

15.10 A business has recently sold a vehicle which had a net book value of £4,000. The provision for depreciation on the vehicle at the time of sale was £6,500. The business made a profit of £250 on the sale. The disposal proceeds were received by bank transfer.

You are to prepare the vehicle disposal account:

Dr **Vehicle Disposal Account** Cr

		£			£

15.11* On 1 January 20-1, Martin Jackson bought a car for £12,000. In his financial statements, which have a year-end of 31 December, he has been depreciating it at 25 per cent per annum using the reducing balance method. On 31 December 20-3 he sells the car for £5,500 (bank transfer received). His accounting policy is to depreciate assets in the year of sale.

You are to show:

(a) The provision for depreciation account for 20-1, 20-2 and 20-3.

(b) The statement of financial position extract at 31 December 20-1 and 20-2.

(c) The asset disposal account.

Round your answer down to whole £s where appropriate.

15.12 Rachael Hall's financial year runs to 31 December. On 1 January 20-8 her accounting records show that she owns a car with an original cost of £12,000 and depreciation to date of £7,200.

On 1 October 20-8, Rachael bought a new car at a cost of £15,000. She traded in the old car at a part-exchange value of £5,500 and paid the balance by bank transfer.

Rachael depreciates vehicles at 20 per cent per year using the straight-line method. Her accounting policy is to charge a full year's depreciation in the year of purchase, but none in the year of sale.

You are to show the following for the year ended 31 December 20-8:

(a) Vehicles account.

(b) Provision for depreciation account – vehicles.

(c) Disposals account – vehicles.

(d) Statement of financial position extract at 31 December 20-8.

15.13 On 1 January 20-9 the following information is taken from the accounting system of Lisa Hall.

	£
• Vehicle (registration number VU64 UUF) at cost	20,000
• Provision for depreciation of Vehicle VU64 UUF	12,500

Lisa purchased a new vehicle (registration number VK19 PZV) on 15 March 20-9 at a cost of £25,000. The garage gave Lisa a part-exchange allowance of £4,000 on vehicle VU64 UUF. Lisa's financial year ends on 31 December. She depreciates vehicles at 12.5% per annum using the straight-line method. Depreciation is calculated on vehicles held at the end of the financial year.

Required:

(a) Calculate the profit or loss made on the disposal of vehicle VU64 UUF.

(b) Prepare the statement of financial position extract as at 31 December 20-9 of Lisa Hall, showing entries arising from the above transactions.

15.14* At the end of her financial year on 31 December 20-5 Sandra Ali, the owner of a business, was preparing financial statements.

The following information had yet to be recorded in the general ledger of Sandra's business.

At 31 December 20-5:

- Advertising expense, £550, was owing.
- Commission income, £85, was due but unpaid.
- Inventory was valued at £25,450.
- The net book value (carrying amount) of computers is £8,400 and depreciation is to be provided on computers at 30% per annum using the reducing balance method.
- The provision for doubtful debts is to be maintained at 2% of trade receivables; at the year end trade receivables totalled £14,000.

You are to record the information in the ledger accounts shown below. Balance the accounts at 31 December 20-5.

GENERAL LEDGER

Dr **Advertising Expenses Account** Cr

20-5			£	20-5			£
Jan	1	Balance b/d	150				
Jan-Dec		Bank	4,528				

Dr **Commission Income Account** Cr

20-5			£	20-5			£
				Jan	1	Balance b/d	55
				Jan-Dec		Bank	1,665

Inventory Account

Dr							Cr
20-5			£	20-5			£
Jan	1	Balance b/d	23,240				

Provision for Depreciation (Computers) Account

Dr							Cr
20-5			£	20-5			£
				Jan	1	Balance b/d	3,600

Provision for Doubtful Debts Account

Dr							Cr
20-5			£	20-5			£
				Jan	1	Balance b/d	200

16 PREPARING SOLE TRADER FINANCIAL STATEMENTS

This chapter brings together all that has been studied on the preparation of financial statements of sole traders – in Chapters 9, 12, and 15.

When preparing financial statements it is important to distinguish between capital expenditure and revenue expenditure. We begin this chapter by looking at the differences between these, and why they are important to financial statements.

We then see how the adjustments to financial statements are applied by looking at a practical worked example of sole trader financial statements, before we move on to study limited companies.

Capital Expenditure and Revenue Expenditure

When preparing financial statements it is important to distinguish between capital expenditure and revenue expenditure.

capital expenditure

Capital expenditure is expenditure incurred on the purchase, alteration or improvement of non-current assets.

Included in capital expenditure are such costs as:

- delivery of non-current assets
- installation of non-current assets
- improvement (but not repair) of non-current assets
- legal costs of buying property

A common example of capital expenditure is the purchase of a car for use in the business.

Note that we use the word 'capitalised' to mean that an item has been treated as capital expenditure.

Capital expenditure is subject always to the application of the accounting concept of materiality (see page 253) – when items in accounts have a low monetary value and it is not worthwhile recording them separately.

revenue expenditure

Revenue expenditure is expenditure incurred on running expenses.

Included in revenue expenditure are the costs of:

- maintenance and repair of non-current assets
- staff training costs
- administration of the business
- selling and distributing the goods or products in which the business trades

An example of revenue expenditure is the cost of fuel for cars used in the business.

capital expenditure and revenue expenditure – the differences

Capital expenditure is shown on the statement of financial position, while revenue expenditure is an expense in the income statement. It is important to classify these types of expenditure correctly in the accounting system. For example, if the cost of the car was shown as an expense in income statement, then profit would be reduced considerably, or even a loss recorded; meanwhile, the statement of financial position would not show the car as a non-current asset – clearly this is incorrect as the business owns the asset.

Study the following examples and the table on the next page; they both show the differences between capital expenditure and revenue expenditure.

- **cost of building an extension to the factory £30,000, which includes £1,000 for repairs to the existing factory**
  - capital expenditure, £29,000
  - revenue expenditure, £1,000 (because it is for repairs to an existing non-current asset)
- **a plot of land has been bought for £20,000, the legal costs are £750**
  - capital expenditure £20,750 (the legal costs are included in the capital expenditure, because they are the cost of acquiring the non-current asset, ie the legal costs are capitalised)
- **the business' own employees are used to install a new air conditioning system: wages £1,000, materials £1,500**
  - capital expenditure £2,500 (an addition to the property); note that, in cases such as this, revenue expenditure, ie wages expense and materials purchases, will need to be reduced to allow for the transfer to capital expenditure
- **own employees used to repair and redecorate the property: wages £500, materials £750**
  - revenue expenditure £1,250 (repairs and redecoration are running expenses)
- **purchase of a new machine £10,000, payment for installation and setting up £250**
  - capital expenditure £10,250 (costs of installation of a non-current asset are capitalised)

Only by allocating capital expenditure and revenue expenditure correctly between the statement of financial position and the income statement can the financial statements report reliably on the financial state of the business. The chart on the next page shows the main items of capital expenditure and revenue expenditure associated with three classes of non-current assets – property, vehicles and machinery/computers/office equipment.

	capital expenditure	revenue expenditure
property	• cost of building/construction • cost of extension • delivery costs on raw materials used • professional fees, eg legal • labour cost of own employees used on building/construction • installation of utilities, eg gas, water, electricity • installation of air conditioning	• insurance of building • general maintenance • repairs • redecoration • depreciation charges
vehicles	• cost of vehicle, including any optional extras • delivery costs • number plates • changes to the vehicle	• fuel • road fund licence • extended warranty • company logo • insurance • servicing and repairs • depreciation charge
machinery/ computers/ office equipment	• cost of asset • delivery costs • installation and testing • modifications to meet specific needs of business • installation of special wiring, etc • computer programs (but can be classified as revenue expenditure if cost is low and will have little impact on financial statements – the accounting concept of materiality)	• insurance of asset • servicing and repairs • consumables – such as paper, ink cartridges, etc • computer programs (or can be classified as capital expenditure if cost is high and will have a large impact on financial statements) • depreciation charge

Financial Statements: Worked Example

Many AQA examination questions focus on aspects of the preparation of financial statements – for example, asking you to prepare an income statement, or a statement of financial position. Some questions may also require the preparation of the full financial statements – income statement, together with a statement of financial position.

Examination questions often include a number of adjustments which need to be incorporated into the financial statements. The diagram on the next page summarises the adjustments and their effect on the financial statements. Remember that the adjustments are made in order to apply the accounting concepts – the diagram already seen in Chapter 14 (on page 256) links the adjustments to the accounting concepts. The objective of making adjustments is to improve the relevance and reliability of financial statements in showing the profit or loss, and the assets and liabilities of the business.

The Worked Example on the next page brings together all of the adjustments that we have seen previously in Chapters 9, 12, and 15. Although in total the Worked Example is more complex than would be required in an examination, it does provide a useful reference point which shows how all the adjustments are incorporated into the financial statements of a sole trader.

The examination questions at the end of this chapter are based on the preparation of financial statements – either from a trial balance or a list of balances – and provide practice to help with your studies.

SUMMARY OF ADJUSTMENTS FOR FINANCIAL STATEMENTS

ADJUSTMENT	INCOME STATEMENT	STATEMENT OF FINANCIAL POSITION
closing inventory	• deduct from purchases in income statement	• current asset
accrual of expenses	• add to expense in income statement	• current liability
prepayment of expenses	• deduct from expense in income statement	• current asset
accrual of income	• add to income in income statement	• current asset
prepayment of income	• deduct from income in income statement	• current liability
provision for depreciation of non-current assets	• expense in income statement	• non-current assets reduced by provision for depreciation to date
irrecoverable debts written off	• expense in income statement	• deduct from trade receivables
recovery of irrecoverable debts	• income in income statement	• add to bank/cash
creation of, or increase in, provision for doubtful debts	• expense in income statement	• trade receivables' figure reduced by total amount of provision
decrease in provision for doubtful debts	• income in income statement	• trade receivables' figure reduced by total amount of provision
goods taken by the owner for own use	• deduct from purchases in income statement	• add to drawings
goods on sale or return	• include in income, but deduct from income if returned	• add unsold goods to inventory

WORKED EXAMPLE: PREPARING SOLE TRADER FINANCIAL STATEMENTS

situation

You are the accountant to Olivia Boulton, a sole trader, who runs a kitchen and cookware shop in Brighton. Her bookkeeper has just extracted the year-end trial balance from the books of account, as follows:

Trial balance of Olivia Boulton as at 31 December 20-2

	Dr	Cr
	£	£
Inventory at 1 January 20-2	50,000	
Purchases	420,000	
Revenue		559,500
Shop expenses	6,200	
Shop wages	33,500	
Telephone expenses	500	
Interest paid	8,000	
Travel expenses	550	
Discount allowed	450	
Discount received		900
Rent income		2,350
Commission income		500
Recovery of irrecoverable debts		250
Property at cost	250,000	
Shop fittings at cost	40,000	
Provision for depreciation of property at 1 Jan 20-2		10,000
Provision for depreciation of shop fittings at 1 Jan 20-2		8,000
Trade receivables	12,100	
Provision for doubtful debts		200
Bank	5,850	
Cash	50	
Capital		125,000
Drawings	24,000	
Loan from bank (repayable in 20-9)		130,000
Trade payables		14,500
	849,200	849,200

You are to prepare the financial statements for Olivia and, to help with this, she gives you the following information:

- at 31 December closing inventory, excluding sale or return goods, was valued at £40,500
- a telephone bill received on 5 January 20-3 showed calls for £100 in 20-2
- in December Olivia paid shop wages of £200 in advance for January
- in December Olivia received rent of £200 from her tenant in advance for January
- commission income of £100 is owing and was received on 10 January

- depreciation on property is at the rate of 2% per annum, using the straight-line method
- depreciation on shop fittings is at the rate of 20% per annum, using the reducing balance method
- Olivia has incurred irrecoverable debts of £100 during 20-2 which she wishes to write off
- a provision for doubtful debts is to be 2.5% of trade receivables
- goods costing £1,500 were supplied to a customer on a sale or return basis for £2,000; none of the goods had been sold by the customer at the year-end
- goods costing £1,000 were taken by Olivia for her own use

Note: In making adjustments for the above information we are ensuring that the financial statements are more relevant and reliable to stakeholders. The adjustments are based on the application of accounting concepts (see page 252) – the concepts applied here include cost, accruals, consistency and prudence.

solution

The financial statements incorporating these adjustments are shown on pages 299 and 300. A summary of the effect of each adjustment is given below.

closing inventory

The adjustment for closing inventory is to:

- deduct £42,000 from purchases in the income statement
- show inventory valued at £42,000 as a current asset in the statement of financial position

accrual of expenses

For the telephone expenses accrued:

- increase the income statement expense by £100 to £600 (ie £500 from the trial balance, plus £100 expenses accrued)
- show £100 accrual of expenses as a current liability (other payables) in the statement of financial position

prepayment of expenses

For the shop wages prepaid:

- reduce the income statement expense by £200 to £33,300 (ie £33,500 from the trial balance, less £200 expenses prepaid)
- show £200 prepayment of expenses as a current asset (other receivables) in the statement of financial position

prepayment of income

For the prepaid rent income:

- reduce the income statement income by £200 to £2,150 (ie £2,350 from the trial balance, less £200 income prepaid)
- show £200 prepayment of income as a current liability (other payables) in the statement of financial position

accrual of income

For the accrued commission income:

- increase the income statement income by £100 to £600 (ie £500 from the trial balance, plus £100 income accrual)
- show £100 accrual of income as a current asset (other receivables) in the statement of financial position

depreciation of non-current assets

The depreciation amounts are:

- property: 2% pa straight-line, ie £250,000 x 2% = £5,000
- shop fittings: 20% pa reducing balance, (£40,000 – £8,000 depreciation to date) x 20% = £6,400

The depreciation is shown in the financial statements as follows:

– in the income statement show (as expenses) provision for depreciation amounts for property £5,000, and shop fittings £6,400

– in the statement of financial position show depreciation amounts being deducted from non-current assets to give net book values as follows:

	£	£	£
	Cost	Depreciation	Net book value
Property	250,000	15,000	235,000
Shop fittings	40,000	14,400	25,600
	290,000	29,400	260,600

Remember that the depreciation column in the statement of financial position comprises depreciation from previous years, plus this year's depreciation (just calculated). For property, depreciation is the trial balance figure of £10,000, plus £5,000 for this year; for shop fittings, it is £8,000 from the trial balance, plus £6,400 for this year.

irrecoverable debts written off

The adjustment to write off irrecoverable debts in the financial statements is as follows:

– record irrecoverable debts written off of £100 as an expense in income statement

– reduce the trade receivables' figure by £100 to £10,000 and show this latter figure as a current asset in the statement of financial position

provision for doubtful debts

A provision for doubtful debts of £200 (see trial balance) is already in existence. As the provision is to be maintained at 2.5% of trade receivables, the provision at the end of the year is £10,000 trade receivables (see above) x 2.5% = £250. Thus an increase of £50 (from £200 to £250) is required; this is shown in the financial statements as follows:

– in income statement record the £50 amount of the increase in provision for doubtful debts as an expense

– in the statement of financial position deduct £250 from the trade receivables' figure of £10,000 to give net trade receivables of £9,750 – it is this amount that is added in to current assets

goods on sale or return

As none of the goods on sale or return had been sold by the customer at the year-end:

– reduce sales revenue by £2,000

– reduce trade receivables by £2,000

– increase closing inventory by £1,500, being the cost price of the goods to Olivia Boulton

goods for own use

As Olivia has taken goods in which the business trades for her own use, the adjustment is:

- deduct £1,000 from purchases in the income statement to give a purchases figure of £419,000
- add £1,000 to owner's drawings in the statement of financial position to give a drawings figure of £25,000

financial statements

The financial statements of Olivia Boulton, incorporating the above adjustments, are shown below.

OLIVIA BOULTON
INCOME STATEMENT FOR THE YEAR ENDED 31 DECEMBER 20-2

	£	£
Revenue		557,500
Opening inventory (1 January 20-2)	50,000	
Purchases	419,000	
	469,000	
Less Closing inventory (31 December 20-2)	42,000	
Cost of sales		427,000
Gross profit		130,500
Add income:		
Discount received		900
Rent income		2,150
Commission income		600
Recovery of irrecoverable debts		250
		134,400
Less expenses:		
Shop expenses	6,200	
Shop wages	33,300	
Telephone	600	
Interest paid	8,000	
Travel expenses	550	
Discount allowed	450	
Depreciation: property	5,000	
shop fittings	6,400	
Irrecoverable debts written off	100	
Increase in provision for doubtful debts	50	
		60,650
Profit for the year		73,750

STATEMENT OF FINANCIAL POSITION AS AT 31 DECEMBER 20-2

	£	£	£
Non-current Assets	Cost	Depreciation	Net book value
Property	250,000	15,000	235,000
Shop fittings	40,000	14,400	25,600
	290,000	29,400	260,600
Current Assets			
Inventory		42,000	
Trade receivables	10,000		
Less provision for doubtful debts	250		
		9,750	
Other receivables		*300	
Bank		5,850	
Cash		50	
		57,950	
Less Current Liabilities			
Trade payables	14,500		
Other payables	**300		
		14,800	
Net Current Assets or Working Capital			43,150
			303,750
Less Non-current Liabilities			
Loan from bank			130,000
NET ASSETS			173,750
FINANCED BY			
Capital			
Opening capital			125,000
Add Profit for the year			73,750
			198,750
Less Drawings			25,000
			173,750

*Other receivables	£	**Other payables	£
Prepayment of expenses	200	Accrual of expenses	100
Accrual of income	100	Prepayment of income	200
	300		300

Tutorial note:

The only adjustment omitted from this Worked Example is the sale of non-current assets, and the resultant calculation of any profit or loss on sale. This topic has been covered already in the previous chapter and there are questions incorporating the sale of non-current assets at the end of both this chapter and the previous one (Chapter 15).

CHAPTER SUMMARY

- Capital expenditure is expenditure incurred on the purchase, alteration or improvement of non-current assets.
- Revenue expenditure is expenditure incurred on running expenses.
- Adjustments are made to financial statements in order to apply the accounting concepts.
- The objective of making adjustments is to improve the relevance and reliability of financial statements.

In recent chapters we have looked at preparing sole trader financial statements, together with a number of adjustments, in some detail. In the next chapter we turn our attention to the financial statements of limited companies.

QUESTIONS

visit
www.osbornebooks.co.uk
to take an online test

An asterisk (*) after the question number means that the answer is given at the end of this book.

16.1 Tara Kassir has bought a new delivery van for use in her business. The invoice received from the garage for the van includes the following items:

	£
Cost of van	11,650
Air conditioning	550
Fitted shelving	350
Road fund licence	165
Cost of extended warranty	220
Tank of fuel	40
Insurance premium	450

Required:

(a) Calculate the total amount of capital expenditure incurred by Tara

(b) Calculate the total amount of revenue expenditure incurred by Tara.

16.2* The following trial balance has been extracted by the bookkeeper of John Barclay at 30 June 20-3:

	Dr	Cr
	£	£
Revenue		864,321
Purchases	600,128	
Sales returns	2,746	
Purchases returns		3,894
Office expenses	33,947	
Salaries	122,611	
Vehicle expenses	36,894	
Discount allowed	3,187	
Discount received		4,951
Commission income		1,245
Rent income		3,350
Trade receivables	74,328	
Trade payables		58,821
Inventory at 1 July 20-2	63,084	
Vehicles	83,500	
Office equipment	23,250	
Property	100,000	
Bank loan (repayable in 20-9)		75,000
Bank	1,197	
Capital		155,000
Drawings	21,710	
	1,166,582	1,166,582

Notes at 30 June 20-3:

- inventory is valued at £66,941
- vehicle expenses owing £1,250
- office expenses prepaid £346
- commission income owing £150
- rent income prepaid £200
- goods costing £250 were taken by John Barclay for his own use

Required:

You are to prepare the income statement of John Barclay for the year ended 30 June 20-3, together with his statement of financial position at that date.

16.3* The following list of balances has been extracted by the bookkeeper of Southtown Supplies, a wholesaling business, at 31 December 20-4:

	£
Opening inventory	70,000
Purchases	280,000
Revenue	420,000
Sales returns	6,000
Purchases returns	4,500
Rent income	2,500
Commission income	1,250
Discount received	750
Discount allowed	500
Electricity	13,750
Salaries	35,600
Post and packing	1,400
Property	120,000
Fixtures and fittings	45,000
Trade receivables	55,000
Trade payables	49,250
Bank balance	5,000
Capital	195,000
Drawings	41,000

Notes at 31 December 20-4:

- inventory is valued at £60,000
- commission income owing £200
- rent income prepaid £300
- electricity owing £350
- salaries prepaid £400

Required:
You are to prepare the income statement of Southtown Supplies for the year ended 31 December 20-4, together with a statement of financial position at that date.

16.4 The following list of balances has been extracted from the books of John Henson at 31 December 20-8:

	£
Purchases	71,600
Revenue	122,000
Inventory at 1 January 20-8	6,250
Vehicle running expenses	1,480
Rent and business rates	5,650
Office expenses	2,220
Discount received	285
Wages and salaries	18,950
Office equipment	10,000
Vehicle	12,000
Trade receivables	5,225
Trade payables	4,910
Capital	20,000
Drawings for the year	13,095
Cash at bank	725

Required:

(a) You are to prepare the income statement of John Henson for the year ended 31 December 20-8, together with his statement of financial position at that date, taking into account:

- closing inventory of £8,500
- office expenses prepaid £120
- vehicle running expenses owing £230
- depreciation of office equipment for the year £1,000
- depreciation of vehicle for the year £3,000

(b) John Henson asks your advice as to whether it would be advantageous to change his business from a sole trader into a private limited company.

16.5* The following trial balance has been extracted by the bookkeeper of James Jenkins, who owns a patisserie and coffee lounge, as at 30 June 20-9:

	Dr	Cr
	£	£
Capital		36,175
Drawings	19,050	
Purchases and revenue	105,240	168,432
Inventory at 1 July 20-8	9,427	
Trade receivables and trade payables	3,840	4,226
Returns	975	1,237
Commission income		2,350
Discounts	127	243
Wages and salaries	30,841	
Vehicle expenses	1,021	
Rent and business rates	8,796	
Heating and lighting	1,840	
Telephone	355	
General expenses	1,752	
Recovery of irrecoverable debts		210
Irrecoverable debts	85	
Vehicle at cost	8,000	
Provision for depreciation on vehicle		3,500
Shop fittings at cost	6,000	
Provision for depreciation on shop fittings		2,400
Provision for doubtful debts		150
Cash	155	
Bank	21,419	
	218,923	218,923

Notes at 30 June 20-9:

- inventory is valued at £11,517
- commission income owing £160
- vehicle expenses owing £55
- rent prepaid £275
- depreciate the vehicle at 25 per cent per annum, using the reducing balance method
- depreciate shop fittings at 10 per cent per annum, using the straight-line method
- the provision for doubtful debts is to be equal to 2.5 per cent of trade receivables

You are to prepare the income statement of James Jenkins for the year ended 30 June 20-9, together with his statement of financial position at that date.

16.6* Liz Blackburn runs a nursing agency. She provides the following information for the year ended 31 December 20-6:

	£
Income from clients	113,490
Wages	62,400
Rent and business rates	8,430
General expenses	9,477
Discount received	388
Discount allowed	307
Trade receivables at 31 December 20-6	10,000
Equipment at cost at 31 December 20-6	12,000
Provision for doubtful debts at 1 January 20-6	400
Provision for depreciation on equipment at 1 January 20-6	4,800

Additional information not yet recorded in the accounts at 31 December 20-6:

(1) Business rates paid in advance amounted to £120.

(2) Rent owing amounted to £600.

(3) Liz maintains a provision for doubtful debts of 3% of trade receivables outstanding at year-end.

(4) Liz provides for depreciation on equipment at 10% per annum using the straight-line method.

Required:

Prepare an income statement for the year ended 31 December 20-6.

17 FINANCIAL STATEMENTS OF LIMITED COMPANIES

In the last few chapters we have looked at a number of adjustments made to the financial statements of sole traders in order to improve their relevance and reliability. In this chapter we turn our attention to limited companies and their financial statements, including:

- aspects of ordinary (equity) shares
- the use of loans and debentures to raise finance
- the concept of reserves, and the differences between capital reserves and revenue reserves
- the layout of a company's income statement, statement of changes in equity, and statement of financial position for internal use

Companies Act 2006

The Companies Act 2006 requires that companies produce financial statements and states the detailed information that must be disclosed. For larger companies the financial statements are audited by external auditors – this is a costly and time-consuming exercise (smaller companies are often exempt from audit). Nevertheless, the audit process enhances the reliability of the financial statements for stakeholders – such as shareholders, trade payables and lenders. The financial statements are filed at Companies House, where they are available for public inspection. The financial statements are available to all shareholders, together with a report on the company's activities during the year.

In this chapter we study the 'internal use' financial statements, rather than being concerned with the accounting requirements of the Companies Act 2006.

Introduction to Limited Company Accounts

The preparation of the financial statements of limited companies is a natural progression from those of sole traders and partnerships. Similar layouts are used for limited companies.

The financial statements comprise:

- an income statement
- a statement of changes in equity
- a statement of financial position

In limited company financial statements the terminology of international accounting standards is widely used. In particular, note the use of 'cash and cash equivalents' for 'bank/cash'.

As we have seen earlier - in Chapter 13 - the main types of limited company are:

- public limited company (Plc)
- private limited company (Ltd)
- company limited by guarantee

The main advantages of setting up in business as a limited company are:

- limited liability
- separate legal entity
- ability to raise finance through an issue of shares
- other advantages include the ability of a company to benefit from economies of scale as it develops into a larger business unit than a sole trader or a partnership.

Ordinary (Equity) Shares

One of the benefits of owning ordinary shares (often calles 'equities') in a limited company is that the shareholders (members) of a company can only lose the amount of their investment. In the event of the company becoming insolvent (going 'bust'), the shareholders' personal assets are not available to pay the company's liabilities.

The amount of a shareholder's investment comprises the money paid for the shares, together with any money unpaid on their shares (unpaid instalments on new share issues, for example). This means that, if the company became insolvent, shareholders would have to pay any unpaid instalments to help pay the liabilities. As this happens very rarely, shareholders are usually in a safe position.

Ordinary shares are the most commonly issued class of share which carry the main 'risks and rewards' of the business. The risks are of losing part or all of the value of the shares if the business loses money or becomes insolvent; the rewards are that they take a share of the profits – in the form of **dividends** – after allowance has been made for all expenses of the business, including loan and debenture interest (see page 311) and taxation. Amounts paid as dividends to ordinary shareholders will vary: when a company makes large profits, it will have the ability to pay higher dividends to the ordinary shareholders; when losses are made, the ordinary shareholders may receive no dividend.

Often dividends are paid twice a year to shareholders. An **interim dividend** is paid just over half-way through the company's financial year and is based on the profits made during the first half of the year. A **final dividend** is paid early in the next financial year and is based on the profits made for the full year. Note that dividends are expressed as either pence per share or a percentage (based on the nominal value of the shares). For example, 5 pence per share is the same as a 5 per cent dividend for shares that have a nominal value of £1; 3 pence per share is the same as a 6 per cent dividend for shares that have a nominal value of 50 pence.

Companies rarely pay out all of their profits in the form of dividends; most retain some profits as reserves. These can always be used to enable a dividend to be paid in a year when the company makes little or no profit, always assuming that the company has sufficient cash in the bank to make the payment. Ordinary shareholders, in the event of the company becoming insolvent, will be the last to receive any repayment of their investment: other liabilities will be paid off first.

Ordinary shares carry voting rights – thus shareholders have a say at the annual general meeting and at any other shareholders' meetings.

Ordinary shares are not normally repayable, so the company will have the finance for the foreseeable future.

A company can issue further ordinary shares if it requires additional capital – subject to the rules of the company permitting this.

advantages and disadvantages of ordinary shares

To the company raising finance, the advantages and disadvantages of issuing ordinary shares need to be considered.

advantages to the company:

- ordinary shares are not normally repayable
- a variable dividend is paid, which is dependent on profits
- if profits are low and a dividend is not paid in one year, the dividend is not carried forward
- in the event of insolvency of the company, ordinary shareholders will be paid off last

disadvantage to the company:

- ordinary shareholders can speak and vote at a general meeting of the company, and each share carries one vote; this could be a problem to the company if the shareholders are dissatisfied

nominal value of shares

Each share has a nominal value – or face value – which is entered in the accounts. Shares may be issued with nominal values of 5p, 10p, 25p, 50p or £1, or indeed for any amount.

Most ordinary shares are described as being fully paid, meaning that the company has received the full amount of the nominal value of each share from the shareholders. Sometimes shares are partly paid, eg nominal value of £1, but 75p paid – this means that the company can make a call on the shareholders, at an agreed time, to pay the extra 25p to make the shares fully paid.

market value of shares

The market value is the price at which issued – or 'secondhand' – shares are traded. For ordinary shares this value can go up or down depending on, amongst other things, the success of the company – the 'risks and rewards' of equity shares. The market value usually bears little relationship to the nominal value. Note that only a small number of limited companies have their shares bought and sold on the Stock Exchange (eg Tesco, BT); the large majority of companies are much smaller and are not quoted on the stock market and will only need to be valued if the company is up for sale.

issue price

This is the price at which shares are issued to shareholders by the company – either when the company is being set up, or at a later date when it needs to raise more funds. The issue price is either 'at par' (ie the nominal value), or above nominal value. In the latter case, the amount of the difference between issue price and nominal value is known as a **share premium** (see page 318): for example – nominal value £1.00; issue price £1.50; therefore share premium is 50p per share. Share premium often comes about when established companies issue additional shares – the new shareholders are paying extra to buy a stake in a profitable business.

bookkeeping entries

The bookkeeping entries to record an issue of ordinary shares at a premium are:

- Dr bank account (with total amount received, ie from shares plus share premium)
- Cr ordinary shares account
- Cr share premium account

Loans and Debentures

In addition to money provided by shareholders, who are the owners of the company, as we have seen earlier (pages 243-247) further funds may be obtained by borrowing long-term, usually in the form of loans or debentures.

loans

Loans are borrowed by companies from lenders (eg banks) and investors on a medium or long-term (non-current) basis. Generally repayments are made throughout the period of the loan, but can often be tailored to suit the needs of the borrower. Lenders often require security for loans so that, if the loan is not repaid, the lender has an asset – such as the company's premises – that can be sold.

debentures

Debentures are formal certificates issued by companies raising long-term finance from lenders and investors. Debenture certificates – or loan notes – issued by large public limited companies are often traded on the Stock Exchange. Most debentures state the date they will be repaid, for example, "debentures 2030-2035" means that repayment will be made by the issuer between the years 2030 and 2035, at a date to be decided by the issuer. Debentures are commonly secured against assets such as property so that, in the event of the company ceasing to trade, the assets could be sold and used to repay the debenture holders.

Loans may carry fixed or variable rates of interest, while debentures are usually at fixed rates that must be paid, just like other business expenses, whether a company makes profits or not. As loan and debenture interest is a business expense, this is shown in the income statement under the heading of 'finance costs'. In the event of the company ceasing to trade, loan and debenture-holders would be repaid before shareholders.

Income Statement and Statement of Changes in Equity

income statement

A limited company uses a similar form of financial statements as a sole trader.

There are two expense items commonly found in the income statement of a limited company that are not found in those of other business types:

- **directors' remuneration** – ie amounts paid to directors; as directors are employed by the company, their pay appears amongst the income statement expenses of the company – this contrasts with the drawings taken by a sole trader which appear in the statement of financial position
- **loan/debenture interest** – as already noted, the interest on loans and debentures is shown as a finance cost in the income statement

Note that a figure is shown in the income statement for **profit from operations** after the deduction of expenses, but before the deduction of finance costs (such as debenture interest, bank and loan interest) and tax. The profit from operations of a company is important to investors, lenders and other stakeholders because it shows them the profit made after deduction of the running expenses (distribution expenses, sales and marketing expenses, and administration expenses) but before finance costs and tax are deducted, ie it shows them the ability of the company to generate profits from its day-to-day activities.

The income statement also shows **profit before tax** and concludes with **profit for the year after tax.**

statement of changes in equity

Limited company financial statements require a further statement – a statement of changes in equity – to show how the profit for the year has been distributed and to provide a link to the statement of financial position. The following statement of changes in equity that deals with a share issue at a premium and retained earnings:

Statement of Changes in Equity for the year ended 31 December 20-1

	Issued share capital	Share premium	Retained earnings	Total
	£	£	£	£
Balances at start	100,000	20,000	30,000	150,000
Profit for the year			25,000	25,000
Dividends paid			(15,000)	(15,000)
Issue of share capital	50,000	10,000	–	60,000
Balances at end	150,000	30,000	40,000	220,000

Notes:

- dividends paid include *interim dividends* (usually paid just over half-way through the financial year) and the previous year's *final dividends* (proposed at the end of the previous year, but paid early in the current financial year)
- an issue of shares – here at a premium (see page 318) – is shown on the statement
- the balance at the end of the year for issued share capital, share premium and retained earnings is shown on the statement of financial position

The diagram on pages 314 and 315 shows the income statement and the statement of changes in equity of Orion Limited as an example. Explanations are set out on the left-hand page.

Statement of Financial Position

The statement of financial position of limited companies follows a similar layout for those of sole traders and partnerships, but the equity section is more complex with the issued shares and various reserves. The diagram on pages 316 and 317 shows the statement of financial position of Orion Limited as an example. Explanations are set out on the left-hand page.

Note that, as with sole trader statements of financial position, there are alternative columnar layouts, for example:

	Non-current assets
plus	Current assets
equals	Total assets

which balances against

	Equity
plus	Non-current liabilities
plus	Current liabilities
equals	Capital and liabilities

Total Equity

On a company statement of financial position, the total equity section represents the stake of the ordinary shareholders in the company and comprises:

- issued ordinary shares
- capital reserves (see page 318)
- revenue reserves (see page 319)

Equity in a company statement of financial position is the same concept as the owner's capital in a sole trader statement of financial position.

Dealing with Dividends in the Financial Statements

Dividends are distributions to the shareholders, who own the company, as a return on their investment. Many companies pay dividends twice a year – an *interim dividend*, which is usually paid just over halfway through the financial year, and a *final dividend* which is paid early in the next financial year. The interim dividend is based on the profits reported by the company during the first half of the year, while the final dividend is based on the profits reported for the full year. The final dividend is proposed by the directors and has to be approved by shareholders at a meeting of the company. Thus the financial calendar for a company with a financial year end of 31 December 20-8 might take the following form:

continued on page 318

Revenue is sales less sales returns, ie the turnover of the company.

Other income could include rental income, cash discount, profit on sale of assets, etc.

The **expenses** of a limited company are usually split between the expenses of distribution, sales and marketing, and administration, although different headings can be used, eg wages, depreciation of assets, etc.

The company has recorded a **profit from operations** (operating profit) of £49,000, before deduction of finance costs (such as debenture interest, bank and loan interest) and tax.

Tax, the corporation tax that a company has to pay, based on its profits, is shown. We shall not be studying the calculations for corporation tax in this book. It is, however, important to see how the tax is recorded in the financial statements.

The company has recorded a **profit for the year after tax**, of £28,000. This amount is taken to the statement of changes in equity.

The **statement of changes in equity** demonstrates how profit for the year is added to the brought forward balance of retained earnings (a revenue reserve), while dividends paid during the year are deducted. The resultant balance of retained earnings at the end of the year is shown in the statement of financial position in the equity section.

New issues of shares are also shown in the statement of changes in equity.

ORION PLC

INCOME STATEMENT FOR THE YEAR ENDED 31 DECEMBER 20-6

	£	£
Revenue		725,000
Opening inventory	45,000	
Purchases	381,000	
	426,000	
Less Closing inventory	50,000	
Cost of sales		(376,000)
Gross profit		349,000
Other income		10,000
		359,000
Expenses:		
Distribution expenses	(85,000)	
Sales and marketing expenses	(100,000)	
Administration expenses	(125,000)	
		(310,000)
Profit/(loss) for the year from operations		49,000
Finance costs		(6,000)
Profit/(loss) for the year before tax		43,000
Tax		(15,000)
Profit/(loss) for the year after tax		28,000

STATEMENT OF CHANGES IN EQUITY FOR THE YEAR ENDED 31 DECEMBER 20-6

	Issued share capital £	Share premium £	Retained earnings £	Total £
Balances at start	400,000	30,000	41,000	471,000
Profit for the year			28,000	28,000
Dividends paid			(20,000)	(20,000)
Balances at end	400,000	30,000	49,000	479,000

The **non-current assets** section of a limited company statement of financial position usually distinguishes between:

intangible non-current assets, which do not have material substance but belong to the company and have value, eg goodwill (the amount paid for the reputation and connections of a business that has been taken over), patents and trademarks; the intangible non-current assets are amortised (depreciated).

property, plant and equipment, which are tangible (ie have material substance) non-current assets and are depreciated over their useful lives.

As well as the usual **current liabilities**, for limited companies, this section also contains the amount of tax to be paid within the next twelve months.

Non-current liabilities are those liabilities that are due to be repaid more than twelve months from the date of the statement of financial position, eg loans and debentures.

Equity is assets minus liabilities, representing the stake of ordinary shareholders in the company.

Issued share capital shows the shares that have been issued. In this statement of financial position, the ordinary shares are described as being fully paid, meaning that the company has received the full amount of the nominal value of each share from the shareholders. Sometimes shares will be partly paid, eg ordinary shares of £1, but 75p paid. This means that the company can make a call on the shareholders to pay the extra 25p to make the shares fully paid.

Capital reserves (see page 318) are created as a result of a non-trading profit, for example, share premium, and cannot be distributed as dividends.

Revenue reserves (see page 319) are retained earnings from the statement of changes in equity and can be distributed as dividends.

Total equity is the stake of the ordinary shareholders in the company. It comprises issued ordinary share capital, plus capital and revenue reserves.

ORION PLC

STATEMENT OF FINANCIAL POSITION AS AT 31 DECEMBER 20-6

Non-current Assets	**Cost**	**Amortisation/ Depreciation**	**Carrying amount**
	£	£	£
Intangible			
Goodwill	50,000	20,000	30,000
Property, plant and equipment			
Freehold land and buildings	280,000	40,000	240,000
Machinery	230,000	100,000	130,000
Fixtures and fittings	100,000	25,000	75,000
	660,000	185,000	475,000
Current Assets			
Inventory			50,000
Trade and other receivables			38,000
Cash and cash equivalents			21,000
			109,000
Less Current Liabilities			
Trade and other payables			(30,000)
Tax liabilities			(15,000)
			(45,000)
Net Current Assets or Working Capital			64,000
			539,000
Less Non-current Liabilities			
7% debentures (repayable in 20-9)			(60,000)
NET ASSETS			479,000
EQUITY			
Issued Share Capital			
400,000 ordinary shares of £1 each fully paid			400,000
Capital Reserve			
Share premium			30,000
Revenue Reserve			
Retained earnings			49,000
TOTAL EQUITY			479,000

Note: the statement of financial position can be presented using a number of columns, as required.

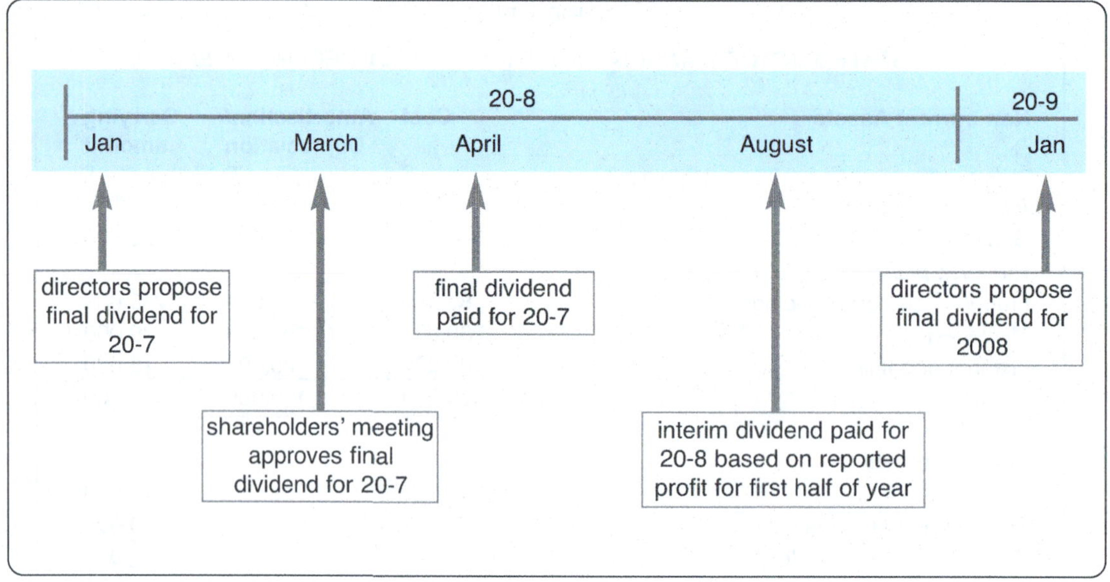

Only the dividends paid during the year can be recorded in the financial statements. In the above example, the dividends paid in April 20-8 (final dividend for the previous year) and August 20-8 (interim dividend for the current year) are recorded in the financial statements for the year ended 31 December 20-8. The proposed final dividend for the year ended 31 December 20-8 is disclosed as a note, stating that it is subject to approval by the shareholders at a company meeting. All dividends for the year which have been paid are shown in the statement of changes in equity.

RESERVES

A limited company rarely distributes all its profits to its shareholders. Instead, it will often keep part of the profits earned each year in the form of reserves. There are two types of reserves:

- capital reserves, which are created as a result of a non-trading profit
- revenue reserves, which are retained profits from the income statement

Note that reserves and changes in reserves are recorded in the statement of changes in equity.

capital reserves

Capital reserves are created as a result of a non-trading profit. Note that capital reserves cannot be used to fund dividend payments.

An example is **share premium**. This comes about when an established company issues additional shares to the public at a higher amount than the nominal value. For example, a company seeks finance for further expansion by issuing additional ordinary shares. The shares have a nominal value of £1 each, but, because it is a well-established company, the shares are issued at £1.50 each. Of this amount, £1 is recorded in the issued share capital section, and the extra 50p is the share premium.

revenue reserves

Revenue reserves are profits from trading activities which have been retained in the company to help build the company for the future.

As revenue reserves have been created from the trading activities of the company, they are available to fund dividend payments (as we have seen on page 312, dividends paid are deducted in the statement of changes in equity).

reserves: profits not cash

It should be noted that reserves – both capital and revenue – are not cash funds to be used whenever the company needs money, but are in fact represented by assets shown on the statement of financial position. The reserves record the fact that the assets belong to the ordinary shareholders via their ownership of the company.

CHAPTER SUMMARY

- Shareholders have limited liability, but will be liable for any money unpaid on their shares.
- The main type of shares that may be issued by companies is ordinary shares.
- Loan capital in the form of loans and debentures is a further source of finance.
- The financial statements of a company include a statement of changes in equity, which follows the income statement.
- The statement of financial position of a limited company includes an equity section which states the ownership of the company by its shareholders:
  - ordinary shares issued
  - capital reserves and revenue reserves
- Capital reserves are created as a result of a non-trading profit and cannot be used to fund dividend payments.
- Revenue reserves are profits from trading activities.

In the next chapter we look at how we can assess business performance by interpreting and analysing the financial statements. To help us in this we shall be calculating financial ratios and other measures.

QUESTIONS

visit
www.osbornebooks.co.uk
to take an online test

An asterisk (*) after the question number means that the answer is given at the end of this book.

17.1* What does the term 'limited' mean in the name of a company?

A	The liability for shareholders is limited to the amount of their investment in the company	
B	The company cannot issue more shares	
C	Ordinary shareholders do not have voting rights in the company	
D	The company cannot take out loans or debentures	

17.2 Distinguish between:

(a) Ordinary shares and debentures.

(b) Nominal value and market value of shares.

(c) Capital reserves and revenue reserves.

17.3 Explain where the following items appear in a limited company's financial statements:

(a) Debenture interest.

(b) Drectors' remuneration.

(c) Corporation tax.

(d) Dividends paid.

(e) Share premium.

(f) Goodwill.

17.4* Chapelporth Limited has a balance of retained earnings of £185,000 at 1 July 20-7, the beginning of its financial year.

The company has made a profit from operations of £135,000 for the year ended 30 June 20-8.

The following payments have been made during the year ended 30 June 20-8:

	£
• debenture interest	12,500
• final ordinary dividend for the year ended 30 June 20-7	30,500
• interim ordinary dividend for the half-year ended 31 December 20-7	18,000

Corporation tax to be paid for the year ended 30 June 20-8 is £48,000.

You are to:

- Complete the income statement from the profit from operations of £135,000 for the year ended 30 June 20-8.
- Prepare the statement of changes in equity for retained earnings for the year ended 30 June 20-8.

17.5 Mason Motors Limited is a second-hand car business. The following information is available for the year ended 31 December 20-1:

- retained earnings at 1 January 20-1 is £100,000
- profit from operations for the year was £75,000
- loan interest of £5,500 was paid
- corporation tax of £20,050 is to be paid on the year's profit
- a dividend of 10% was paid on the issued ordinary share capital of £100,000

You are to:

(a) Complete the income statement from the profit from operations of £75,000 for the year ended 31 December 20-1.

(b) Prepare the statement of changes in equity for retained earnings for the year ended 31 December 20-1.

(c) State how you would reply to one of the directors of the company who asks if the retained earnings could be used to rebuild the garage forecourt.

17.6* The following figures are taken from the accounting records of Jobseekers Limited, a recruitment agency, at the end of the financial year on 31 December 20-6:

	£
Issued share capital (£1 ordinary shares) fully paid	100,000
Property at cost	175,000
Depreciation of property to date	10,500
Office equipment at cost	25,000
Depreciation of office equipment to date	5,000
Goodwill at cost	20,000
Amortisation* of goodwill to date	6,000
Inventory	10,750
Trade and other receivables	42,500
Trade and other payables	17,250
Cash and cash equivalents	1,950
Bank loan (repayable in 20-9)	55,000
Profit for the year after tax	68,200
Corporation tax owing for the year	14,850
Ordinary dividend paid	10,000
Retained earnings at 1 January 20-6	8,400

* amortisation is similar to depreciation

You are to prepare the statement of changes in equity for the year ended 31 December 20-6, together with a statement of financial position at that date.

17.7 Playfair Limited prepares its financial statements to 31 December each year. At 31 December 20-3 its trial balance was as follows:

	£000	£000
Issued share capital (£1 ordinary shares) fully paid		380
Share premium		50
Plant and equipment at cost	800	
Trade receivables	350	
Trade payables		160
Accruals		30
Prepayments	40	
Cash and cash equivalents	140	
Loan (non-current)		200
Inventory at 1 January 20-3	250	
Administrative expenses	110	
Purchases	1,650	
Revenue		2,340
Loan interest paid	40	
Distribution expenses	240	
Accumulated depreciation on plant and equipment		230
Dividends paid	50	
Retained earnings at 1 January 20-3		260
Provision for doubtful debts at 1 January 20-3		20
	3,670	3,670

Further information:

- Inventory at 31 December 20-3 cost £280,000.
- Depreciation of plant and equipment is to be charged at the rate of 20 per cent per annum on cost and allocated equally between distribution costs and administrative expenses.
- The provision for doubtful debts, an administrative expense, is to be increased to £40,000.
- The corporation tax charge for the year has been calculated as £30,000.

Your are to prepare the financial statements of Playfair Limited for the year to 31 December 20-3.

17.8* The following is the summarised draft statement of financial position of Trevaunance Limited as at 30 June 20-4:

	Cost	Depreciation	Carrying amount
	£000	£000	£000
Non-current assets	1,500	840	660
Current assets		380	
Less Current liabilities		220	160
			820
Ordinary share capital			500
Retained earnings			320
			820

Depreciation has been charged on non-current assets at 25% for the year using the straight-line method.

After preparing the draft statement of financial position, the directors of Trevaunance Limited wish to incorporate the following in the financial statements:

(a) Office expenses due but unpaid at the year-end amounted to £15,000.

(b) Depreciation of non-current assets is to be changed to a rate of 20% for the year using the straight-line method.

(c) Closing inventory has been overvalued by £5,000.

(d) Corporation tax of £28,000 is to be paid on the year's profit.

Required:

Using the table below show the effect, ie increase/decrease/no change, and state the amount that any amendments resulting from notes (a) to (d) above will have on the profit for the year and the statement of financial position of Trevaunance Limited.

Note	Profit for the year	Retained earnings	Total equity	Current assets	Current liabilities
(a)					
(b)					
(c)					
(d)					

17.9* The trading section of the income statement for Glinka Ltd for the year ended 30 June 20-2 has been completed. It showed a gross profit of £155,100.

The following balances remained in the books of account of Glinka Ltd at 30 June 20-2:

	£
Bank loan repayable 20-6	30,000
Ordinary shares of 25p each	50,000
Cash and cash equivalents	18,120
Inventory	40,208
Operating expenses	90,755
Loan interest paid	500
Non-current assets at cost	150,000
Provision for depreciation at 1 July 20-1	37,500
Trade payables	22,310
Trade receivables	65,174
Retained earnings	52,847
Share premium	5,000

Additional information:

- The five year bank loan was taken out last year and interest is payable at the rate of 5% per annum.
- It is the company policy to depreciate non-current assets using the reducing balance method at the rate of 25% per annum.
- The directors have been advised that there should be a provision for corporation tax for the year ended 30 June 20-2. It is estimated that this should be 20% of the profit before tax.
- On 20 June 20-2 the directors paid a dividend of 10p per share. Apart from in the bank account, this has not been recorded in the books of account.
- On 25 June 20-2 the directors issued 80,000 new ordinary shares at a price of 40p per share. The issue was fully subscribed and, apart from in the bank account, this has not been recorded in the books of account.

(a) Complete the income statement of Glinka Ltd for the year ended 30 June 20-2.

GLINKA LTD
INCOME STATEMENT FOR THE YEAR ENDED 30 JUNE 20-2

	£	£
Gross profit		155,100
Expenses:		

(b) Prepare the statement of changes in equity of Glinka Ltd for the year ended 30 June 20-2.

GLINKA LTD
STATEMENT OF CHANGES IN EQUITY FOR THE YEAR ENDED 30 JUNE 20-2

	Share capital £	Share premium £	Retained earnings £	Total £

(c) Prepare the statement of financial position of Glinka Ltd as at 30 June 20-2.

GLINKA LTD
STATEMENT OF FINANCIAL POSITION AS AT 30 JUNE 20-2

	£	£	£

18 FINANCIAL RATIOS

Financial ratios, and other measures, are used to interpret the financial statements of businesses in order to assess strengths and weaknesses. A business needs to be performing well in areas of profitability, liquidity, efficiency, and capital structure.

In this chapter we examine:

- the importance of interpretation of financial statements
- the main financial ratios and performance indicators
- the difference between profit and cash
- a commentary on trends shown by the main financial ratios
- how to report on the overall financial situation of a business
- limitations in the use of financial ratios

INTERESTED PARTIES

The use of financial ratios to interpret financial statements is not always made by an accountant; interested parties (stakeholders) include:

- **managers** or **owners** of the business, who need to make financial decisions affecting the future development of the business
- **banks**, who are being asked to lend money to finance the business
- **suppliers**, who want to know if they are likely to get paid
- **customers**, who wish to be assured of continuity of supplies in the future
- **shareholders** of a limited company, who wish to be assured that their investment is sound
- prospective **investors** in a limited company, who wish to compare comparative strengths and weaknesses
- the **owner** of a business, who wishes to make comparisons with other businesses
- **employees** and **trade unions**, who wish to check on the financial prospects of the business
- **government** and **government agencies**, eg HM Revenue & Customs, that wants to check it is receiving the amount due for VAT and the tax payable on the profits of the business

In all of these cases, the interested parties will be able to calculate the main ratios, percentages and performance indicators. By doing this, the strengths and weaknesses of the business will be highlighted and appropriate conclusions can be drawn as to whether or not the business is meeting the expectations of stakeholders.

Types of Financial Ratios and Measures

The general term 'financial ratios' is usually used to describe the calculations aspect of interpretation of financial statements. The term 'ratio' is, in fact, partly misleading because the performance indicators include percentages, time periods, as well as ratios in the strict sense of the word.

The main themes covered by financial ratios are:

- profitability – the relationship between profit and sales revenue, assets and capital employed
- liquidity – the stability of the business on a short-term basis
- efficiency – the effective and efficient use of assets and liabilities
- capital structure – the stability of the business on a long-term basis

Making Use of Financial Ratios

It is important when examining a set of financial statements and using financial ratios to relate them to reference points or standards. These points of reference might be to:

- establish trends from past years, so providing a standard of comparison
- compare against other businesses in the same industry
- compare with standards assumed to be satisfactory by the interested party, eg a bank

Above all, it is important to understand the relationships between ratios: one ratio may give an indication of the state of the business but, before drawing conclusions, this needs to be supported by other ratios. Ratios can highlight symptoms, but the cause will then need to be investigated.

Another use of ratios is to estimate the likely future profit for the year or statement of financial position of a business. For example, it might be assumed that the same gross profit percentage as last year will also apply next year; thus, given an estimated increase in revenue, it is a simple matter to estimate gross profit. In a similar way, by making use of ratios, profit for the year and the statement of financial position can be forecast.

Now study the illustration on the next two pages. It shows the ways in which the profitability of a business is assessed. The first page sets out the calculation of the ratios and the next page highlights the figures that are used in calculating them. Then read the section 'Profitability' which follows on page 332.

PROFITABILITY RATIOS

$$\textbf{Gross profit margin} = \frac{\text{Gross profit}}{\text{Revenue}} \times \frac{100}{1}$$

$$\textbf{Gross profit mark-up} = \frac{\text{Gross profit}}{\text{Cost of sales}} \times \frac{100}{1}$$

$$\textbf{Expenses in relation to revenue} = \frac{\text{Expenses}}{\text{Revenue}} \times \frac{100}{1}$$

$$\textbf{Profit in relation to revenue} = \frac{\text{Profit before tax}}{\text{Revenue}} \times \frac{100}{1}$$

Return on capital employed (sole trader)

$$= \frac{\text{Profit before interest}}{\text{Capital employed*}} \times \frac{100}{1}$$

*capital + non-current liabilities (note: either opening or closing capital could be used)

Return on capital employed (limited company)

$$= \frac{\text{Profit from operations}}{\text{Capital employed*}} \times \frac{100}{1}$$

*equity + non-current liabilities (note: either opening or closing equity could be used)

Mithian Trading Company Limited

INCOME STATEMENT

for the year ended 31 December 20-7

	£000s	£000s
Revenue		1,430
Opening inventory	200	
Purchases	1,000	
	1,200	
Less Closing inventory	240	
Cost of sales		960
Gross profit		470
Expenses:		
Distribution expenses	(150)	
Administration expenses	(140)	
		(290)
Profit for the year from operations		180
Finance costs		(10)
Profit for the year before tax		170
Tax		(50)
Profit for the year after tax		120

Statement of changes in equity (extract)

Retained earnings	
Balance at start	180
Profit for the year	120
	300
Dividends paid	(100)
Balance at end	200

STATEMENT OF FINANCIAL POSITION (extract)

	£000s
Capital employed (ordinary share capital + reserves + non-current liabilities)	1,550

Notes: Items used in the ratios on the opposite page are shown in bold type on a blue background

PROFITABILITY

One of the main objectives of a business is to make a profit. Profitability ratios examine the relationship between profit and revenue, assets, equity and capital employed. Before calculating the profitability ratios, it is important to read the income statement in order to review the figures.

The key profitability ratios are shown on the previous two pages. We will be calculating the accounting ratios from these in the Worked Example (pages 340-345).

gross profit margin

$$\frac{\textbf{Gross profit}}{\textbf{Revenue}} \times \frac{100}{1}$$

This ratio expresses, as a percentage, the gross profit (revenue minus cost of sales) in relation to sales revenue. For example, a gross profit margin of 20 per cent means that for every £100 of revenue made, the gross profit is £20.

The gross profit margin should be similar from year-to-year for the same business. It will vary between different types of businesses, eg the gross profit margin on jewellery is considerably higher than that on food. A significant change from one year to the next, particularly a fall in the percentage, requires investigation into the cost of sales (including purchase prices) and selling prices.

Gross profit margin and mark-up (see below) – and also net profit margin (see next page) – need to be considered in context. For example, a supermarket may well have a lower gross profit margin than a small corner shop but, because of the supermarket's much higher sales revenue, the amount of profit will be much higher. Whatever the type of business, gross profit – both as an amount and a percentage – needs to be sufficient to cover the overheads (expenses), and then to give an acceptable return on capital employed (see page 334).

gross profit mark-up

$$\frac{\textbf{Gross profit}}{\textbf{Cost of sales}} \times \frac{100}{1}$$

This ratio expresses, as a percentage, the gross profit in relation to cost of sales. For example, a gross profit mark-up of 25 per cent means that for every £100 of purchases made, the gross profit is £25. Gross profit mark-up should be similar from year-to-year for the same business, although it will vary between different types of businesses. Any significant change needs investigation into the cost of sales (including purchase prices) and selling prices.

It is quite common for a business to establish its selling price by reference to either a margin or a mark-up. The difference between the two is that:

- margin is a percentage profit based on the selling price
- mark-up is a profit percentage added to buying or cost price

For example, a product is bought by a retailer for £100; the retailer sells it for £125, ie

cost price	+	gross profit	=	selling price
£100	+	£25	=	£125

The **margin** is:

$$\frac{\text{gross profit}}{\text{selling price}} \times \frac{100}{1} = \frac{£25}{£125} \times \frac{100}{1} = \mathbf{20\%}$$

The **mark-up** is:

$$\frac{\text{gross profit}}{\text{cost price}} \times \frac{100}{1} = \frac{£25}{£100} \times \frac{100}{1} = \mathbf{25\%}$$

Notice here that gross profit margin and mark-up look at the same information, but from a different viewpoint: with margin, it is the gross profit related to the selling price; with mark-up, it is the gross profit related to the buying price (cost of sales).

expenses in relation to revenue

$$\frac{\textbf{Expenses}}{\textbf{Revenue}} \times \frac{\mathbf{100}}{\mathbf{1}}$$

Here the expenses (overheads) of a business are expressed as a percentage of revenue. The ratio should fall as revenue increases – this is because not all expenses are variable, ie increase in direct proportion to the increase in revenue.

Note that each expense or overhead falls into one of three categories of cost:

- fixed costs, eg rent, council tax
- variable costs, eg commission
- semi-variable costs, eg car hire, telephone expenses

Fixed costs remain constant despite other changes. Variable costs alter with changed circumstances, such as increased sales. Semi-variable costs combine both a fixed and a variable element, eg hire of a car at a basic (fixed) cost, with a variable cost per mile. It is important to appreciate the nature of costs when interpreting accounts: for example, if revenue this year is twice last year's figure, not all expenses will have doubled.

Any expense item from the income statement can be expressed as a percentage of revenue. For example, if advertising is £50,000 and revenue is £500,000 then the percentage is 10 per cent; if it is found to be 20 per cent next year then this could indicate that an increase in advertising has failed to produce a proportionate increase in revenue.

Note that the behaviour of costs is discussed in more detail in Chapter 20.

profit in relation to revenue

$$\frac{\textbf{Profit before tax}}{\textbf{Revenue}} \times \frac{\mathbf{100}}{\mathbf{1}}$$

As with gross profit margin, the percentage of profit in relation to revenue should be similar from year-to-year for the same business, and should also be comparable with other firms in the same line of business. Profit in relation to revenue should, ideally, increase from year-to-year, which indicates that the income statement expenses are being kept under control. Any significant fall should be investigated to see if it has been caused by:

- a fall in gross profit margin
- and/or an increase in one particular expense, eg wages and salaries, advertising, etc

return on capital employed (ROCE)

This compares the profit before interest/finance costs of a business with the amount of capital invested in the business by the owner. The percentage return is best thought of in relation to other investments – such as the interest on a savings account. A person running a business is investing a sum of money in that business, and the profit is the return that is achieved on that investment. However, it should be noted that the risks in running a business are considerably greater than depositing the money with a bank, and an additional return to allow for the extra risk is needed.

For **sole traders** return on capital employed is:

$$\frac{\textbf{Profit before interest}}{\textbf{Capital employed}} \times \frac{\textbf{100}}{\textbf{1}}$$

Here capital employed is the owner's capital plus non-current liabilities. Note that either opening capital or closing capital could be used in the calculation.

For **limited companies** return on capital employed is:

$$\frac{\textbf{Profit from operations}}{\textbf{Capital employed}} \times \frac{\textbf{100}}{\textbf{1}}$$

Here capital employed is equity (ordinary share capital plus reserves) plus non-current liabilities. Note that either opening equity or closing equity could be used in the calculation.

the difference between profit and cash

This section has looked at the profitability of a business, ie the ability of the business to generate profit. Many people who use financial statements are also interested in cash flows – the ability to generate cash. There is an important difference between profit and cash – it is possible to have a highly profitable company that is using more cash than it is generating so that its bank balance is falling (or its overdraft is increasing). Liquidity (which we shall be looking at in the next section) is important: it is often a lack of cash (a lack of liquidity) that causes most businesses to fail.

To distinguish between cash and profit:

- **cash** is the actual amount of money held in the bank or as cash
- **profit** is a calculated figure which shows the surplus of income over expenditure for the year; it takes note of adjustments for accruals and prepayments and non-cash items such as depreciation and provision for doubtful debts.

Various transactions have an unequal effect on cash and profit as shown by the examples in the following diagram:

Effect on profit		Transaction	Effect on cash	
increase	decrease		increase	decrease
		• purchase of non-current assets		✓
	✓	• depreciation of non-current assets		
		• issue of new shares	✓	
		• payment of dividends		✓
		• raising of a loan	✓	
		• repayment of a loan		✓
✓		• increase in inventory		✓
	✓	• decrease in inventory	✓	
		• increase in trade receivables		✓
		• decrease in trade receivables	✓	
	✓	• increase in provision for doubtful debts		
✓		• reduction in provision for doubtful debts		
		• increase in trade payables	✓	
		• decrease in trade payables		✓

LIQUIDITY

Liquidity ratios measure the financial stability of the business, ie the ability of the business to operate on a short-term basis. For this we focus our attention on the current assets and current liabilities sections of the statement of financial position.

The key liquidity ratios follow. We will be calculating the accounting ratios from these in the Worked Example on pages 340-345.

net current assets and liquid capital

Net current assets = Current assets – Current liabilities

Net current assets, or working capital, is needed by all businesses in order to finance day-to-day trading activities. Sufficient net current assets enables a business to hold adequate inventory, allow a measure of credit to its customers (trade receivables), and to pay its suppliers (trade payables) as payments fall due.

Liquid capital = (Current assets – Inventory) – Current liabilities

Liquid capital omits inventory, because it is the most illiquid (ie furthest from cash) current asset. Liquid capital provides a direct comparison between the short-term assets of trade receivables and bank/cash, and the short-term liabilities of trade payables, tax and bank overdraft.

explanation continued on page 338

LIQUIDITY RATIOS

Current ratio* = $\dfrac{\text{Current assets}}{\text{Current liabilities}}$

* also known as the working capital ratio

Liquid capital ratio* = $\dfrac{\text{Current assets} - \text{inventory}}{\text{Current liabilities}}$

* also known as the acid test or quick ratio

EFFICIENCY RATIOS

Rate of inventory turnover = (days) $\dfrac{\text{Average inventory*}}{\text{Cost of sales}} \times 365 \text{ days}$

Rate of inventory turnover = (times per year) $\dfrac{\text{Cost of sales}}{\text{Average inventory*}}$

*usually taken as: (opening inventory + closing inventory) ÷ 2; alternatively, if opening inventory figure is not available, use closing inventory from the statement of financial position in the calculation

Trade receivable days = $\dfrac{\text{Trade receivables}}{\text{Credit sales}} \times 365 \text{ days}$

Trade payable days = $\dfrac{\text{Trade payables}}{\text{Credit purchases}} \times 365 \text{ days}$

CAPITAL STRUCTURE RATIO

Capital gearing = $\dfrac{\text{Non-current liabilities}}{\text{Issued share capital + Reserves + Non-current liabilities}} \times \dfrac{100}{1}$

Mithian Trading Company Limited
STATEMENT OF FINANCIAL POSITION
as at 31 December 20-7

Non-Current Assets	£000s Cost	£000s Depreciation	£000s Carrying amount
Property	950	100	850
Fixtures and fittings	300	120	180
Vehicles	350	100	250
	1,600	320	1,280
Current Assets			
Inventory			240
Trade and other receivables			150
Cash and cash equivalents			135
			525
Less Current Liabilities			
Trade payables			(205)
Other payables (tax)			(50)
			(255)
Net Current Assets			270
			1,550
Less Non-Current Liabilities			
10% Debentures			(100)
NET ASSETS			1,450
EQUITY			
Issued Share Capital			
1,250,000 ordinary shares of £1 each, fully paid			1,250
Revenue Reserve			
Retained earnings			200
TOTAL EQUITY			1,450

INCOME STATEMENT (extract)

	£000s
Cost of sales	960
Revenue	1,430
Purchases	1,000

Note: Items used in ratios are shown in bold type with a blue background.

current ratio (or working capital ratio)

$$\text{Current ratio*} = \frac{\text{Current assets}}{\text{Current liabilities}}$$

*expressed as X:1

The current ratio uses figures from the statement of financial position and measures the relationship between current assets and current liabilities. Although there is no ideal net current asset ratio, an acceptable ratio for a 'traditional' business is about 2:1, ie £2 of current assets to every £1 of current liabilities. However, a business in the retail trade may be able to work with a lower ratio, eg 1.5:1 or even less, because it deals mainly in sales for cash and so does not have a large figure for trade receivables. A current ratio can be too high: if it is above 3:1 an investigation of the make-up of current assets and current liabilities is needed: eg the business may have too much inventory, too many trade receivables, or too much cash at the bank.

liquid capital ratio (or acid test ratio)

$$\text{Liquid capital ratio*} = \frac{\text{Current assets} - \text{Inventory}}{\text{Current liabilities}}$$

*expressed as X:1

The liquid capital ratio (also known as the acid test or quick ratio) uses the current assets and current liabilities from the statement of financial position, but inventory is omitted. This is because inventory is the most illiquid current asset: it has to be sold, turned into trade receivables, and then the cash has to be collected from the trade receivables. Thus the liquid capital ratio provides a direct comparison between trade receivables/cash and short-term liabilities. The balance between liquid assets, that is trade receivables and cash, and current liabilities should, ideally, be about 1:1, ie £1 of liquid assets to each £1 of current liabilities. This means that a business is expected to be able to pay its current liabilities from its liquid assets; a figure below 1:1, eg 0.75:1, indicates that the firm would have difficulty in meeting pressing demands from trade payables. However, as with the current ratio, some businesses are able to operate with a lower liquid capital ratio than others.

EFFICIENCY

Efficiency ratios measure how well the management of a business controls the current assets and liabilities of the business – that is inventory, trade receivables and trade payables.

The key efficiency ratios are shown below. We will be calculating the accounting ratios from these in the Worked Example (pages 340-345).

rate of inventory turnover (days)

$$\frac{\text{Average inventory}}{\text{Cost of sales}} \times 365 \text{ days}$$

Rate of inventory turnover (days) is the number of days' inventory held on average. This figure will depend on the type of goods sold by the business. For example, a market trader selling fresh flowers, who finishes each day when sold out, will have an inventory turnover of one day. By contrast, a jewellery shop – because it may hold large quantities of jewellery – will have a much slower inventory turnover, perhaps sixty or ninety days, or longer. Nevertheless, inventory turnover must not be too long, bearing in mind the type of business. A business which is improving will seek to reduce the number of days' inventory it holds, when comparing one year with the previous one, or with the inventory turnover of similar businesses. This indicates that it is more efficient at managing its inventory.

Inventory turnover can also be expressed as number of times per year:

$$\textbf{Rate of inventory turnover (times per year)} = \frac{\textbf{Cost of sales}}{\textbf{Average inventory}}$$

An inventory turnover of, say, twelve times a year means that about thirty days' inventory is held. Note that inventory turnover can only be calculated where a business buys and sells goods; it cannot be used for a business that provides a service.

Note: average inventory is normally calculated as opening inventory + closing inventory ÷ 2.

trade receivable days

$$\frac{\textbf{Trade receivables}}{\textbf{Credit sales}} \times \textbf{365 days}$$

This calculation shows how many days, on average, trade receivables take to pay for goods sold to them by the business. It should link to the credit terms offered to customers, eg net 30 days. Trade receivable days can be compared with that for the previous year, or with that of a similar business. In the UK, most trade receivables should make payment within about 30 days; however, with international trade, it will take longer for the proceeds to be received. Over time, a business will seek to reduce the trade receivable days, showing that it is more efficient at collecting the money that is due to it.

trade payable days

$$\frac{\textbf{Trade payables}}{\textbf{Credit purchases}} \times \textbf{365 days}$$

This calculation is the opposite aspect to that of trade receivables: here we are measuring the speed it takes to pay trade payables. It should link to the credit terms offered by suppliers, eg net 30 days. While trade payables can be a useful temporary source of finance, delaying payment too long may cause problems, such as stopping the delivery of supplies. This ratio is most appropriate for businesses that buy and sell goods; it cannot be used for a business that provides a service; it is also difficult to interpret when a business buys in some goods and, at the same time, provides a service, eg an hotel. Generally, though, we would expect to see the trade payable days period longer than the trade receivable days, ie money is being received from trade receivables before it is paid out to trade payables. Over time, a business should seek to maintain the same trade payable payment period, and possibly increase it slightly if better terms can be negotiated with suppliers.

CAPITAL STRUCTURE

Capital structure focuses on the long-term financing of the business – contained in the statement of financial position sections for non-current liabilities and equity.

capital gearing

$$\text{Capital gearing} = \frac{\text{Non-current liabilities}}{\text{Issued share capital} + \text{Reserves} + \text{Non-current liabilities}} \times \frac{100}{1}$$

Whilst the current and liquid capital ratios focus on whether the business can pay its way in the short-term, capital gearing is concerned with long-term financial stability. Here we measure how much of the business is financed by non-current liabilities. The higher the capital gearing percentage, the less secure will be the ordinary share capital of the business and, therefore, the future of the business. This is because non-current liabilities are costly in terms of interest payments (particularly if interest rates are variable). It is difficult to set a standard for an acceptable capital gearing: in general terms most investors (or lenders) would not wish to see a capital gearing percentage of greater than 50%.

WORKED EXAMPLE: FINANCIAL RATIOS

In the Worked Example which follows, we will look at the set of financial statements of a limited company. For clarity, one year's statements are given although, in practice, more than one year should be used. The comments given indicate what should be looked for when analysing and interpreting a set of financial statements.

situation

The following are the financial statements of Mithian Trading Company Limited. The business trades in office supplies and sells to the public through three retail shops in its area; it also delivers direct to businesses in the area from its modern warehouse on a local business park.

Using financial ratios and measures to analyse the financial statements, prepare a report for a potential investor in the company.

Mithian Trading Company Limited

INCOME STATEMENT

for the year ended 31 December 20-7

	£000s	£000s
Revenue		1,430
Opening inventory	200	
Purchases	1,000	
	1,200	
Less closing inventory	240	
Cost of sales		960
Gross profit		470
Expenses:		
Distribution expenses	(150)	
Administration expenses	(140)	
		(290)
Profit for the year from operations		180
Finance costs		(10)
Profit for the year before tax		170
Tax		(50)
Profit for the year after tax		120

Statement of changes in equity (extract)

Retained earnings	
Balance at start	180
Profit for the year	120
	300
Dividends paid	(100)
Balance at end	200

Mithian Trading Company Limited

STATEMENT OF FINANCIAL POSITION

as at 31 December 20-7

Non-Current Assets	£000s Cost	£000s Depreciation	£000s Carrying amount
Property	950	100	850
Fixtures and fittings	300	120	180
Vehicles	350	100	250
	1,600	320	1,280
Current Assets			
Inventory			240
Trade and other receivables			150
Cash and cash equivalents			135
			525
Less Current Liabilities			
Trade payables			(205)
Other payables (tax)			(50)
			(255)
Net Current Assets			270
			1,550
Less Non-Current Liabilities			
10% Debentures			(100)
NET ASSETS			1,450
EQUITY			
Issued Share Capital			
1,250,000 ordinary shares of £1 each, fully paid			1,250
Revenue Reserve			
Retained earnings			200
TOTAL EQUITY			1,450

solution

REPORT

To: Potential investor
From: Student Accountant
Date: Today
Subject: Mithian Trading Company Limited – report on financial statements

I have used financial ratios and measures to analyse the financial statements using the main themes of profitability, liquidity, efficiency and capital structure.
Please note that all money amounts shown are in £000s.

PROFITABILITY

Gross profit margin

$$\frac{£470}{£1,430} \times \frac{100}{1} = 32.87\%$$

Gross profit mark-up

$$\frac{£470}{£960} \times \frac{100}{1} = 48.96\%$$

Expenses in relation to revenue

$$\frac{£290}{£1,430} \times \frac{100}{1} = 20.28\%$$

Profit in relation to revenue

$$\frac{£170}{£1,430} \times \frac{100}{1} = 11.89\%$$

Return on capital employed

$$\frac{£180}{£1,250 + £200 + £100} \times \frac{100}{1} = 11.61\%$$

The gross profit margin and mark-up, and profit in relation to revenue seem to be acceptable figures for the type of business, although comparisons should be made with those of the previous accounting period. A business should always aim at least to hold its margin and mark-up with, ideally, a small improvement. A significant fall may indicate a poor buying policy, poor pricing (perhaps caused by competition), and the causes should be investigated.

Expenses seem to be quite a high percentage of revenue – comparisons need to be made with previous years to see if they are increasing. As they are likely to be a relatively fixed cost, it would seem that the business could increase revenue without a corresponding increase in expenses.

Return on capital employed is satisfactory, but could be better. At 11.61% it is less than two percentage points above the ten per cent cost of the debentures.

LIQUIDITY

Current ratio

$$\frac{£525}{£255} = 2.06:1$$

Liquid capital ratio

$$\frac{(£525 - £240)}{£255} = 1.12:1$$

The net current asset and liquid capital ratios are excellent: they are slightly higher than the expected 'norms' of 2:1 and 1:1 respectively (although many companies operate successfully with lower ratios).

EFFICIENCY

Rate of inventory turnover (days)

$$\frac{(£200 + £240) \div 2 \times 365}{£960} = 83.6 \text{ days}$$

Rate of inventory turnover (times per year)

$$\frac{£960}{(£200 + £240) \div 2} = 4.36 \text{ times per year}$$

Trade receivable days

$$\frac{£150 \times 365}{£1,430} = 38.3 \text{ days}$$

Trade payable days

$$\frac{£205 \times 365}{£1,000} = 74.8 \text{ days}$$

The inventory, trade receivable and trade payable ratios show up the main weakness of the company: not enough business is passing through for the size of the company. The rate of inventory turnover is very low for an office supplies business: the inventory is turning over only every 83 days – surely it should be faster than this. Trade receivable days are acceptable on the face of it – 30 days would be better – but quite a volume of the revenue will be made through the retail outlets in cash. This amount should, if known, be deducted from the revenue before calculating trade receivable days: thus the period is, in reality, longer than that calculated. Trade payable days is very slow for this type of business – long delays could cause problems with suppliers in the future.

CAPITAL STRUCTURE

Capital gearing

$$\frac{£100}{£1,250 + £200 + £100} \times \frac{100}{1} = 6.45\%$$

The capital gearing percentage is low: anything up to 50% could be seen. With a low percentage of 6.45% this indicates that the company could borrow more money if it wished to finance expansion plans. There are plenty of non-current assets for a lender – such as a bank – to take as security for a loan.

CONCLUSION

This appears to be a profitable business, although there may be some scope for cutting down somewhat on the income statement expenses. The business offers a reasonable return on capital employed, although things could be improved.

The company is liquid and has good current and liquid capital ratios. The main area of weakness is in the use of inventories, trade payables and trade receivables. It appears that the company could do much to reduce the days for inventory turnover and trade receivable days; at the same time trade payables could be paid faster.

Capital gearing is low – a good sign during times of variable interest rates – and there is scope for borrowing more money to finance expansion plans.

It does seem that there is much scope for expansion within the structure of the existing company. As the benefits of expansion flow through to the financial statements, the ratios will show an improvement from their present leisurely performance.

A potential investor must consider whether the directors of Mithian Trading Company Limited have the ability to focus on the weaknesses shown by financial ratios and take steps to improve the business.

Limitations in the Use of Financial Ratios

Although ratios and measures can usefully highlight strengths and weaknesses, it should always be considered as a part of the overall assessment of a business, rather than as a whole. We have already seen the need to place ratios in context and relate them to a reference point or standard. The limitations of financial ratios should always be borne in mind.

retrospective nature of ratios

Financial ratios are usually retrospective, based on previous performance and conditions prevailing in the past. They may not necessarily be valid for making forward projections: for example, a large customer may become insolvent, so threatening the business with an irrecoverable debt, and also reducing revenue in the future.

differences in accounting policies

When the financial statements of a business are compared, either with previous years' figures, or with figures from a similar business, there is a danger that the comparative statements are not drawn up on the same basis as those currently being worked on. Different accounting policies, in respect of depreciation and inventory valuation for instance, may well result in distortion and invalid comparisons.

inflation

Inflation may prove a problem, as most financial statements are prepared on an historic cost basis, that is, assets and liabilities are recorded at their original cost. As a result, comparison of figures from one year to the next may be difficult. In countries where inflation is running at high levels any form of comparison becomes practically meaningless.

reliance on standards

We have already mentioned guideline standards for some financial ratios, for instance 2:1 for the current ratio. There is a danger of relying too heavily on such suggested standards, and ignoring other factors in the statement of financial position. An example of this would be to criticise a business for having a low current ratio when the business sells the majority of its goods for cash and consequently has a very low trade receivables figure: this would in fact be the case with many well-known and successful retail companies.

other considerations

Economic: The general economic climate and the effect this may have on the nature of the business, eg in an economic downturn retailers are usually the first to suffer, whereas manufacturers feel the effects later.

State of the business: The director's report for a limited company should be read in conjunction with the financial statements to ascertain an overall view of the state of the business. Of great importance are the products of the company and their stage in the product life cycle, eg is a car manufacturer relying on old models, or is there an up-to-date product range which appeals to buyers?

Comparing like with like: Before making comparisons between 'similar' businesses we need to ensure that we are comparing 'like with like'. Differences, such as the acquisition of assets – renting property compared with ownership, leasing vehicles compared with ownership – will affect the profitability of the business and the structure of the statement of financial position; likewise, the long-term financing of a business – the capital gearing – will also have an effect.

CHAPTER SUMMARY

The key ratios are summarised in this chapter on pages 330 and 336.

- Financial ratios and measures use numerical values – percentages, time periods, ratios – extracted from the financial statements of businesses.
- Financial ratios can be used to measure:
  - profitability
  - liquidity
  - efficiency
  - capital structure
- Comparisons need to be made with previous financial statements, or those of similar businesses.
- There are a number of limitations to be borne in mind when drawing conclusions from financial ratios:
  - retrospective nature, based on past performance
  - differences in accounting policies
  - effects of inflation when comparing year-to-year
  - reliance on standards
  - economic and other factors

In the next section of this book we see how businesses use management accounting techniques to assist with decision-making, planning and control.

QUESTIONS

visit www.osbornebooks.co.uk to take an online test

An asterisk (*) after the question number means that the answer is given at the end of this book.

Tutorial note: unless stated otherwise, calculate ratios and percentages to two decimal places and round days to the nearest whole day.

18.1* The following information is taken from the income statements of two plcs:

	Amero plc	Britz plc
	£m	£m
Revenue	55.7	32.3
Cost of sales	(49.1)	(20.2)
GROSS PROFIT	6.6	12.1
Expenses	(5.0)	(7.4)
PROFIT FROM OPERATIONS	1.6	4.7
Note: Capital employed	£8.8m	£34.3m

You are to calculate, for each company:

- gross profit margin
- gross profit mark-up
- expenses in relation to revenue
- profit in relation to revenue
- return on capital employed

18.2* The following is taken from the statement of financial positions of two plcs:

	Cawston plc	Dunley plc
	£m	£m
Inventory	3.8	4.1
Trade receivables	4.5	0.7
Bank/(bank overdraft)	(0.4)	6.3
Trade payables	5.1	10.7
Non-current liabilities	3.2	2.1
Ordinary share capital	4.5	8.4
Reserves	1.4	4.7
Notes:		
Revenue for year	43.9	96.3
Purchases for year	32.4	85.1
Cost of sales for year	33.6	84.7

(a) **You are to** calculate, for each company:

- current ratio
- liquid capital ratio
- trade receivable days

- trade payable days
- rate of inventory turnover (days)
- capital gearing percentage

(b) One company runs department stores, the other is a chemical manufacturer. Which is which? Why is this?

18.3 The following information relates to two businesses, Exton and Frimley:

	Exton	Frimley
	£000s	£000s
INCOME STATEMENT (EXTRACTS)		
Revenue	3,057	1,628
Cost of sales	(2,647)	(911)
Gross profit	410	717
Expenses	(366)	(648)
Profit for the year	44	69

	Exton	Frimley
	£000s	£000s
SUMMARISED STATEMENTS OF FINANCIAL POSITION		
Non-Current Assets	344	555
Current Assets		
Inventory	242	237
Trade and other receivables	6	269
Cash and cash equivalents	3	1
	251	507
Current Liabilities	(195)	(212)
Net Current Assets	56	295
NET ASSETS	400	850
EQUITY		
Capital	400	850

One business operates a supermarket; the other is an engineering company. You are to calculate the following financial ratios for both businesses:

(a) gross profit margin

(b) gross profit mark-up

(c) expenses in relation to revenue

(d) profit in relation to revenue

(e) inventory turnover (use statement of financial position figure as average inventory)

(f) current ratio

(g) liquid capital ratio

(h) trade receivable days

(i) return on capital employed

Indicate which business you believe to be the supermarket and which the engineering company. Briefly explain the reasons for your choice based on the ratios calculated and the accounting information.

18.4* Ann, Bee and Cat are proposing to set up a limited company with a share capital of £150,000. They will be the only shareholders and originally planned to invest in the share capital using Ratio 1 below. However, circumstances have changed and they have to use Ratio 2.

	Ann	Bee	Cat
Ratio 1	2	2	1
Ratio 2	7	5	3

What difference will it make to Bee's investment when Ratio 2 is chosen?

A	Invests £10,000 less	
B	Invests £10,000 more	
C	Invests £12,000 less	
D	Invests £12,000 more	

18.5 The following balances have been extracted from the books of account of a business for the year ended 30 June 20-4:

	£
Closing inventory	18,000
Opening inventory	16,000
Purchases	122,000
Revenue	180,000

(a) State the formula for the mark-up percentage.

(b) Calculate the mark-up percentage.

(c) State the formula to calculate the rate of inventory turnover in days.

(d) Calculate the rate of inventory turnover.

18.6 Distinguish between the following terms:

(a) Gross profit margin and gross profit mark-up.

(b) Current ratio and liquid capital ratio.

(c) Cash and profit.

(d) Return on capital employed and capital gearing.

18.7* The following figures are extracted from the trial balance of Haque Limited as at 31 December 20-8:

	Dr	Cr
	£	£
Revenue		96,000
Purchases	56,000	
Inventory at 1 January 20-8	8,400	
Trade receivables	10,250	
Trade payables		6,000
Bank		1,865
Cash	450	

Notes:

- Inventory at 31 December 20-8 was valued at £5,200
- A customer who owes £2,450 has gone into liquidation and is not expected to be able to pay off any of the debt. No adjustment has been made for this in the above figures.

Required:

(a) Define the terms:
- net current assets
- liquid capital

(b) State the formula to be used for:
- current ratio
- liquid capital ratio
- trade receivable days
- trade payable days

(c) Calculate the following for Haque Limited:
- current ratio
- liquid capital ratio
- trade receivable days
- trade payable days

(d) Assess the effect on the liquidity and liquidity ratios of Haque Limited of
- writing off the debt for £2,450
- reducing the value of inventory over the year

18.8 Tick the boxes to indicate which of the following current assets will be included in the calculation of:

- the current ratio
- the liquid capital ratio

	Current ratio	Liquid capital ratio
Trade receivables		
Inventory		
Cash and cash equivalents		
Other receivables		

18.9 The following accounting ratios have been calculated for two different businesses for the year ended 30 June 20-7:

	Green Ltd	Hawke Ltd
Current ratio	1.1:1	1.8:1
Liquid capital ratio	0.6:1	0.9:1
Profit in relation to revenue	3%	12%
Rate of inventory turnover (times per year)	20 times	5 times
Return on capital employed	3%	6%

One business is a supermarket; the other is a furniture store.

Required:

(a) State the formula used to calculate each accounting ratio.

(b) Indicate which business you believe to be the supermarket and which the furniture store. Briefly explain the reasons for your choice based on the financial ratios.

(c) Write a note to the owner of Green Limited suggesting two ways in which the performance of the business could be improved.

18.10 A friend of yours, Samantha Smith, owns a shop selling children's clothes. You are helping Samantha to understand her financial statements which have been prepared by her accountant. She says to you: "I cannot understand why my bank overdraft has increased in a year when I have made such a good profit".

Required:

(a) Explain to Samantha the difference between profit and cash.

(b) Give two examples to explain how a business can make a good profit during a year when the bank balance reduces or the bank overdraft increases.

18.11* The following information is available for Tanveer Limited.

	Year ended 30 June 20-6		Year ended 30 June 20-7	
	£	£	£	£
Revenue		200,000		300,000
Opening inventory	20,000		30,000	
Purchases	170,000		255,000	
	190,000		285,000	
Closing inventory	(30,000)		(40,000)	
Cost of sales		160,000		245,000
Gross profit		40,000		55,000

Required:

(a) Calculate the rate of inventory turnover for each year. State the formula used.

(b) Calculate the gross profit margin for each year. State the formula used.

(c) Assess the profitability of Tanveer Limited by comparing the performance for the years ended 30 June 20-6 and 30 June 20-7.

18.12 The following information relates to Parkes Ltd as at 31 December 20-3.

	£
Ordinary shares of £1 each fully paid	300,000
Share premium	60,000
Retained earnings as at 31 December 20-3	210,000

During the next financial year the business intends to expand.

The directors are considering two proposals to raise finance:

Proposal 1 – to issue 150,000 ordinary shares of £1 each at a price of £2.50 per share

or Proposal 2 – to arrange a long-term bank loan of £300,000 and an overdraft of £75,000.

The forecast profit from operations for the year ending 31 December 20-4 is £45,000.

Required:

(a) State the formula used to calculate the Return on Capital Employed (ROCE).

(b) Calculate the Return on Capital Employed (ROCE) for **each** of the proposals.

(c) Write a report to an existing ordinary shareholder of Parkes Ltd analysing the effects of each proposal.

Management Accounting

This section of the book introduces techniques of management accounting which assist with the financial decision-making, planning and control of businesses. The following topics are covered:

- an introduction to budgeting and budgetary control
- the behaviour of costs and the use of marginal costing
- the calculation and interpretation of break-even methods
- the use of marginal costing in decision-making situations

19 BUDGETING AND BUDGETARY CONTROL

Budgeting is used by businesses as a method of financial planning for the future. Budgets are prepared for main areas of the business – purchases, sales (revenue), production, labour, trade receivables, trade payables, cash – and provide detailed plans of the business for the next three, six or twelve months.

In this chapter we shall be examining:

- the need for budgeting in business organisations
- methods of budgeting – incremental budgeting and zero-based budgeting
- the benefits of budgets and budgetary control
- the limitations of budgets and budgetary control
- the use of accounting techniques in the preparation and analysis of budgets for the income statement and the statement of financial position
- use of budgets in planning and control

The Need for Budgeting in Business Organisations

Business organisations need to plan for the future. In large businesses such planning is very formal while, for smaller businesses, it will be less formal. Planning for the future falls into three time scales:

- **long-term**: from about three years up to, sometimes, as far as twenty years ahead
- **medium-term**: one to three years ahead
- **short-term**: for the next year

Clearly, planning for these different time scales needs different approaches: the further on in time, the less detailed are the plans. In the medium and longer term, a business will establish broad **business objectives**. Such objectives do not have to be formally written down, although in a large business they are likely to be. In smaller businesses, objectives will certainly be considered and discussed by the owners or managers. Planning takes note of these broader business objectives and sets out how these are to be achieved in the form of detailed plans known as **budgets**.

In this chapter we are concerned with planning for the more immediate future, ie the next financial year.

What is a Budget?

A budget is a financial plan for a business, prepared in advance.

A budget may be set in money terms, eg a sales budget of £500,000, or it can be expressed in terms of units, eg a purchases budget of 5,000 units to be bought.

Budgets can be **income** budgets for money received, eg a sales budget, or **expenditure** budgets for money spent, eg a purchases budget.

Most budgets are prepared for the next financial year (the **budget period**), and are usually broken down into shorter time periods, commonly four-weekly or monthly. This enables **budgetary control** to be exercised over the budget: the actual results can be monitored against the budget, and variances between the two can be investigated and corrective action taken where appropriate.

Methods of Budgeting

When setting budgets there are two alternative methods that can be used, either:

- incremental budgeting, or
- zero-based budgeting

incremental budgeting

In an incremental budget the previous budget figures are used as a basis and a small percentage added on (the 'increment') to allow for general rises in costs brought about by inflation. This type of budgeting works reasonably well in situations where the area budgeted for is stable but has the major disadvantage that it does not analyse why costs and revenues occur; thus inefficiencies and overspending remain in the budget.

Incremental budgeting is carried out in the following way:

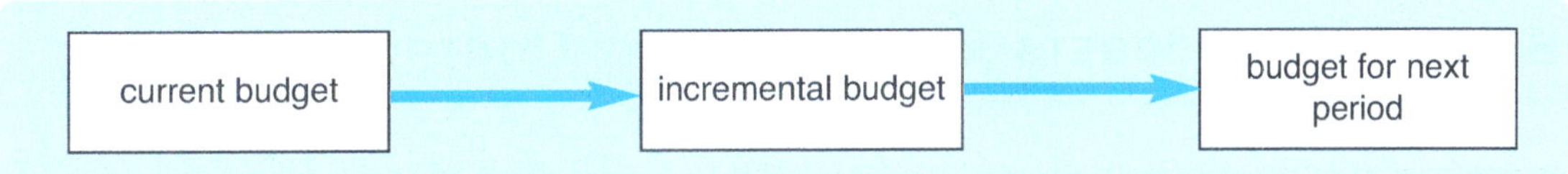

advantages of incremental budgeting

- generally quick and easy to prepare
- most suitable for stable businesses where an incremental increase can be applied to the previous period's figures, eg increase in wages and salaries

disadvantages of incremental budgeting

- inefficiencies and overspending remain in the budget
- activities may continue that are uneconomic, eg components made 'in-house' when it would be cheaper to buy in
- budget holders may often seek to spend their budgeted expenditure in order to ensure that the next period's budget is the same – or a larger – amount

zero-based budgeting

The other alternative when setting budgets is to 'start from scratch'. The budget starts from zero, and each item going into the budget has to be justified by the budget holder – normally the manager of the department. This ensures that inefficiencies and overspending can be identified and avoided. It is, however, a time-consuming procedure, and is hardly feasible every year. Some businesses therefore adopt the policy of using zero-based budgeting from time-to-time and incremental budgeting in the intervening years.

Zero-based budgeting is carried out in the following way:

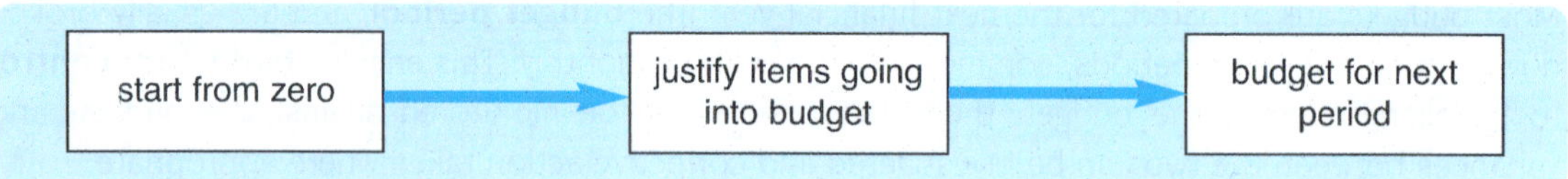

advantages of zero-based budgeting

- each item going into the budget has to be justified
- budget holders have to consider how the budget links to the objectives of the business within the business environment
- a range of staff will participate in the budgeting process which may prove to be motivating
- inefficiencies and overspending can be identified and avoided so that business resources are used more efficiently

disadvantages of zero-based budgeting

- time-consuming to prepare – may demotivate staff
- more difficult to prepare than incremental budgeting – budget holders may need to be trained
- not cost-effective to prepare each year
- focus is on the next period's budget rather than the longer term

Benefits of Budgets and Budgetary Control

Budgets provide benefits both for the business and for its managers and staff:

the budget assists planning

By formalising objectives through a budget, a business can ensure that its plans are achievable. It will be able to decide what is needed to produce the output of goods and services, and to make sure that everything will be available at the right time.

the budget communicates and co-ordinates

Because a budget is agreed by the business, all the relevant managers and staff will be working towards the same end.

When the budget is being set, any anticipated problems should be resolved and any areas of potential confusion clarified. All departments should be in a position to play their part in achieving the overall goals.

the budget helps with decision-making

By planning ahead through budgets, a business can make decisions on how much output – in the form of goods or services – can be achieved. At the same time, the cost of the output can be planned and changes can be made where appropriate.

the budget can be used to monitor and control

An important reason for producing a budget is that management is able to use budgetary control to monitor and compare the actual results (see diagram below). This is so that action can be taken to modify the operation of the business as time passes, or possibly to change the budget if it becomes unachievable.

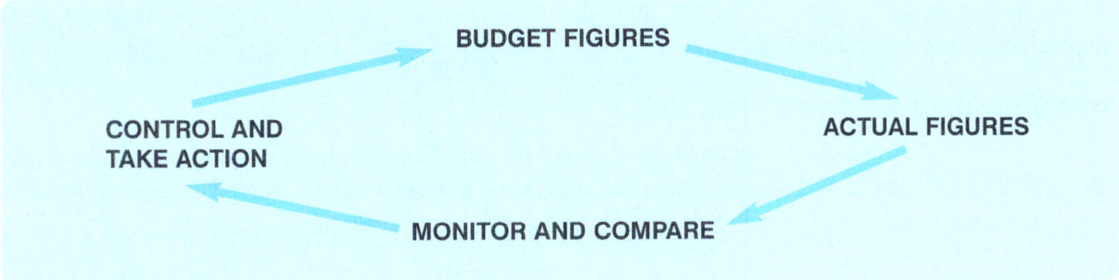

the budget can be used to motivate

A budget can be part of the techniques for motivating managers and other staff to achieve the objectives of the business. The extent to which this happens will depend on how the budget is agreed and set, and whether it is thought to be fair and achievable. The budget may also be linked to rewards (for example, bonuses) where targets are met or exceeded.

Limitations of Budgets and Budgetary Control

Whilst most businesses will benefit from the use of budgets, there are a number of limitations of budgets to be aware of:

the benefit of the budget must exceed the cost

Budgeting is a fairly complex process and some businesses – particularly small ones – may find that the task is too much of a burden in terms of time and other resources, with only limited benefits. Nevertheless, many lenders – such as banks – often require the production of budgets as part of the business plan. As a general rule, the benefit of producing the budget must exceed its cost.

budget information may not be accurate

It is essential that the information going into budgets should be as accurate as possible. Anybody can produce a budget, but the more inaccurate it is, the less use it is to the business as a planning and control mechanism. Great care needs to be taken with estimates of sales – often the starting point of the budgeting process – and costs. Budgetary control is used to compare the budget against what actually happened – the budget may need to be changed if it becomes unachievable.

the budget may demotivate

Employees who have had no part in agreeing and setting a budget which is imposed upon them, will feel that they do not own it. As a consequence, the staff may be demotivated. Another limitation is that employees may see budgets as either a 'carrot' or a 'stick', ie as a form of encouragement to achieve the targets set, or as a form of punishment if targets are missed.

budgets may lead to disfunctional management

A limitation that can occur is that employees in one department of the business may over-achieve against their budget and create problems elsewhere. For example, a production department might achieve extra output that the sales department finds difficult to sell. To avoid such disfunctional management, budgets need to be set at realistic levels and linked and co-ordinated across all departments within the business.

budgets may be set at too low a level

Where the budget is too easy to achieve it will be of no benefit to the business and may, in fact, lead to lower levels of output and higher costs than before the budget was established. Budgets should be set at realistic levels, which make the best use of the resources available.

What Budgets are Prepared?

Budgets are planned for specific sections of the business: these budgets can then be controlled by a **budget holder**, who may be the manager or supervisor of the specific section. Such budgets include:

- purchases budget – what the business needs to buy to make/supply the goods it expects to sell
- sales (revenue) budget – what the business expects to sell
- production budget – how the business will make/supply the goods it expects to sell
- labour budget – the cost of employing the people who will make/supply the goods
- cash budget – how much money will be flowing in and out of the bank account

The end result of the budgeting process is often the production of a **master budget**, which takes the form of budgeted financial statements – budgeted income statement – and budgeted statement of financial position. The master budget is the 'master plan' which links together all the other budgets. The Worked Examples that follow show how the accounting techniques studied so far are used in the preparation and analysis of budgets for the income statement and the statement of financial position.

Note that, in this chapter, we focus our attention on the budgeted financial statements – the further budgets are studied in our other book, Accounting for AQA A-level Part 2.

WORKED EXAMPLE: BUDGETING THE INCOME STATEMENT

situation

Jayne Slater is in business selling a single product online to credit customers. Her actual income statement for the year ended 30 June 20-7 was:

	£	£
Revenue (12,000 units)		180,000
Opening inventory (2,000 units)	12,000	
Purchases (13,000 units)	91,000	
Closing inventory (3,000 units)	(21,000)	
Cost of sales		82,000
Gross profit		98,000
Less expenses:		
Wages	6,000	
General expenses	5,500	
Rent	5,000	
Carriage out (£1.00 per unit)	12,000	
Depreciation	4,000	
		32,500
Profit for the year		65,500

Jayne is in the process of preparing her budgeted income statement for the year ended 30 June 20-8 and has identified the following changes compared to the actual results, above, for the year ended 30 June 20-7:

1. The unit selling price to customers will be increased by 8%. This is expected to decrease the number of sales units by 4%.
2. The unit purchase price will increase by 50p.
3. The number of units of closing inventory will be reduced by 10%.
4. Wages are expected to increase by 2.0%.
5. General expenses, because of efficiency measures, are expected to fall by 10%.
6. Rent for the year will increase to £6,000.
7. Carriage out will increase by 10% per unit
8. Depreciation will be £3,600 for the year

Prepare the budgeted income statement for Jayne Slater for the year ended 30 June 20-8, taking into account the changes identified.

solution

The budgeted income statement, together with workings, is shown below:

JAYNE SLATER
BUDGETED INCOME STATEMENT FOR THE YEAR ENDED 30 JUNE 20-8

	£	£
Revenue (11,520 units at £16.20)		186,624
Opening inventory (3,000 units at £7.00)	21,000	
Purchases (11,220 units at £7.50)	84,150	
Closing inventory (2,700 units at £7.50)	(20,250)	
Cost of sales		84,900
Gross profit		101,724
Less expenses:		
Wages (£6,000 x 1.02)	6,120	
General expenses (£5,500 x 0.9)	4,950	
Rent (as stated)	6,000	
Carriage out (£1.10 per unit sold)	12,672	
Depreciation (as stated)	3,600	
		33,342
Profit for the year		68,382

Analysis of Jayne's budgeted income statement:

- Revenue is budgeted to increase by £6,624, the fall in the number of units sold being more than balanced out by the increase in selling prices.
- Cost of sales is budgeted to increase by £2,900, with an increase in the unit purchase price and a reduction in closing inventory.
- Gross profit is budgeted to increase by £3,724.
- The expenses total is budgeted to increase by £842, with increases in wages, rent and carriage out, and decreases in general expenses and depreciation.
- Profit for the year is budgeted to increase by £2,882.

Note that financial ratios and measures could also be calculated.

WORKED EXAMPLE: BUDGETING THE STATEMENT OF FINANCIAL POSITION

situation

Jayne Slater's actual statement of financial position as at 30 June 20-7 was:

	£	£
Non-current Assets		40,000
Less depreciation for the year		4,000
Net book value		36,000
Current Assets		
Inventory	21,000	
Trade receivables	15,000	
Bank	8,250	
	44,250	
Less Current Liabilities		
Trade payables	22,750	
Net Current Assets		21,500
NET ASSETS		57,500
FINANCED BY		
Capital		
Opening capital		56,500
+ Profit for the year		65,500
– Drawings		64,500
		57,500

Jayne asks for your assistance in preparing her budgeted statement of financial position as at 30 June 20-8 and has identified the following changes compared to the actual results, above, as at 30 June 20-7. You will also need to make use of her budgeted income statement, just prepared, for certain information.

1. Trade receivables take, on average, one month to pay.
2. Jayne pays trade payables, on average, after two months.
3. During the year, Jayne plans to take drawings of £60,000 from the business bank account.

Note that all Jayne's purchases and sales are made on credit.

Prepare the budgeted statement of financial position for Jayne Slater as at 30 June 20-8 taking into account the changes identified.

solution

The budgeted statement of financial position, together with workings, is shown below.

JAYNE SLATER
BUDGETED STATEMENT OF FINANCIAL POSITION AS AT 30 JUNE 20-8

	£	£
Non-current Assets		36,000
Less depreciation for the year (income statement)		3,600
Net book value		32,400
Current Assets		
Inventory (income statement)	20,250	
Trade receivables (£186,624 ÷ 12)	15,552	
Bank (see page 363)	11,705	
	47,507	
Less Current Liabilities		
Trade payables (£84,150 ÷ 6)	14,025	
Net Current Assets		33,482
NET ASSETS		65,882
FINANCED BY		
Capital		
Opening capital		57,500
Add Profit for the year (income statement)		68,382
Less Drawings		60,000
		65,882

To calculate the closing bank balance at 30 June 20-8, use the following layout:

	£	£
Opening bank balance (from actual sfp)		8,250
Add receipts from trade receivables:		
opening trade receivables	15,000	
+ revenue (from income statement)	186,624	
- closing trade receivables	15,552	
		186,072
Less payments to trade payables:		
opening trade payables	22,750	
+ purchases (from income statement)	84,150	
– closing trade payables	14,025	
		(92,875)
Less expenses (from income statement):		
wages	6,120	
general expenses	4,950	
rent	6,000	
carriage out	12,672	
		(29,742)
Note that depreciation is excluded because it is a non-cash expense		
Less drawings taken by Jayne Slater		(60,000)
Closing bank balance (to budgeted sfp)		11,705

Analysis of Jayne's budgeted statement of financial position:

- Non-current assets are budgeted at a net book value of £32,400 – Jayne appears to be using reducing balance depreciation.
- Current assets are budgeted to increase by £3,257 – in particular the reduction in inventory of £750 and the increase in the bank balance of £3,455 are to the benefit of the business, but are slightly offset by the increase in trade receivables of £552.
- Trade payables are budgeted to decrease by £8,725 – a considerable reduction on the actual figure, and which could put a strain on the bank balance.
- Jayne's budgeted payment terms for trade receivables of one month and trade payables of two months works well in her favour, provided she can achieve such terms.
- Jayne's stake in the business is budgeted to increase by £8,382.

Note that financial ratios and measures could also be calculated.

THE USE OF BUDGETS IN PLANNING AND CONTROL

As we have seen earlier, budgets are used as a method of financial planning for a business. Once the planning process has been completed and the budget is approved by the owner of the business or its senior managers, then it becomes the official plan of the business. During the period of the budget the process of budgetary control uses the budget as a control mechanism – as illustrated by the diagram on page 357.

An important aspect with which budgetary planning and control is concerned is in comparing actual results for costs, revenues and profit with what was planned to happen in the budget. This comparison leads to the calculation of **variances**.

A variance is the budgeted cost, revenue or profit minus the actual cost, revenue or profit:

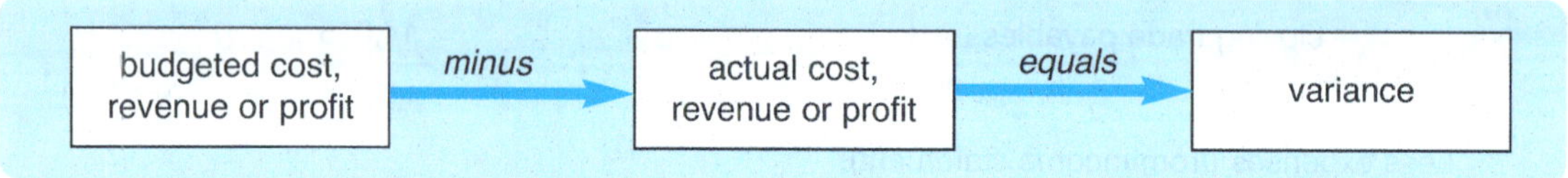

Variances can be either **favourable** or **adverse**:

- **favourable variances**
  - a favourable cost variance is where actual costs are lower than budgeted costs
  - a favourable revenue variance is where actual revenues are higher than budgeted revenues
  - a favourable profit variance is where actual profit is higher than budgeted profit
- **adverse variances**
  - an adverse cost variance is where actual costs are higher than budgeted costs
  - an adverse revenue variance is where actual revenues are lower than budgeted revenues
  - an adverse profit variance is where actual profit is lower than budgeted profit

Examples of variances:

- budgeted cost of £5,000; actual cost £4,500 = £500 favourable cost variance
- actual revenue £74,000; budgeted revenue £75,000 = £1,000 adverse revenue variance
- budgeted profit £24,000; actual profit £26,000 = £2,000 favourable profit variance

Variances are reported to the appropriate manager or managers in the business. For example:

- a labour cost variance will be reported to the human resources manager and the production manager
- a materials cost variance will be reported to the purchasing manager and the production manager
- a sales revenue variance will be reported to the sales manager

management by exception

The control systems of a business will set down procedures for acting on variances, but only for significant variances. This type of system is known as **management by exception**, ie acting on variances that are exceptional. Managers will normally work to **tolerance limits** – a tolerance limit is an acceptable percentage variance on the budgeted amount. If a cost or revenue exceeds the tolerance limit, the variance will be significant and investigative action will need to be taken.

For example, the budgeted labour cost for a production department is £50,000 a month, with a tolerance limit of 5 per cent set. If labour costs in any one month exceed £50,000 x 5%, ie a variance of £2,500, action will have to be taken and the cause investigated.

Variances against budgeted cost, revenue or profit need to be reported to the appropriate level of management within the business. For example, a one per cent increase in the cost of materials will be referred to the purchasing manager; by contrast, a fall in sales of 50 per cent will be referred to the owner or to the senior management of the business.

CHAPTER SUMMARY

- A budget is a financial plan for a business, prepared in advance.
- Budgets are used to plan and control the business.
- Incremental budgeting and zero-based budgeting are alternative methods used to set budgets.
- Budgets – for income or expenditure – are prepared for each section of the business – purchases, sales (revenues), production, labour, cash, income statement, statement of financial position.
- Budgetary planning is the process of setting the budget for the next period, using either incremental budgeting or zero-based budgeting.
- Budgetary control uses the budgets to monitor actual results with budgeted figures.
- Responsibility for budgets is given to managers and supervisors – the budget holders.
- The calculation of variances is an important aspect of budgeting and control.
- A variance is the budgeted cost, revenue or profit minus the actual cost, revenue or profit.
- Variances are reported to the appropriate manager or managers.
- Significant variances are reported to the appropriate level of management for investigative action to be taken.

The next chapter looks at the costing technique of marginal costing, which categorises costs by how they behave.

QUESTIONS

visit
www.osbornebooks.co.uk
to take an online test

An asterisk (*) after the question number means that the answer is given at the end of this book.

19.1* Which of the following statements apply better to either incremental budgeting or zero-based budgeting?

statements	incremental budgeting	zero-based budgeting
The previous budget figures are used as a basis for the next budget period		
Each item going into the budget has to be justified by the budget holder		
Inefficiencies and overspending may remain in the budget		
May not be cost-effective to prepare each year		

19.2 Classic Furniture is a manufacturer of reproduction 'antique' furniture. It is owned by Helen Sutton as a sole trader business. There are four employees and annual sales revenue is approximately £500,000 per year.

Required:

(a) Explain two benefits of budgetary control to Helen Sutton.

(b) Suggest three budgets which Helen could use in the business to provide an adequate system of budgetary control.

(c) Advise Helen of the relevant factors to consider when implementing budgetary control.

19.3* For each of the following statements calculate the amount of the variance and indicate whether it is favourable or adverse.

statements	variance	favourable variance	adverse variance
Actual costs £2,000; budgeted costs £2,500			
Actual revenue £25,000; budgeted revenue £22,500			
Actual profit £12,000; budgeted profit £14,000			
Budgeted costs £10,000; actual costs £11,000			

19.4 The income statement for the year ended 31 December 20-5 of Fraser and Co, which sells a single product online, was:

	£	£
Revenue (250,000 units)		4,000,000
Opening inventory (16,000 units)	120,000	
Add Purchases (254,000 units)	2,540,000	
Less Closing inventory (20,000 units)	200,000	
Cost of sales		2,460,000
Gross profit		1,540,000
Less Expenses:		
Wages	250,000	
General expenses	290,000	
Rent	75,000	
Depreciation	90,000	
Carriage outwards (£1.50 per unit)	375,000	
		1,080,000
Profit for the year		460,000

Additional information for the year ending 31 December 20-6:

1. The unit selling price will decrease by 10%. This is expected to increase the number of sales units by 20%.
2. The supplier of the product will give a discount of 4% on last year's price.
3. The ratio of units of closing inventory to sales units will be the same in both years. Closing inventory is to be valued at the cost price for the year.
4. Wages are expected to increase by 2.0%.
5. General expenses, because of efficiency measures, are expected to fall by 1.5%.
6. Rent is fixed for the year at £75,000.
7. 20 per cent reducing balance depreciation for the year is to be calculated on the second year of ownership of non-current assets with a cost price of £450,000.
8. Carriage outwards will, because of inflation, increase to £1.75 per unit sold.

Required:

(a) Prepare the budgeted income statement for Fraser and Co for the year ending 31 December 20-6, taking into account the changes identified.

Fraser and Co

Budgeted Income Statement for the year ending 31 December 20-6

	£	£

Workings:

(b) Explain **two** benefits to Fraser and Co of preparing a budgeted income statement.

19.5* The statement of financial position of Jan Leung as at 31 December 20-2 was:

	£	£
Non-current Assets		250,000
Less depreciation for the year		50,000
Net book value		200,000
Current Assets		
Inventory	14,000	
Trade receivables	45,000	
Bank	9,000	
	68,000	
Less Current Liabilities		
Trade payables	14,000	
Net Current Assets		54,000
NET ASSETS		254,000
FINANCED BY		
Capital		
Opening capital		251,500
Add Profit for the year		27,500
Less Drawings		25,000
		254,000

Jan Leung asks for your assistance in preparing her budgeted statement of financial position as at 31 December 20-3. She has identified the following changes compared to the actual results, above, as at 31 December 20-2:

1. Currently, trade receivables take, on average, two months to pay. Jan intends to reduce this to one-and-a-half months.
2. Currently, Jan pays trade payables, on average, after one month. She has now negotiated to pay after two months.
3. During the year, Jan plans to take drawings of £30,000 from the business bank account.

You note the following from Jan's budgeted income statement for 20-3:

- all sales and purchases are made on credit
- revenue £336,000
- purchases £180,000
- closing inventory is one month's purchases
- expenses £122,500 (this includes the amount for depreciation, being the second year reducing balance on all of the non-current assets)

(a) Prepare the budgeted statement of financial position of Jan Leung as at 31 December 20-3, taking into account the changes identified.

Jan Leung
Budgeted Statement of Financial Position as at 31 December 20-3

	£	£

Workings:

(b) Show your calculation of the budgeted closing bank balance as at 31 December 20-3.

20 MARGINAL COSTING AND BREAK-EVEN

Marginal costing is an accounting technique used by businesses to help in decision-making situations. It is particularly used by manufacturing businesses to distinguish between those costs that are fixed (ie do not increase as output increases) and those costs that are variable (ie do vary as output increases).

In this chapter we cover:

- the terms 'direct costs' and 'indirect costs'
- the nature of costs – fixed, stepped, semi-variable and variable
- marginal cost
- contribution and break-even

Direct and Indirect Costs

Businesses incur many different kinds of cost in the production of goods or the provision of services – the 'output' of the business. Some costs can be identified directly with each unit of output. For example:

- direct materials, eg the cost of components used in making cars
- direct labour, eg the wages of workers on a production line in a factory

These are termed **direct costs**. Costs which cannot be identified directly with each unit of output are **indirect costs** or overheads. We can therefore define these two types of cost as follows:

direct costs can be identified directly with units of output

indirect costs (overheads) are all costs other than those identified as 'direct costs'; they cannot be identified directly with units of output

There are many examples of overheads, including:

- telephone charges
- insurance premiums
- cost of wages of non-production staff, such as managers, secretaries, accountants and so on
- running costs of delivery vehicles
- depreciation charge for non-current assets

FIXED, STEPPED, SEMI-VARIABLE AND VARIABLE COSTS

It is important to appreciate the **behaviour** of costs – in particular to understand that not all costs increase or decrease directly in line with increases or decreases in output. Costs are:

- fixed, or
- stepped, or
- semi-variable, or
- variable

The diagram below shows the differences between these.

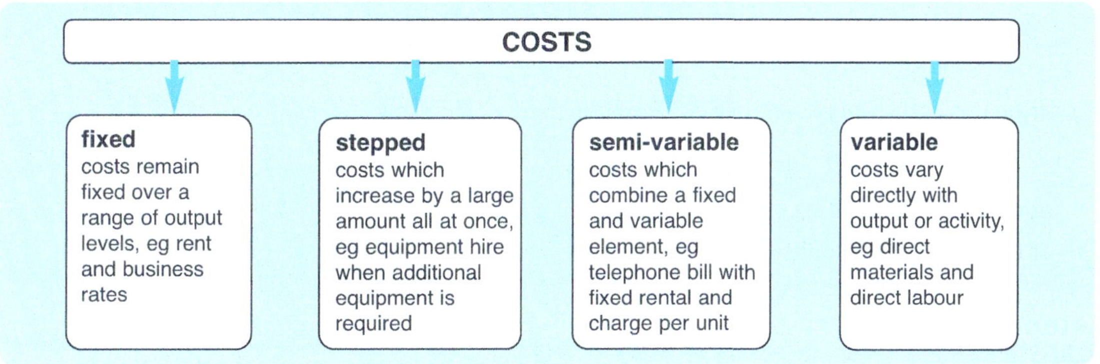

It is important to know how costs are affected by changes in the level of output. For example, a business decides to increase its output by 25% – will all costs increase by 25%? Fixed costs, such as rent and business rates, are likely to remain unchanged, provided that there is capacity for the increased output within the existing building. Variable costs, such as direct materials and direct labour, are likely to increase by 25% as they generally vary directly with output (unless any economies of scale can be achieved). Semi-variable costs, such as the telephone bill, will increase as the extra business generates more phone calls and internet usage; however, the increase should certainly be much less than 25%.

fixed costs

These are costs that do not normally change when the level of output changes. For example, the cost of insuring a car factory against business risks will not vary in line with the number of cars produced – it is a fixed cost and varies with time rather than activity.

Note that total cost is shown on the vertical axis and output or activity on the horizontal axis.

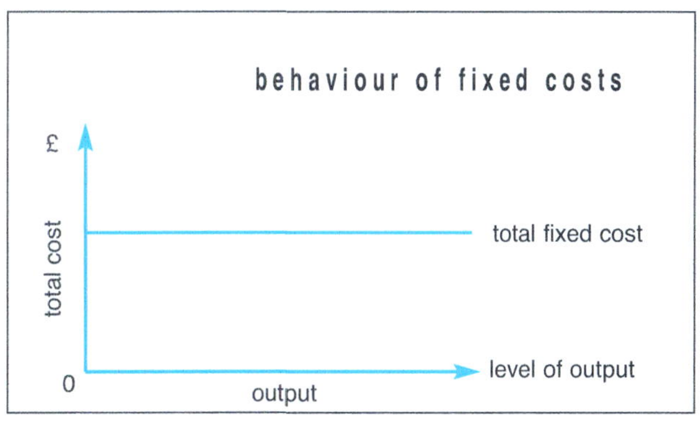

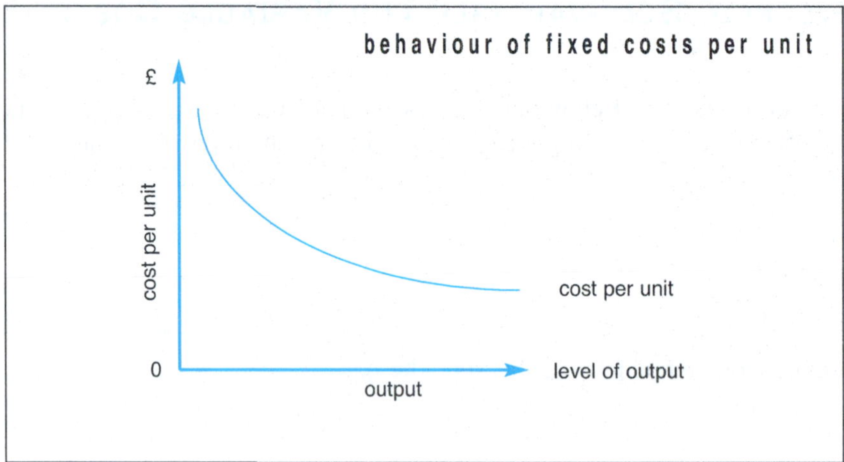

For fixed costs, the *cost per unit* falls as output increases, as follows:

For example, with rent of £40,000 per year:

- at output of 4,000 units, equals £10 per unit
- at output of 10,000 units, equals £4 per unit

stepped costs

Fixed costs do not remain fixed at all levels of production. For example, a decision to double production is likely to increase the fixed costs – an increase in factory rent, for example, because an additional factory may need to be rented. Fixed costs are often described as *stepped fixed costs*, because they increase by a large amount all at once; graphically, the cost behaviour is shown as a step:

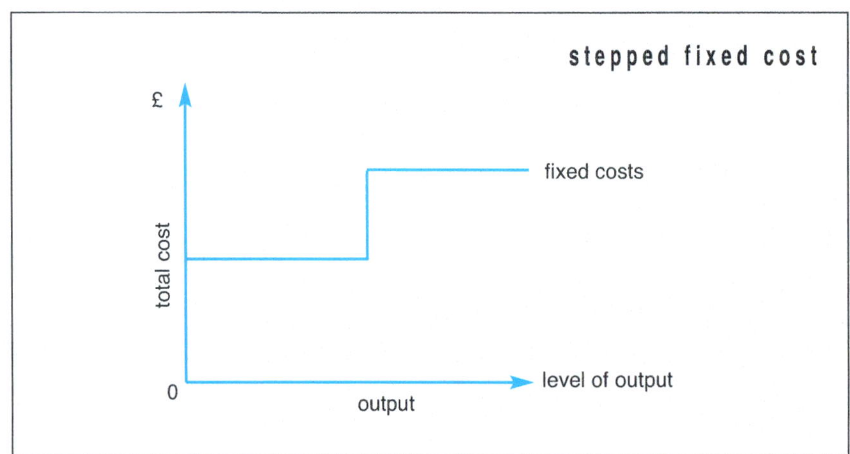

semi-variable costs

These are costs where a part of the cost acts as a variable cost, and a part acts as a fixed cost. For example, some fuel bills are semi-variable: there is a fixed 'standing charge' and a variable 'unit charge'.

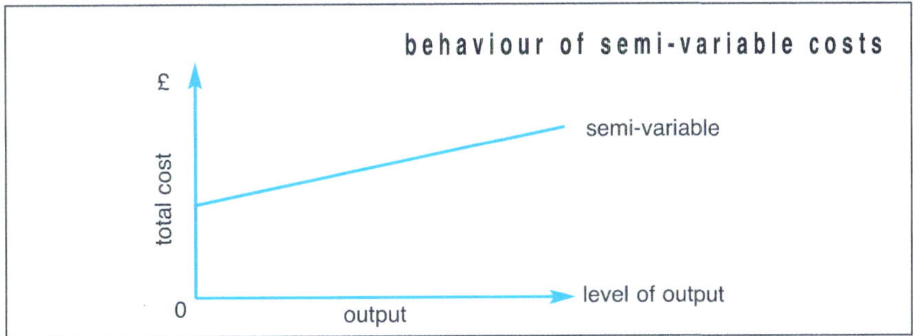

Note that the fixed element of semi-variable costs can increase as a stepped cost.

variable costs

These are the costs where the total cost varies in proportion with output or activity. For example, if a car manufacturer makes more cars it will use more metal – a variable cost. Note however that the cost per unit remains constant at all levels of output (unless any economies of scale can be achieved).

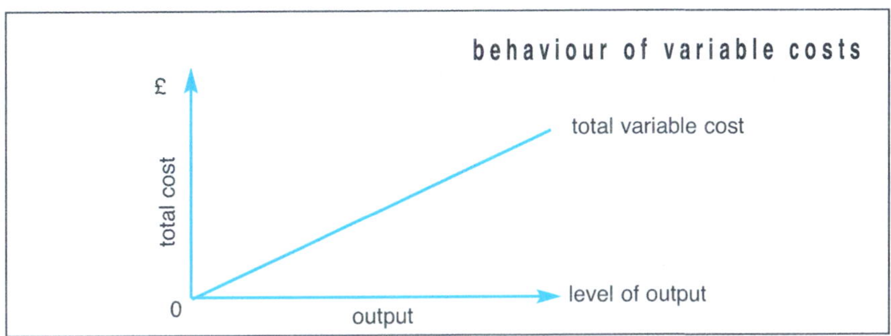

MARGINAL COST AND CONTRIBUTION

To help with decision-making, costs are classified as either variable costs or fixed costs (semi-variable costs are divided into their fixed and variable components). For example, a car manufacturer will need to identify:

- the variable costs of each car
- the total fixed costs of running the business over a period of time

The classification of costs as fixed or variable is used in **marginal costing** to work out how much it costs to produce each extra unit of output.

marginal cost is the cost of producing one extra unit of output

The marginal cost for a car manufacturer is therefore the cost of producing one extra car.

Marginal cost is often – but not always – the total of the variable costs of producing a unit of output. For most purposes, marginal costing is not concerned with fixed costs (such as the rent of a factory); instead it is concerned with variable costs – direct materials, direct labour, direct expenses, and variable production overheads – which increase as output increases. For most decision-making, the marginal cost of a unit of output is, therefore, the variable cost of producing one more unit.

Knowing the marginal cost of a unit of output enables the managers of a business to focus on the **contribution** provided by each unit. The contribution is the amount of money coming in from sales after marginal/variable costs have been paid. The formula for calculating contribution is:

sales revenue minus variable costs = contribution

Contribution can be calculated on a per unit basis, or for a batch of output (eg 1,000 units), or the total for the whole business.

It follows that the difference between the sales revenue and the variable costs of the units sold in a period is the **total contribution** that the sales of all the units in the period make towards the fixed costs of the business. Once these are covered, the remainder of the contribution is profit.

Thus a business can work out its profit, using a marginal costing statement, for any given period from the total contribution and fixed costs figures:

total contribution minus total fixed costs = profit

A marginal costing statement can be prepared in the following format:

	sales revenue
minus	variable costs
equals	contribution
minus	fixed costs
equals	profit

Note from the marginal costing statement how the contribution goes firstly towards the fixed costs and, when they have been covered, secondly contributes to profit.

The relationship between marginal costing, contribution and profit is shown in the Worked Example which follows.

WORKED EXAMPLE: MARGINAL COSTING

situation

The Wyvern Bike Company makes 100 bikes each week and its costs are as follows:

Direct materials	£3,000
Direct labour	£2,500
Indirect costs	£3,500

Investigations into the behaviour of costs has revealed the following information:

- direct materials are variable costs
- direct labour is a variable cost
- of the indirect costs, £1,500 is a fixed cost, and the remainder is a variable cost

The selling price of each bike is £120.

You are to:

- calculate the marginal cost of producing each bike
- show the expected contribution per bike
- prepare a marginal costing statement to show clearly the total contribution and the total profit each week

solution

Marginal cost per bike

Variable costs per unit:	£
direct materials (£3,000 ÷ 100)	30
direct labour (£2,500 ÷ 100)	25
indirect costs (£2,000* ÷ 100)	20
marginal cost per bike	75

* £3,500 – £1,500 fixed costs

Contribution per bike

	selling price per bike	120
minus	variable cost per bike	75
equals	contribution per bike	45

Marginal costing statement

		£	£
	sales £120 x 100 bikes		12,000
minus	variable costs:		
	direct materials	3,000	
	direct labour	2,500	
	indirect costs	2,000	
			7,500
equals	total contribution		4,500
minus	fixed costs (indirect costs)		1,500
equals	profit for the week		3,000

BREAK-EVEN

Break-even is the point at which neither a profit nor a loss is made.

Break-even is the output level (units manufactured or services provided) at which the revenue from sales is just enough to cover all the costs. Break-even is the point at which the profit (or loss) is zero. The output level can be measured in a way that is appropriate for the particular business; it is commonly measured in units of output.

The formula for break-even in units of output is:

$$\frac{\text{fixed costs (£)}}{\text{*contribution per unit (£)}} = \text{break-even point (in units of output)}$$

* selling price – variable costs

In order to calculate break-even, we need to know:

- selling price (per unit)
- costs of the product
  - variable costs (such as materials, labour) per unit
  - overhead costs, and whether these are fixed or variable
- limitations, such as maximum production capacity, maximum sales

The Worked Example of Fluffy Toys Limited which follows shows how the break-even point can be determined.

WORKED EXAMPLE: BREAK-EVEN

situation

Fluffy Toys Limited manufactures soft toys, and is able to sell all that can be produced. The variable costs (materials and direct labour) for producing each toy are £10 and the selling price is £20 each. The fixed costs of running the business are £5,000 per month.

- How many toys need to be produced and sold each month for the business to cover its costs, ie to break-even?
- What is the break-even revenue amount?

solution

This problem can be solved by calculation or by means of a graph. Which method is used depends on the purpose for which the information is required:

- the **calculation method** is quick to use and is convenient for seeing the effect of different cost structures on break-even point
- the **graph method** is used for making presentations – for example, to the directors of a company – because it shows in a visual form the relationship between costs and sales revenue, and the amount of profit or loss at different levels of production

Often the calculation or table methods are used before drawing a graph. By doing this, the break-even point is known and suitable scales can be selected for the axes of the graph in order to give a good visual presentation.

calculation method

The contribution per unit is:

	sales revenue	£20
minus	variable costs	£10
equals	contribution	£10

Each toy sold gives a contribution (selling price, less variable costs) of £10. This contributes towards the fixed costs and, in order to break-even, the business must have sufficient £10 'lots' to meet the fixed costs. Thus, with fixed costs of £5,000 per month, the break-even calculation is:

$$\frac{\text{fixed costs (£)}}{\text{contribution per unit (£)}} = \frac{\text{£5,000}}{\text{£10}} = \text{500 toys each month}$$

- The break-even point (in units of output) is 500 toys each month.
- The break-even revenue amount is:
  break-even output x selling price per unit = 500 toys x £20 = £10,000

graph method

To help with the graph method we will first calculate the costs and revenues at a range of outputs to demonstrate their behaviour.

units of output	fixed costs A	variable costs B	total cost C	revenue D	profit/(loss)
			A + B		D – C
	£	£	£	£	£
100	5,000	1,000	6,000	2,000	(4,000)
200	5,000	2,000	7,000	4,000	(3,000)
300	5,000	3,000	8,000	6,000	(2 000)
400	5,000	4,000	9,000	8,000	(1,000)
500	5,000	5,000	10,000	10,000	nil
600	5,000	6,000	11,000	12,000	1,000
700	5,000	7,000	12,000	14,000	2,000

The graphical presentation uses the money amounts of fixed costs, variable costs, and revenue from the calculations above.

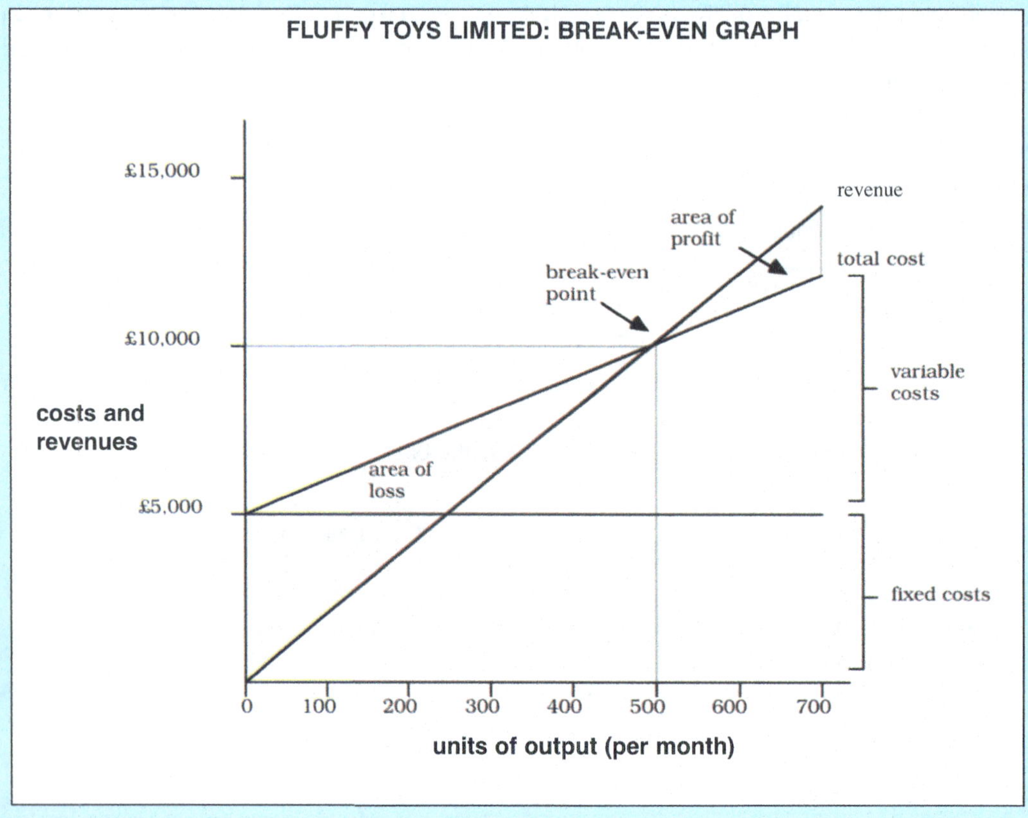

notes to the graph

- It is usual for the vertical axis to show money amounts, while the horizontal axis shows units of output/sales – the reason for this is that the amount of money depends on the volume of activity, ie output/sales.
- The fixed costs are unchanged at all levels of output, in this case they are £5,000.
- The variable costs commence, on the vertical axis, *from the fixed costs amount,* not from 'zero'. This is because the cost of producing zero units is the fixed costs.
- The fixed costs *and* the variable costs added together form the *total costs line.*
- The point at which the total cost and revenue lines cross is the break-even point.
- From the graph we can read off the break-even point both in terms of units of output, 500 units on the horizontal axis, and in revenue and total costs, £10,000 on the vertical axis.
- The 'proof' of the break-even chart is to use a marginal costing statement:

		£
	revenue (500 units at £20 each)	10,000
minus	variable costs (500 units at £10 each)	5,000
equals	contribution	5,000
minus	monthly fixed costs	5,000
equals	profit/loss	nil

Interpretation of Break-even

When interpreting break-even, it is all too easy to concentrate solely on the break-even point. The graph, for example, tells us much more than this: it also shows the profit or loss at any level of output/sales contained within the graph. To find this, simply measure the gap between sales revenue and total costs at a chosen number of units, and read the money amounts off on the vertical axis (above break-even point it is a profit; below, it is a loss). For example, the graph in the Worked Example shows a profit or loss at:

- 650 units = £1,500 profit
- 600 units = £1,000 profit
- 400 units = £1,000 loss

Break-even analysis, whether by calculation or by graph, can be used by all types of businesses, as well as other organisations. For example, a shop will wish to know the sales it has to make each week to meet costs; a sports centre will wish to know the ticket sales that have to be made to meet costs; a club or society might wish to know how many raffle tickets it needs to sell to meet the costs of prizes and of printing tickets.

Once the break-even point has been reached, the additional contribution forms the profit. For example, if the business considered in the Worked Example was selling 650 toys each month, it would have a total contribution of 650 x £10 = £6,500; of this the first £5,000 will be used to meet fixed costs, and the remaining £1,500 represents the profit (which can be read off the break-even graph). This can be shown in a marginal costing statement as follows:

		£
	revenue (650 units at £20 each)	13,000
minus	variable costs (650 units at £10 each)	6,500
equals	contribution (to fixed costs and profit)	6,500
minus	monthly fixed costs	5,000
equals	profit for month	1,500

A quick way of calculating the profit or loss is to use the following formula:

(selling price – variable costs) per unit x volume* – fixed costs = profit or loss

* the level of output or activity

ie (£20 – £10) x 650 – £5,000 = £6,500 – £5,000 = £1,500 profit

Uses of Break-even Analysis

Break-even analysis is used by businesses in a variety of situations:

before starting a new business

The calculation of break-even point is important in order to see the level of sales needed by the new business in order to cover costs, or to make a particular level of profit. The feasibility of achieving the level can then be considered by the owner of the business, and other parties such as the bank manager.

when making changes within a business

The costs of a major change will need to be considered by the owners and/or managers. For example, a large increase in production will, most likely, affect the balance between fixed and variable costs. Break-even analysis will be used as part of the planning process to ensure that the business remains profitable.

to measure profits and losses

Within the limitations of break-even analysis, profits and losses can be estimated at different levels of output from current production. Note that this can be done only where the new output is close to current levels and where there is no major change to the structure of costs.

to answer 'what if?' questions

Questions such as 'what if sales fall by 10 per cent?' and 'what if fixed costs increase by £1,000?' can be answered – in part at least – by break-even analysis. The effect on the profitability of the business can be seen, subject to the limitations noted earlier. A question such as 'what if sales increase by 300 per cent?' is such a fundamental change that it can only be answered by examining the effect on the nature of the fixed and variable costs and then re-calculating break-even.

to evaluate alternative viewpoints

There are often different ways of production; this is particularly true of a manufacturing business. For example, a product could be made:

- either by using a labour-intensive process, with a large number of employees supported by basic machinery, or
- by using expensive machinery in an automated process with very few employees.

In the first case, the cost structure will be high variable costs (labour) and low fixed costs (depreciation of machinery). In the second case, there will be low variable costs and high fixed costs. Break-even analysis can be used to examine the relationship between the costs which are likely to show a low break-even point in the first case, and a high break-even point in the second. In this way, the management of the business is guided by break-even analysis; management will also need to know the likely sales figures, and the availability of money with which to buy the machinery.

LIMITATIONS OF BREAK-EVEN ANALYSIS

The problem of break-even analysis is the assumption that the relationship between sales revenue, variable costs and fixed costs remains the same at all levels of production. This is a rather simplistic view because, for example, in order to increase sales, a business will often need to offer bulk discounts, so reducing the sales revenue per unit at higher levels. The limitations of break-even analysis can be summarised as follows:

- the assumption is made that all output is sold. There is no point in preparing the cost data, calculating the break-even point, and estimating the profits to be made if the product will not sell in sufficient quantities
- the presumption is made that there is only one product. While separate break-even analysis can be made for different products, it is difficult to make the calculations for a mix of products
- all costs and revenues are expressed in terms of straight lines. However, this relationship is not always so. As indicated above, selling prices may vary at different quantities sold; in a similar way,

variable costs alter at different levels as advantage is taken of the lower prices to be gained from bulk buying, and/or more efficient production methods

- fixed costs do not remain fixed at all levels of output; instead, there may be stepped costs
- it is not possible to extrapolate the graph or calculation; 'extrapolation' means extending the lines on the graph beyond the limits of the activity on which the graph is based. For example, in the Worked Example, the graph cannot be extended to, say, 1,000 units of output and the profit read off at this point. The relationship between sales revenues and costs will be different at much higher levels of output – different methods of production might be used, for example
- the profit or loss shown by the graph or calculations is probably only true for figures close to current output levels – the more that output changes from current figures, the less accurate will be the expected profit or loss
- external factors – such as the state of the economy, interest rates, the rate of inflation, etc – are not considered by break-even analysis
- a further disadvantage of break-even analysis is that it concentrates too much attention on the break-even point. While this aspect is important, other considerations such as ensuring that the output is produced as efficiently as possible, and that costs are kept under review, are just as important

CHAPTER SUMMARY

- Direct costs can be identified directly with each unit of output.
- Indirect costs (overheads) cannot be identified directly with specific units of output.
- By behaviour, costs are fixed, or stepped, or semi-variable, or variable when compared to output.
- A fixed cost remains fixed over a range of output levels and varies with time rather than activity.
- A stepped fixed cost increases by a large amount all at once.
- A variable cost varies directly with output.
- A semi-variable cost combines a fixed and variable element.
- The marginal cost is the cost of producing one extra unit of output.
- Knowing the marginal cost of a unit of output enables the managers of a business to focus on the contribution of each unit.
- Contribution = sales revenue minus variable costs.

- A business can work out its profit, using a marginal costing statement, for any given period from the total contribution and fixed cost figures:

  total contribution minus total fixed costs = profit or loss

- Break-even is the point at which neither a profit nor a loss is made.

- The relationship between sales revenue, and fixed costs and variable costs is used to ascertain the break-even point, by means of a calculation or a graph.

- The break-even calculation is:

$$\frac{\textit{fixed costs (£)}}{\textit{contribution per unit (£)}} = \textit{break-even point (number of units)}$$

- Break-even analysis can show:
  - break-even point in units of output
  - break-even point in value of sales
  - profit or loss at a given level of output/sales

- Break-even analysis is often used:
  - before starting a new business
  - when making changes to a business
  - to measure profits or losses
  - to answer 'what if?' questions
  - to evaluate alternative viewpoints

- The limitations of break-even analysis are that:
  - the assumption is made that all output is sold
  - the presumption is that there is only one product
  - costs and revenues are expressed in straight lines
  - fixed costs do not remain fixed at all levels of output
  - it is not possible to extrapolate the break-even graph or calculation
  - the profit or loss is probably only true for figures close to current output levels
  - external factors are not considered
  - it concentrates too much on break-even point

In the next chapter we look at the use of marginal costing in decision-making situations.

QUESTIONS

visit **www.osbornebooks.co.uk** to take an online test

An asterisk (*) after the question number means that the answer is given at the end of this book.

20.1* Which one of the following is the correct method for calculating contribution?

A	Sales revenue minus fixed costs	
B	Sales revenue multiplied by variable costs	
C	Sales revenue minus variable costs	
D	Fixed costs plus variable costs	

20.2 Choose the correct description for each of the three terms in the table below.

Select your entries for the 'Description' column from the following list.

The cost of producing one extra unit of output

Break-even units x selling price per unit

A fixed cost that increases by a large amount all at once

Sales revenue minus variable costs

The point at which there is neither a profit nor a loss

The point at which selling price equals variable costs

Contribution plus fixed costs

Cost where a part is variable and a part is fixed

Cost that does not normally change when the level of output changes

Sales returns minus variable costs

Costs where the cost per unit increases as output increases

Costs where the total cost varies in proportion with output

Contribution minus fixed costs

Term	Description
Break-even	
Fixed cost	
Marginal cost	

20.3* A business has forecast its electricity expense for the year to be £1,600. This consists of a fixed element which is ¼ of the total cost; the remaining ¾ are variable based on usage of electricity. Another supplier of electricity offers to reduce the fixed element by ¼, but the variable cost of electricity will increase by 10%.

How much will the forecast electricity expense be from the other supplier, assuming usage of electricity does not change?

A	£1,320	
B	£1,500	
C	£1,620	
D	£1,820	

20.4 Bert Peters is the owner of a petrol filling station. He provides you with the following information:

cost of petrol from oil company	£1.20 per litre
selling price	£1.25 per litre
fixed costs each week	£750

(a) Complete the following table showing Bert Peter's weekly costs, revenue and profit or loss:

units of output (litres)	**fixed costs** £	**variable costs** £	**total cost** £	**revenue** £	**profit/(loss)** £
0					
5,000					
10,000					
15,000					
16,000					
17,000					
18,000					
19,000					
20,000					

(b) Prove the break-even point of Bert Peter's business by calculation.

20.5* The following is the break-even chart of a business which makes and sells a single product.

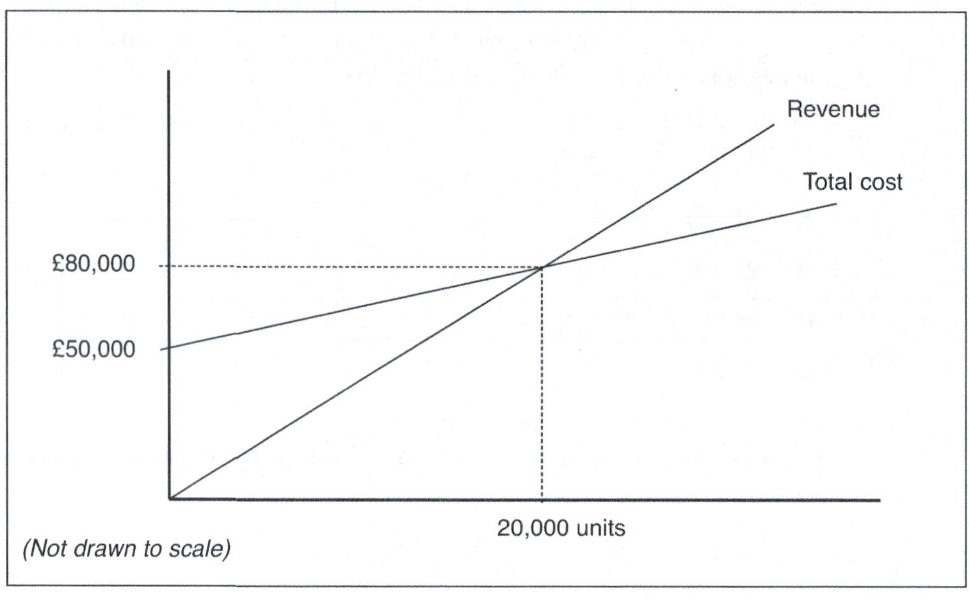

(a) Calculate the selling price per unit of the product.

(b) Calculate the variable cost per unit.

(c) State the formula used to calculate contribution per unit.

(d) Calculate the contribution per unit.

(e) Calculate the forecast profit if 25,000 units are manufactured and sold.

20.6* Westlake Limited makes a product which is coded WL15. The selling price of product WL15 is £24 per unit and the total variable cost is £16 per unit. Westlake Limited estimates that the fixed costs per quarter associated with this product are £1,760.

(a) Calculate the break-even point, in units per quarter, for product WL15.

[ ] units

(b) Calculate the estimated profit, in £ per quarter, if Westlake Limited makes and sells 520 units of product WL15.

£ [ ]

20.7 Angrave Limited makes a product which is numbered AN02. The selling price of product AN02 is £22 per unit and the total variable cost is £14 per unit. Angrave Limited estimates that the fixed costs per quarter associated with this product are £12,000.

(a) Calculate the break-even point, in units per quarter, for product AN02.

[ ] units

(b) Calculate the break-even sales revenue, in £ per quarter, for product AN02.

£ [ ]

(c) Calculate the estimated profit, in £ per quarter, if Angrave Limited makes and sells 2,250 units of product AN02.

£ [ ]

(d) If Angrave Limited increases the selling price of AN02 by £1, what will be the impact on the break-even point, assuming no change in the number of units sold?

The break-even point will increase	
The break-even point will stay the same	
The break-even point will decrease	

20.8* Croome Limited makes controllers for hot water systems – both domestic and commercial use. The company has prepared a budget for the next quarter for one of its controllers, CC8. This budget is based on producing and selling 1,000 batches.

One of the customers of Croome Limited has indicated that it may be significantly increasing its order level for controller CC8 for the next quarter and it appears that activity levels of 1,500 units and 1,800 units are feasible.

Complete the table below and calculate the budgeted total profit of CC8 at the different activity levels.

Units produced and sold	**1,000**	**1,500**	**1,800**
	£	£	£
Revenue	45,000		
Variable costs:			
• Direct materials	10,000		
• Direct labour	12,000		
• Overheads	8,000		
Semi-variable costs:			
• Variable element	2,000		
• Fixed element	2,000		
Total cost	34,000		
Total profit	11,000		

21 DECISION-MAKING SITUATIONS

In this chapter we see how marginal costing is used in decision-making situations. These situations are:

- make or buy decisions
- acceptance of additional work
- price setting
- optimum use of scarce resources
- closing of a potentially loss-making line or production department
- target profit

INTRODUCTION

In the long term every business that seeks to make profits must cover its costs and make a profit from the sale of its output. However, it is common to use marginal cost to help with the analysis of 'what if' situations. Nevertheless, an important point to bear in mind is that, overall, if the business is to be profitable, the selling prices used must give sufficient contribution to meet its fixed costs and provide an acceptable level of profit.

We have already seen in the previous chapter that the marginal cost is the cost of producing one extra unit of output. Marginal costing techniques recognise that fixed costs vary with time rather than activity. For example, the rent of premises relates to a certain time period – such as a week, month or year – and remains unchanged whether there are 100 units of output or 300 (always assuming that the capacity of the premises is at least 300 units). By contrast, one extra unit of output will incur an increase in the variable costs, such as direct materials and direct labour; this increase is the marginal cost.

A knowledge of marginal costing helps with decision-making situations in the forms of:

- make or buy decisions
- acceptance of additional work
- price setting
- optimum use of scarce resources

- closing of a potentially loss-making line or production department
- target profit

The key to each of these, as we shall see shortly, is the contribution from the sale of units of output. Contribution is calculated as:

	selling price
minus	marginal cost
equals	contribution to fixed costs and profit

We have already seen, in the previous chapter, how contribution is used as part of the calculation for break-even.

It is important to note that decision-making situations include a consideration of non-financial matters. For example, the effect on the business, its employees, and the local economy needs to be considered.

MAKE OR BUY DECISIONS

A make or buy decision is a management decision whether to make a product, or supply a service, 'in-house', or to buy in the product/service from an outside supplier.

Examples of make or buy decisions include:

- a car manufacturer needing many different components to make the car – some components will be manufactured in-house while others will be bought from outside suppliers
- a hospital facing the decision whether to provide a payroll accounting service itself, or to buy in the service from an outside contractor

There are a number of considerations before taking a make or buy decision, including:

- for how long will we need this product or service?
- can we find a supplier to make the product or provide the service for us?
- is the supplier's product or service to the specification that we require?
- how much do we want to be reliant on another business?
- what are the costs involved in the decision and the effect on our profits?
- what happens if there are problems with the supplier, eg poor quality, late delivery?
- what happens at the end of the make or buy contract?

the effect on fixed and variable costs

Make or buy decisions affect the cost structure of the business, particularly the relationship between fixed and variable costs. For example, a business seeking to increase output can:

- either expand its own production facilities – which will mainly affect its fixed costs (ie rent of premises, depreciation of new machinery and equipment), with a smaller effect on variable costs

- or buy in from outside suppliers – which will mainly affect its variable costs (ie bought in units are classed as direct materials), with a smaller effect on fixed costs

The first course of action takes a long-term view and assumes that the increase in production can be sustained for a number of years. The second course of action is rather more flexible (ie the number of units bought in can be varied to meet demand) and could be either a long-term arrangement, or for the short-term with, perhaps, the possibility of expanding in-house production facilities in the future.

the use of marginal costing

When considering make or buy decisions, comparisons need to be made between:

- the marginal cost of the product from in-house supply

  and

- the price quoted by the outside supplier

The lower price is, in financial terms, the better choice; however there may well be non-financial aspects to consider, such as quality, reliability, etc.

opportunity cost

Opportunity cost is the benefit that is foregone when a particular course of action is taken.

In make or buy decisions we must consider the resources used (eg factory or office space, machines and equipment) when goods or services are provided in-house. The use of these resources may cause other work to be lost or curtailed. The loss of contribution from this other work needs to be added to the marginal cost in order to make the decision. The make or buy decision is expressed now as a comparison between:

- the marginal cost of making the product in-house, plus the contribution from lost or curtailed work

  and

- the price quoted by the outside supplier

The lower price is the better choice in financial terms.

WORKED EXAMPLE: A MAKE OR BUY DECISION

situation

Wyvern Alarms Limited manufactures high quality security alarms called 'Wyvern Super'. These are sold to alarm companies who install and maintain them.

Until now, Wyvern Alarms has been proud of its in-house production line – materials are bought in, and all manufacturing and assembly is carried out at its factory in Wyvern. The company is finding that demand for its products is increasing. The point has been reached when decisions must be taken about buying in components from outside suppliers.

The management accountant of Wyvern Alarms has obtained a price from a potential supplier for control boxes. These comprise a metal box with a hinged, lockable cover. The box is spray painted in white, with the company logo applied by means of a transfer. It is not considered that quality will be compromised if this item is bought in from an outside supplier.

These are the two alternatives:

1 The cost of making each control box in-house at the current level of 5,000 units each year is:

	£
direct materials	2.50
direct labour	5.50
variable overheads	1.50
fixed overheads	5.50
total cost	15.00

There is no other use for the specialist production machinery required to make this product.

2 An outside supplier has quoted a price of £10 per unit (based on Wyvern's requirements of 5,000 units each year).

Should the management of Wyvern Alarms 'make' or 'buy' ?

solution

The marginal cost of producing each control box is:

	£
direct materials	2.50
direct labour	5.50
variable overheads	1.50
marginal cost	9.50

The comparison is then:

- marginal cost of in-house manufacturer, £9.50 x 5,000 units = £47,500
- price quoted by outside supplier, £10 x 5,000 units = £50,000

As there is no other use for the production machinery currently being used, the decision should be to continue making this component in-house.

Note that if there was an alternative use for the production machinery, the comparison then becomes:

- marginal cost of in-house manufacture, plus contribution from alternative work
- price quoted by outside supplier

In this Worked Example, a contribution of more than £2,500 per year from the production machinery, would make the buy-in a better financial proposition. However, before making the final decision, the management of Wyvern Alarms need to consider social accounting issues, such as making employees redundant, the effect on their local community.

ACCEPTANCE OF ADDITIONAL WORK

Once a business is profitable at its current level of output, to increase its profits it can make additional sales at a selling price above marginal cost, but below absorption cost (the full cost of manufacturing, ie materials, labour, and all variable and fixed overheads), and so increase its profits. However, in order to increase profits, the additional sales must be sourced from spare production capacity within the business. For example, if in order to sell 1,000 extra units, a new factory has to be bought with a production capacity of one million units, then it seems unlikely that the additional sales will prove to be profitable!

The key to increasing profit from the acceptance of additional work is to ensure that a contribution to profit is made from the additional work. The Worked Example below illustrates this principle.

WORKED EXAMPLE: ACCEPTING ADDITIONAL WORK

situation

The Wyvern Bike Company produces 100 bikes a week, and sells them for £200 each. Its costs are as follows:

weekly costs for producing 100 bikes

	£
Direct materials (£40 per bike)	4,000
Direct labour (£50 per bike)	5,000
	9,000
Fixed overheads	5,000
TOTAL COST	14,000

The management of the company has been approached by a mail order warehouse which wishes to buy:

- ***either* 50 bikes each week at a price of £120**
- ***or* 100 bikes each week at a price of £80**

The bikes can be produced in addition to existing production, with no increase in overheads. The additional work is not expected to affect the company's existing sales. How would you advise the management?

solution

The *cost price* of producing one bike is £140 (£14,000 ÷ 100 bikes) – this is the absorption cost. The mail order warehouse is offering either £120 or £80 per bike. On the face of it, with a cost price of £140, both orders should be rejected. However, as there will be no increase in fixed overheads, we can use *marginal costing* to help with decision-making.

The *marginal cost* per bike is £90 (direct materials £40, plus direct labour £50 per bike), and so any contribution, ie selling price less marginal cost, will be profit:

- **50 bikes at £120 each**

  Although below cost price, the offer price of £120 is above the marginal cost of £90 and increases profit by the amount of the £30 extra contribution, ie (£120 – £90) x 50 bikes = £1,500 extra profit.

- **100 bikes at £80 each**

  This offer price is below cost price of £140 and marginal cost of £90; therefore there will be a fall in profit if this order is undertaken of (£80 – £90) x 100 bikes = £1,000 reduced profit.

weekly income statements

	Existing production of 100 units	Existing production + 50 units @ £120 each	Existing production + 100 units @ £80 each
	£	£	£
Revenue (per week):			
100 bikes at £200 each	20,000	20,000	20,000
50 bikes at £120 each	–	6,000	–
100 bikes at £80 each	–	–	8,000
	20,000	26,000	28,000
Less production costs:			
Direct materials (£40 per unit)	4,000	6,000	8,000
Direct labour (£50 per unit)	5,000	7,500	10,000
Fixed overheads	5,000	5,000	5,000
PROFIT	6,000	7,500	5,000

The conclusion is that the first order from the mail order warehouse should be undertaken, and the second declined.

summary

The general rule about accepting additional work is that there needs to be a contribution to profit. Other factors to consider are:

- the additional work should not take the place of products or services that can be sold at above cost price
- there must be spare capacity to produce the additional products or services

- customers who pay normal prices must not be aware of the special prices being offered for additional work
- if marginal costing is used for special prices, it may be difficult to maintain normal prices for other customers
- a customer buying at special prices may undercut the prices charged by other customers who have bought at normal prices

In the short-term a business may choose to sell some of its output at below marginal cost, ie at a negative contribution. This will have the effect of reducing profit but might be done in order to:

- use as a 'loss leader' (a product sold cheaply, often below cost) to attract customers who, it is expected, will then buy other, profitable, items
- develop relations with new customers and/or markets, with the intention of increasing prices in the future
- sell a range of products, eg a garage might service cars cheaply with the expectation that any faults found will be repaired at their normal charges
- keep together a skilled workforce in times of economic slowdown
- ensure continual availability of the product or service

Note that a negative contribution is only sustainable in the short-term and, in the longer-term, additional work must make a contribution to profit.

PRICE SETTING

A price is the amount of money that is agreed between a buyer and a seller which enables the exchange of a product – goods or a service – to take place.

There are three main factors that a business must consider when deciding the price at which to sell its products or services:

- *the need to make a profit* – in the long-term, selling price must be higher than total cost
- *prices of competing products or services* – the selling price is determined largely by the price charged by other suppliers of the product or service
- *under-used capacity* – selling some of the output at a cut price, eg selling unsold tickets cheaply at a theatre just before the performance, or off-peak travel on trains and buses

For each of these factors which determine price, there is a related pricing strategy:

- *the need to make a profit* – the pricing strategy is *cost-plus pricing*
- *prices of competing products* – the pricing strategy is *market led pricing/competitive pricing*
- *under-used capacity* – the pricing strategy is *marginal cost/contribution pricing*

cost-plus pricing

The calculation for cost-plus pricing is:

cost price + profit = selling price

Cost price is usually calculated on the basis of total cost, but can also be on the basis of marginal cost.

market-led pricing

When a business has a product or service for which there is considerable demand and over which it has sole rights, it may be able to set and maintain its own price level (subject to government intervention on the grounds of monopoly pricing). Most businesses, however, must set their prices in comparison with other suppliers of the same or similar products and services – in other words, they must use competitive pricing. In the economy of the free market, buyers will tend to buy from the supplier than can produce the product, or supply the service, at least cost. Thus, in an ideal world (but not always in reality), inefficient suppliers will be forced out of the market and, in order to re-establish themselves, will have to look carefully at their costings and/or production techniques.

There are many examples of market-led or competitive pricing, some of which benefit the buyer:

- **the price of similar products**

  Supermarket shelves, as an example, often contain 'rival' brands of the same product, eg tins of baked beans, cans of cola drink. Whilst each manufacturer will always tell you that their product is infinitely superior to that of their rivals, market-led pricing means that there is little, if any, difference in price. Whilst supermarket 'own brand' products are usually cheaper, the pricing is still market-led, ie a smaller margin below the price of branded goods.

- **the price of seasonal products, such as fresh fruit**

  Usually the market leads the price, eg a supplier of strawberries cannot charge significantly more than the competitors.

- **price cutting**

  In recent years there have been many examples of price cutting started by one retailer and then spreading across the whole industry, ie the price cutting has been market led. Examples include air fares, clothes and holidays.

marginal cost/contribution pricing

Marginal cost is useful in price setting because it determines the minimum price to be charged for products or services. This is appropriate for pricing additional sales at a special reduced rate after sales have already been made at the normal selling price. The rule is simple: once fixed costs have been covered by the contribution from normal sales, then additional sales must cover, as a minimum, their variable costs – at above variable cost, the contribution will be profit.

Optimum Use of Scarce Resources

Scarce resources, or limiting factors, are those aspects of a business which limit output.

Examples of scarce resources include:

- availability of materials
- availability of skilled labour
- availability of productive capacity, eg machine hours
- availability of storage facilities
- finance
- the quantity of the output which can be sold – whether a manufactured product or a service

At any one time there is usually one main scarce resource. It is essential to minimise its effect by optimising resources and maximising profit. After one scarce resource has been dealt with, another one then affects the business – for example, once a shortage of materials has been resolved, the scarce resource might well become a lack of skilled labour.

Where a business sells more than one product, under normal circumstances it will be best to switch output to the product that gives the highest contribution in relation to sales. For example, a company makes two products, Exe and Wye, with the following costs and revenues:

	Product	Exe £	Wye £
	Sales revenue per unit	100	200
minus	Variable costs per unit	60	140
equals	Contribution per unit	40	60

With no limiting factors, the company should concentrate on making and selling product Exe. The reason for this is that the contribution/sales percentage is 40 per cent (£40 ÷ £100) when compared with product Wye, where it is 30 per cent (£60 ÷ £200).

Where there is a scarce resource, for example the availability of skilled labour, a business will switch production to the product which gives the highest contribution from each unit of the limiting factor (eg contribution per direct labour hour). Thus the key to optimising the use of scarce resources is to:

maximise the contribution per unit of scarce resources

Following this rule will always maximise profits. Where there is a maximum level of output for the selected product, this product should be produced to the full if possible, and any units of scarce resources which remain unused should be 'spilled over' to the next best product. This is illustrated in the Worked Example which follows.

WORKED EXAMPLE: OPTIMUM USE OF SCARCE RESOURCES

situation

Sound Systems Limited is a small company which makes reproduction radios to 1930s' designs (but with 21st century sound quality!). Two models are made – the 'Windsor' and the 'Buckingham'. Both products require skilled direct labour which cannot be increased in the short term. Demand for the company's products is increasing rapidly and, while the company is taking steps to train new employees, the managing director is unsure of the 'mix' of products that should be produced each week.

Costs and revenues are as follows:

		Windsor £	Buckingham £
	Sales revenue per unit	50	100
minus	Variable costs per unit	30	70
equals	Contribution per unit	20	30

- each radio takes two direct labour hours to make
- the number of direct labour hours each week is 260
- the weekly fixed overheads of the business are £2,000
- demand for the Windsor model is currently 100 radios per week, and for the Buckingham it is 80 radios per week

Give the production manager your recommendations for next week's production, supporting your views with a forecast income statement.

solution

Ignoring, for the moment, the scarce resource of direct labour, the better model for the company to produce is the Windsor, because this gives a higher contribution/sales ratio (see page 406):

- Windsor: £20 contribution on £50 of sales = 40 per cent
- Buckingham: £30 contribution on £100 of sales = 30 per cent

However, as direct labour is the scarce resource, the company should maximise the contribution from each hour of direct labour, as follows:

		Windsor	Buckingham
	Contribution per unit	£20	£30
	Direct labour hours per unit	2	2
equals	Contribution per direct labour hour	£10	£15
	Ranking	2	1

To optimise use of the scarce resource of direct labour, the company should produce all of the Buckingham model that can be sold, ie 80 per week, as follows:

	Total hours available per week	260
minus	80 units of Buckingham at 2 hours each	160
equals	hours remaining to produce units of Windsor	100

Therefore production of Windsor will be 100 hours ÷ 2 hours = 50 units per week

The weekly production plan of Sound Systems Limited will be 50 units of Windsor and 80 units of Buckingham. However, by taking this action, insufficient Windsor models will be produced to meet demand. This may make it difficult to re-establish the Windsor in the market when full production of this model can be resumed following the completion of training of new employees.

The forecast income statement for next week will be as follows:

		Windsor £	**Buckingham** £	**Total** £
	Sales revenue:			
	50 Windsor at £50 per unit	2,500		2,500
	80 Buckingham at £100 per unit		8,000	8,000
		2,500	8,000	10,500
minus	Variable costs:			
	50 Windsor at £30 per unit	1,500		1,500
	80 Buckingham at £70 per unit		5,600	5,600
equals	Contribution	1,000	2,400	3,400
minus	Fixed overheads			2,000
equals	Profit			1,400

summarising the use of scarce resources

The procedures for decision-making with scarce resources are:

- calculate the *contribution per unit of scarce resource* to make the decision as to which product to manufacture – the one with the highest contribution per unit of scarce resource will maximise profits
- calculate the income statement using the *number of units of output* (and not the number of units of scarce resource)
- where there is a maximum level of output for the selected product, use as much of the scarce resource as possible, and then 'spill over' any unused scarce resource to the next best product (as in the Worked Example)

Note that, where there are scarce resources, fewer of one or more products will be produced causing a shortfall in the market. It may be difficult to re-establish these products when full production can be resumed after the availability of the scarce resource has been resolved. The problem is that often customers want availability of all products and, if one isn't fully available, they won't buy the others (think of a store closing its carpet department and the effect on sales in the furniture department).

Closing of a Potentially Loss-Making Line or Production Department

"Shall we close down X?"

This question applies to both a manufacturer looking at a loss-making line or production department as well as to a department store considering a loss-making department.

Marginal costing can be used to compare the contribution made by a line or production department to the overall profitability of the business, as the following worked example shows:

WORKED EXAMPLE: A LOSS-MAKING PRODUCT?

situation

The following information is given for S & T Manufacturing Limited, a two-product (S & T) company, for last year:

	S	T	Total
	£	£	£
Revenue	100,000	200,000	300,000
Variable costs	90,000	135,000	225,000
Contribution	10,000	65,000	75,000
Fixed costs*	20,000	40,000	60,000
Profit/(Loss)	(10,000)	25,000	15,000

** apportioned to each product on the basis of revenue*

Should S & T Manufacturing Limited close the loss-making production department S?

solution

On the basis of the information given, production department S should be closed because it is making a loss. However, this may be a simplistic solution as, using marginal costing, we can see that the product makes a contribution to fixed costs.

If department S is closed, it is likely that most of the fixed costs of the business will continue – this reduces the profit for the business to:

	T
Revenue	200,000
Variable costs	135,000
Contribution	65,000
Fixed costs £20,000 + £40,000	60,000
Profit	5,000

This shows that profits of the company may fall from £15,000 to £5,000 if department S is closed. It seems, therefore, that department S should be retained.

Other factors will have to be considered, for example, sales of product T may be linked to sales of product S.

This Worked Example shows the need to analyse the contribution made by each line or production department to the fixed costs and the overall profitability of the business.

closure problems

The following points should be considered in the decision-making situation for closing a loss-making line or production department:

- check that the basis of apportionment of fixed costs is appropriate to each line or production department
- can the price of the loss-maker's products be increased to make it profitable?

  Perhaps it is a superior product to those of competitors in terms of quality or features
- can sales of the loss-maker be increased (eg with marketing), costs reduced (eg cheaper buying prices of materials), or a more efficient production process used (eg more automation)?
- if the loss-maker is to be closed, what will take its place?

  Perhaps the unused capacity can be diverted to another – more profitable – product. If so, do the workforce have the necessary skills to be transferred to another product?
- what will happen to the fixed costs currently being charged to the loss-maker?

  These will have to be borne by the other parts of the business – there may be a reduction in some fixed costs, eg administration, but other fixed costs, eg factory rent, are likely to continue in full
- will closure of the loss-maker have an adverse effect on the rest of the business?

  For example, closure of a store's carpet department could well reduce sales in the curtain department because customers may prefer to buy both together from a store that offers both lines
- if the loss-maker is to be closed, is it to be a permanent or temporary closure? If permanent, there are likely to be closure costs (eg redundancy payments to staff) and revenues (eg sale of non-current assets and inventory), or can staff, non-current assets and inventory be transferred to other lines or production departments? A temporary closure might be considered if it is thought that selling and marketing conditions will improve in a year or two

The general rules when considering closure of a loss-maker are:

- if a contribution is being made to fixed costs, it should not be closed
- if no contribution is being made to fixed costs, then it should be considered for closure (but check that the basis of apportionment of fixed costs is appropriate to each line or production department)

Target Profit

A decision-making situation which is a further development of break-even is to calculate the output that needs to be sold in order to give a certain amount of profit – the **target profit**. This is calculated as follows:

$$\frac{\text{fixed costs (£) + target profit (£)}}{\text{contribution per unit (£)}} = \text{number of units of output}$$

WORKED EXAMPLE: TARGET PROFIT

situation

Fluffy Toys Limited manufactures soft toys, and is able to sell all that can be produced. The variable costs (materials and direct labour) for producing each toy are £10 and the selling price is £20 each. The fixed costs of running the business are £5,000 per month. How many toys need to be produced and sold each month for the business to achieve a target profit of £2,000?

solution

If Fluffy Toys Limited requires a profit of £2,000 per month, the calculation is:

$$\frac{\text{£5,000 + £2,000}}{\text{£10}} = \text{700 units, with a sales value of £14,000*}$$

*700 units at £20 each = £14,000

This target profit can then be shown by means of a profit statement as follows:

		£
	sales revenue (700 units at £20 each)	14,000
minus	variable costs (700 units at £10 each)	7,000
equals	contribution (to fixed costs and profit)	7,000
minus	monthly fixed costs	5,000
equals	target profit for month	2,000

Alternatively, it can be calculated as follows:

(sales revenue – variable costs) per unit x volume – fixed costs = profit

ie (£20 – £10) x 700 – £5,000 = £7,000 – £5,000 = £2,000

Note that target profit can also be calculated by making use of the contribution sales ratio (see next page).

contribution sales ratio

The contribution sales (CS) ratio – also known as the profit volume (PV) ratio – expresses the amount of contribution in relation to the amount of the selling price:

$$\frac{\text{contribution (£)}}{\text{selling price (£)}} = \text{contribution to sales ratio}$$

The ratio, or percentage, can be calculated on the basis of a single unit of production or for the whole business.

If fixed costs are known, we can use the CS ratio to find the sales revenue at which the business breaks-even, or the sales revenue to give a target amount of profit.

WORKED EXAMPLE: CONTRIBUTION SALES RATIO

Referring back to Fluffy Toys Limited, the CS ratio (per unit) is:

$$\frac{\text{contribution (£)}}{\text{selling price (£)}} = \frac{\text{£10*}}{\text{£20}} = 0.5 \text{ or } 50\%$$

* selling price £20 – variable costs £10 = contribution £10

Fixed costs are £5,000 per month, so the sales revenue needed to break-even is:

$$\frac{\text{fixed costs (£)}}{\text{CS ratio}} = \frac{\text{£5,000}}{\text{0.5 (see above)}} = \underline{\text{£10,000}}$$

As the selling price is £20 per toy, we can get back to the break-even in units of output as follows: £10,000 ÷ £20 = 500 units

If the directors of Fluffy Toys Limited wish to know the sales revenue that must be made to achieve a target profit of £2,000 per month, the CS ratio is used as follows:

$$\frac{\text{fixed costs + target profit}}{\text{CS ratio}} = \text{required level of sales}$$

$$\frac{\text{£5,000 + £2,000}}{0.5} = \underline{\text{£14,000}}$$

As the selling price is £20 per toy, we can get to the units of output as follows:

£14,000 ÷ £20 = 700 units to achieve a target profit of £2,000.

Marginal Costing: Other Points

In this chapter we have seen how marginal costing techniques can be useful in decision-making situations. Nevertheless, there are a number of points that must be borne in mind:

- **fixed costs must be covered**

  The total contribution from output needs to cover the fixed costs of the business and provide a profit. A balance needs to be struck between the output that is sold at above marginal cost and the output that is sold at absorption cost.

- **separate markets for marginal cost**

  It is sensible business practice to separate out the markets where marginal cost is used. For example, a business would not quote a price based on absorption cost to retailer A and a price based on marginal cost to retailer B, when A and B are both in the same town! It would be better to seek new markets in which to sell with prices based on marginal cost.

- **effect on customers**

  One of the problems of using marginal cost pricing to attract new business is that it is difficult to persuade the customer to pay closer to, or above, absorption cost later on. Thus one of the dangers of using marginal cost is that profit margins can be squeezed quite dramatically if the technique is used too widely.

- **problems of product launch on marginal cost basis**

  There is great temptation in business to launch a new product at the keenest possible price – below absorption cost (but above marginal cost). If the product is highly successful, it could well alter the cost structure of the business. However, it could also lead to the collapse of sales of older products so that most of the company's sales are derived from output priced on the marginal cost basis – it may then be difficult to increase prices to above absorption cost levels.

- **special edition products**

  Many businesses use marginal costing techniques to sell off older products at a keen price. For example, car manufacturers with a new model due in a few months' time will package the old model with 'special edition' badging and sell it at a low price (but above marginal cost).

CHAPTER SUMMARY

- A business, seeking to make a profit, must cover its costs and make a profit from the selling prices of its output.
- Marginal costing is used in decision-making situations.
- A make or buy decision is a management decision whether to make a product/supply a service 'in-house', or to buy in the product/service from an outside supplier.
- Make or buy decisions compare the marginal cost of making the product in-house, plus the contribution from lost or curtailed work, with the price quoted by the outside supplier. The lower price is the better choice in financial terms.
- Acceptance of additional work is where a business is able to sell output as 'special orders' at a price above marginal cost, but below cost price (absorption cost) – always provided that the fixed costs are covered by the contribution from normal sales.
- The factors to consider when setting a selling price for products or services are:
  - the need to make a profit
  - prices of competing products or services
  - the availability of any under-used capacity
- The main price setting strategies are:
  - cost-plus pricing
  - market-led pricing/competitive pricing
  - marginal cost/contribution pricing
- Scarce resources, or limiting factors, are those aspects of a business which limit output. Scarce resources should be allocated to the output which maximises the contribution per unit of scarce resources.
- When considering closure of a potential loss-making part of a business, marginal costing should be used to ascertain whether or not a contribution is being made to fixed costs.
- Target profit calculates the required sales revenue in order to give a certain amount of profit.
- Using marginal costing techniques, decision makers must bear in mind:
  - fixed costs must be covered
  - separate markets for marginal cost
  - effect on customers
  - problems of product launch on a marginal cost basis
  - special edition products

QUESTIONS

visit
www.osbornebooks.co.uk
to take an online test

An asterisk (*) after the question number means that the answer is given at the end of this book.

21.1* A supplier to a business has quoted a price of £20 per unit to supply a component used by the business. The marginal cost of manufacturing the component in-house is £18 per unit. If the component is bought in from the supplier:

A	Profits will increase	
B	Profits will decrease	
C	Profits will be unchanged	
D	Losses will decrease	

21.2 A make or buy decision compares:

A	The total cost of making the product in-house and the price quoted by the outside supplier	
B	The marginal cost of making the product in-house and the price quoted by the outside supplier	
C	The selling price of the product made in-house and the price quoted by the outside supplier	
D	The marginal cost of making the product in-house and the total cost of making the product in-house	

21.3 Pentland Pumps Limited manufactures electric pumping equipment used in industry and agriculture. At present all parts are made in-house from raw materials. The company is considering buying in pump motors from an outside supplier in order to release facilities for a new product, an 'olde worlde' handpump for decorative (and practical) use.

The following information is available:

- the cost of making each pump motor in-house at the current level of production of 3,500 pumps per year is:

	£
direct materials	40.00
direct labour	25.00
variable overheads	20.00
fixed overheads	15.00
total cost	100.00

- an outside supplier has quoted a price of £95 per motor
- if pump motors are bought in from an outside supplier, the company will be able to make 750 'olde worlde' handpumps each year, with a selling price of £250 per unit and variable costs of £150 per unit

You are to advise the management of Pentland Pumps Limited whether or not, in financial terms, the motors should be bought in from the outside supplier.

21.4* Westfield Limited makes 2,000 units of product Exe each month. The company's costs are:

monthly costs for making 2,000 units of Exe (£)	
direct materials	6,000
direct labour	4,000
fixed overheads	8,000
total cost	18,000

Each unit of Exe is sold for £12.

The management of the company has been approached by a buyer who wishes to purchase:

- *either* 200 units of Exe each month at a price of £6 per unit
- *or* 500 units of Exe each month at a price of £4 per unit

The extra units can be produced in addition to existing production, with no increase in overheads. The special order is not expected to affect the company's existing sales.

You are to prepare monthly income statements showing current profits and the expected profits from the two proposed options. Using this data, advise the management of Westfield Limited as to the best course of action.

21.5* Popcan Limited manufactures and sells a soft drink which the company sells at 25p per can. Currently output is 150,000 cans per month, which represents 75 per cent of production capacity. The company has an opportunity to use the spare capacity by producing the product for a supermarket chain which will sell it under their own label. The supermarket chain is willing to pay 18p per can.

You are to prepare, from the data set out below, monthly income statements showing current profits and the expected profits from the new proposal. Using this data, advise the management of Popcan Limited as to whether the supermarket's offer should be accepted.

POPCAN LIMITED	
Costs per can	
	pence
Direct materials	5
Direct labour	5
Variable overheads	4
Fixed* overheads	6

* fixed overheads are apportioned on the basis of current output

21.6* BrightLight Limited manufactures and sells a specialist lighting unit used in hospital operating theatres. The lighting unit has a selling price of £400 per unit and, in the current year, the company expects to sell 5,000 units.

The variable costs per unit are:

	£
Material R: 2 kilos at £30 per kilo	60.00
Material S: 1 litre at £40 per litre	40.00
Skilled labour: 4 hours at £18.00 per hour	72.00
Semi-skilled labour: 6 hours at £14.00 per hour	84.00
Total variable cost per unit	256.00

Budgeted fixed overheads for the current year are £528,600 and the budgeted profit for the year is £191,400.

BrightLight Limited has received an enquiry from a potential overseas customer. This customer wishes to place an order for 2,000 units if a total sales price of £626,500 is agreed and delivery takes place within three months, which is before the end of BrightLight Limited's financial year. The potential customer is prepared to pay in full using bank guaranteed systems once BrightLight Limited presents shipping and insurance documents for the order, the costs of which must be paid by BrightLight Limited, expected to be £30,500.

If the potential overseas customer is satisfied with quality standards and delivery terms there is the expectation that future orders will be placed for around 3,000 units each year.

In considering these orders, the following information may be useful:

- The directors of BrightLight Limited have been looking to develop overseas sales.
- For the current year, skilled labour is forecast to be under-utilised by 1,650 hours. It

is intended to retain the skilled labour in the company and to continue paying them for the company's standard 36-hour week.

- Any shortfall in skilled labour hours would be worked as overtime at a premium of £8 per hour, paid in addition to the hourly rate.
- The wages of non-production employees are included within fixed overheads.
- Additional materials and semi-skilled labour at current prices and rates are readily available.

You are to evaluate the financial and non-financial implications of the proposed order from the overseas customer. Include a justified recommendation as to whether the order should be accepted or rejected.

21.7* When the selling price is determined largely by the price charged by other suppliers of the product, the pricing strategy is:

A	Cost-plus pricing	
B	Marginal cost pricing	
C	Market led pricing	
D	Contribution pricing	

21.8* KeepDry Limited manufactures waterproof coats.

The company currently produces 1,000 coats a month.

The costs per coat are:

Materials: 4 metres @ £12 per metre

Labour: 3 hours @ £15 per hour

Total fixed costs are £33,180 monthly.

The company uses cost-plus pricing and the selling price is set at 150% of the total cost per coat.

If production exceeds 1,100 coats in any one month, overtime will be paid at a rate of £22 per hour for each extra labour hour worked.

The company has received an order from a new customer. This order will increase total production for each of the following months to 1,200 coats.

Required:

(a) Calculate the total cost per coat if the order is accepted and 1,200 coats are produced.

(b) Calculate the change between the new selling price and the original selling price.

(c) Explain one effect of this change in selling price on the company's present customers.

21.9* Dean Limited makes two products – Aye and Bee. Both products are made from the same type of direct material. This material is currently in short supply. At present the company can obtain only 500 kilos of the direct material each week. The production manager wishes to know the 'mix' of products that should be produced each week. The information available is:

	Product	**Aye**	**Bee**
	Sales revenue per unit	£150	£200
minus	Variable costs per unit	£120	£150
equals	Contribution per unit	£30	£50
	Kilos of direct material per unit	2	4
	Demand per week (in units)	200	150

The weekly fixed overheads of the business are £4,000.

Required:

Advise the production manager of your recommendations for next week's production. Support your views with a budgeted income statement.

21.10* Sesame Shoes Limited manufactures shoes at its factory in Wyvern. It has three shoe ranges – the 'Madrid', the 'Paris', and the 'Rome'. The expected monthly costs and sales information for each range is as follows:

The total expected monthly fixed costs relating to the production of all shoes are £72,800.

Product	**'Madrid'**	**'Paris'**	**'Rome'**
Sales and production units*	5,000	3,000	500
Machine hours per month	2,500	1,200	375
Total sales revenue	£150,000	£120,000	£30,000
Total direct materials	£50,000	£45,000	£10,000
Total direct labour	£25,000	£24,000	£6,000
Total variable overheads	£10,000	£9,000	£1,250

*note: a unit is a pair of shoes

Required:

(a) Complete the table on the next page to show for each product range the expected contribution per unit.

Product	'Madrid' £	'Paris' £	'Rome' £
Sales revenue per unit			
minus: Variable costs per unit			
Direct materials			
Direct labour			
Variable costs per unit			
equals: Contribution per unit			

(b) If the company only manufactures the 'Madrid' range, calculate the number of units it would need to make and sell each month to cover the fixed costs of £72,800.

(c) The breakdown of a machine used in the manufacture of shoes has reduced available machine time from 4,075 to 3,000 hours. The finance director asks you to calculate the contribution of each unit (pair of shoes) per machine hour.

Using the data from (a), complete the table below.

Product	'Madrid'	'Paris'	'Rome'
Contribution per unit			
Machine hours per unit			
Contribution per machine hour			

(d) Using the data from (c), calculate how many units of each of product ranges 'Madrid', 'Paris', and 'Rome' the company should make and sell in order to maximise its profits using 3,000 machine hours.

21.11 You work as an accounts assistant for Gold and Partners, an accountancy practice which has three offices in districts of the city. The offices are at Triangle, South Toynton and St Faiths. The accounting system has been set up to show costs and fee income for each of the three offices of the practice.

The following information has been extracted from the accounting system:

	Triangle	**South Toynton**	**St Faiths**
	£000	£000	£000
Costs: materials	75	70	80
labour	550	600	760
Fee income	960	720	1,320
Fixed costs*	144	108	198
*apportioned to each branch office on the basis of fee income			

(a) The accounts supervisor of Gold and Partners knows that one of the offices is making a loss. She asks you to present the accounting information for the partners to show the costs and profit or loss for each office of the practice.

(b) For the office that is making a loss, the accounts supervisor asks you to give her a note of the points she should make to the partners regarding closure of that office.

21.12* The following information is available for the single product manufactured by a business.

Selling price per unit	£15.40
Variable costs per unit	£8.60
Fixed costs	£35,000
Budgeted production	10,000 units

How many units must the business make and sell to produce a target profit of £25,000?

A	3,677 units	
B	5,148 units	
C	8,824 units	
D	10,000 units	

21.13 The accountant of Frowan Limited has produced the following budgeted income statement for the period January - March 20-4:

	£	£
Revenue (80,000 units at £2.50 each)		200,000
Variable costs	120,000	
Fixed costs	50,000	
		170,000
Profit for the period		30,000

(a) What is the contribution sales ratio for Frowan Limited?

(b) Calculate the number of units that must be made and sold for Frowan Limited to break-even.

(c) If the directors of Frowan Limited require the company to achieve a profit of £40,000 for the period, how many units will need to be sold and at what total revenue?

Answers to Selected Questions

Answers to questions marked with an asterisk (*) are provided in this section. These are set out in the fully worked layout that should be used, which is very important in accounting.

Answers to all other questions are available to tutors who adopt this textbook for their students. For further information, visit the Tutor Resources section at www.osbornebooks.co.uk

CHAPTER 1 What is financial accounting?

1.1

(a) ledger
(b) trade receivable
(c) trade payable
(d) sales journal
(e) cash book
(f) general ledger
(g) assets – liabilities = capital
(h) business entity

1.8

capital	£20,000
capital	£10,000
liabilities	£7,550
assets	£14,100
liabilities	£18,430
assets	£21,160

1.9

(a) Owner started in business with capital of £10,000 in the bank
(b) Bought office equipment for £2,000, paying from the bank
(c) Received a loan of £6,000 into the bank
(d) Bought a van for £10,000, paying from the bank
(e) Owner introduces £2,000 additional capital into the bank
(f) Loan repayment of £3,000 made from the bank

CHAPTER 2 Double-entry bookkeeping: first principles

2.2

Bank Account

Dr					Cr
20-2		£	20-2		£
1 May	Capital	6,000	4 May	Machinery	3,500
12 May	L Warner: loan	1,000	6 May	Office equipment	2,000
17 May	Commission income	150	10 May	Rent paid	350
			15 May	Wages	250
			20 May	Drawings	85
			25 May	Wages	135

Capital Account

Dr					Cr
20-2		£	20-2		£
			1 May	Bank	6,000

Machinery Account

Dr					Cr
20-2		£	20-2		£
4 May	Bank	3,500			

Office Equipment Account

Dr					Cr
20-2		£	20-2		£
6 May	Bank	2,000			

Rent Paid Account

Dr					Cr
20-2		£	20-2		£
10 May	Bank	350			

Lucy Warner: Loan Account

Dr					Cr
20-2		£	20-2		£
			12 May	Bank	1,000

Wages Account

Dr					Cr
20-2		£	20-2		£
15 May	Bank	250			
25 May	Bank	135			

Commission Income Account

Dr					Cr
20-2		£	20-2		£
			17 May	Bank	150

Drawings Account

Dr					Cr
20-2		£	20-2		£
20 May	Bank	85			

2.4

Bank Account

Dr					Cr
20-2		£	20-2		£
1 Mar	Capital	6,500	4 Mar	Office equipment	1,000
5 Mar	Bank loan	2,500	7 Mar	Wages	250
8 Mar	Commission income	150	10 Mar	Rent paid	200
			12 Mar	Drawings	175
			15 Mar	Van	6,000

Capital Account

Dr					Cr
20-2		£	20-2		£
			1 Mar	Bank	6,500

Office Equipment Account

Dr					Cr
20-2		£	20-2		£
4 Mar	Bank	1,000			

Bank Loan Account

Dr					Cr
20-2		£	20-2		£
			5 Mar	Bank	2,500

Wages Account

Dr					Cr
20-2		£	20-2		£
7 Mar	Bank	250			

Commission Income Account

Dr					Cr
20-2		£	20-2		£
			8 Mar	Bank	150

Rent Paid Account

Dr					Cr
20-2		£	20-2		£
10 Mar	Bank	200			

Drawings Account

Dr					Cr
20-2		£	20-2		£
12 Mar	Bank	175			

Van Account

Dr					Cr
20-2		£	20-2		£
15 Mar	Bank	6,000			

CHAPTER 3 Double-entry bookkeeping: further transactions

3.2

Bank Account

Dr					Cr
20-1		£	20-1		£
1 Feb	Capital	3,000	3 Feb	Purchases	100
2 Feb	Sales	250	5 Feb	Wages	150
7 Feb	Sales	300	12 Feb	Purchases	200
15 Feb	J Walters: loan	1,000	20 Feb	Computer	1,950
25 Feb	Sales	150	27 Feb	Wages	125

Capital Account

Dr					Cr
20-1		£	20-1		£
			1 Feb	Bank	3,000

Sales Account

Dr					Cr
20-1		£	20-1		£
			2 Feb	Bank	250
			7 Feb	Bank	300
			25 Feb	Bank	150

Purchases Account

Dr					Cr
20-1		£	20-1		£
3 Feb	Bank	100			
12 Feb	Bank	200			

Wages Account

Dr					Cr
20-1		£	20-1		£
5 Feb	Bank	150			
27 Feb	Bank	125			

J Walters: Loan Account

Dr					Cr
20-1		£	20-1		£
			15 Feb	Bank	1,000

Computer Account

Dr					Cr
20-1		£	20-1		£
20 Feb	Bank	1,950			

3.3

Bank Account

		Debit	Credit	Balance
20-1		£	£	£
1 Feb	Capital	3,000		3,000 Dr
2 Feb	Sales	250		3,250 Dr
3 Feb	Purchases		100	3,150 Dr
5 Feb	Wages		150	3,000 Dr
7 Feb	Sales	300		3,300 Dr
12 Feb	Purchases		200	3,100 Dr
15 Feb	J Walters: loan	1,000		4,100 Dr
20 Feb	Computer		1,950	2,150 Dr
25 Feb	Sales	150		2,300 Dr
27 Feb	Wages		125	2,175 Dr

3.4

Purchases Account

Dr					Cr
20-1		£	20-1		£
4 Jan	AB Supplies Ltd	250			
20 Jan	Bank	225			

AB Supplies Ltd

Dr					Cr
20-1		£	20-1		£
15 Jan	Bank	250	4 Jan	Purchases	250

Sales Account

Dr					Cr
20-1		£	20-1		£
			5 Jan	Bank	195
			7 Jan	Cash	150
			17 Jan	L Lewis	145

Bank Account

Dr					Cr
20-1		£	20-1		£
5 Jan	Sales	195	15 Jan	AB Supplies Ltd	250
10 Jan	J Johnson: loan	1,000	20 Jan	Purchases	225
29 Jan	L Lewis	145	31 Jan	Mercia Office Supplies Ltd	160

Cash Account

Dr					Cr
20-1		£	20-1		£
7 Jan	Sales	150	22 Jan	Wages	125

J Johnson: Loan Account

Dr					Cr
20-1		£	20-1		£
			10 Jan	Bank	1,000

L Lewis

Dr					Cr
20-1		£	20-1		£
17 Jan	Sales	145	29 Jan	Bank	145

Wages Account

Dr					Cr
20-1		£	20-1		£
22 Jan	Cash	125			

Office Equipment Account

Dr					Cr
20-1		£	20-1		£
26 Jan	Mercia O S Ltd	160			

Mercia Office Supplies Ltd

Dr					Cr
20-1		£	20-1		£
31 Jan	Bank	160	26 Jan	Office equipment	160

CHAPTER 4 Business documents

4.1 (a) purchase order
(b) invoice
(c) cash discount
(d) trade discount
(e) net
(f) credit note
(g) statement of account

4.6 (a) (i) Trade discount is the amount sometimes allowed as a reduction in price:
- to businesses, often in the same trade (but not to the general public)
- for buying in bulk (this discount is also known as bulk discount)
- by wholesalers, as a discount off list price to retailers

(ii) Cash discount (also known as settlement discount) is given, for prompt payment, if prearranged, and is indicated on the invoice when it applies.

(b) Invoice total: £400.00

Workings:

£500 – 20% = £400

(c) Queenstown Retail will pay £380.00 (£400.00 x 95%) for settlement in full within 14 days

CHAPTER 5 Balancing accounts – the trial balance

5.3 (a)

LORNA FOX
Trial balance as at 31 March 20-2

	Dr	Cr
	£	£
Purchases	96,250	
Sales (Revenue)		146,390
Sales returns	8,500	
Administration expenses	10,240	
Wages	28,980	
Telephone	3,020	
Interest paid	2,350	
Travel expenses	1,045	
Premises	125,000	
Machinery	40,000	
Trade receivables	10,390	
Bank overdraft		1,050
Cash	150	
Trade payables		12,495
Loan from bank		20,000
Drawings	9,450	
Capital		155,440
	335,375	335,375

(b) See Chapters 2 and 3 and page 65. The explanation should be appropriate for someone who does not understand accounting.

5.4 (a) principle
(b) mispost/commission
(c) original entry
(d) compensating
(e) reversal of entries
(f) omission

5.6 A

6.1 (a)

Purchases Journal

Date	Details	Invoice	Reference	Amount
20-6				£
1 Feb	Flair Clothing			520
4 Feb	Modernwear			240
18 Feb	Quality Clothing			800
28 Feb	Flair Clothing			200
28 Feb	Total for month			1,760

Sales Journal

Date	Details	Invoice	Reference	Amount
20-6				£
2 Feb	Wyvern Fashions			200
10 Feb	Zandra Smith			160
15 Feb	Just Jean			120
23 Feb	Zandra Smith			320
24 Feb	Wyvern Fashions			80
26 Feb	Mercian Models			320
28 Feb	Total for month			1,200

(b)

PURCHASES (PAYABLES) LEDGER

Flair Clothing

Dr				Cr	
20-6		£	20-6		£
			1 Feb	Purchases	520
			28 Feb	Purchases	200

Modernwear

Dr				Cr	
20-6		£	20-6		£
			4 Feb	Purchases	240

Quality Clothing

Dr				Cr	
20-6		£	20-6		£
			18 Feb	Purchases	800

SALES (RECEIVABLES) LEDGER

Wyvern Fashions

Dr				Cr	
20-6		£	20-6		£
2 Feb	Sales	200			
24 Feb	Sales	80			

Zandra Smith

Dr				Cr	
20-6		£	20-6		£
10 Feb	Sales	160			
23 Feb	Sales	320			

Just Jean

Dr				Cr	
20-6		£	20-6		£
15 Feb	Sales	120			

Mercian Models

Dr				Cr	
20-6		£	20-6		£
26 Feb	Sales	320			

GENERAL LEDGER

Purchases Account

Dr				Cr	
20-6		£	20-6		£
28 Feb	Purchases journal	1,760			

Sales Account

Dr				Cr	
20-6		£	20-6		£
			28 Feb	Sales journal	1,200

6.4 (a)

Sales Journal

Date	Details	Invoice	Reference	Amount
20-2				£
5 Jan	Mereford College	1093	SL 201	3,900.00
7 Jan	Carpminster College	1094	SL 202	8,500.00
14 Jan	Carpminster College	1095	SL 202	1,800.50
14 Jan	Mereford College	1096	SL 201	2,950.75
20 Jan	Carpminster College	1097	SL 202	3,900.75
22 Jan	Mereford College	1098	SL 201	1,597.85
31 Jan	Total for month			22,649.85

Purchases Journal

Date	Details	Invoice	Reference	Amount
20-2				£
2 Jan	Macstrad plc	M1529	PL 101	2,900.00
3 Jan	Amtosh plc	A7095	PL 102	7,500.00
18 Jan	Macstrad plc	M2070	PL 101	1,750.00
19 Jan	Amtosh plc	A7519	PL 102	5,500.00
31 Jan	Total for month			17,650.00

Sales Returns Journal

Date	Details	Credit note	Reference	Amount
20-2				£
13 Jan	Mereford College	CN109	SL 201	850.73
27 Jan	Mereford College	CN110	SL 201	593.81
31 Jan	Total for month			1,444.54

Purchases Returns Journal

Date	Details	Credit note	Reference	Amount
20-2				£
10 Jan	Macstrad plc	MC105	PL 101	319.75
12 Jan	Amtosh plc	AC 730	PL 102	750.18
23 Jan	Macstrad plc	MC120	PL 101	953.07
31 Jan	Total for month			2,023.00

(b)

SALES (RECEIVABLES) LEDGER

Mereford College (account no 201)

Dr					Cr
20-2		£	20-2		£
1 Jan	Balance b/d	705.35	13 Jan	Sales Returns	850.73
5 Jan	Sales	3,900.00	27 Jan	Sales Returns	593.81
14 Jan	Sales	2,950.75	31 Jan	Balance c/d	7,709.41
22 Jan	Sales	1,597.85			
		9,153.95			9,153.95
1 Feb	Balance b/d	7,709.41			

Carpminster College (account no 202)

Dr					Cr
20-2		£	20-2		£
1 Jan	Balance b/d	801.97	31 Jan	Balance c/d	15,003.22
7 Jan	Sales	8,500.00			
14 Jan	Sales	1,800.50			
20 Jan	Sales	3,900.75			
		15,003.22			15,003.22
1 Feb	Balance b/d	15,003.22			

PURCHASES (PAYABLES) LEDGER

Macstrad plc (account no 101)

Dr					Cr
20-2		£	20-2		£
10 Jan	Purchases returns	319.75	1 Jan	Balance b/d	1,050.75
23 Jan	Purchases returns	953.07	2 Jan	Purchases	2,900.00
31 Jan	Balance c/d	4,427.93	18 Jan	Purchases	1,750.00
		5,700.75			5,700.75
			1 Feb	Balance b/d	4,427.93

Amtosh plc (account no 102)

Dr					Cr
20-2		£	20-2		£
12 Jan	Purchases returns	750.18	1 Jan	Balance b/d	2,750.83
31 Jan	Balance c/d	15,000.65	3 Jan	Purchases	7,500.00
			19 Jan	Purchases	5,500.00
		15,750.83			15,750.83
			1 Feb	Balance b/d	15,000.65

GENERAL LEDGER

Sales Account

Dr 20-2		£	20-2		Cr £
			31 Jan	Sales journal	22,649.85

Purchases Account

Dr 20-2		£	20-2		Cr £
31 Jan	Purchases journal	17,650.00			

Sales Returns Account

Dr 20-2		£	20-2		Cr £
31 Jan	Sales returns journal	1,444.54			

Purchases Returns Account

Dr 20-2		£	20-2		Cr £
			31 Jan	Purchases returns journal	2,023.00

6.6 (a) Credit note

(b) 8 x £50 = £400 – £80 (trade discount) = £320

(c) Sales returns journal
Amount £320

6.7 **C**

6.8

Transaction	Source document	Book of prime entry
(a) Goods purchased on credit from a supplier	Purchase invoice	Purchases journal
(b) Goods sold on credit to a customer	Sales invoice	Sales journal
(c) Faulty goods returned to a supplier	Credit note received	Purchases returns (returns outwards) journal
(d) Payment made by cheque to a supplier	Cheque counterfoil	Cash book
(e) Purchase on credit of a new machine for use in the factory	Purchase invoice	General journal, or analysed purchases journal
(f) Faulty goods returned by a customer	Credit note issued	Sales returns (returns inwards) journal
(g) Bank transfer received from a customer	Bank statement	Cash book

6.10

	Source document	Book of prime entry	Account to be debited	Account to be credited
(a)	invoice received	purchases journal	purchases	A Cotton
(b)	invoice issued	sales journal	D Law	sales
(c)	paying in slip counterfoil	cash book	bank	sales
(d)	credit note received	purchases returns journal	A Cotton	purchases returns
(e)	bank statement	cash book	gas	bank
(f)	credit note issued	sales returns journal	sales returns	D Law

6.11 **D**

6.12 **A**

7.1 *Main responsibilities of the cashier*

- Recording receipts and payments by cheque, by bank transfer and in cash
- Issuing receipts for cash (and sometimes cheques) received
- Making authorised cash payments (except for low-value expenses payments)
- Preparing cheques and bank transfer payments for signature and/or authorisation
- Paying cash and cheques received into the bank
- Controlling the firm's cash, either in a cash till or cash box
- Ensuring that all transactions passing through the cash book are supported by documentary evidence
- Checking the accuracy of the cash and bank balances at regular intervals
- Liaising with the other accounts staff

Qualities of a cashier

- Accuracy – in writing up the cash book, in cash handling, and in ensuring that payments are made only against correct documents and appropriate authorisation
- Security – of cash and cheque books, and correct authorisation of payments
- Confidentiality – that all cash/bank transactions, including cash and bank balances, are kept confidential

7.2 (a)

Dr **Cash Book** Cr

Date	Details	Ref	Discount allowed	Cash	Bank	Date	Details	Ref	Discount received	Cash	Bank
20-2			£	£	£	20-2			£	£	£
1 Jun	Balance b/d			280		1 Jun	Balance b/d				2,240
3 Jun	G Wheaton		5		195	8 Jun	F Lloyd		10		390
5 Jun	T Francis		2	53		10 Jun	Wages			165	
16 Jun	Bank	C		200		12 Jun	A Morris		3	97	
18 Jun	H Watson		30		640	16 Jun	Cash	C			200
28 Jun	M Perry		6		234	20 Jun	R Marks				78
30 Jun	K Willis			45		24 Jun	D Farr		2		65
30 Jun	Balance c/d				1,904	26 Jun	Telephone			105	
						30 Jun	Balance c/d			211	
			43	578	2,973				15	578	2,973
1 Jul	Balance b/d			211		1 Jul	Balance b/d				1,904

(b)

Dr **Discount Allowed Account** Cr

20-2		£	20-2		£
30 Jun	Cash book	43			

Dr **Discount Received Account** Cr

20-2		£	20-2		£
			30 Jun	Cash book	15

7.5 (a)

Dr **Andrew Lim Cash Book** Cr

Date	Details	Discount allowed	Cash	Bank	Date	Details	Discount received	Cash	Bank
20-3		£	£	£	20-3		£	£	£
1 Apr	Balance b/d		100.00		1 Apr	Balance b/d			633.86
4 Apr	Southern Stores Ltd			476.82	2 Apr	A-Z Ltd	5.00		195.00
6 Apr	O Parry Ltd	3.45		223.89	3 Apr	Teme Traders			256.22
7 Apr	Frobisher & Co			361.28	4 Apr	Akhtar Ltd	4.25		146.13
7 Apr	Cash sales		968.27		6 Apr	Wyvern Wares Ltd			108.25
7 Apr	Cash			817.453	7 Apr	City Council			176.50
					7 Apr	Bank charges			33.47
					7 Apr	Bank interest			62.35
					7 Apr	Wages		124.50	
					7 Apr	Office stationery		26.32	
					7 Apr	Bank		817.45	
					7 Apr	Balances c/d		100.00	167.66
		3.45	1,068.27	1,879.44			9.25	1,068.27	1,879.44
8 Apr	Balances b/d		100.00	167.66					

7.7

	Source document	Book of prime entry	Ledger account to be debited	Ledger account to be credited
Sold goods on credit to a customer	Sales invoice	Sales journal	Trade receivables/Sales ledger control account*	Sales
Faulty goods returned to the supplier	Purchases credit note	Purchases returns journal	Trade payables/ Purchases ledger control account*	Purchases returns
Cash sales paid into the bank	Bank paying-in slip counterfoil	Cash book	Bank	Sales
Standing order payment for rent	Bank statement	Cash book	Rent paid	Bank
Purchase of office stationery paid for by bank transfer	Cheque counterfoil/ invoice	Cash book	Stationery	Bank

* see Chapter 11

7.9 C

7.10 A

CHAPTER 8 Bank reconciliation statements

8.1 C

8.2 A

8.3

TOM REID
BANK RECONCILIATION STATEMENT AS AT 31 DECEMBER 20-7

	£
Balance at bank as per cash book	200
Add: unpresented cheque	
B Kay cheque no. 345126	20
	220
Less: amount not yet credited	
J Hill	13
Balance at bank as per bank statement	207

8.6 (a) - (c)

CASH BOOK

Date	Details	Bank	Date	Cheque no	Details	Bank
20-4		£	20-4			£
1 May	Balance b/f	3,652	4 May	451762	Smith and Company	751
26 May	J Ackland	832	4 May	451763	Bryant Limited	268
28 May	Stamp Limited	1,119	7 May	451764	Curtis Cars	1,895
14 May	*Perran Taxis*	*2,596*	7 May	451765	Parts Supplies	1,045
			18 May		*Wyvern Council*	*198*
			20 May		*A1 Insurance*	*1,005*
			25 May		*Okaro and Company*	*254*
			25 May		*Bank charges*	*20*
			31 May		*Balance c/d*	*2,763*
		8,199				*8,199*
1 Jun	*Balance b/d*	*2,763*				

(d)

MILESTONE MOTORS
BANK RECONCILIATION STATEMENT AS AT 31 MAY 20-4

	£	£
Balance at bank as per cash book		2,763
Add: unpresented cheque no 451764		1,895
		4,658
Less: amounts not yet credited		
J Ackland	832	
Stamp Limited	1,119	
		1,951
Balance at bank as per bank statement		2,707

8.7 (a)

Cash Book

Dr					Cr
Date	Details	£	Date	Details	£
1 Apr	Balance b/d	2,620	2 Apr	Durning Supplies	1,320
14	Sales banked	2,410	16	Central Cement Co	850
16	Sales banked	1,240	28	Abbott & Co	390
30	Sales banked	1,030	29	Wages	1,280
30	*L Dove (Bacs)*	*455*	*130*	*Wyvern Finance*	*245*
			30	*Bank charges*	*45*
			30	*Aydee Traders (dishonoured cheque)*	*340*
			31	*Balance c/d*	*3,285*
		7,755			*7,755*
1 May	*Balance b/d*	*3,285*			

(b)

BLENHEIM BUILDERS
BANK RECONCILIATION STATEMENT AS AT 30 APRIL 20-3

	£	£
Balance at bank as per cash book		3,285
Add: unpresented cheques		
Abbott & Co	390	
Wages	1,280	
		1,670
		4,955
Less: amount not yet credited		
Sales banked		1,030
Balance at bank as per bank statement		3,925

(c) A dishonoured cheque is one that has been refused payment by the payer's bank, often due to insufficient funds in the payer's bank account.

9.1

MATTHEW LLOYD
INCOME STATEMENT
FOR THE YEAR ENDED 31 DECEMBER 20-8

	£	£
Revenue		125,890
Opening inventory	–	
Purchases	94,350	
Less Closing inventory	5,950	
Cost of sales		88,400
Gross profit		37,490
Less expenses:		
Office rent	4,850	
Heating and lighting	2,120	
Wages and salaries	10,350	
		17,320
Profit for the year		20,170

STATEMENT OF FINANCIAL POSITION AS AT 31 DECEMBER 20-8

	£	£	£
Non-current Assets			
Office equipment			8,500
Vehicles			10,750
			19,250
Current Assets			
Inventory		5,950	
Trade receivables		3,950	
Bank		4,225	
Cash		95	
		14,220	
Less Current Liabilities			
Trade payables		1,750	
Net Current Assets or Working Capital			12,470
NET ASSETS			31,720
FINANCED BY			
Capital			
Opening capital			20,000
Add Profit for the year			20,170
			40,170
Less Drawings			8,450
			31,720

9.3

Business A:	gross profit £8,000, profit for the year £4,000
Business B:	gross profit £17,000, expenses £7,000
Business C:	revenue £36,500, profit for the year £6,750
Business D:	purchases £25,500, expenses £9,800
Business E:	opening inventory £8,350, loss for the year £1,700
Business F:	closing inventory £4,600, expenses £15,000

9.4

JOHN ADAMS
INCOME STATEMENT
FOR THE YEAR ENDED 31 DECEMBER 20-7

	£	£
Revenue		259,688
Opening inventory	14,350	
Purchases	114,472	
	128,822	
Less Closing inventory	16,280	
Cost of sales		112,542
Gross profit		147,146
Less expenses:		
Office rent	13,718	
Heating and lighting	12,540	
Wages and salaries	42,614	
Vehicle expenses	5,817	
Advertising	6,341	
		81,030
Profit for the year		66,116

STATEMENT OF FINANCIAL POSITION AS AT 31 DECEMBER 20-7

	£	£
Non-current Assets		
Property		75,000
Office equipment		33,000
Vehicles		21,500
		129,500
Current Assets		
Inventory	16,280	
Trade receivables	23,854	
Bank	1,235	
Cash	125	
	41,494	
Less Current Liabilities		
Trade payables	17,281	
Net Current Assets or Working Capital		24,213
		153,713
Less Non-current Liabilities		
Loan from bank		35,000
NET ASSETS		118,713
FINANCED BY		
Capital		
Opening capital		62,500
Add Profit for the year		66,116
		128,616
Less Drawings		9,903
		118,713

9.6

GINA CAMPBELL
INCOME STATEMENT
FOR THE YEAR ENDED 31 DECEMBER 20-4

	£	£	£
Revenue (Sales)			125,642
Less Sales returns			1,347
Net revenue			124,295
Opening inventory		8,220	
Add Purchases	55,261		
Less Purchases returns	2,105		
		53,156	
Add Carriage inwards		622	
		61,998	
Less Closing inventory		9,156	
Cost of sales			52,842
Gross profit			71,453
Less expenses:			
Carriage outwards		1,233	
Wages		40,112	
Other expenses		10,397	
			51,742
Profit for the year			19,711

9.7 **B**

10.1

Date	Details	Reference	Dr	Cr
20-8			£	£
1 May	Vehicle	GL	6,500	
	Fixtures and fittings	GL	2,800	
	Inventory	GL	4,100	
	Cash	GL	150	
	Loan from husband	GL		5,000
	Capital	GL		8,550
			13,550	13,550
	Assets and liabilities at the start of business			

10.3

	book of prime entry	debit	credit
(a)	purchases journal	purchases account	Temeside Traders
(b)	sales journal	Malvern Models	sales account
(c)	general journal	office equipment account	A-Z Computers Ltd
(d)	sales returns journal	sales returns account	Johnson Bros
(e)	cash book	bank account	Melanie Fisher
(f)	cash book	cash account	sales account
(g)	cash book	drawings account	cash account
(h)	cash book	Stationery Supplies Ltd	bank account
(i)	general journal	irrecoverable debts written off account	J Bowen
(j)	purchases returns journal	I Johnson	purchases returns account

10.5

	Date	Details	Reference	Dr	Cr
				£	£
(a)		Office expenses	GL	85	
		Suspense	GL		85
		Omission of entry in office expenses account			
(b)		Suspense	GL	78	
		Photocopying	GL		78
		Photocopying	GL	87	
		Suspense	GL		87
				165	165
		Payment for photocopying £87 entered in photocopying account as £78			
(c)		Suspense	GL	100	
		Sales returns	GL		100
		Overcast on ...(date)... now corrected			
(d)		Commission income	GL	25	
		Suspense	GL		25
		Commission income entered twice in commission income account			

Suspense Account

Dr			Cr		
20-8		£	20-8		£
30 Sep	Trial balance difference	19	(a)	Office expenses	85
(b)	Photocopying	78	(b)	Photocopying	87
(c)	Sales returns	100	(d)	Commission income	25
		197			197

10.6 **C**

10.7 **C**

10.8 **B**

10.9 **A**

10.11 (a)

Suspense Account

Dr Date	Details	£	Date	Details	Cr £
20-3			20-3		
30 Jun	Trial balance difference	215	30 Jun	Rent paid	650
30 Jun	Purchases	250	30 Jun	Wages	580
30 Jun	Wages	850	30 Jun	Discount allowed	85
		1,315			1,315

(b)

- An error which affects both the debit and credit side of the trial balance by the same amount will not be revealed by the trial balance.
- Examples of errors not revealed by the trial balance (note: the question asks for one only):
  - error of omission
  - mispost/error of commission
  - error of original entry (or transcription)
  - reversal of entries
  - error of principle
  - compensating error

CHAPTER 11 Control accounts

11.1

Sales Ledger Control Account

Dr 20-1		£	20-1		Cr £
1 Jun	Balances b/d	17,491	30 Jun	Sales returns	1,045
30 Jun	Credit sales	42,591	30 Jun	Payments received	39,024
			30 Jun	Cash discount allowed	593
			30 Jun	Irrecoverable debts written off	296
			30 Jun	Balances c/d	19,124
		60,082			60,082
1 Jul	Balances b/d	19,124			

11.2

Purchases Ledger Control Account

Dr 20-2		£	20-2		Cr £
30 Apr	Purchases returns	653	1 Apr	Balances b/d	14,275
30 Apr	Payments made to trade payables	31,074	30 Apr	Credit purchases	36,592
30 Apr	Cash discount received	1,048			
30 Apr	Contra: sales ledger	597			
30 Apr	Balances c/d	17,495			
		50,867			50,867
			1 May	Balances b/d	17,495

11.4 C

11.5

Sales Ledger Control Account

Dr Date	Details	£	Date	Details	Cr £
20-5			20-5		
1 Jun	Balance b/d	180,824	30 Jun	Bank	96,214
30 Jun	Sales	118,600	30 Jun	Discount allowed	300
			30 Jun	Sales returns	650
			30 Jun	Irrecoverable debt	350
			30 Jun	Balance c/d	201,910
		299,424			299,424
1 Jul	Balance b/d	201,910			

11.6 (a) Benefits include:

- prevention of fraud
- making the preparation of financial statements easier
- location of errors within sales ledger and purchases ledger
- instant information of trade receivables' or trade payables' totals

(b)

Sales Ledger Control Account

Dr 20-6		£	20-6		Cr £
30 Sep	Balance b/d	15,540	30 Sep	Discount allowed	16
30 Sep	Sales	220	30 Sep	Adjustment to balance	90
30 Sep	Purchases returns	150	30 Sep	Balance c/d	15,804
		15,910			15,910
1 Oct	Balance b/d	15,804			

12.3 (a)

Sales Account

Dr					Cr
20-4		£	20-4		£
31 Dec	Jamal Stores	300	10 Dec	Jamal Stores	1,500
31 Dec	Income statement	1,200			
		1,500			1,500
20-5			20-5		
			1 Jan	Jamal Stores	300

Trade receivable: Jamal Stores

Dr					Cr
20-4		£	20-4		£
10 Dec	Sales	1,500	22 Dec	Bank	1,200
			31 Dec	Sales	300
		1,500			1,500
20-5			20-5		
1 Jan	Sales	300			

Bank

Dr					Cr
20-4		£	20-4		£
22 Dec	Jamal Stores	1,200			

(b)

- The cost price of the unsold goods will be included in the closing inventory used in Severn Services' income statement and statement of financial position.
- The reason for this treatment is because legal title to the unsold goods remains with the supplier who has not transferred the 'risks and rewards of ownership' to Jamal Stores.

12.4

	Amount to be subtracted from draft profit £	Amount to be added to draft profit £
Business rates	2,510	
Rent of premises	4,650	

Workings:

Business rates: £2,250 + £110 + £150

Rent: £5,300 – £250 – £400

12.5 (a)

Rent and Business Rates Account

Dr					Cr
20-8		£	20-8		£
31 Dec	Balance b/d	10,862	31 Dec	Income statement	10,612
			31 Dec	Balance c/d	250
		10,862			10,862
20-9			20-9		
1 Jan	Balance b/d	250			

Electricity Account

Dr					Cr
20-8		£	20-8		£
31 Dec	Balance b/d	2,054	31 Dec	Income statement	2,164
31 Dec	Balance c/d	110			
		2,164			2,164
20-9			20-9		
			1 Jan	Balance b/d	110

Salaries Account

Dr					Cr
20-8		£	20-8		£
31 Dec	Balance b/d	55,891	31 Dec	Income statement	56,256
31 Dec	Balance c/d	365			
		56,256			56,256
20-9			20-9		
			1 Jan	Balance b/d	365

(b)

DON SMITH

INCOME STATEMENT FOR THE YEAR ENDED 31 DECEMBER 20-8

	£	£
Revenue		257,258
Opening inventory (1 January 20-8)	18,471	
Purchases	138,960	
	157,431	
Less Closing inventory (31 December 20-8)	14,075	
Cost of sales		143,356
Gross profit		113,902
Add Discount received		591
		114,493
Less expenses:		
Rent and business rates	10,612	
Electricity	2,164	
Telephone	1,695	
Salaries	56,256	
Vehicle expenses	10,855	
Discount allowed	478	
		82,060
Profit for the year		32,433

STATEMENT OF FINANCIAL POSITION AS AT 31 DECEMBER 20-8

	£	£	£
Non-current Assets			
Vehicles			22,250
Office equipment			7,500
			29,750
Current Assets			
Inventory		14,075	
Trade receivables		24,325	
Other receivables		250	
		38,650	
Less Current Liabilities			
Trade payables	19,684		
Bank overdraft	1,083		
Other payables	475	21,242	
Net Current Assets or Working Capital			17,408
NET ASSETS			47,158
FINANCED BY			
Capital			
Opening capital			30,000
Add Profit for the year			32,433
			62,433
Less Drawings			15,275
			47,158

12.6 A letter incorporating the following points:

- Depreciation is a measure of the amount of the fall in value of non-current assets over a time period.
- It is a systematic method of charging against profits over the life of an asset.
- When the asset is sold, adjustments can be made for any inaccuracies in the estimates of depreciation.
- A recognised system which fits with the accounting concepts (see Chapter 14) of going concern, accruals, consistency and prudence.

12.7 (a)

	year ended 30 June 20-2	year ended 30 June 20-3
	£	£
Profit before depreciation	18,700	33,100
Depreciation of non-current assets	5,000	5,000
Profit after depreciation	13,700	28,100

(b)

	as at 30 June 20-2	as at 30 June 20-3
	£	£
Non-current assets at cost	50,000	50,000
Less provision for depreciation to date	5,000	10,000
Net book value (carrying amount)	45,000	40,000

12.9 (a)

Dr **Irrecoverable Debts Written Off Account** Cr

20-8		£	20-8		£
31 Dec	P Ross	55	31 Dec	Income statement	210
31 Dec	J Ball	105			
31 Dec	L Jones	50			
		210			210

12.9 (b)

- *Income statement (expenses)*
  irrecoverable debts written off £210
  Explanation: profit for the year is reduced by £210
- *Statement of financial position*
  trade receivables £20,000
  workings: £20,210 – £210 irrecoverable debts = £20,000 net trade receivables
  Explanation: current assets are reduced by £210

12.11 **D**

CHAPTER 13 Business organisations and financing

13.1 Advantages of a sole trader business:

- the owner has independence
- all profits belong to the owner
- personal service and supervision are available at all times
- the business is easy to establish legally

Disadvantages of a sole trader business:

- the owner has unlimited liability
- all losses are the owner's responsibility
- expansion is limited
- there may be limited access to finance
- the owner usually has to work long hours, with few holidays
- there may be limited expertise within the business
- if the owner becomes ill the business will be affected

Possible future developments:

- form a partnership
- form a private limited company

13.4

	Ron	Sue	Tom
Ratio of 1 : 1 : 1	£50,000	£50,000	£50,000
Ratio of 2 : 1 : 1	£75,000	£37,500	£37,500
Ratio of 1 : 2 : 2	£30,000	£60,000	£60,000

13.5 (a) The shareholders

(b) The directors

(c) If the company becomes insolvent (goes 'bust') the most the shareholders can lose is the amount of their investment, together with any money unpaid on their shares (unpaid instalments on new share issues, for example).

13.10 (a) **Funding of increased net current assets**

Bank overdraft:

- an ideal financing method for funding the net current assets (working capital) requirements of an expanding business
- if whole £25,000 overdraft used for full twelve months, interest will be £2,000 (£25,000 x 8%)
- the actual interest charge may well be lower as it is calculated on a daily basis on the actual amount overdrawn
- security will be required by the bank to safeguard the borrowing
- interest rates can be higher than bank loan rates
- an overdraft is repayable on demand if the bank wants the borrowing repaid

Bank short-term loan:

- a twelve-month loan can be arranged to provide net current asset (working capital) finance
- usually loan repayments are made on a monthly basis, but it may be possible to arrange a 'repayment holiday' to delay early repayments
- if whole £25,000 loan used for full twelve months, interest would be £1,500 (£25,000 x 6%)
- security will be required by the bank to safeguard the borrowing

Other considerations:

- will £25,000 be sufficient?
- the budgeted financial statements could prove to be incorrect
- arrangement fees will be charged by the bank for both forms of borrowing
- on the face of it, the bank short-term loan is cheaper than an overdraft but will depend on how much of the overdraft facility is used
- can net current assets (working capital) be managed more efficiently (eg reduced inventory and trade receivables, increased trade payables) to reduce the financing requirement?
- will the planned expansion continue into future years?

(b) **Funding the purchase of new premises**

- the company will save rental payments of £24,000 per year (£2,000 x 12 months)
- the finance director proposes borrowing £350,000, being 50% of the cost, although most lenders would be prepared to finance up to 70%
- the interest cost per year will be £14,000, giving a net saving of £10,000 over rental costs
- the 10-year term suggested by the finance director is very reasonable as the term could be up to 25 years
- an arrangement fee will be charged by the lender
- security will be required by the lender, usually the property being financed
- repayments on the commercial mortgage – capital and interest – will have to be made for ten years, usually on a monthly basis (which makes for easy budgeting)
- the other half of the cost of the new premises needs to be financed, possibly through a share issue or directors' loans. Do the three directors have private funds for this, or are there new shareholders that will contribute?
- if new shares are issued to other parties, the directors' holdings will be diluted as they will no longer own the whole company

- are there likely to be sufficient future profits to pay dividends?
- the benefit of using shares to fund part of the purchase cost is that repayments do not need to be made to shareholders
- the issue of debentures – loan notes – is another source of finance, subject to finding a lender; the disadvantage of debentures, from the company's viewpoint, is that interest must always be paid on time even when losses are made

CHAPTER 14 Accounting concepts and inventory valuation

14.3 **D**

14.4 **C**

14.5 (a) Prudence concept: inventory valuation should be at lower of cost and net realisable value, ie £10,000 in this case.

(b) Business entity concept: car is an asset of John's firm, not a personal asset (in any case personal assets, for sole traders and partnerships, might well be used to repay debts of firm).

(c) Prudence concept: the irrecoverable debt should be written off in the income statement (so reducing profit), and the statement of financial position figure for trade receivables should be £27,500 (which is closer to the amount he can expect to receive from trade receivables).

(d) Accruals concept: expenses and income must be matched, therefore it must go through the old year's financial statements.

(e) Going concern concept: presumes that business will continue to trade in the foreseeable future: alternative is 'gone concern' and assets may have very different values.

14.6 **B**

14.7 (a) £220 + £750 + £290 + £35,500 = £36,760

Note: replacement cost is not applicable here

(b) Prudence

(c) Net realisable value is the actual or estimated selling price of the goods (less any further costs such as repairs and replacement parts, selling and distribution).

CHAPTER 15 Further aspects of financial statements

15.1 **C**

15.2 (a)
- £400 is to be included as income, which is added to gross profit in the income statement account for the year ended 31 December 20-8.
- £400 will be included as income, which will be added to gross profit in the income statement for the year ended 31 December 20-9.
- £400 is to be shown as a prepayment of income in the current liabilities (other payables) section of the statement of financial position as at 31 December 20-8.

(b) The accounting concept to be applied is accruals (or matching).

15.4

Dr	**Bank Account**		Cr
	£		£
Recovery of irrecoverable debts	50		

Dr	**Recovery of Irrecoverable Debts**		Cr
	£		£
		Bank	50

15.6 (a) *20-1 increasing the provision*
- new provision is £8,000 x 5% = £400
- existing provision is £300
- therefore increase in provision is £100

20-2 decreasing the provision
- new provision is £7,000 x 5% = £350
- existing provision is £400
- therefore decrease in provision is £50

(b) *20-1 Extracts from financial statements produced for year ended 30 June:*
- income statement: expense of £100
- statement of financial position: trade receivables £8,000 – £400 = £7,600

20-2 Extracts from financial statements produced for year ended 30 June:
- income statement: income of £50
- statement of financial position: trade receivables £7,000 – £350 = £6,650

15.8 (a) *profit for the year*

	£
Increase in provision for doubtful debts	(50)
Irrecoverable debts written off	(235)
Recovery of irrecoverable debts	115
Change in profit	(170)

Profit is now £21,060 – £170 = £20,890

(b) *net current assets (working capital)*

	£
Trade receivables decrease £50 + £235	(285)
Bank increase	115
Decrease in net current assets	(170)

(c) *bank balance*

Bank balance increases by £115 from the recovery of irrecoverable debts

15.9 **B**

15.11 (a)

Provision for Depreciation Account – Car

Dr		£			Cr £
20-1			20-1		
31 Dec	Balance c/d	3,000	31 Dec	Income statement	3,000
20-2			20-2		
31 Dec	Balance c/d	5,250	1 Jan	Balance b/d	3,000
			31 Dec	Income statement	2,250
		5,250			5,250
20-3			20-3		
31 Dec	Disposals	6,937	1 Jan	Balance b/d	5,250
			31 Dec	Income statement	1,687
		6,937			6,937

(b) **STATEMENT OF FINANCIAL POSITION AS AT 31 DECEMBER 20-1**

	£	£	£
Non-current Assets	Cost	Prov for dep'n	Net book value
Car	12,000	3,000	9,000

STATEMENT OF FINANCIAL POSITION AS AT 31 DECEMBER 20-2

	£	£	£
Non-current Assets	Cost	Prov for dep'n	Net book value
Car	12,000	5,250	6,750

(c) **Disposals Account – Car**

Dr		£			Cr £
20-3			20-3		
31 Dec	Car	12,000	31 Dec	Provision for depreciation	6,937
31 Dec	Income statement (profit on sale)	437	31 Dec	Bank	5,500
		12,437			12,437

15.14

GENERAL LEDGER

Advertising Expenses Account

Dr 20-5			£	20-5			Cr £
Jan	1	Balance b/d	150	Dec	31	Income statement	5,228
Jan-Dec		Bank	4,528				
Dec	31	Balance c/d	550				
			5,228				5,228
20-6				20-6			
				Jan	1	Balance b/d	550

Commission Income Account

Dr 20-5			£	20-5			Cr £
Dec	31	Income statement	1,805	Jan	1	Balance b/d	55
				Jan-Dec		Bank	1,665
				Dec	31	Balance c/d	85
			1,805				1,805
20-6				20-6			
Jan	1	Balance b/d	85				

Dr **Inventory Account** Cr

20-5			£	20-5			£
Jan	1	Balance b/d	23,240	Dec	31	Income statement	23,240
Dec	31	Income statement	25,450	Dec	31	Balance c/d	25,450
			48,690				48,690
20-6				20-6			
Jan	1	Balance b/d	25,450				

Dr **Provision for Depreciation (Computers) Account** Cr

20-5			£	20-5			£
Dec	31	Balance c/d	6,120	Jan	1	Balance b/d	3,600
				Dec	31	Income statement W1	2,520
			6,120				6,120
20-6				20-6			
				Jan	1	Balance b/d	6,120

Dr **Provision for Doubtful Debts Account** Cr

20-5			£	20-5			£
Dec	31	Balance c/d	280	Jan	1	Balance b/d	200
				Dec	31	Income statement W2	80
			280				280
20-6				20-6			
				Jan	1	Balance b/d	280

W1 Provision for depreciation: 30% x (£12,000 – £3,600) = £2,520
W2 Provision for doubtful debts: £14,000 x 2% = £280 – £200 = £80 increase

16.2

JOHN BARCLAY

INCOME STATEMENT FOR THE YEAR ENDED 30 JUNE 20-3

	£	£	£
Revenue			864,321
Less Sales returns			2,746
Net revenue			861,575
Opening inventory		63,084	
Purchases (less £250 goods for own use)	599,878		
Less Purchase returns	3,894		
		595,984	
		659,068	
Less Closing inventory		66,941	
Cost of sales			592,127
Gross profit			269,448
Add income:			
Discount received			4,951
Commission income			1,395
Rent income			3,150
			278,944
Less expenses:			
Office expenses		33,601	
Salaries		122,611	
Vehicle expenses		38,144	
Discount allowed		3,187	
			197,543
Profit for the year			81,401

STATEMENT OF FINANCIAL POSITION AS AT 30 JUNE 20-3

	£	£	£
Non-current Assets			
Property			100,000
Vehicles			83,500
Office equipment			23,250
			206,750
Current Assets			
Inventory		66,941	
Trade receivables		74,328	
Other receivable		*496	
Bank		1,197	
		142,962	
Less Current Liabilities			
Trade payables	58,821		
Other payables	**1,450		
		60,271	
Net Current Assets or Working Capital			82,691
			289,441
Less Non-current Liabilities			
Bank loan			75,000
NET ASSETS			214,441
FINANCED BY			
Capital			
Opening capital			155,000
Add Profit for the year			81,401
			236,401
Less Drawings (plus £250 goods for own use)			21,960
			214,441

*Other receivables	£
prepayment of expenses	346
accrual of income	150
	496

**Other payables	£
accrual of expenses	1,250
prepayment of income	200
	1,450

16.3

SOUTHTOWN SUPPLIES

INCOME STATEMENT FOR THE YEAR ENDED 31 DECEMBER 20-4

	£	£	£
Revenue			420,000
Less Sales returns			6,000
Net revenue			414,000
Opening inventory		70,000	
Purchases	280,000		
Less Purchases returns	4,500		
		275,500	
		345,500	
Less Closing inventory		60,000	
Cost of sales			285,500
Gross profit			128,500
Add income:			
Discount received			750
Rent income			2,200
Commission income			1,450
			132,900
Less expenses:			
Discounts allowed		500	
Electricity		14,100	
Salaries		35,200	
Post and packing		1,400	
			51,200
Profit for the year			81,700

STATEMENT OF FINANCIAL POSITION AS AT 31 DECEMBER 20-4

	£	£	£
Non-current Assets			
Property			120,000
Fixtures and fittings			45,000
			165,000
Current Assets			
Inventory		60,000	
Trade receivables		55,000	
Other receivables		*600	
Bank		5,000	
		120,600	
Less Current Liabilities			
Trade payables	49,250		
Other payables	**650		
		49,900	
Net Current Assets or Working Capital			70,700
NET ASSETS			235,700
FINANCED BY			
Capital			
Opening capital			195,000
Add Profit for the year			81,700
			276,700
Less Drawings			41,000
			235,700

*Other receivables	£
prepayment of salaries	400
accrual of income	200
	600

**Other payables	£
accrual of expenses	350
prepayment of income	300
	650

16.5

JAMES JENKINS

INCOME STATEMENT FOR THE YEAR ENDED 30 JUNE 20-9

	£	£	£
Revenue			168,432
Less Sales returns			975
Net revenue			167,457
Opening inventory		9,427	
Purchases	105,240		
Less Purchases returns	1,237		
		104,003	
		113,430	
Less Closing inventory		11,517	
Cost of sales			101,913
Gross profit			65,544
Add income:			
Commission income			2,510
Discount received			243
Recovery of irrecoverable debts			210
Reduction in provision for doubtful debts			54
			68,561
Less expenses:			
Discount allowed		127	
Wages and salaries		30,841	
Vehicle expenses		1,076	
Rent and business rates		8,521	
Heating and lighting		1,840	
Telephone		355	
General expenses		1,752	
Irrecoverable debts		85	
Provision for depreciation:			
vehicle		1,125	
shop fittings		600	
			46,322
Profit for the year			22,239

STATEMENT OF FINANCIAL POSITION AS AT 30 JUNE 20-9

	£	£	£
Non-current Assets	Cost	Depreciation	Net book value
Vehicle	8,000	4,625	3,375
Shop fittings	6,000	3,000	3,000
	14,000	7,625	6,375
Current Assets			
Inventory		11,517	
Trade receivables	3,840		
Less Provision for doubtful debts	96		
		3,744	
Other receivables		435	
Bank		21,419	
Cash		155	
		37,270	
Less Current Liabilities			
Trade payables	4,226		
Other payables	55		
		4,281	
Net Current Assets or Working Capital			32,989
NET ASSETS			39,364
FINANCED BY			
Capital			
Opening capital			36,175
Add Profit for the year			22,239
			58,414
Less Drawings			19,050
			39,364

Workings

- Provision for doubtful debts: £3,840 trade receivables x 2.5% provision = £96, which is deducted from £150 existing provision = £54 reduction in provision for doubtful debts
- Provision for depreciation of shop fittings: £6,000 x 10% = £600
- Provision for depreciation of vehicle: £8,000 – £3,500 depreciation to date = £4,500 x 25% = £1,125
- Other receivables: accrual of commission income £160 + prepayment of rent £275 = £435

16.6

LIZ BLACKBURN
INCOME STATEMENT FOR THE YEAR ENDED 31 DECEMBER 2006

	£	£
Revenue:		
Income from clients		113,490
Add income:		
Reduction in provision for doubtful debts		100
Discount received		388
		113,978
Less expenses:		
Wages	62,400	
Rent and business rates	8,910	
General expenses	9,477	
Discount allowed	307	
Provision for depreciation: equipment	1,200	
		82,294
Profit for the year		31,684

Workings:

- Provision for doubtful debts: £10,000 trade receivables x 3% provision = £300, which is deducted from £400 existing provision = £100 reduction in provision for doubtful debts
- Rent and business rates: £8,430 – £120 prepayment + £600 accrual = £8,910
- Provision for depreciation: £12,000 x 10% = £1,200

17.1 A

17.4

CHAPELPORTH LIMITED
INCOME STATEMENT (EXTRACT) FOR THE YEAR ENDED 30 JUNE 20-8

	£
Profit for the year from operations	135,000
Finance costs	(12,500)
Profit for the year before tax	122,500
Tax	(48,000)
Profit for the year after tax	74,500

STATEMENT OF CHANGES IN EQUITY (EXTRACT)
FOR THE YEAR ENDED 30 JUNE 20-8

	Issued share capital £	Share premium £	Retained earnings £	Total £
Balance at start			185,000	185,000
Profit for the year			74,500	74,500
Dividends paid			(48,500)	(48,500)
Balance at end			211,000	211,000

17.6

JOBSEEKERS LIMITED
STATEMENT OF CHANGES IN EQUITY FOR THE YEAR ENDED 31 DECEMBER 20-6

	Issued share capital £	Share premium £	Retained earnings £	Total £
Balance at start	100,000		8,400	108,400
Profit for the year			68,200	68,200
Dividends paid			(10,000)	(10,000)
Balance at end	100,000		66,600	166,600

STATEMENT OF FINANCIAL POSITION AS AT 31 DECEMBER 20-6

	£	£	£
Non-current Assets	Cost	Depreciation	Carrying amount
Intangible			
Goodwill	20,000	6,000	14,000
Property, plant and equipment			
Property	175,000	10,500	164,500
Office equipment	25,000	5,000	20,000
	220,000	21,500	198,500
Current Assets			
Inventory			10,750
Trade and other receivables			42,500
Cash and cash equivalents			1,950
			55,200
Less Current Liabilities			
Trade and other payables			(17,250)
Tax liabilities			(14,850)
			(32,100)
Net Current Assets or Working Capital			23,100
Less Non-current Liabilities			
Bank loan			(55,000)
NET ASSETS			166,600
EQUITY			
Issued Share Capital			
100,000 ordinary shares of £1 each fully paid			100,000
Revenue Reserve			
Retained earnings			66,600
TOTAL EQUITY			166,600

17.8

Note	Profit for the year	Retained earnings	Total equity	Current assets	Current liabilities
(a)	decrease £15,000	decrease £15,000	decrease £15,000	no change	increase £15,000
(b)	increase £75,000*	increase £75,000	increase £75,000	no change	no change
(c)	decrease £5,000	decrease £5,000	decrease £5,000	decrease £5,000	no change
(d)	decrease £28,000	decrease £28,000	decrease £28,000	no change	increase £28,000

*£1,500,000 x 25% = £375,000; £1,500,000 x 20% = £300,000; reduction in depreciation = £75,000

17.9 (a)

GLINKA LTD
INCOME STATEMENT FOR THE YEAR ENDED 30 JUNE 20-2

	£	£
Gross profit		155,100
Expenses:		
Operating expenses	90,755	
Depreciation	[1] 28,125	
		(118,880)
Profit for the year from operations		36,220
Finance costs		[2] (1,500)
Profit for the year before tax		34,720
Tax		[3] (6,944)
Profit for the year after tax		27,776

1 Depreciation: (£150,000 – £37,500) x 25%
2 Finance costs: £30,000 x 5%
3 Tax: £34,720 x 20%

(b)

GLINKA LTD
STATEMENT OF CHANGES IN EQUITY FOR THE YEAR ENDED 30 JUNE 20-2

	Share capital £	Share premium £	Retained earnings £	Total £
Balances at start	50,000	5,000	52,847	107,847
Profit for the year			27,776	27,776
Dividends paid			(20,000)	(20,000)
Issue of shares	20,000	12,000		32,000
Balances at end	70,000	17,000	60,623	147,623

(c)

GLINKA LTD
STATEMENT OF FINANCIAL POSITION AS AT 30 JUNE 20-2

	£ Cost	£ Depreciation	£ Carrying amount
Non-current Assets			
Non-current assets	150,000	[1] 65,625	84,375
Current Assets			
Inventory		40,208	
Trade receivables		65,174	
Cash and cash equivalents		18,120	
		123,502	
Less Current Liabilities			
Trade payables	22,310		
Other payables	[2] 7,944		
		(30,254)	
Net Current Assets			93,248
			177,623
Less Non-current Liabilities			
Bank loan			(30,000)
NET ASSETS			147,623
EQUITY			
Issued Share Capital			
280,000 ordinary shares of 25p each fully paid			70,000
Capital Reserve			
Share premium			17,000
Revenue Reserve			
Retained earnings			60,623
TOTAL EQUITY			147,623

1 Depreciation: £37,500 + £28,125
2 Other payables: loan interest £1,000 owing + tax provision £6,944

18.1

	Amero plc	Britz plc
• gross profit margin	11.85%	37.46%
• gross profit mark-up	13.44%	59.90%
• expenses in relation to revenue	8.98%	22.91%
• profit in relation to revenue	2.87%	14.55%
• return on capital employed	18.18%	13.70%

18.2 (a)

	Cawston plc	*Dunley plc*
• current ratio	1.51:1	1.04:1
• liquid capital ratio	0.82:1	0.65:1
• trade receivable days	37 days	3 days
• trade payable days	57 days	46 days
• rate of inventory turnover (days)	41 days	18 days
• capital gearing percentage	35.16%	13.82%

(b) Cawston plc is the chemical manufacturer, while Dunley plc runs department stores.

All of the ratios for Cawston are close to the benchmarks for a manufacturing business: eg current and liquid capital ratios, although a little low, are near the 'accepted' figures of 2:1 and 1:1, respectively. The rate of inventory turnover shows quite a high level of inventory being held; trade receivable days indicate that most sales are on credit; trade payable days are rather high. The capital gearing percentage is acceptable – medium geared.

For Dunley plc, the ratios indicate a business that sells most of its goods on cash terms: low current and liquid capital ratios, with minimal trade receivable days. The rate of inventory turnover is speedy, whilst trade payables are paid after 46 days (approximately one-and-a-half months). The capital gearing percentage is low, indicating that there is scope for future borrowing should it be required.

18.4 **A**

18.7 (a) *Net current assets*

Current assets – Current liabilities

Net current assets, or working capital, are needed by all businesses in order to finance day-to-day trading activities. Sufficient net current assets enable a business to hold adequate inventory, allow a measure of credit to its customers (trade receivables), and to pay its suppliers (trade payables) on time.

Liquid capital

(Current assets – Inventory) – Current liabilities

Liquid capital is calculated in the same way as net current assets, except that inventory is omitted. This is because inventory is the most illiquid current asset. Liquid capital provides a direct comparison between the short-term assets of trade receivables and bank/cash, and the short-term liabilities of trade payables and bank overdraft.

(b)

- Current ratio = $\frac{\text{Current assets}}{\text{Current liabilities}}$
- Liquid capital ratio = $\frac{\text{(Current assets – Inventory)}}{\text{Current liabilities}}$
- Trade receivable days = $\frac{\text{Trade receivables}}{\text{Credit sales}}$ x 365 days
- Trade payable days = $\frac{\text{Trade payables}}{\text{Credit purchases}}$ x 365 days

(c)

- Current ratio £13,450* = $\frac{\text{£13,450*}}{\text{£7,865**}}$ = 1.71 : 1

  *(10,250 – 2,450) + 450 + 5,200

  **6,000 + 1,865

- Liquid capital (acid test) ratio = $\frac{\text{£13,450 – £5,200 (inventory)}}{\text{£7,865}}$ = 1.05:1
- Trade receivable days = $\frac{\text{£7,800*}}{\text{£96,000}}$ x 365 days = 29.66 days

  *10,250 – 2,450 (irrecoverable debt written off)

- Trade payable days = $\frac{\text{£6,000}}{\text{£56,000}}$ x 365 days = 39.11 days

(d) *Writing off the debt for £2,450*

- Writing off the debt as irrecoverable has reduced trade receivables to £7,800, and current assets from £15,900 to £13,450.
- The effect of this is that the current ratio has been reduced from 2.02:1 to 1.71:1.
- The effect on the liquid capital ratio has been a reduction from 1.36:1 to 1.05:1.
- By writing off the irrecoverable debt, liquidity ratios have reduced quite significantly.

Reducing the value of inventory over the year

- Inventory has reduced from £8,400 to £5,200.
- Had the higher level of inventory been maintained, the current ratio at the year's end would have been £16,650*/£7,865 = 2.12:1.

  *(10,250 – 2,450) + 450 + 8,400
- The liquid capital ratio would be unchanged – because inventory is excluded.
- A change in the level of inventory affects the current ratio but has no effect on the liquid capital ratio.

18.11 (a) *Formula*

$$\text{Rate of inventory turnover} = \frac{\text{Average inventory}}{\text{Cost of sales}} \times 365 \text{ days} \quad \text{or} \quad \frac{\text{Cost of sales}}{\text{Average inventory}}$$

Ratio calculations

20-6

$$\frac{£25{,}000^*}{£160{,}000} \times 365 \text{ days} = 57.03 \text{ days} \quad \text{or} \quad \frac{£160{,}000}{£25{,}000} = 6.40 \text{ times per year}$$

*(£20,000 + £30,000) ÷ 2

20-7

$$\frac{£35{,}000^*}{£245{,}000} \times 365 \text{ days} = 52.14 \text{ days} \quad \text{or} \quad \frac{£245{,}000}{£35{,}000} = 7 \text{ times per year}$$

*(£30,000 + £40,000) ÷ 2

(b) *Formula*

$$\text{Gross profit margin} = \frac{\text{Gross profit}}{\text{Revenue}} \times \frac{100}{1}$$

Ratio calculations

20-6

$$\frac{£40{,}000}{£200{,}000} \times \frac{100}{1} = 20\%$$

20-7

$$\frac{£55{,}000}{£300{,}000} \times \frac{100}{1} = 18.33\%$$

(c) Gross profit margin has fallen from 20% in 20-6 to 18.33% in 20-7. Despite this fall, gross profit has increased from £40,000 in 20-6 to £55,000 in 20-7. The explanation for this apparent contradiction is that revenue has increased from £200,000 to £300,000 – an increase of a half – perhaps as a result of reducing the selling prices. As gross profit margin has fallen, so cost of sales as a percentage of revenue has increased from 80% to 81.67%.

Rate of inventory turnover has improved – from 57.03 days in 20-6 to 52.14 days in 20-7. This indicates that, despite an increase of £10,000 in average inventory, inventory is moving more quickly – a good sign, which links in with the increase of one-half in revenue.

Overall, the business is increasing its revenue and gross profit – at the same time inventory turnover is improving.

19.1

statements	incremental budgeting	zero-based budgeting
The previous budget figures are used as a basis for the next budget period	✔	
Each item going into the budget has to be justified by the budget holder		✔
Inefficiencies and overspending may remain in the budget	✔	
May not be cost-effective to prepare each year		✔

19.3

statements	variance £	favourable variance	adverse variance
Actual costs £2,000; budgeted costs £2,500	500	✔	
Actual revenue £25,000; budgeted revenue £22,500	2,500	✔	
Actual profit £12,000; budgeted profit £14,000	2,000		✔
Budgeted costs £10,000; actual costs £11,000	1,000		✔

19.5

(a)

Jan Leung
Budgeted Statement of Financial Position as at 31 December 20-3

	£	£
Non-current Assets		200,000
Less depreciation for year W1		40,000
Net book value		160,000
Current Assets		
Inventory W2	15,000	
Trade receivables W3	42,000	
Bank (see part (b))	71,500	
	128,500	
Less Current Liabilities		
Trade payables W4	30,000	
Net Current Assets		98,500
NET ASSETS		258,500
FINANCED BY		
Capital		
Opening capital		254,000
Add Profit for the year W5		34,500
Less Drawings		30,000
		258,500

Workings:

W1 20% reducing balance depreciation
W2 Purchases £180,000 ÷ 12
W3 Revenue £336,000 ÷ 8 (ie 1.5 months)
W4 Purchases £180,000 ÷ 12
W5 Revenue £336,000 – Cost of sales £179,000 (Opening inventory £14,000 + Purchases £180,000 – Closing inventory £15,000) – Expenses £122,500

(b) Calculation of budgeted closing bank balance as at 31 December 20-3.

	£	£
Opening bank balance (31 December 20-2)		9,000
Add receipts from trade receivables:		
opening trade receivables	45,000	
+ revenue	336,000	
– closing trade receivables	42,000	
		339,000
Less payments to trade payables:		
opening trade payables	14,000	
+ purchases	180,000	
– closing trade payables	30,000	
		(164,000)
Less expenses:		
income statement	122,500	
– depreciation for the year	40,000	
		(82,500)
Less drawings taken by Jan Leung		(30,000)
Closing bank balance (31 December 20-2)		71,500

note that depreciation for the year is excluded because it is a non-cash expense

CHAPTER 20 Marginal costing and break-even

20.1 **C**

20.3 **C** £1,620, ie fixed cost £300 + variable cost £1,320

20.5
(a) £4.00 per unit, ie £80,000 ÷ 20,000 units
(b) £1.50 per unit, ie (£80,000 – £50,000) ÷ 20,000 units
(c) Sales revenue per unit – variable costs per unit
(d) £2.50 per unit, ie £4.00 – £1.50
(e) £12,500 forecast profit, ie (£2.50 x 25,000 units) – £50,000 fixed costs

20.6
(a) 220 units, ie £24 – £16 = £8 contribution per unit; £1,760 fixed costs ÷ £8
(b) £2,400, ie 520 units x £8 contribution = £4,160 – £1,760 fixed costs

20.8

Units produced and sold	**1,000**	**1,500**	**1,800**
	£	£	£
Revenue	45,000	67,500	81,000
Variable costs:			
• Direct materials	10,000	15,000	18,000
• Direct labour	12,000	18,000	21,600
• Overheads	8,000	12,000	14,400
Semi-variable costs:			
• Variable element	2,000	3,000	3,600
• Fixed element	2,000	2,000	2,000
Total cost	34,000	50,000	59,600
Total profit	11,000	17,500	21,400

21.1 B

21.4 The marginal cost per unit of Exe is £5 (direct materials £3 + direct labour £2), and so any contribution, ie selling price less marginal cost, will be profit:

- *200 units at £6 each*

The offer price of £6 is above the marginal cost of £5 and increases profit by the amount of the £1 extra contribution, ie (£6 – £5) x 200 units = £200 extra profit.

- *500 units at £4 each*

This offer price is below the marginal cost of £5; therefore there will be a fall in profit if this order is undertaken of (£4 – £5) x 500 units = £500 reduced profit.

WESTFIELD LIMITED
monthly income statements

	Existing production of 2,000 units	**Existing production + 200 units @ £6 each**	**Existing production + 500 units @ £4 each**
	£	£	£
Revenue (per month):			
2,000 units at £12 each	24,000	24,000	24,000
200 units at £6 each	–	1,200	–
500 units at £4 each	–	–	2,000
	24,000	25,200	26,000
Less production costs:			
Direct materials (£3 per unit)	6,000	6,600	7,500
Direct labour (£2 per unit)	4,000	4,400	5,000
Fixed costs	8,000	8,000	8,000
PROFIT	6,000	6,200	5,500

The conclusion is that the first special order should be accepted, and the second declined.

21.5

POPCAN LIMITED
monthly income statements

	Existing production of 150,000 cans	**Existing production + 50,000 cans at 18p each**
	£	£
Revenue (per month):		
150,000 cans at 25p each	37,500	37,500
50,000 cans at 18p each	–	9,000
	37,500	46,500
Less production costs:		
Direct materials (5p per can)	7,500	10,000
Direct labour (5p per can)	7,500	10,000
Overheads – variable (4p per can)	6,000	8,000
– fixed*	9,000	9,000
PROFIT	7,500	9,500

*6p x 150,000 cans = £9,000

The offer from the supermarket chain should be accepted because:

- the marginal cost of producing each can is 14p (direct materials 5p, direct labour 5p, variable production overheads 4p)
- the offer price is 18p per can, which is above marginal cost, and gives a contribution of 4p
- profits increase by the amount of the extra contribution, ie (18p – 14p) x 50,000 cans = £2,000 extra profit

21.6

Financial implications

	£	£
Revenue 2,000 units x £313.25		626,500
Less variable costs:		
Material R: 2,000 x £60	120,000	
Material S: 2,000 x £40	80,000	
Skilled labour: *6,350 hours at £26	165,100	
Semi-skilled labour 12,000 hours at £14	168,000	
		533,100
		93,400
Less shipping and insurance		30,500
Profit on order		62,900

*Skilled labour	
2,000 x 4 hours	8,000 hours
Less unutilised hours	1,650 hours
	6,350 hours

- The order would produce a significant increase in the company's profit of (£62,900 ÷ £191,400) x 100 = 32.9%. At the same time, it meets the objective of developing overseas sales and could be the entry into other overseas markets.
- For the order, the selling price is being discounted to £313.25 per unit when compared with a normal price of £400 per unit. Existing customers may learn of this and may well seek their own discounts.
- Potential future orders are larger, but much will depend on the price per unit.
- Are there any foreign exchange rate issues? If the order is priced and paid for in £s there is no problem.
- Future orders may not be paid in full upon shipping – in any case, credit control checks should be made on buyers. BrightLight Limited may wish to take out export credit insurance for their overseas business.
- If large orders are received in future years, BrightLight Limited must consider if it has the capacity to handle them. If not, consideration and the cost implications of adding more capacity should be made.
- There will be net current asset (working capital) considerations of this year's potential order and future orders. For example, increased inventory, trade payables, trade receivables, together with additional cash requirements to pay wages.

Non-financial implications

- Will skilled employees be prepared to work the necessary overtime hours at the rate suggested?
- The potential order this year has to be produced within three months and this will put pressure on employees and all aspects of the business.
- Will existing production and customer service suffer during the three-month period?
- Will quality of the product be maintained for both the overseas and current customers? What happens if the overseas customer is dissatisfied with quality?
- Is it possible to assess the likelihood of future orders materialising and at what selling price?
- If future orders materialise, the company needs to recruit and train new skilled labour. Is such labour available and what will be the training costs? More semi-skilled labour will also be required.
- Are material suppliers able to meet the requirements of increased orders? There is the potential to negotiate discounts with suppliers.
- Are there further overseas markets for BrightLight Limited to consider?

21.7 C

21.8 (a) Total cost per coat if 1,200 units are produced:

		£
Materials	4 metres @ £12 per metre x 1,200 units	57,600
Labour	3 hours @ £15 per hour x 1,100 units	49,500
	3 hours @ £22 per hour x 100 units	6,600
PRIME COST		113,700
Indirect fixed costs		33,180
TOTAL COST		146,880

Total cost per coat £146,880 ÷ 1,200 coats = £122.40

(b) Original selling price:

	£
Materials per coat	48.00
Labour per coat	45.00
Fixed costs per coat £33,180 ÷ 1,000 coats	33.18
TOTAL COST PER COAT	126.18
Profit 50%	63.09
SELLING PRICE PER COAT	189.27

Total cost per coat – see (a) above	122.40
Profit 50%	61.20
SELLING PRICE PER COAT	183.60

∴ the new selling price is £5.67 less than the original selling price.

(c) Effect on company's present customers:

- will be pleased with reduction in the price they pay to buy the coats
- will be concerned to ensure that, with the increase in output, quality of the coats is maintained
- will wish to be assured that supplies will be maintained and may question the ability of KeepDry Ltd to use overtime as a solution in the medium term to increase output

21.9 Production of Aye and Bee

- Materials used in the production of both products are in short supply and the company can only obtain 500 kgs each week. These materials need to be used to the best advantage of the company.
- With insufficient direct materials there is a scarce resource (or a limiting factor). To make best use of this scarce resource to produce profits for the company, the contribution (selling price – variable costs) from each kg of direct material must be maximised.
- The contribution from producing each unit of Aye is £30. As this product requires two kgs of material, the contribution per kg is £30 ÷ 2 kgs = £15.
- The contribution from producing each unit of Bee is £50. As this product requires four kgs of material, the contribution per kg is £50 ÷ 4 kgs = £12.50.
- To make best use of the scarce resource of direct material, the company should produce all of product Aye that can be sold, ie 200 per week. This will take 400 kgs of materials (200 units x 2 kgs each) and will leave 100 kgs available to produce 25 of product Bee (25 units x 4 kgs each).
- If this production plan is followed, insufficient output of product Bee will be produced to meet demand. This may make it difficult to re-establish it in the market when full production of this product can be resumed, once the shortage of direct materials has been resolved.

Conclusion

- Based on the concept of maximising the contribution from each kg of material (the scarce resource), the optimum production plan for next week should be:

  200 units of product Aye

  25 units of product Bee

- This will give a budgeted income statement for next week as follows:

		Aye	Bee	Total
		£	£	£
	Revenue:			
	200 product Aye at £150 per unit	30,000		30,000
	25 product Bee at £200 per unit		5,000	5,000
		30,000	5,000	35,000
less	Variable costs:			
	200 product Aye at £120 per unit	24,000		24,000
	25 product Bee at £150 per unit		3,750	3,750
equals	Contribution	6,000	1,250	7,250
less	Fixed costs			4,000
equals	Profit			3,250

21.10 (a)

Product	'Madrid'	'Paris'	'Rome'
	£	£	£
Sales revenue per unit	30	40	60
Minus variable costs per unit			
Direct materials	10	15	20
Direct labour	5	8	12
Variable costs per unit	2	3	2.50
Equals contribution per unit	13	14	25.50

(b) Break-even point for the 'Madrid' range is:

$$\frac{\text{fixed costs (£)}}{\text{contribution per unit (£)}} = \frac{£72{,}800}{£13} = 5{,}600 \text{ units}$$

(c)

Product	'Madrid'	'Paris'	'Rome'
	£	£	£
Contribution per unit	£13	£14	£25.50
Machine hours per unit	0.5	0.4	0.75
Contribution per machine hour	£26	£35	£34

(d)

- Machine hours are the scarce resource here, with 3,000 hours available.
- To maximise profits, the company should maximise the contribution from each machine hour.
- The preferred order is 'Paris' (at £35 contribution per machine hour), 'Rome' (at £34), and 'Madrid' (at £26).
- Optimum production plan:

	Total hours available per month	3,000
less	'Paris', 3,000 units x 0.4 hours per unit	1,200
		1,800
less	'Rome', 500 units x 0.75 hours per unit	375
equals	hours remaining to produce 'Madrid'	1,425

Therefore production of 'Madrid' at 0.5 hours per unit will be 2,850 units. This production plan does not allow for full production of the 'Madrid' range.

21.12 C

Index